CONT

Lake Matheson reflections Photo: Tourism West Coast

TRIP PLANNING

North Island travel time and distances	ii
South Island travel time and distances	iii
20 top things to do in New Zealand	iv
25 must-see attractions	v
DOC campsites	vi

NATIONAL PARKS MAPS

Te Araroa – The Long Pathway	viii
Te Urewera National Park	ix
Tongariro National Park	x
Arthur's Pass National Park	xi
Kahurangi National Park	xii
Mount Aspiring National Park	xiii
Aoraki/Mt Cook & Westland Tai Poutini National Parks	xiv
Nelson Lakes National Park	xv

NORTH ISLAND REGIONAL MAPS

Far North	map	1-2
Kauri Coast & Whangarei	map	3-4
Kaipara Harbour & Kowhai Coast	map	5-6
Auckland & Coromandel	map	7-8
Waikato	map	9-10
Central Waikato	map	11-12
Rotorua & Bay of Plenty	map	13-14
Eastern Bay of Plenty & East Cape	map	15-16
North Taranaki & Taumarunui	map	17-18
Taupo	map	19-20
Hawke's Bay & Gisborne	map	21-22
Taranaki and River Region	map	23-24
South Taranaki	map	25-26
Napier & Hastings	map	27-28
Manawatu & Horowhenua	map	29-30
Manawatu & Wairarapa	map	31-32
Wellington & South Wairarapa	map	33-34
Cook Strait	map	35
Great Barrier Island	map	36

SOUTH ISLAND REGIONAL MAPS

Nelson	map	37-38
Nelson & Marlborough	map	39-40
Buller & Tasman	map	41-42
Marlborough	map	43-44
Central West Coast	map	45-46
Kaikoura & Hurunui	map	47-48
Glacier Country	map	49-50
Arthur's Pass	map	51-52
Central Canterbury	map	53-54
Ashburton & Christchurch	map	55-56
Southern West Coast	map	57-58
Mackenzie Region	map	59-60
Timaru & Ashburton	map	61-62
Northern Fiordland	map	63-64
Queenstown, Wanaka & Central Otago	map	65-66
Southern Canterbury & Northern Otago	map	67-68
Central Fiordland	map	69-70
Southland & Central Otago	map	71-72
Central Otago & Dunedin	map	73-74
Southern Fiordland	map	75-76
Southland	map	77-78
Coastal Otago	map	79
Stewart Island	map	80

NORTH ISLAND CITY & SUBURBS MAPS

Bay of Islands	map	81
Russell	map	82
Paihia	map	83
Whangarei CBD	map	84
Whangarei Suburbs	map	85
Kerikeri CBD	map	86
Auckland CBD	map	87
North Shore Suburbs	map	88
West Auckland Suburbs	map	89
East & South Auckland Suburbs	map	90
Hamilton CBD	map	91
Hamilton Suburbs	map	92
Tauranga CBD	map	93
Tauranga Suburbs	map	94
Rotorua CBD	map	95
Rotorua Suburbs	map	96
Taupo CBD	map	97
Taupo Suburbs	map	98
Gisborne CBD	map	99
Gisborne Suburbs	map	100
Napier CBD	map	101
Hastings CBD	map	102
Napier / Hastings Suburbs	map	103
Palmerston North CBD	map	104
Palmerston North Suburbs	map	105
New Plymouth CBD	map	106
New Plymouth Suburbs	map	107
Wanganui CBD	map	108
Wanganui Suburbs	map	109
Wellington Suburbs	map	110
Wellington CBD	map	112

SOUTH ISLAND CITY & SUBURBS MAPS

Picton CBD	map	113
Picton Suburbs	map	114
Nelson CBD	map	115
Nelson Suburbs	map	116
Blenheim CBD	map	117
Greymouth CBD	map	118
Christchurch CBD	map	119
Christchurch Suburbs	map	120
Timaru CBD	map	121
Oamaru CBD	map	122
Dunedin CBD	map	123
Dunedin Suburbs	map	124
Queenstown CBD	map	125
Queenstown Suburbs	map	126
Invercargill CBD	map	127
Invercargill Suburbs	map	128

MOTORHOME DUMP STATIONS

Motorhome Park/Caravan Park with dump station (wastewater disposal site)	129
Motorhome Public Dump Station (Wastewater Disposal Site)	131
Index	133
Legends	Inside back cover

north island travel time and distances

Distances are shown in kilometres and assume the most direct route on sealed roads where possible.
Travelling times are shown in hours & minutes and are calculated for a driver travelling at 80-100 km/hr on open stretches, with an allowance for rest stops.

From \ To	Cape Reinga	Chateau Tongariro	Dargaville	Gisborne	Hamilton	Hicks Bay	Kaitaia	Masterton	Napier	New Plymouth	Paihia	Palmerston North	Rotorua	Taupo	Taumarunui	Tauranga	Thames	Waikaremoana	Waitomo Caves	Wanganui	Wellington	Whakatane	Whangarei
Auckland	444 / 8:15	342 / 5:35	182 / 8:20	496 / 1:55	124 / 9:20	500 / 9:05	321 / 6:00	626 / 9:20	424 / 6:35	365 / 7:40	237 / 3:50	521 / 4:05	235 / 4:45	282 / 4:05	284 / 4:45	201 / 3:50	115 / 7:50	390 / 3:10	198 / 7:50	457 / 3:10	652 / 8:00	295 / 9:15	166 / 4:55
Cape Reinga	•	786 / 13:50	290 / 5:25	940 / 16:35	568 / 10:10	944 / 17:20	112 / 2:15	1070 / 17:35	868 / 14:50	809 / 14:35	216 / 4:30	967 / 15:55	679 / 11:50	726 / 12:20	728 / 13:00	645 / 11:35	559 / 10:05	834 / 14:50	642 / 11:25	901 / 16:15	1096 / 17:30	739 / 13:10	267 / 5:15
Chateau Tongariro		•	524 / 8:40	431 / 6:55	218 / 3:40	468 / 8:25	663 / 11:35	314 / 4:20	234 / 4:00	251 / 4:20	579 / 9:50	178 / 3:10	417 / 2:50	94 / 1:30	58 / 3:45	250 / 4:40	311 / 5:05	283 / 2:45	158 / 2:45	138 / 4:45	338 / 4:15	263 / 8:35	508 / —
Dargaville			•	678 / 11:25	306 / 5:00	682 / 12:10	178 / 3:40	808 / 12:25	606 / 9:40	547 / 9:25	126 / 2:20	705 / 10:45	417 / 6:40	464 / 7:10	466 / 7:50	383 / 6:25	297 / 4:55	572 / 10:55	380 / 6:15	639 / 11:05	834 / 12:20	477 / 8:00	55 / 1:05
Gisborne				•	385 / 6:30	176 / 4:20	817 / 14:20	452 / 6:45	221 / 3:25	582 / 8:20	733 / 12:35	397 / 6:05	274 / 4:50	337 / 5:25	446 / 7:20	291 / 5:00	402 / 7:05	167 / 2:55	435 / 7:30	469 / 7:15	534 / 8:15	201 / 3:25	662 / 11:20
Hamilton					•	389 / 7:55	445 / 7:55	504 / 7:25	298 / 4:40	241 / 4:25	361 / 6:10	397 / 5:45	111 / 1:40	158 / 2:10	160 / 2:50	109 / 1:55	110 / 1:50	266 / 5:55	74 / 1:15	326 / 6:05	528 / 7:30	196 / 3:05	290 / 4:55
Hicks Bay						•	821 / 15:05	628 / 10:25	397 / 7:05	586 / 11:10	737 / 13:20	573 / 9:45	278 / 5:35	362 / 6:55	450 / 8:50	295 / 5:45	406 / 7:50	343 / 6:35	439 / 8:15	582 / 10:40	710 / 11:55	205 / 3:25	666 / 12:05
Kaitaia							•	947 / 15:20	745 / 12:35	686 / 12:20	109 / 2:15	844 / 13:40	556 / 9:35	603 / 10:05	605 / 10:45	522 / 9:20	436 / 7:50	711 / 13:50	519 / 9:10	778 / 14:00	973 / 15:15	616 / 10:55	155 / 3:05
Masterton								•	231 / 3:20	341 / 5:15	863 / 13:35	107 / 1:40	430 / 6:35	346 / 5:15	342 / 5:20	502 / 8:05	563 / 8:25	413 / 6:30	442 / 8:00	179 / 2:50	100 / 1:50	515 / 8:00	792 / 12:20
Napier									•	410 / 6:15	661 / 10:50	176 / 2:40	224 / 3:50	140 / 2:30	252 / 4:55	296 / 3:30	357 / 5:20	182 / 3:10	309 / 5:05	248 / 3:50	313 / 4:45	309 / 7:00	590 / 9:35
New Plymouth										•	602 / 10:35	234 / 3:35	308 / 5:35	305 / 5:25	193 / 3:30	309 / 5:40	343 / 6:15	463 / 10:00	181 / 3:30	162 / 2:25	352 / 5:35	393 / 6:20	531 / 9:20
Paihia											•	760 / 11:55	472 / 7:50	519 / 8:20	521 / 9:00	438 / 7:35	352 / 6:05	627 / 12:05	435 / 7:25	694 / 12:15	889 / 13:30	532 / 9:10	71 / 1:15
Palmerston North												•	323 / 4:55	239 / 4:00	235 / 5:25	395 / 6:20	456 / 6:45	358 / 6:15	335 / 5:20	72 / 1:10	142 / 2:10	408 / 6:45	689 / 10:40
Rotorua													•	84 / 1:20	172 / 2:50	83 / 1:30	168 / 2:45	155 / 4:25	161 / 2:45	304 / 4:25	454 / 6:30	85 / 1:25	401 / 6:35
Taupo														•	112 / 1:55	156 / 2:25	217 / 3:10	189 / 4:35	169 / 2:35	220 / 3:05	370 / 5:10	169 / 2:45	448 / 7:05
Taumarunui															•	227 / 4:05	288 / 4:40	301 / 6:30	100 / 1:55	166 / 3:15	356 / 5:15	257 / 4:15	450 / 7:45
Tauranga																•	111 / 2:05	238 / 5:45	149 / 2:30	376 / 6:35	526 / 8:00	94 / 1:35	367 / 6:20
Thames																	•	323 / 6:55	173 / 3:05	425 / 6:55	587 / 8:20	205 / 3:40	281 / 4:50
Waikaremoana																		•	316 / 7:00	430 / 7:00	495 / 8:00	240 / 5:40	556 / 10:50
Waitomo Caves																			•	266 / 5:10	456 / 7:10	243 / 4:05	364 / 6:10
Wanganui																				•	190 / 2:45	389 / 5:10	623 / 10:00
Wellington																					•	539 / 7:55	818 / 12:15
Whakatane																						•	461 / 7:55
Whangarei																							•

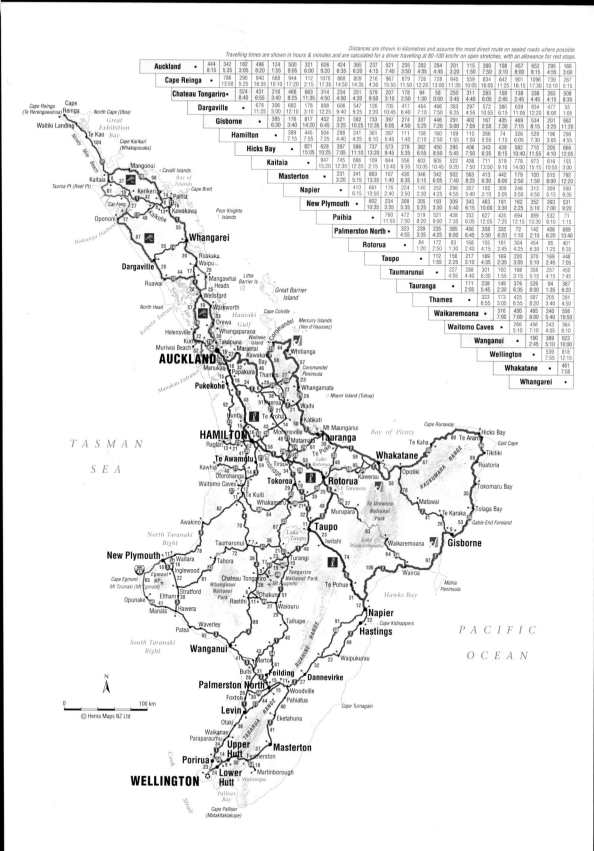

TASMAN SEA

PACIFIC OCEAN

N

0 ____ 100 km

© Hema Maps NZ Ltd

Distances are shown in kilometres and assume the most direct route on sealed roads where possible.
Travelling times are shown in hours & minutes and are calculated for a driver travelling at 80-100 km/hr on open stretches, with an allowance for rest stops.

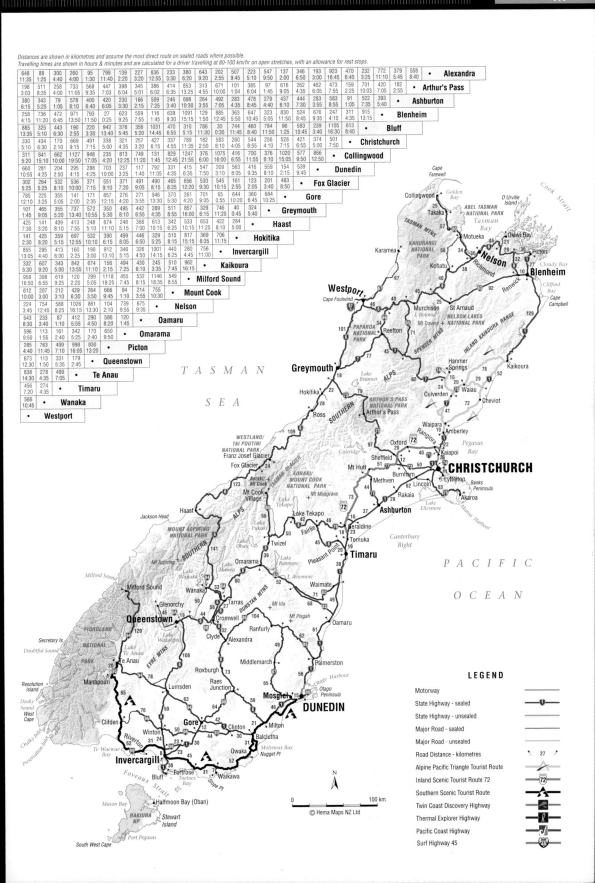

Travel time and distance chart (each cell: distance in km / travelling time in h:min, listed in order across each row)

From	Distances (km) / times (h:min)
Alexandra	648 11:35 · 88 1:25 · 300 4:40 · 260 4:00 · 95 1:30 · 799 11:40 · 139 2:20 · 227 3:20 · 836 12:55 · 233 3:30 · 380 6:20 · 643 9:20 · 202 2:55 · 507 9:45 · 223 5:10 · 547 9:50 · 137 2:00 · 346 6:50 · 193 3:00 · 923 16:45 · 470 6:40 · 232 3:25 · 772 11:10 · 379 5:45 · 558 8:40
Arthur's Pass	198 3:03 · 511 8:35 · 258 4:00 · 733 9:35 · 568 7:03 · 447 7:03 · 398 6:04 · 345 5:01 · 386 6:02 · 414 6:35 · 853 13:25 · 313 4:55 · 671 10:00 · 101 1:04 · 385 6:04 · 97 1:45 · 616 9:05 · 262 4:35 · 462 6:05 · 473 7:55 · 159 2:25 · 701 10:03 · 420 7:05 · 182 2:55
Ashburton	380 6:15 · 343 5:25 · 79 1:05 · 578 8:10 · 400 6:40 · 420 6:05 · 230 3:30 · 166 2:15 · 509 7:25 · 246 3:40 · 698 10:30 · 264 3:55 · 492 7:05 · 283 4:45 · 478 8:45 · 279 4:40 · 437 6:10 · 444 7:30 · 283 3:55 · 583 8:55 · 91 1:05 · 522 7:35 · 393 5:40
Blenheim	258 4:15 · 736 11:20 · 472 6:45 · 971 13:50 · 793 11:50 · 27 0:25 · 559 9:25 · 116 1:45 · 639 7:55 · 1091 15:15 · 129 1:50 · 885 12:45 · 363 5:50 · 647 10:45 · 323 5:50 · 830 11:50 · 524 10:45 · 676 9:35 · 247 4:10 · 311 4:35 · 915 13:15
Bluff	885 13:35 · 325 5:10 · 443 6:30 · 190 2:55 · 220 3:30 · 942 13:40 · 376 5:45 · 356 5:20 · 1031 14:45 · 470 6:55 · 310 5:15 · 786 11:30 · 30 0:30 · 744 10:40 · 460 8:40 · 784 11:50 · 96 1:25 · 583 10:45 · 239 3:40 · 1105 16:30 · 613 8:40
Christchurch	330 5:10 · 434 6:30 · 170 2:10 · 669 9:15 · 491 7:15 · 338 5:00 · 321 4:35 · 257 3:20 · 427 6:15 · 337 4:55 · 789 11:35 · 182 2:50 · 583 8:10 · 260 4:05 · 544 8:55 · 256 4:10 · 528 7:15 · 421 6:55 · 374 5:00 · 501 7:50
Collingwood	311 5:20 · 841 15:10 · 662 10:00 · 1127 19:50 · 948 17:05 · 235 4:20 · 813 12:25 · 749 11:20 · 131 1:45 · 829 12:45 · 1247 21:55 · 376 6:00 · 1075 16:00 · 416 6:55 · 700 11:55 · 376 6:10 · 1020 15:05 · 577 9:50 · 866 12:50
Dunedin	660 10:55 · 281 4:25 · 204 4:25 · 295 4:25 · 288 4:25 · 703 10:00 · 237 3:25 · 117 1:40 · 792 11:05 · 331 4:35 · 415 6:35 · 547 7:50 · 209 3:10 · 416 8:05 · 559 9:35 · 154 8:10 · 539 9:45
Fox Glacier	302 5:25 · 264 5:25 · 532 8:10 · 536 10:00 · 371 7:20 · 551 9:05 · 371 8:15 · 491 8:25 · 490 12:20 · 465 9:30 · 656 10:15 · 530 2:55 · 545 2:05 · 161 3:40 · 123 8:10 · 201 2:15 · 483 8:50
Gore	785 12:10 · 225 3:25 · 355 5:05 · 141 2:00 · 171 2:35 · 857 12:15 · 276 4:20 · 271 3:55 · 946 13:30 · 370 5:30 · 261 4:20 · 701 9:05 · 65 0:55 · 240 6:45 · 360 10:25 · 684
Greymouth	101 1:45 · 465 9:05 · 355 5:20 · 737 13:40 · 572 10:55 · 350 5:30 · 495 8:10 · 442 6:55 · 289 4:35 · 511 8:55 · 857 16:00 · 329 6:15 · 746 11:20 · 40 0:45 · 324 5:40
Haast	425 7:30 · 141 3:20 · 409 8:10 · 413 7:30 · 248 5:10 · 674 11:10 · 248 5:15 · 368 7:00 · 613 10:15 · 342 6:25 · 533 10:15 · 653 11:25 · 422 8:10 · 284 5:00
Hokitika	141 2:30 · 425 8:20 · 359 5:15 · 697 12:55 · 532 10:10 · 390 6:15 · 490 8:05 · 446 6:50 · 329 5:25 · 515 8:15 · 817 15:15 · 369 6:35 · 706 11:15
Invercargill	855 13:05 · 295 4:40 · 413 6:00 · 160 2:25 · 190 3:30 · 912 13:10 · 346 5:15 · 326 4:50 · 1001 14:15 · 440 6:25 · 280 4:45 · 756 11:00
Kaikoura	332 5:30 · 607 9:20 · 343 5:00 · 842 13:55 · 674 11:10 · 156 2:15 · 494 7:25 · 430 6:10 · 245 3:35 · 510 7:45 · 962 16:15
Milford Sound	958 16:50 · 398 6:55 · 619 9:25 · 120 2:20 · 299 5:05 · 1118 18:25 · 455 7:45 · 532 8:15 · 1146 18:35 · 549 8:55
Mount Cook	612 10:00 · 207 3:10 · 212 3:10 · 429 6:30 · 264 3:50 · 666 9:45 · 94 1:10 · 214 3:55 · 755 10:30
Nelson	224 3:45 · 754 12:45 · 588 8:25 · 1026 16:15 · 861 13:30 · 104 2:10 · 739 9:55 · 675 9:35
Oamaru	543 8:30 · 233 3:40 · 87 1:10 · 412 5:55 · 290 4:50 · 586 8:20 · 120 1:45
Omarama	596 9:50 · 113 1:55 · 161 2:40 · 342 5:25 · 170 2:40 · 650 9:50
Picton	285 4:40 · 763 11:45 · 499 7:10 · 998 16:05 · 830 13:20
Queenstown	673 12:30 · 113 1:50 · 331 5:35 · 179 2:45
Te Anau	838 14:30 · 278 4:35 · 499 7:05
Timaru	456 7:20 · 274 4:35
Wanaka	566 10:45
Westport	

LEGEND

- Motorway
- State Highway - sealed
- State Highway - unsealed
- Major Road - sealed
- Major Road - unsealed
- Road Distance - kilometres — 27
- Alpine Pacific Triangle Tourist Route
- Inland Scenic Tourist Route 72 — 72
- Southern Scenic Tourist Route
- Twin Coast Discovery Highway
- Thermal Explorer Highway
- Pacific Coast Highway
- Surf Highway 45

0 — 100 km

N

© Hema Maps NZ Ltd

discover new zealand

20 top things to do

1 Great Walks

There are six DOC Great Walks in the South Island: Abel Tasman Coastal Track, Heaphy Track, Kepler Track, Milford Track, Rakiura Track and Routeburn Track. Every year about 14,000 people complete the Milford Track. The North Island has three DOC Great Walks: Waikaremoana, Tongariro Northern Circuit and Whanganui Journey (a canoe trip).

2 Ski

The South Island has numerous skiing areas, including Queenstown and Lake Wanaka, as well as many areas around the Southern Alps. The North Island has three skifields: Whakapapa, Turoa and Maunganui. Whakapapa is New Zealand's largest ski field. The season in New Zealand generally runs between July and September.

3 Follow wine trails

The Hawke's Bay region is the North Island's largest wine producing area, with other major areas including Waiheke Island, Kumeu, Warkworth/ Matakana, Gisborne and Martinborough. The South Island's largest wine producing region is Marlborough, and Central Otago and the Waipara Valley are other booming areas.

4 Cruise

Around the Bay of Islands and Auckland you can charter a yacht or join a boat cruise. Another popular tour is from Russell or Paihia out to the Hole in the Rock. On the South Island, cruising is a good way to experience the numerous sounds in both the Fiordland and Marlborough regions.

5 See wildlife

Throughout New Zealand kiwis are on display at various locations, including the Kiwi House, Rainbow Springs, Mt Bruce National Wildlife Centre, the Kiwi and Birdlife Park, the National Kiwi Centre, the Orana Wildlife Park and Willowbank Reserve. The South Island's West Coast has New Zealand's only white heron nesting site, and colonies of both blue and yellow-eyed penguins. See fur seals at Cape Foulwind, the Southern Encounter Aquarium in Christchurch and the world's only mainland colony of royal albatross on the Otago Peninsula.

6 Sample local produce

Te Puke is the 'capital' for kiwifruit. Try mussels and oysters at the Coromandel, shellfish at the Pouto Lighthouse, kumara at Dargaville, honey in Warkworth, bacon and ham in Pokeno and cheese in Eltham. Visit orchards and olive groves in the Hawke's Bay region. Around the South Island sample rock lobster at Kaikoura, Havelock's greenshell mussels, the internationally-famous Bluff oysters, Mapua's smoked fish and Stirling's cheese. Buy seafood in Nelson, stone fruit in Central Otago and cheese, chocolate and Barker's fruit products in Geraldine.

7 Scenic flights

A scenic flight is the perfect way to see the South Island's more remote scenery, like the Fiordland region's sounds, the glaciers of the southern West Coast and the Southern Alps. It's also a good way to see Australasia's highest mountain and the southern hemisphere's longest glacier in Mt Cook National Park.

8 Participate in adventure activities

New Zealand is a wonderful country to experience adventure activities, like sky diving, bungy jumping, jet boating, mountain biking, bridge climbing, sky jumping, kayaking, parapenting, skiing, white-water rafting, four-wheel driving, diving, gliding and hot-air ballooning.

9 Bushwalk and tramp

Tramp in the Waipoua and Waitangi forests, Waitakere and Hunua ranges, Whakarewarewa Forest, Egmont and Whanganui national parks, and the Tararua Ranges on the North Island. Tongariro Crossing is one of the best day-walks. Around the South Island, tramp in the Abel Tasman, Kahurangi, Rakiura and Fiordland national parks. The Otago Central Rail Trail and Tuatapere Hump Ridge Track are other highlights.

10 The TranzAlpine train journey

Although it's a spectacular journey, winding through amazing scenery, the TranzAlpine train journey takes just four hours. It is a great way to travel between Greymouth on the west coast and Christchurch on the east.

11 See geothermal phenomenon and hot pools

Around Rotorua and Taupo there are numerous geothermal parks, and the world-famous Pohutu Geyser. Hot pool complexes are near Gisborne, the Bay of Plenty, Tongariro National Park, Waiwera Hot Springs, Morere Hot Springs, Tokaanu, Lake Taupo and Te Aroha. The South Island has Hanmer Springs and Maruia Springs Thermal Resort.

12 Shop

Auckland has good designer shopping, Wellington offers excellent urban shopping, and smaller cities have artworks, gourmet food products and quality knitwear. Both Christchurch and Dunedin have excellent urban shopping while other South Island towns and cities have artworks and gourmet food products. On the West Coast, pick up some jade (greenstone) jewellery.

13 Fish

Try catching trout at Turangi – the trout town of New Zealand – as well as at Lake Waikaremoana, Lake Maraetai, Whirinaki Forest Park, Kaweka Forest Park, Lake Taupo, Tongariro River, Waitahanui River and Tauranga Taupo River. Head to Whangaroa Harbour or Tutukaka for game-fishing. To catch brown trout and salmon on the South Island head to: rivers like the Buller, Karamea, Waitaki, Taieri, Clutha and Pomehaka and lakes including Rotoiti, Rotoroa, Roxburgh, Wanaka, Hawea, Te Anau, Manapouri and Brunner. The Matuara River, near Gore, is known as 'the brown trout fishing centre of Southland'. Rakaia is world renowned as a salmon fishing area.

14 Experience Maori culture

Cultural experiences can be found in Waitangi, Auckland and Rotorua. There are numerous historic pa sites and marae around the East Coast and Maori craft at Tokomaru Bay. Rewa's Village, Tamaki Maori Village and Howick Historical Village also provide interesting insights. On the South Island, see a Maori pa site at Matangi Awhea, Whakatu Marae, Te Waikoropupu Springs (a Maori sacred place) and Te Awhina Marae.

15 Bungy jump

On the North Island, bungy jump off the Auckland Harbour Bridge or leap from New Zealand's first purpose-built platform bungy jump at Taupo. At Mount Hutt, on the South Island, try a ski or snowboard bungy. At 134m, the Nevis Highwire bungy jump, near Queenstown, is the highest in Australasia.

16 Surf

On the rough west coast, board surfers enjoy the breaks of Opunake, Raglan, Piha, Muriwai and Ahipara. Highly recommended surfing venues on the east coast include: Castle Point, Gisborne, Mt Maunganui, Whangamata, Hot Water Beach, Mangawhai Heads, Waipu Cove and Sandy Bay.

17 Cave

The Waitomo region has extensive cave systems and caves can also be found at Waipu, Waiomio, Nikau Caves and Kawiti Caves. New Zealand's deepest cave, Nettlebed, is located in the South Island's Kahurangi National Park. Mt Owen Bulmer Caves, Ngarua Caves, Oparara Basin, Honeycomb Hill Cave and Te Ana-au Caves are also popular.

18 Golf

Premium golf experiences are offered at Kauri Cliffs in Northland, Gulf Harbour north of Auckland and Wairakei near Taupo. Paraparaumu Beach Golf Links is New Zealand's number one ranked course. There's a great golf course in Amberley on the South Island, and some of New Zealand's toughest holes at the Clearwater Resort's golf course in Christchurch.

19 Scenic drives

The North Island has three scenic tourist routes: Twin Coast Discovery Highway, Thermal Explorer Highway and Pacific Coast Highway. Mauao and Mount Maunganui Beach has the best beach and coastline of the Bay of Plenty. Travel through the South Island on the Alpine Pacific Triangle touring route, Inland Scenic Route 72 and Southern Scenic Highway. The Milford Road is known as one of the world's best alpine roads.

20 Mountain bike rides

Popular spots on the North Island are Woodhill, Waiheke Island, Rotorua's Whakarewarewa Forest, and the Hunua Ranges and Tapapakanga regional parks. One of the best routes is the 42nd Traverse. On the South Island, around Nelson, Reefton, Queenstown, Alexandra, Christchurch and Naseby there are numerous tracks. Good routes include the Queen Charlotte Walkway and the Otago Central Rail Trail.

25 must-see attractions

Lord of the Rings movie-set locations
See where Middle Earth was filmed. Throughout this atlas major filming locations are shown with a 🎬 symbol.

Cape Reinga lighthouse (1 A1)
The meeting point of the Tasman Sea and the Pacific Ocean

Kerikeri's old buildings (4 A8)
New Zealand's oldest stone building (1833) and New Zealand's oldest house (1822)

Poor Knights Islands Marine Reserve (4 E13)
One of the world's finest dive locations – off the coast from Tutukaka.

Auckland (7 D4)
Sky Tower, MOTAT, Kelly Tarlton's Antarctic Encounter and Underwater World, Auckland Zoo, Rainbow's End Adventure Park, Waiheke and Rangitoto Island, Bungy off the Harbour Bridge, museums, galleries

Cathedral Cove and the Coromandel Peninsula (8 D13)
Beautiful beaches for swimming, fishing and boating

Waitomo Caves (11 H5)
Glow-worms, caving, black-water rafting

Mount Tarawera (13 H6)
See the Buried Village, visit the museum and walk between the excavated dwellings

Rotorua (13 G4)
Geothermal attractions, including hot springs, mud pools and geysers

Cruise to White Island (14 E11)
Take a cruise from Whakatane to New Zealand's most active volcano

Lake Taupo area (19 E4)
Wild trout fishery, geothermal and volcanic areas to explore, bungy jump, waterfalls

Mount Taranaki (23 D5)
New Zealand's 'most climbed mountain' at 2517m.

Tongariro National Park (26 A12)
Whakapapa skifield, active and extinct volcanoes, tramping

Wellington (33 F1)
New Zealand's capital: Te Papa Museum, Wellington Zoo, seal colony, Embassy Theatre, Wellington Cable Car, Carter

Observatory, Wellington Botanical Gardens, Capital E

Marlborough region (40)
Wineries, kayaking and cruising on the Sounds

Pancake Rocks blowholes (45 B5)
Limestone rocks and blowholes that make a spectacular spouting display

Franz Josef (49 G6) and Fox (49 H4) glaciers
Experience massive rivers of ice on foot or by helicopter

Mt Cook National Park (59 A7)
Tasman Glacier, the southern hemisphere's longest glacier, and Aoraki (Mt Cook), Australasia's highest mountain at 3754m

Lake Tekapo (60 D10)
Turquoise glacial lake best seen from the historic Church of the Good Shepherd

Christchurch (56 D10)
Hagley Park, tram rides, Avon River, garden tours, Southern Encounter Aquarium, Antarctic Centre, Gondola, Art Gallery

Dunedin (74 H11)
Larnach Castle, Victorian and

Edwardian architecture, Royal Albatross Centre, Penguin Place, Taieri Gorge Railway, garden tours, Otago Museum, Otago Peninsula

Curio Bay (78 H11)
Fossilised forest which is believed to date from the Jurassic age; in the Catlins

Invercargill's Queens Park (127 A3)
80ha park in the CBD, with a golf course, Southland Museum and Art Gallery, aviary, Japanese garden and rose garden

Queenstown (65 H4) and Wanaka (66 D8)
Ski fields, adventure activities, Skyline gondola complex, TSS Earnslaw cruise on Lake Wakatipu, wine trails, Skippers Canyon, scenic flights, Mount Aspiring National Park, lakes Wanaka and Hawea, Rob Roy Glacier, Puzzling World, Wanaka Beerworks, Rippon Vineyard

Milford Sound (63 C7)
Bowen Falls, Stirling Falls, Mitre Peak, bottlenose dolphins, fur seals, Fiordland crested penguins, cruises, kayaking, diving, Milford Deep underwater observatory.

Legend

Icon	Meaning	Icon	Meaning	Icon	Meaning
🚰	Drinking Water	🏞	Picnic Area	💧	Stream Water
🚻	Toilets	🗑	Rubbish Disposal	🚶	Walking Track
🔥	Fireplace/BBQ	🚿	Shower		

- Fully serviced Campgrounds have flush toilets, tap water, showers, rubbish collection, picnic tables and usually some powered sites. Many have barbecues or fireplaces, a kitchen, laundry and shop.
- A fee is charged at most DOC campsites.

Northland

Name	Ref
Cable Bay	4 A11
Forest Pools	3 B6
Kapowairua (Spirits Bay)	1 A2
Maitai Bay	2 F7
Otamure Bay	4 D13
Puketi	2 K11
Puriri Bay	4 C12
Raetea North Side	3 A4
Rarawa	1 E4
Sunset Bay	4 A11
Taputaputa	1 A1
Trounson Kauri Park	3 G5
Uretiti	4 J13
Urupukapuka Bay	4 A11
Waikahoa Bay, Mimiwhangata	4 D12

Auckland

Name	Ref
Akapoua Bay	36 D4
Awana Beach	36 D5
Harataonga	36 D5
Home Bay	6 J12
Medlands Beach	36 E5
Motuihe	7 D6
Motuora	6 F11
Whangapoua	36 C4

Waikato

Name	Ref
Booms Flat	8 G12
Broken Hills	8 G13
Catleys	8 G12
Fantail Bay	8 A9
Fletcher Bay	8 A10
Hotoritori	8 G12
Kakaho	19 C2
Ngaherenga	18 B13
Piropiro	18 C12
Port Jackson	8 A10
Shag Stream	8 H12
Stony Bay	8 A10
Totara Flat	8 G12
Trestle View	8 G12
Waikawau Bay	8 B11
Wainora	8 G12
Wentworth	8 J14
Whangaiterenga	8 G12

Bay of Plenty

Name	Ref
Dickey Flat	10 F10
Hot Water Beach	13 H6
Lake Tarawera Outlet	13 H6
Mangamate	20 D11
Okahu Roadend	20 D12
Rerewhakaaitu-Ash Pit Road	13 J6
Rerewhakaaitu-Brett Road	13 J6
Sanctuary	20 D11

East Coast

Name	Ref
Anaura Bay	16 J11
Boulders	15 G3
Manganuku	14 J14
Mokau Landing	21 E2
Omahuru (Ogilvies)	14 J12
Orangihikoia	20 D14
Rosie's Bay	21 E2
Te Pakau (8 Acre)	14 H12
Te Taita O Makoro	21 D2
Waikaremoana Motor Camp	21 E3 — Fully serviced
Whitikau	15 G5

Tongariro/Taupo

Name	Ref
Army Road	19 G6
Clements Clearing	19 G6
Clements Roadend	19 G6
Kaimanawa Road	19 J3
Kakapo	19 G6
Mangahuia	18 J12
Mangawhero	26 C11
Pokaka Mill	18 H12
Te Iringa	19 G6
Urchin	19 J3
Whakapapa Motor Camp	26 A12 — Fully Serviced

Whanganui

Name	Ref
Kawhatau	27 G5
Ohinepane	18 G9
Whakahoro	18 H9

Wellington

Name	Ref
Bucks Road	33 C6
Catchpool Valley	33 F3
Holdsworth	34 B7
Kiriwhakapapa	34 A8
Otaki Forks	33 A5
Putangirua Pinnacles	33 G5
Waikawa	29 H5
Waiohine Gorge	33 B7

Hawkes Bay

Name	Ref
Everetts	20 J11
Glenfalls	20 J10
Kumeti	30 B11
Lake Tutira	28 A12
Lawrence	28 C8
Kuripapango	27 C7
Mangatutu Hot Springs	28 A8
Waikare River Mouth	28 A13

There are many more places to stay in the great outdoors managed by Department of Conservation. For details of Great Walks, walk in campsites near huts, information about huts or any other conservation information contact your nearest visitor centre or visit the DOC website: www.doc.govt.nz

DOC Hotline 0800 362 468 For fire, search and rescue call 111

Nelson/Marlborough

Campsite	Grid ref
Acheron Accommodation House	47 E6
Aussie Bay	40 G9
Butchers Flat	39 H6
Camp Bay	40 F11
Canaan Downs	38 F9
Cobb Cottage	43 J5
Cobb River	37 H6
Coldwater Stream	43 J2
Courthouse Flat	42 B8
Cowshed Bay	40 G10
D'Urville Island	40 B9
Elaine Bay	40 E8
Ferndale	40 F10
French Pass	40 C9
Harvey Bay	40 E8
Kauauroa Bay	40 E10
Kawatiri	42 F11
Kenepuru Head	40 F11
Kerr Bay	42 G13 — Fully serviced
Kowhai Point	43 E3
Lake Rotoroa	42 G11
Lake Tennyson	47 C4
Marfells Beach	44 E12
Mill Flat	43 C7
Moetapu Bay	40 G9
Momorangi Bay	40 G9 — Fully serviced
Nikau Cove	40 F10
Onamalutu	40 J8
Pelorus Bridge	39 H6 — Fully serviced
Picnic Bay	40 F10
Rarangi	40 J10
Ratimera Bay	40 G11
Robin Hood Bay	40 H11
Siberia	42 C11
Totaranui	38 D9
Waimaru	40 E10
Waiona Bay	40 D9
West Bay	43 F1
Whatamango Bay	40 G11
Whites Bay	40 J10

*Except for kitchen and hot showers

Canterbury

Campsite	Grid ref
Ahuriri Bridge	67 A4
Andrews Shelter	52 B10
Avalanche Creek Shelter	52 B8
Craigieburn Shelter	52 D9
Deer Valley	46 E13
Grey River	53 D7
Greyneys	52 B8
Hawdon Valley	52 B9
Klondyke Corner	52 C8
Lake Taylor Camping Area	46 J12
Loch Katrine Camping Area	46 H12
Mt Nimrod	60 J13
Orari	61 E4
Otaio Gorge	68 B11
Peel Forest	61 C5 — Fully serviced
Pioneer Park	61 F2
Temple	59 F4
Waihi Gorge	61 E4
White Horse Hill	59 B6
Wooded Gully	52 E14

West Coast

Campsite	Grid ref
Gillespies Beach	49 G3
Goldsborough	45 H3
Hans Bay	45 J3
Kohaihai	37 H2
Lake Ianthe	50 C9
Lake Mahinapua	45 J1
Lake Paringa	58 B12
Lyell	41 G6
Marble Hill	46 D12
Ottos/MacDonalds	49 F6
Slab Hut Creek	46 B9

Otago

Campsite	Grid ref
Boundary Creek	58 J10
Cameron Flat	58 G11
Glencoe	68 J10
Homestead	66 E14
Kidds Bush	66 A9
Kinloch	64 F12
Lake Sylvan	64 E11
Macetown	65 F6
Moke Lake	64 H14
Pleasant Flat	58 E12
Purakaunui Bay	79 H2
Skippers Township	65 F4
St Bathans Domain	67 F2
Tawanui	78 E13
Trotters Gorge	74 B13
Twelve Mile Delta	64 H13

Southland

Campsite	Grid ref
Cascade Creek	64 G10
Deer Flat	64 H9
Henry Creek	70 B12
Kiosk Creek	64 H9
Lake Gunn	64 F10
Mackay Creek	64 J9
Mavora Lakes	71 B4
Monowai	70 H10
Piano Flat	72 E11
Smithy Creek	64 G9
Thicket Burn	76 D10
Totara	64 J9
Upper Eglinton	64 G9
Walker Creek	64 J9

Cape Reinga Lighthouse

Land's End, Bluff

Base image © Geographx 2006

Te Araroa – The Long Pathway

A New Zealand-long walking track – Te Araroa, meaning the Long Pathway – is taking shape from Cape Reinga to Bluff. This edition of Hema's New Zealand Road Atlas shows sections of it.

The track will be 3,000 kms long – a project headed by the private Te Araroa Trust and its eight regional trusts. Seventy percent of the distance is open for walking on existing north-south tracks though some are not yet signed with Te Araroa logos, and most are not yet linked. A further 13 percent of the trail is walkable on back-roads which connect trailheads. In consultation with local authorities and Department of Conservation (DOC) conservancies, Te Araroa Trust designed the North Island route in 1997, using many existing tracks and mapping possible linking routes.

In 2000 the Trust financed and constructed its first link track, 18km up the Waikato River. Since then, Te Araroa Trust and Te Araroa regional trusts, usually in cooperation with local authorities, have opened over 400km of new linking track, some 13% of the total distance. The DOC tracks en route are now mostly marked up with Te Araroa logos. Many of them are in the South Island, where Te Araroa Trust completed a route design in 2002. The latest track developments and trail maps for many of the walkable sections are available on Te Araroa's website www.teararoa.org.nz.

History

Much of Te Araroa's route crosses countryside and coast that is legally walkable, for example on road reserve that has been surveyed off but not built, or coastline, or down rivers where canoes are recommended, or across DOC land that is not tracked. If these 'paper' roads, beaches, forests and water sections such as the Whanganui River are included, the trail route can be described as 93% legally negotiable. For reasons of safety though, these additional routes are not shown, for they do not yet have proper definition.

Also, some of the tracks that are shown, for example the routes through the Tararua or Richmond Ranges, should be attempted by experienced trampers only.

River crossings are another hazard. At major rivers, Te Araroa Trust simply declares a 'safety zone' and it's up to individual trampers whether they cross and how. For at least two South Island rivers, the crossing is best done by 4WD vehicle or jet boat. Te Araroa Trust recommends that any trampers who attempt remote tracks or significant river crossings should first consult with the local area office of DOC. It advises that trampers must always fill in intentions forms in every hut and shelter they pass, even if they don't intend staying there. The Trust also recommends that trampers should take advantage of mountain safety and river crossing courses, available through www.mountainsafety.org.nz.

Safety

The New Zealand-long tramping route was once an aim of the New Zealand Walkways Commission set up in 1975 to encourage walkway development. The Commission put in place 130 new short tracks, but did not progress a New Zealand-long trail. NZWC was formally abolished in 1990, when control of walkways was handed over to DOC, but the Department did not pursue the long trail idea.

In the mid 1990s the long trail project was revived by a newspaper campaign headed by journalist and tramper Geoff Chapple. Te Araroa Trust was formed as keeper of the vision. At first the Trust saw its role only as encouraging those with the necessary resources to undertake construction of their sections – mainly district, city and regional councils – but in 2000 the trust became a track builder.

In 2002 the Mayors Taskforce for Jobs – an organisation which aims to stimulate employment, and includes most New Zealand district and city councils – made Te Araroa a priority project. That same year DOC signed a Memorandum of Understanding with Te Araroa Trust by which the Department agreed to support the goal, and in 2007 the Government voted DOC $3.8 million to finance construction of Te Araroa on DOC estate.

Te Araroa Trust acts now as an advisor for participating councils and DOC, as well as continuing its own track scoping, financing, and building using a construction manager and many volunteers.

Te Araroa Trust intends to open the track in December 2010.

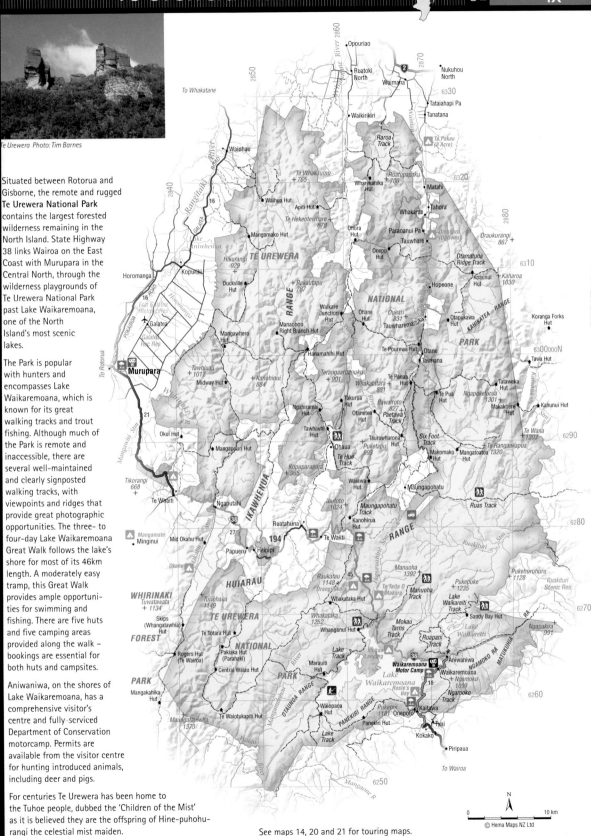

Te Urewera Photo: Tim Barnes

Situated between Rotorua and Gisborne, the remote and rugged **Te Urewera National Park** contains the largest forested wilderness remaining in the North Island. State Highway 38 links Wairoa on the East Coast with Murupara in the Central North, through the wilderness playgrounds of Te Urewera National Park past Lake Waikaremoana, one of the North Island's most scenic lakes.

The Park is popular with hunters and encompasses Lake Waikaremoana, which is known for its great walking tracks and trout fishing. Although much of the Park is remote and inaccessible, there are several well-maintained and clearly signposted walking tracks, with viewpoints and ridges that provide great photographic opportunities. The three- to four-day Lake Waikaremoana Great Walk follows the lake's shore for most of its 46km length. A moderately easy tramp, this Great Walk provides ample opportunities for swimming and fishing. There are five huts and five camping areas provided along the walk – bookings are essential for both huts and campsites.

Aniwaniwa, on the shores of Lake Waikaremoana, has a comprehensive visitor's centre and fully-serviced Department of Conservation motorcamp. Permits are available from the visitor centre for hunting introduced animals, including deer and pigs.

For centuries Te Urewera has been home to the Tuhoe people, dubbed the 'Children of the Mist' as it is believed they are the offspring of Hine-puhohu-rangi the celestial mist maiden.

See maps 14, 20 and 21 for touring maps.

© Hema Maps NZ Ltd

0   10 km

N

Tongariro National Park

Lake Lahar, Mt Ruapehu Photo: Donna Blaber

Containing both active and extinct volcanoes, **Tongariro National Park** is New Zealand's oldest national park and a World Heritage area. In Peter Jackson's Lord of the Rings films, the Park's dramatic landscape was the setting for Mordor and Mount Ngauruhoe made an appearance as Mount Doom.

Forming the Park's heart are the active volcanoes: Mt Tongariro with its red, raw craters; the charred cinder cone of Mt Ngauruhoe; and majestic Mt Ruapehu's snowy crown and sinister crater lake. Scenic flights provide excellent views of the mountains' diverse peaks.

The cream of the Park's hikes is the 17km Tongariro Crossing, which provides an opportunity to experience some of the most scenic volcanically active areas. There is the option to climb to the summit of Mt Ngauruhoe or Mt Tongariro en route. It is not a round trip so transport must be arranged at one end, or you can catch a shuttle bus from Turangi, Whakapapa Village or National Park Village.

During the summer, guided walks take you to NZ's largest active volcanic crater lake at Mt Ruapehu's summit, or you can 'self-hike' the Skyline Walk, a one-and-a-half-hour round trip, or the dramatic Meads Wall Walk. Other popular walks include the Tama Lakes and Taranaki Falls.

In winter, snow falls in the Park and Mt Ruapehu has three skifields: Whakapapa, Turoa and Tukino.

See maps 18, 19, 26 and 27 for touring maps.

Trampers and climbers flock to **Arthur's Pass National Park** for its amazing ridges, screes, deep valleys, waterfalls, glaciers and gorges. Sitting right in the heart of the national park, Arthur's Pass village has basic facilities and several accommodation options. The excellent DOC headquarters has detailed maps of all the tracks in the area and enthusiastic trampers can enquire here about overnight trips. There's also a small museum, which gives some historical background, and an old Cobb and Co coach on display. Nearby, at the Alpine Chapel, you can gain great views of the Avalanche Creek Waterfall.

Since Arthur Dobson surveyed the pass in 1864, it has been a popular route linking Westland and Christchurch. Skiers, trampers and climbers have been frequenting the region since the railway was completed in the early 1920s. During the summer experienced climbers flock to Arthur's Pass to climb nearby mountains including Mt Rolleston, Mt Murchison and Mt Franklin. In winter the park is transformed by snow, making it popular with skiers and climbers.

Make sure you stop at the lookout point above the pass to see the native mountain parrots called keas and gain excellent views before heading downhill to Otira where the Caley Art Gallery has a good collection of oil paintings, hand blown glass, greenstone (jade) and Maori carvings.

See maps 45, 46, 51 and 52 for touring maps.

Arthur's Pass Photo: Donna Blaber

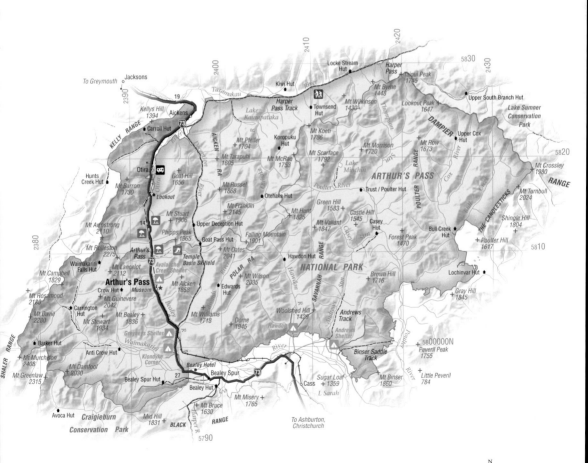

© Hema Maps NZ Ltd

0 ———— 10 km

N

Karamea Waterfall

The vast **Kahurangi National Park** is a 400,000 hectare wilderness of native forest and nikau palms that is a haven for adventure activities. The park contains New Zealand's deepest cave: Nettlebed.

Many tracks cross this isolated park, including the Heaphy Great Walk and the Wangapeka Track. It takes four to six days to complete this Great Walk, and DOC provides seven huts and six campsites. Many a hiker emerges from the national park reporting sightings of great spotted kiwi, short and long tailed bats, and giant land snails. The quiet township of Karamea is both the beginning and the end point of the Heaphy Track.

The beginning of the Heaphy Track provides one of the region's nicest short walks. A suspension bridge crosses the Kohaihai River accessing a 40-minute side-loop that winds through an amazing nikau palm grove where these beautiful palms thrust their smooth, ringed trunks from the pure white sands of a lagoon.

See maps 37, 38 and 42 for touring maps.

Gates of Haast Photo: Peter Mitchell

Key Summit along the Routeburn Track. This magnificent view is also easily accessible from the Milford Road.

See maps 57, 58, 64 and 65 for touring maps.

Part of Te Wahipounamu, the Southwest New Zealand World Heritage Area, **Mount Aspiring National Park** has many scenic walks including the Cascade Saddle Route and Rees-Dart Track, a moderately difficult four to five day tramp along the Rees and Dart rivers. Stunning mountain scenery, alpine landscapes and the Dart Glacier are all seen en route. It is also possible to climb Mount Aspiring (Tititea), but peaks such as these and the glaciers are best explored with experienced guides from a reputable trekking and climbing company.

The Routeburn Great Walk journeys through Mount Aspiring National Park and down over Harris Saddle into the Fiordland National Park. The 32km track takes two to three days to complete, and four huts and two campsites are provided along the way.

From Wanaka, SH6 follows the northern shores of Lake Wanaka towards Makarora before the incredibly scenic drive heads through Mount Aspiring National Park then hugs the Haast River into the small settlement of Haast, on the west coast. Be sure to stop at the Gates of Haast to see the river tumbling down over massive boulders.

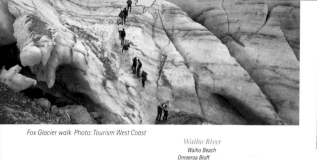

Fox Glacier walk Photo: Tourism West Coast

Aoraki/Mt Cook.

© Hema Maps NZ Ltd

N
0   10 km

Hooker Valley Track. The Blue Lakes to the Tasman Glacier viewpoint track offers stunning views of the glacier's lunar-like landscape. If you're looking to conquer Aoraki/Mt Cook (3754m) or Mt Tasman (3498m), Alpine Guides can lead you to either summit. Those tackling longer hikes should check in at the DOC Visitors' Centre for a weather update, as conditions can change fast, no matter what the season.

The incredibly scenic drive to Mt Cook via SH80 skirts the shores of Lake Pukaki beneath the textured slopes of the Ben Ohau Range. The tiny alpine village of Mount Cook is an ideal base from which to explore the **Aoraki/Mt Cook National Park**, which boasts Australasia's highest mountain (Mt Cook) and the rumbling Tasman Glacier, the Southern Hemisphere's longest frozen river of ice.

During the winter heli-skiing is a popular pastime and various companies provide options for guided tours. Skiers can also land on the 27km-long Tasman Glacier in a ski plane. Heli-hiking on Mt Dark's rugged ridges and wide open basins is available year round.

In the summer visitors can enjoy 4WD journeys, rock climbing and hiking or an informative cruise on Tasman Glacier Lake, beneath the terminus of the glacier. There are a number of good family walks that leave from the village, including the Bowen Bush Walk, Glencoe Walk, Kea Point and

The **Westland Tai Poutini National Park** encompasses the Fox and Franz Josef glaciers, whose icy tongues are surrounded by rainforest. To really experience these massive rivers of ice, take a guided tour or take a helicopter ride for a bird's-eye view.

From Franz Josef it's a short drive to the glacier's car park. To gain a good view of the Franz Josef Glacier hike to Sentinel Rock (around 10 minutes) or hike the 3km Glacier Valley Walk to the terminal face (around an hour and a half return). You can join a guided tour and hike up the face of the glacier to explore stunning ice-blue tunnels on the world's steepest and fastest-flowing commercially guided glacier.

Helicopter flights and guided walks of the Fox Glacier are also on offer and it takes around five minutes' hiking from the car park to gain a view of the glacier or 30 minutes to get close to the terminal face.

See maps 49, 50, 59 and 60 for touring maps.

Nelson Photo: Donna Blaber

St Arnaud, right at the doorstep of **Nelson Lakes National Park**, provides a great base for trampers exploring the park's various tracks including the four- to seven-day Travers-Sabine Circuit. The two- to three-day hike to Lake Angelus, a stunning alpine pond, is also popular. There are also several excellent day hikes, including the Lake Rotoiti Circuit, Mount Robert loop track, St Arnaud Range track, and Whisky Falls track. A commercial water-taxi service on the lake whisks hikers to and from various points or provides cruises of the lake on demand. The latest weather report, maps, hut tickets and hunting permits are available from the DOC visitor centre in St Arnaud.

Located on the lake edge, the Rotoiti Nature Recovery Project is an important conservation site. The Bellbird and Honeydew tracks provide an insight into this work and honey-dew nectar can be seen literally dripping from the beech trees.

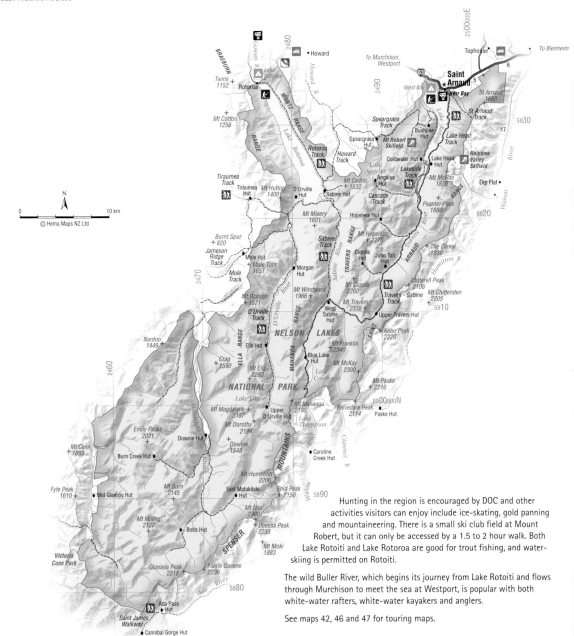

Hunting in the region is encouraged by DOC and other activities visitors can enjoy include ice-skating, gold panning and mountaineering. There is a small ski club field at Mount Robert, but it can only be accessed by a 1.5 to 2 hour walk. Both Lake Rotoiti and Lake Rotoroa are good for trout fishing, and water-skiing is permitted on Rotoiti.

The wild Buller River, which begins its journey from Lake Rotoiti and flows through Murchison to meet the sea at Westport, is popular with both white-water rafters, white-water kayakers and anglers.

See maps 42, 46 and 47 for touring maps.

map
1

NORTH ISLAND

Far North

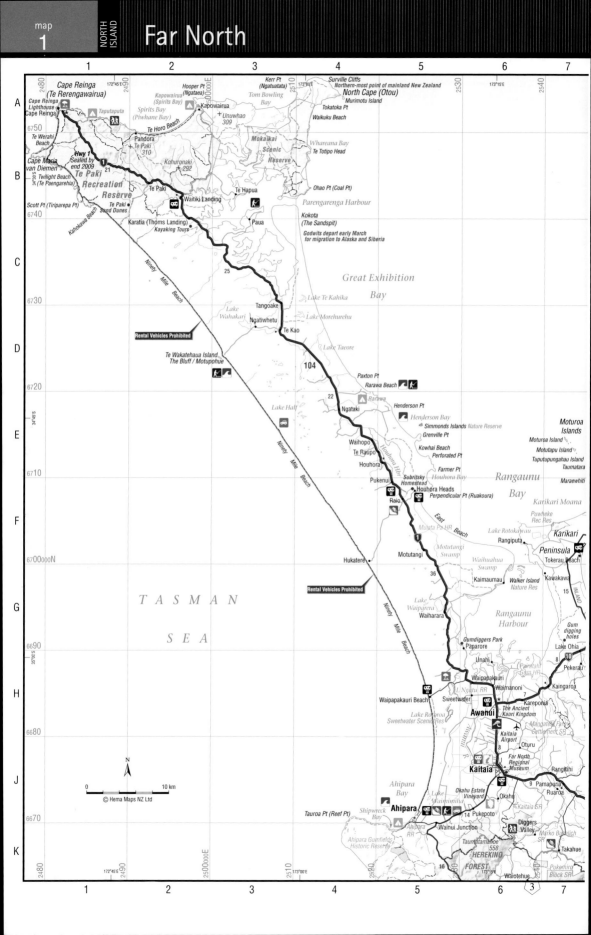

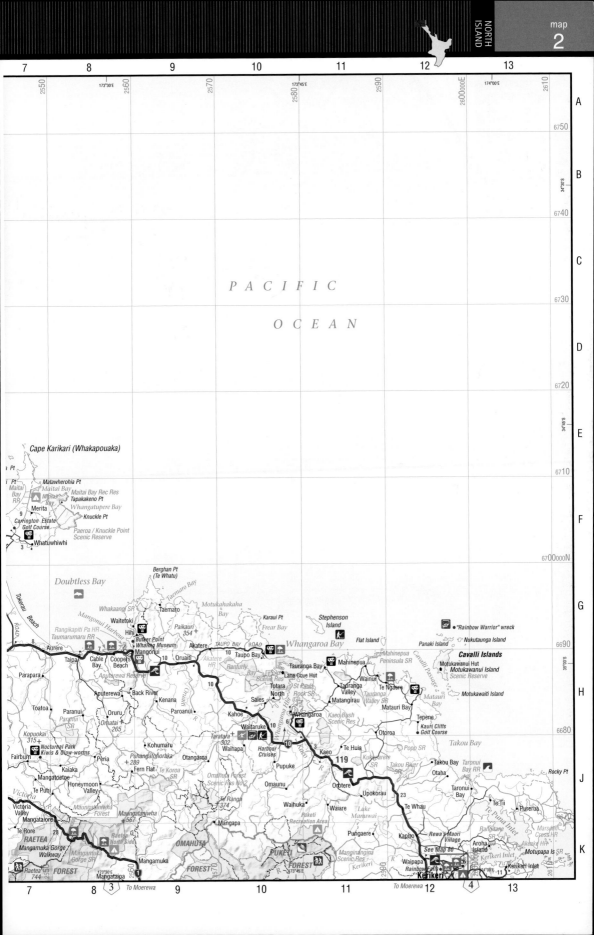

map
3
NORTH ISLAND
Kauri Coast & Whangarei

© Hema Maps NZ Ltd

TASMAN SEA

0   10 km

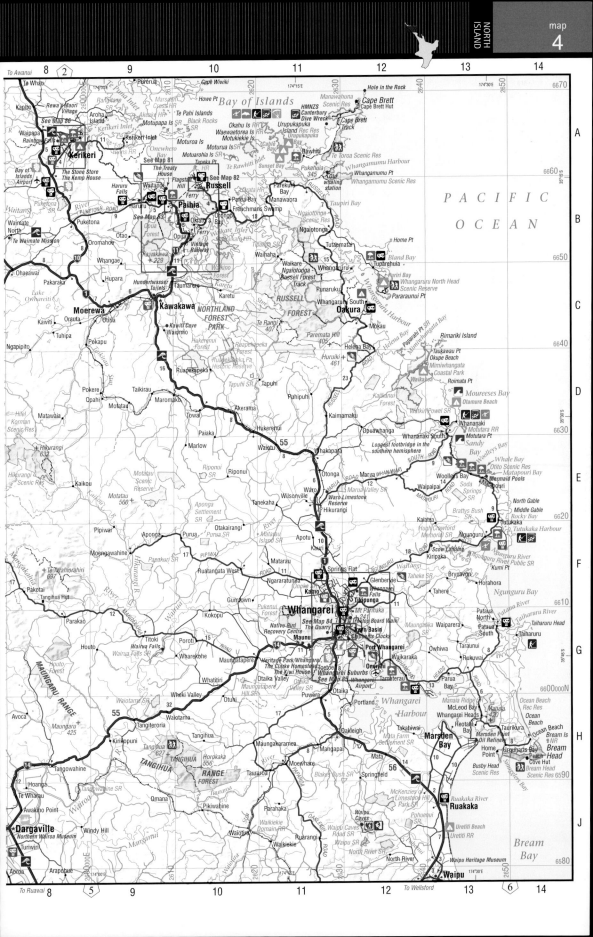

map
5
NORTH ISLAND
Kaipara Harbour & Kowhai Coast

To Dargaville

Tasman Sea

$T\ A\ S\ M\ A\ N$

$S\ E\ A$

6580
6570
6560
6550
6540
6530
6520
6510
6500000N
6490

173°45'E
174°00'E
174°15'E

36°00'S
36°15'S
36°30'S
36°45'S

2580
2590
260000mE
2610
2620
2630
2640

Rehutai
Mahuta
Aoroa
Arapohue
Okahu
North River
Aratapu
Mititai
Montgomeres Memorial Bush SR
Maungaraho Rock
Taipuhi
Braigh
Te Kopuru
Tokatoka
Rehia
Parahi
Parahi SR
Pukekohe Hill Scenic Res
Mareretu
Waipu Gorge Scenic Res
Tatarariki
Tokatoka SR
Ararua
Redhill
Repia
Naumai
Whenuanui
Smoky Hill Scenic Res
Paparoa
Paparoa Stm
Wairere
Brynderwyn
Glinks Gully
Land Yachting
Koremoa
Raupo
Matakohe
The Kauri Museum
Pahi & Pahi River SR
Huarau
Maungaturoto
Pukekaroro
Maungaturoto SR
Tikinui
Ruawai
Mapau
Te Kowhai
Pahi
Whakapirau
Upper Pahi River SR
Marohemo
Taingaehe
Hukatere
Giant Moreton Bay Fig Tree
Te Opu SR
Whakapirau River SR
Hukatere SR
Arapaoa
Arapaoa River
Tanoa
Batley
Otamatea River
Rototuna
Lake Rototuna
Kellys Bay
Tinopai
Otamatea River
Oruawharo
Port Albert
The Bluff
Puketotara Peninsula
Oneriri
Minesdale Historic Church
Lake Karaka
Lake Hamuhamu
Wharehine
Lake Mokeno
Lake Rotokawau
Okahukura
Burma Road Scenic Res
Lake Whakaneke
Lake Kanono
Pouto Point
Tapora
Okahukura Peninsula
Hiki Stream SR
North Head
Pouto Lighthouse
Kaipara North Head Lighthouse Hist Res
Kaipara Head
Okahukura Rec Res
Te Ngaio Pt
Karaka Pt
Orongo Pt
Kaipara Entrance
South Head
Moturemu Island Scenic Reserve
57
Wainui Inlet
Te Kawau Pt
South Head
Lake Ototoa Scenic Reserve
Tokotoroto Pt
Kakanui Pt
Te Oneone Rangitira Beach
SOUTH HEAD ROAD
Lake Kuwakatai
Waioneke
Mairetahi
Lake Kereta
Shelly Beach
Oyster Pt
Kaukapakapa SR
Beware of rips when swimming
Parkhurst
Parakai Hot Springs
Parakai
Helensville
Te Pua
Woodhill Forest
Wharepapa
Muriwai Beach
Woodhill
Woodhill Tree Adventure Park
Muriwai Regional Park

Kaipara

Kaipara Harbour

Otamatea River

Paparoa Stm

N

0   10 km

© Hema Maps NZ Ltd

12
28
44
16
18
22
8
13
2
7
11
5
20
17
10

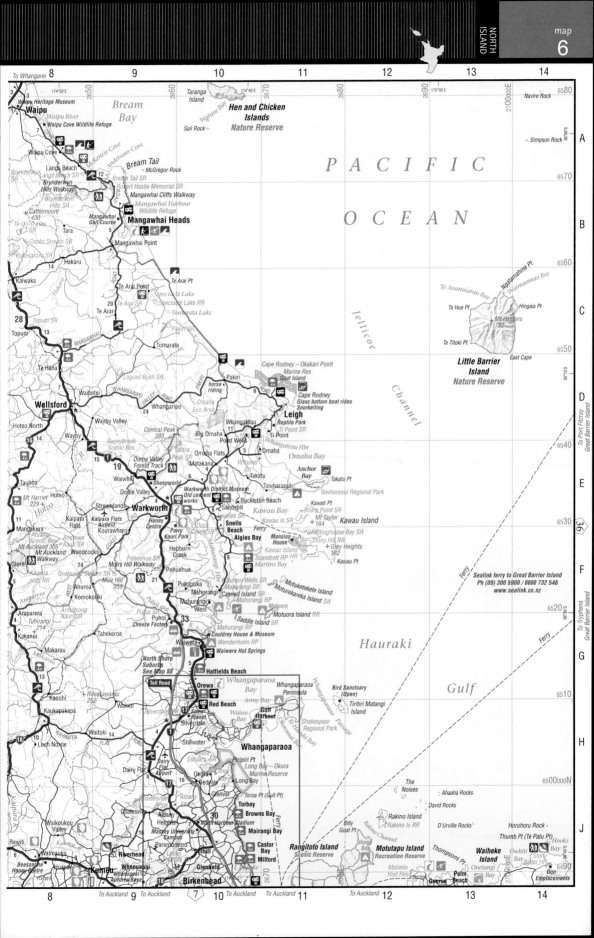

map
7
NORTH ISLAND
Auckland & Coromandel

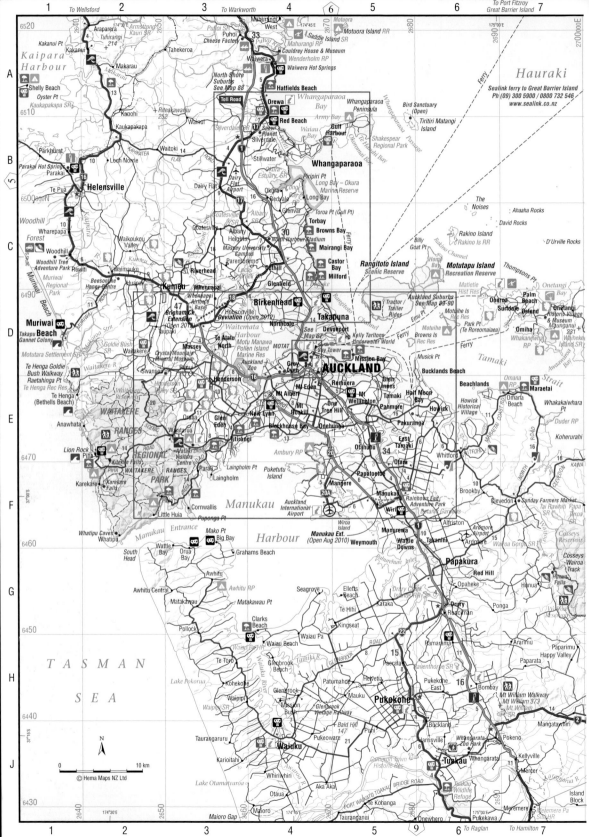

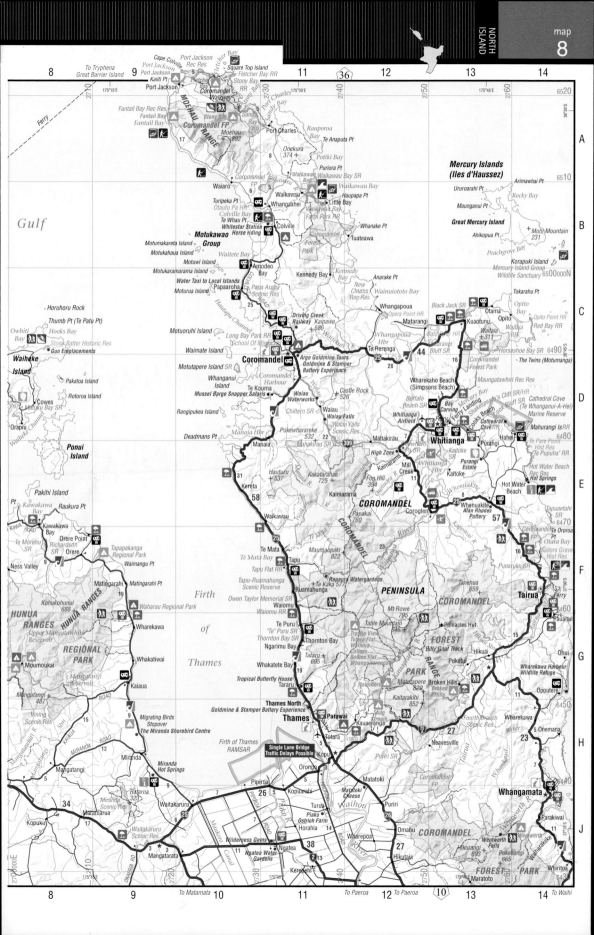

map

9

NORTH ISLAND

Waikato

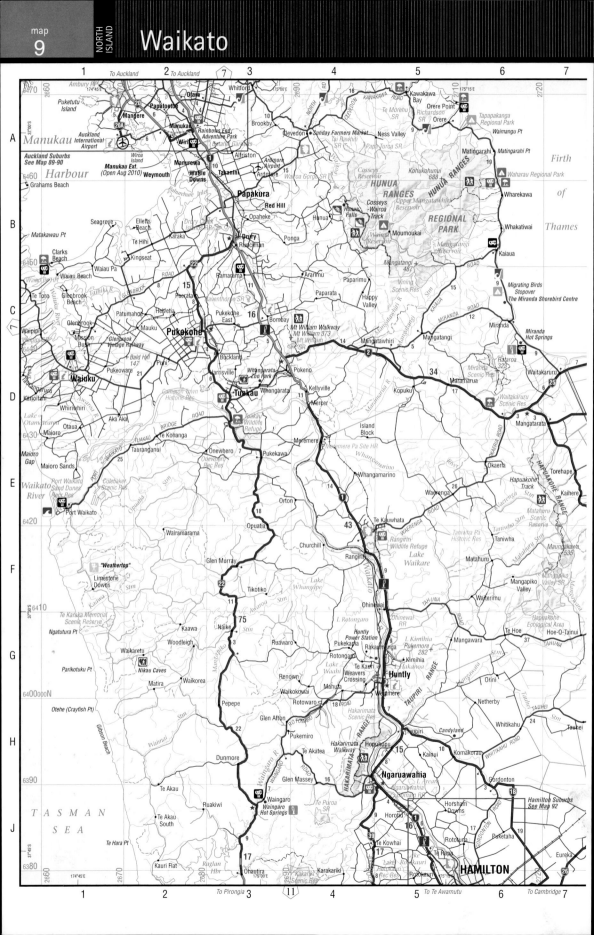

7 To Coromandel 8 9 10 To Whitianga 11 12 13

Waikawau
Te Mata
Te Mata Bay
Tapu
Tapu Flat RR
Maumaupaki 822
Papakai 760
COROMANDEL PENINSULA
Tapuaetahi Scenic Res
To Ororoa Pt
Otara Bay
Sailors Grave Historic Reserve
Pohutukawa Grove RR
Twin Kauris SR
The Aldermen Islands
Nature Reserve

A

Tapu-Ruamahunga Scenic Reserve
Owen Taylor Memorial SR
Waiomu
Waiomu RR
Te Kaka Watergardens
Rapaura
Ruamahunga
Tanehua 659
COROMANDEL
Tairua
Paku 79 Ferry
Shoe Island (Motuhoa)

N

Te Puru
'Te' Puru SR
Thornton Bay SR
Ngarimu Bay
Thornton Bay
Mt Rowe 795
Table Mountain 846
Pinnacles Hut
FOREST
Billy Goat Track
Hikuai
Puketui
Pauanui
Pauanui 387

Slipper Island

0   10 km
© Hema Maps NZ Ltd

B

Whakatete Bay
Tropical Butterfly House
Tararu
Taparu 695
Hotoritori
Motutapere 828
Broken Hills
RANGE
Kaitarakihi 852
PARK
Ohui

Opoutere
Opoutere Beach Recreation Reserve
Wharekawa Harbour Wildlife Refuge
Wharekawa Harbour

PACIFIC

Thames North
Goldmine & Stamper Battery Experience
Thames
Parawai
Totara
Kauaeranga
Shag Stream
Fourth Branch Scenic Res
Wharekawa

OCEAN

C

Firth of Thames RAMSAR
Single Lane Bridge Traffic Delays Possible
Kopu
Orongo
Smith St
Puriri SR
Coromandel FP
Neavesville
Tairua River
Whenuakite
Onemana
Onemana Scenic Res
Charter Boats
Boat Cruises
Swimming with Dolphins

Pipiroa
Kopuarahi
Matatoki
Turua
Matatoki Cheese
Puriri
Coromandel FP
Whangamata
Whangamata Harbour
Whangamata Islands Sanctuary

D

Wilderness Gems
Ngatea
Ngatea Water Gardens
Horahia
Piako Ostrich Farm
Wharepoa
Omahu
Hikutaia
COROMANDEL
Wentworth Falls
Wentworth Valley
Parakiwai
Te Karetu Pt
Te Ramarama SR
Waiharakeke
Waimama RR
Whiritoa

HAURAKI PLAINS
Kerepehi
Maratoto
FOREST
Hikutangi 693
Pukehangi 665
Whakamoehau 750
Otonga Pt
Mataora Bay

Tuhua (Mayor Island) Marine Res

E

Komata
Netherton
Golden Cross
Komata Reefs
PARK
RANGE
28
Homunga Bay
Orokawa Scenic Reserve
Orokawa Bay

Opuahan 355
Mayor Island (Tuhua)
Tokimataa Pt

Patetonga
Awaiti
Paeroa
L & P Bottle
Waitekauri
Martha Gold & Silver Mine
Waihi
Golden Valley

F

Patetonga Rec Res
Te Moananui
Tirohia
Karangahake Gorge
Karangahake 544
Puketawa 548
Mackaytown
Karangahake
Waikino
Dickey Flat
Waitawheta
Goldfields Railway
Waihi Waterlily Gardens
Waihi Gold Mining Museum & Arts Centre
Rain Rides
Waimata
Waihi Beach
Island View
Hot Springs
Pios Beach
Bowentown
Bowentown Domain RR
Katikati Entrance

Waiti
Tahuna
Te Aroha Aerodrome
Tahuna RR
Otway
Mangaiti
Mangaiti SR
Daly's Clearing Hut
Athenree
Athenree HB
Tuapiro Point RR
Kauri Point Hist Res

G

Hangawera 302
Springdale
Elstow
Mangakino Track
KAIMAI-MAMAKU
Waitawheta Hut
Tahawai
Woodlands
Matakana Island

Morrinsville
Kuranui
Te Aroha
Bath Houses
Soda Geyser
Waihou
Waiorongomai
Wairakau
FOREST
Te Aroha 952
Pahiko 788
Te Rereatukahia Hut
Sapphire Springs
Katikati
Murais Town
Tauranga
Omokoroa Beach
Gerald Grapp Hill

H

Mangateparu
Te Puninga
Te Aroha West
Waitoa
Tatuanui
Waiorongomai
Shaftesbury
Motutapere Hut
Motutapere 746
Sapphire Springs RR
Katikati Lavender
Aongatete
Harbour
Matahui Pt
Rangiwaea Island
Omokoroa
Pahoia
Plummers Point
Fernland Spa Mineral Pools

Motumaoho
Tahuroa
Kiwitahi Station
Ngarua
Hungahunga
Gordon
Kauritatahi Hut
Ngatamahinerua 849
Waipuna
Minden Scenic Res
Minden
Te Puna
Wairoa
Bethlehem
Tauranga
Gate Pa
Te Puke

J

Kuranui
Kiwitahi
WALTON
Walton
Matamata Aerodrome
Wardville
Wairere Falls SR
Gordon Park
Turangaomoana
Maurihoro Scenic Res
Whakamarama
Puketoki Scenic Res
Tauriko
Greerton
Waimapu
Welcome Bay

7 8 9 To Matamata 10 11 12 To Tirau 13

map
11

NORTH ISLAND

Central Waikato

1 2 3 To Pukekohe 4 9 5 To Huntly 6 7

N

0 10 km

© Hema Maps NZ Ltd

A

B

C

D

E

F

G

H

J

Major places: Ngaruawahia, HAMILTON (See Map 91), Raglan, Te Awamutu, Kihikihi, Pirongia, Kawhia, Otorohanga, Waitomo Caves, Te Kuiti, Tokanui

Hamilton Suburbs See Map 92

PIRONGIA FOREST PARK

Raglan Harbour, Aotea Harbour, Kawhia Harbour

Kawhia Museum Boat Cruises History Tours
Te Puia Springs

Waingaro Hot Springs

Horse riding

Bridal Veil Falls (Waireinga)

Piripiri Caves
Mangapohue Natural Bridge
Marokopa Falls
Waitomo Caves Museum of Caves
Shearing Shed
Aultura Gardens & Wildlife Park
The Kiwi House
Woodlyn Park

Shearing Capital of the World

Lake Taharoa, Lake Harihari, Lake Ngaroto, Lake Serpentine Rec Res, Lake Rotomanu, Lake Maratoto, Lake Rotokauri

HAKARIMATA RANGE
TAUPIRI RA

To New Plymouth 5 To Tokoroa 6 18 7

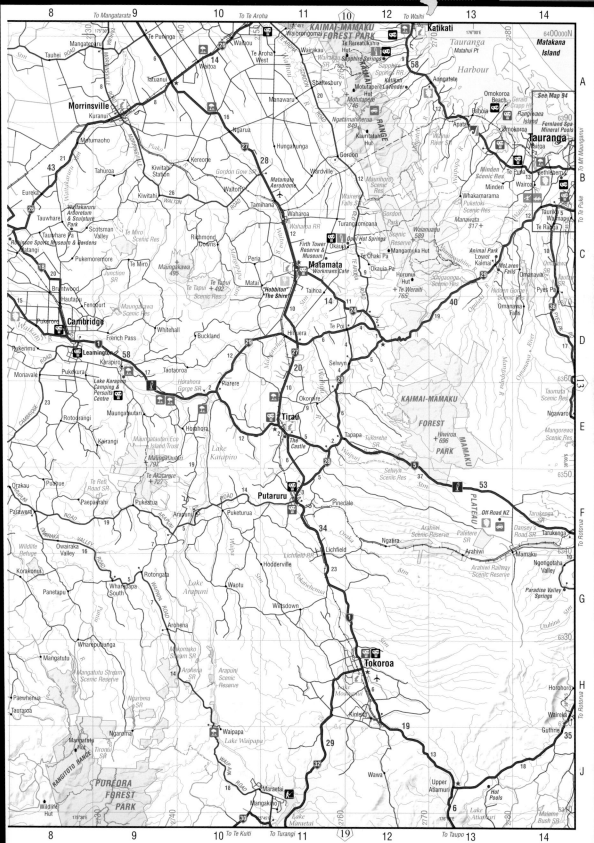

To Mangatarata
To Te Aroha
To Waihi

KAIMAI-MAMAKU FOREST PARK

Katikati
Tauranga Matakana Island
Harbour

Te Puninga
Mangateparu
Tauhei
Waihou
Wairakau
Waiorongomai
Te Rereatukahia Hut
Matahui Pt
Matakana Island

Waitoa
Te Aroha West
Sapphire Springs
Katikati Hut
Motutapere Lavender
Aongatete

Morrinsville
Tatuanui
Manawaru
Shaftesbury
Motutapere 746
Omokoroa Beach
See Map 94

Kuranui
Ngatamahinerua 849
Pahoia
Rangiwaea Island
Fernland Spa Mineral Pools

Motumaoho
Ngarua
Kauritatahi Hut
Apata
Omokoroa
Tauranga

43
Tahuroa
Kiwitahi Station
Hungahunga
Gordon
Waitoa
Te Puke
Bethlehem

Eureka
Kiwitahi
Walton
Wardville
Mourihoro Scenic Res
Minden Scenic Res
Te Puna
Wairoa

Waitakaruru Arboretum & Sculpture Park
Tamihana
Waharoa
Wairere Falls SR
Whakamarama
Puketoki Scenic Res
Minden

Tauwhare
Scotsman Valley
Waharoa RR
Turangaomoana
Gordon Park Scenic Reserve
Manawata 317

Robinson Sports Museum & Gardens
Matangi
Richmond Downs
Firth Tower Reserve & Museum
Okauia
Opal Hot Springs
Waianuadu 589
Animal Park Lower Kaimai

Pukemoremore
Te Miro
Peria
Matamata
Te Ohaki SR
Mangamuka Hut
McLaren Falls
Omanawa

Bruntwood
Hautapu
Maungakawa 495
Workmans Cafe
Okauia Pa
Horonui Hut
Ongaonga Scenic Res
Omanawa Falls

Cambridge
Whitehall
"Hobbiton" "The Shire"
Taihoa
Te Weraiti 765
40
Hidden Gorge Scenic Res

Pukerimu
Fencourt
Te Tapui 492 Scenic Res
Hinuera
Te Poi
Pyes Pa

Leamington
French Pass
Buckland
Selwyn
Omanawa

Pukekura
Karapiro
Taotaoroa
Okoroire
KAIMAI-MAMAKU
Taumata Scenic Res

Monavale
Lake Karapiro Camping & Persuits Centre
Piarere
Tirau
FOREST
Ngawaro

Rotoorangi
Horahora Gorge SR
The Castle
Tapapa
Hiwiroa 696
Mangorewa Scenic Res

Kairangi
Horahora
Tukorehe
PARK

Maungatautari
Maungatautari Eco Island Trust
Matingatautari 797
Tapa
Selwyn Scenic Res
Dansey's Road SR
Tarukenga

Orakau
Puahue
Te Reti Road SR
Te Akatarere 727
Putaruru
Pinedale
Off Road NZ
PLATEAU

Parawera
Paepaerahi
Pukeatua
Puketurua
Ngatira
Arahiwi Scenic Reserve
Pafetere SR
Mamaku

Wildlife Refuge
Owairaka Valley
Rotongata
Lichfield
Lichfield RR
Arahiwi
Ngongotaha Valley

Korakonui
Panetapu
Wharepapa South
Lake Arapuni
Waotu
Hodderville
Arahiwi Railway Scenic Reserve
Paradise Valley Springs

Arohena
Wiltsdown
Horohoro

Wharepuhunga
Makomako Stream Scenic Reserve
Arapuni Scenic Reserve
Tokoroa
Waireka

Mangatutu
Ngaroma SR
Kinleith
Guthrie

Paewhenua
Tauraroa
RANGITOTO RANGE
Tironui SR
Waipapa
Lake Waipapa
Wawa
Upper Atiamuri
Hot Pools

Mangatutu Hut
PUREORA FOREST PARK
Maraetai
Mangakino
Lake Maraetai
To Te Kuiti
To Turangi
To Taupo
Lake Atiamuri
Maleme Bush SR

Wildlife Hut

To Te Aroha
To Waihi
To Mt Maunganui
To Te Puke
To Rotorua
To Te Kuiti
To Turangi
To Taupo

map
13
NORTH ISLAND

Rotorua & Bay of Plenty

Katikati
Tauranga
Mt Maunganui
Omanu Beach
Papamoa Beach
Te Puke
Te Puke Vintage Auto Barn
Blokart Landsailing Centre
Makatu
Little Waihi
Pukehina
Pukehina Beach
Okurei Pt
Ohinepanea
Motiti Island
Motuhaku Island (Schooner Rocks)
Motunau Island (Plate Island)
Tumu Bay
Taumaika Pt
Tauranga Suburbs See Map 94

KAIMAI-MAMAKU FOREST PARK
MAMAKU PLATEAU

Rotorua
Ngongotaha
Lake Rotorua
Rotorua Museum
The Bath House
Orchid Gardens
Rotorua Airport
Hannahs Bay
Rotorua Suburbs See Map 96

Lake Rotoiti
Lake Rotoehu
Lake Rotoma
Lake Rotomahana
Lake Tarawera
Lake Okataina
Lake Tikitapu
Lake Rotokakahi

Whakarewarewa Thermal Valley
Pohutu Geyser
The Buried Village
Waimangu Volcanic Valley
Wai-O-Tapu Thermal Area
Lady Knox Geyser
Kerosene Creek Thermal Area
Waikite Valley Hot Pools & Thermal Area
Tamaki Maori Village

To Waihi
To Matamata
To Putaruru
To Tirau
To Tokoroa
Tokoroa
To Taupo
To Murupara

PACIFIC OCEAN

Bay of Plenty

Whakaari / White Island
New Zealand's most
frequently active volcano

N

0   10 km
© Hema Maps NZ Ltd

Tokata Island   Rurima Island
                 Moutoki Island

Moutohora Island
No Access
Permit Required

Pikowai
Kohioawa
Beach
59
Ohinekoao RR
Ohinekoao
Scenic Res
Matata
Scenic Res
Matata

5
Awakaponga
19
Thornton
Thornton Beach Park RR

Dolphin Safaris
White Island Tours
Whakatane
Wairere
Waterfall

Piripai
Paroa
6
13
2
4
Edgecumbe
30
Poroporo
Pahou
Kohi Point Scenic Res
Te Rangi HR
Te Paripari Pa HR

Otakiri
10
10
Awakeri
Ohope
SR
Ohope
Ohiwa
Oyster Farm
Ohiwa
Ohiwa
Hbr
Port Ohope
Port Ohope RR
Waiotahi Spit SR
Waiotahi Spit HR
Waiotahi Beach
Dolphin Safaris

Manawahe
34
Awakeri Springs
Awakeri
Uretara Is SR
Ohiwa
Kukumoa
Omarumutu

13
9
Awakeri
Hot Springs
White Pine
Bush
Mokorua
Bush SR
11
Wainui
Motuotu Is NR
19
Tablelands
Tirohanga
11

12
3
30
White Pine
Bush
15
Cheddar Valley
Kutarere RR
Kutarere
Opotiki
Hospital Hill
Waiaua

Te Teko
13
Waiotane
Scenic Res
Waingarara
Kererutahi
Kutarere
Waiotahi
Marae
Paerata Ridge
Woodlands
Apanui
Waiaua
School
Reserve

Ohepu
Taneatua
Stanley
Falls SR
Kotare SR
Matekerepu
Hist Res
Waiotahi
SR
Waiotahi
Valley
Taketakerau
2000 year old
Puriri Tree
Otara
Waioeka Pa

Parimahana
SR
9
Kawerau
Te Mahoe
Opouriao
Waimana Gorge
Scenic Reserve
9
Matahapa
Hokutaia
Domain RR
Hine Rae HR
Marawairau
Scenic Res
Zohs Acquisition
Scenic Res

7
34
Putauaki
(Mt Edgecumbe)
821
Ruatoki
North
19
Nukuhou
North
58
2
Matahanea
41
Waioeka
Gorge
Boulders
+697
6330

Matahina
17
Waimana
Tataiahapi Pa
Tanatana
Te Pakau
(8. Acre)
Tukaigiuka
Scenic Res
Maungawhiorangi
814
Oktore
Scenic
Reserve
Turaetoko
914
Te Waiti Hut
Te Waiti Hill
1011
6320

Lake
Matahina
Waikirikiri
Raroa
Track
Matahi
Ruatupakuu
706
2

Waiohau
16
Te Whakaumu
+765
Wharekahika
Whakarae
Tahora
Oponae
Wairata
Waioeka
Gorge
SR
Waioeka
Gorge
Scenic
Reserve

Pahekeheke Stm
Waihua Hut
Apiti Hut
Te Hekeotewhare
678
Ohora
Hut
Paraoanui Pa
Tauwhare
Oraukurangi
867
Waoeka
Gorge
SR

TE UREWERA
Mangamako Hut
Onepu
Hut
Omahuru (Ogilvies)
Koaunui Kaharoa
1830
Kotepato
Hut
Okahuata
958
10
29

NATIONAL PARK
Hikurangi
929
Koputiki
Duckville
Hut
Rakautapu
767
Otamatuna
Ridge Track
Otamatuna Hut

Horomanga
20
21

To Te Kaha
To Gisborne

map
15
NORTH ISLAND
Eastern Bay of Plenty & East Cape

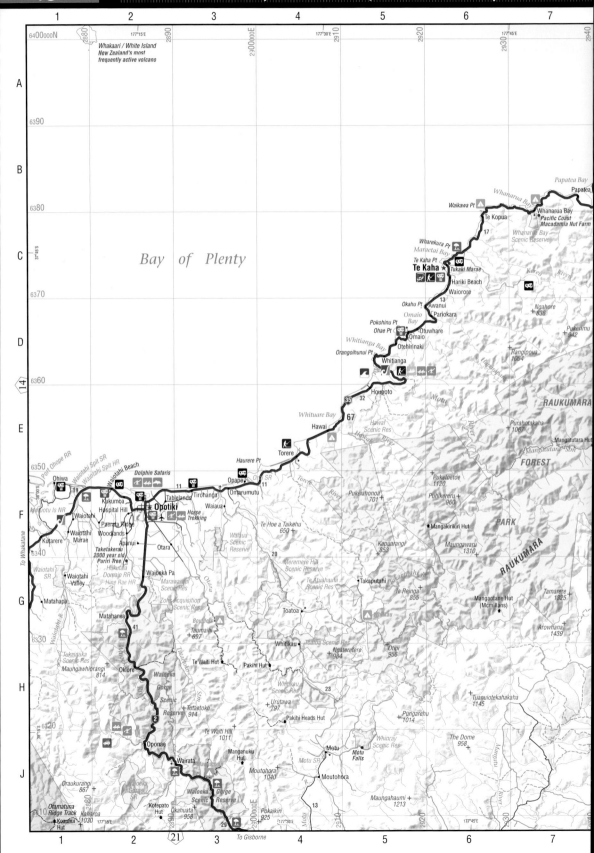

Whakaari / White Island
New Zealand's most
frequently active volcano

Bay of Plenty

Papatea Bay
Papatea

Waikawa Pt
Te Kopua
Whanarua Bay
Pacific Coast
Macadamia Nut Farm
17
Whanarua Bay
Scenic Reserve

Wharekura Pt
Maraetai Bay
Te Kaha Pt
Te Kaha ★
Tukaki Marae
Hariki Beach
Waiorore

Okahu Pt
Awanui
13
Pariokara

Pokohinu Pt
Omaio
Bay
Ohae Pt
Otuwhare
Omaio
Otehirinaki
Orangoihunui Pt
Whitianga Bay
Whitianga

Ngahore
836

Pukennu
942

Rangipoua
1064

RAUKUMARA

Houpoto
35 32
67
Whituare Bay
Hawai
*Hawai
Scenic Res*

Purahotakaha
1067

Mangatutara Str
Mangatutara Str

FOREST

Haurere Pt
Torere
Opape
Omarumutu
11 11
Orini SR

Puketoetoe
1120
Puhikereru
960

Port Ohope RR
Ohiwa
Waiotahi Spit SR
Waiotahi Spit HR
Waiotahi Beach
Dolphin Safaris
Kukumoa
Hospital Hill
Tablelands
Tirohanga
Waiaua
Motu Is NR
Waiotahi
Opotiki
*Horse
Trekking*
Paerata Ridge
Woodlands
Apanui
*Taketakerau
2000 year old
Puriri Tree*
Otara
*Hikurangi
Domain RR Hine Rae HR*
Waioeka Pa
*Marawainui
Scenic Res*
Kutarere
Waiotahi
Marae
Matahapa
Matahanea
41
Waiotahi
SR
Waiotahi
Valley
Oklore

Te Hoe a Taikehu
650
20
*Meremere Hill
Scenic Reserve*
*Te Atuahaua
Scenic Res*
Takaputahi
Toatoa
*Zone Acquisition
Scenic Res*
Boulders
Taumaini
697
Te Waiti Hut
Whitikau
Pakihi Hut
*Ngateretere
984*
Toatoa Scenic Res
Otipi
956
Te Reinga
855
*Whinray
Scenic Res*
Mangaotane Hut
(Mcmillans)
Tamarere
1325
Arowhana
1439

Mangakirikiri Hut
Kapuarangi
853
Maungawaru
1310
Puketoetoe

RAUKUMARA

Pukeiahonoa
701
Pukeiahonoa

Tuaiguka
Scenic Res
Maungawhiorangi
814
2
*Waioeka
Gorge
Scenic
Reserve*
Tutaetoko
914
Te Waiti Hill
1011
Urutawa
797
Pakihi Heads Hut
23
Tuanuiotekahakaha
1145

Oponae
Wairata
*Waioeka
Gorge
SR*
Kotepato
Hut
*Waioeka
Scenic
Gorge
Reserve*
Okahuata
958
Pokaikiri
925
Manganuku
Hut
Moutohora
1040
Motu SR
Moutohora
*Motu
Falls*
Maungahaumi
1213
*Whinray
Scenic Res*
The Dome
958

Oraukurangi
867
*Otamatuna
Ridge Track*
Koanui
1030
Kaharoa
Koanui
Hut
10
29
13
21
To Gisborne

map
17
NORTH ISLAND
North Taranaki & Taumarunui

N

0   10 km

© Hema Maps NZ Ltd

TASMAN SEA

North Taranaki Bight

HERANGI RANGE

Maungamangero 806
Waitanguru
Taumatamahoe
Mangaohae Stream SR
Haku
Mangaotaki
Rararimu Stream Scenic Reserve
Te Marama Scenic Res
Mangatoa Scenic Res
Leitchs Hut
Waikawau
Mangaotaki Scenic Res
Waikawau
Mangaorongo SR
Grand Canyon Nature Reserve
Paemako SR
Manganui Gorge Scenic Res
Huikomako Scenic Reserve
Mahoenui Scenic Reserve
23
67
Mangaotaki Gorge Scenic Res
Manganui Road Scenic Reserve
Mahoenui
3
Awakino SR
Arorangi Scenic Reserve
26
Mangaroa SR
Awakino
Mokau
Mokau SR
Mackford
Mokau Scenic Reserve
Tainui SR
Mokau River Scenic Reserve
Mokau River Scenic Reserve
Pura SR
Tawhitiraupeka 533
Mohakatino R
22
Umukaha Point Rec Res
Pou Tehia HR
Tongaporutu
Hutiwai Stm
Mt Roa 376
Waitaanga
Mangaroa SR
19
Whitecliffs Walkway
Ahititi
Okau
Kotare
N.G. Tucker Scenic Res
Pukearuhe HR
Mt Davidson SR
Mt Messenger
Kotare Scenic Res
Te Rerepahupahu Falls
Waiaraia
Pukearuhe
Mt Messenger 310
32
Mt Damper Falls
Mt Damper 528
Tatu
Pukearuhe Scenic Res
16
Rerekapa Hut
Rerekapa Track
Rerekapa Falls
Okau SR
Mimi SR
Uruti
Mironui Scenic Res
Moki SR
Rerekapa Falls Rec Res
Mangapapa Stream Scenic Reserve
Waitoetoe RR
Mimi R
Uruti Domain Scenic Res
Miro SR
Lancaster SR
30
16
84
Okoki Pa Hist Res
Uruti SR
Tangarakau Scenic Res
Tangarakau Gorge
Waitara
Motunui
Onaero
Urenui
Waitara R
Tahora SR
Moki Tunnel
Tahora
Raekohua Falls
Tangarakau
Brixton
Manukorihi RR
Onaero River SR
Okoki
Matau SR
Puketapu PHR
Kaipikari
Sentry Hill
Tikorangi
Awa-te-take Pa HR
Pehu Scenic Res
Mangare Scenic Res
17
Kohuratahi
Huirangi
Awa-te-take SR
Pukemgiora Pa HR
Mangapaka Scenic Res
Kohura SR
Marco
Lepperton
Everett Park Scenic Res
Rimutauteka Scenic Res
Omaero R
Urenui R
Awahou Scenic Res
Whangamomona
3A
Waitara River
Whangamomona Scenic Reserve
Putikituna SR
Inglewood
Tarata
Purangi
Matau
Pohokura
40
Fun Ho! National Toy Museum
Kaimata
Purangi SR
Forgotten World Highway
43
10
Norfolk
Ratapiko
Lake Ratapiko
Waitara River
Mokau Stm
Mokoly R
Whangamomona R
Whangamonona R

To New Plymouth
To Stratford

23
11
3
25

8 9 10 11 12 12 13 14

To Te Kuiti

175°00'E   175°15'E   175°30'E

PUREORA FOREST PARK

To Tokoroa

A

Tanehopuwai
Eight Mile Junction
Waiteti
Mokau River
Waipa River
Ahoroa SR
Wildlife Hut

Arapae
Puketutu
Kahuwera SR
15
30

Piopio
Kopaki
Mangaokewa
Waipa Valley
Horokino
Pouakani SR
24

Te Mapara
16
Aratoro
KOPAKI ROAD
Mangaokewa Road Scenic Reserve
84
Barryville

Paemako
Ngatamahine
Mangapehi
Mangapehi SR
Benneydale
Herekawe Scenic Res
Tiroa
22
Pureora
Ngaherenga
Titiraupenga 1042

B

Aria
Taumatiti SR
Puketapu HR
Totoro SR
Turaerae SR
Porootarao
Maraeroa
Pureora 1165
Kakaho

Mokauiti
Mapiu
Tapuwae
Ongarue R
Ongarue SR
Bog Inn Hut
6290

Whareroa Stream SR
29
Tangitu
Waimiha
Piropiro
Piropiro
Ketemaringi 939
Weraroa 1088
Tihoi

C

Pukenewa SR
Puketehi Scenic Res
4
Waihuka SR
Maramataha R
Waione Stm
PUREORA
Tuhingamata 884
50

Waitaka Scenic Res
70
Tapuiwahine
FOREST
Waihaha Hut
32
Waihaha SR

D

Hapu SR
Tangitu SR
Mangatupoto
Ongarue
RANGE
Pakihi 902
Waihaha R
HAUHUNGAROA
Hauhungaroa Hut
Waihaha SR

Matiere
Tuhua
Okahukura SR
Te Koura
Mangakahu Valley
PARK
Tuhua 1042
Te Hiapo 950
Whanganui

E

Nihoniho
26
ROAD
Rangi SR
25
Okahukura
Hikurangi Scenic Res
Hikurangi 771
Ngakonui
Taringamotu Valley
Oruaiwi
Hauhungaroa 1078
Te Aputa
Te Raina
6260

F

Ohura
10
Mangaparo
Ohura SR
Pokoera SR
Oruatira SR
Otunui
Taringamotu
Taumarunui / Raurimu RR
Lairdvale
Echolands
Meringa
Pureora Forest Park
Kuratau Junction
Lake Kuratau

Taumarunui
Taumaruiti
Manunui
Pungapunga
Ngapuke
43
Waituhi-Kuratau Scenic Reserve
Moerangi
41

8
Te Raianga SR
Tunnel Hill SR
Aukopae Tunnel
Te Whakarae
Tunakotekote
Piriaka
Kakahi
The Ratas SR
41
18
6250

G

Nevis Lookout
Tokirima
72
Aukopae
43
Ohinepani
Te Maire
11
Hikumutu
Piriaka Lookout
Whakapapa Island Scenic Reserve
Kuharua 1129
Waihi Hot Springs
21

Heao
Koiro
Kokakonui SR
Wall SR
Hikumutu SR
Whakapapa Gorge Scenic Reserve
Whanganui River
Pukepoto Ecological Area
Mangahouhou
Kakaramea 1300

Opatu
Kirikau
Te Ruatine Scenic Reserve
Kawautahi
Owhango
43
Ohinetonga Scenic Res
Otamajutara Stream SR
Lake Otamangakau
TONGARIRO NP

H

Whakahoro Hut
Whakahoro
Maungaroa
Papapotu SR
Retaruke
Ngamoturiki SR
Owairua SR
4
Oio
Ten Man Hut
Te Porete Pa Hist Res
Pihanga SR
Tongariro
Papakai
Otukou
Lake Rotoaira
46
19

Kaitieke
36
Hukapapa
Taurewa 1076
Sir Edmund Hilary Outdoor Pursuits Centre
Ketetahi
49
Taurewa
17
Tongariro Crossing
6230

Retaruke Upper
Oio SR
Kooini Scenic Res
Mansons Siding
42nd Traverse
Ketetahi Hut
Mt Tongariro 1967
Tongariro Northern Circuit

J

Te Mata 585
Riamaki (Upper Ruatiti)
Pairawahipi Scenic Reserve
Upper Retaruke Valley SR
Raurimu
Manga Te Puhi SR
Raurimu Spiral
Raurimu Spiral Scenic Reserve
47
Mountain Air Scenic Flights
National Park Climbing Wall
Ketetahi Hot Springs
"Plains of Gorgoroth"
Mt Ngauruhoe 2287
"Mount Doom"
Oturere Hut
Blue Lake
Upper Tama Lake

9
Mangahuia
48
Chateau Tongariro
Whakapapa Village
Lower Tama Lake
Waihohonu Hut

5
TONGARIRO NATIONAL PARK
Whakapapa Motor Camp
6220

Waikune
175°00'E
175°15'E
To Raetihi
26
175°30'E

8 9 10 11 12 13 14

To Tokoroa
To Turangi
To Rangipo

map
19
NORTH ISLAND
Taupo

© Hema Maps NZ Ltd

0   10 km

PUREORA FOREST PARK

To Te Kuiti
Barryville
Pureora
Pureora 1165
Bog Inn Hut
Weraroa 1088
Tuhingamata 884
Waihaha Hut
Te Hiapo 950
Hauhungaroa 1078
Te Aputa
Te Raina
Moerangi
Kuratau Junction
Mangahouhou
Otamarautara Scenic Res
Tongariro
Papakai
Ketetahi Hot Springs
"Plains of Gorgoroth"
Mt Tongariro 1967
Mangatepopo Hut
Mt Ngauruhoe 2287 "Mount Doom"
TONGARIRO NATIONAL PARK
Lower Tama Lake
Upper Tama Lake
Waihohonu Hut
Tongariro Northern Circuit
Blue Lake
Tongariro Crossing
Lake Rotoaira
Lake Rotopounamu
Pihanga 1325
Kakaramea 1300
Tokaanu
Waihi
Waihi Hot Springs
Thermal Area & Hot Pools
Tokaanu Thermal Park Rec Res
Picnic Area Scenic Lookout
Turangi
Tongariro National Trout Centre
Climbing Wall
Hautu Village
Stump Bay Scenic Res
Rangipo
Kuharua 1129
Omori
Pukawa
Kopeopou Stream SR
Gardiners RR
Morunga SR
Delta RR
Waimarino RR
Motudapa
Echo Cliffs
Te Rangawha Pt
Te Rangiita
Motutere
Motutere SR
Waitetoko
Waitetoko SR
Orbatua
Oruanui RR
Hatepe
Hinemaiaia Scenic Res
Motutaiko Island
Te Kohaiakahu Pt
Waitahanui
Awaroa Rec Res
Five Mile Bay RR
Taupo Airport
Wharewaka
Waipahihi
Waipahihi Botanical Reserve SR
Taupo Hot Springs
Thermal Baths
Taupo
Nukuhau
Broadlands Road Geothermal SR
Tauhara 1088
Tauhara Mountain SR
Taupo Bungy
Huka Falls
Huka Prawn Park
Volcanic Activity Centre
Wairakei
Craters of the Moon
International Golf Course
Geothermal Village
Geothermal Area
Aratiatia Rapids
Aratiatia Rapids SR
Aratiatia Rapids Rec Res
Rotokawa
Acacia Bay
Taupo Courthouse
Whakaipo Bay SR
Whakaipo Point RR
Kinloch
Kawakawa Pt
Kawakawa Bay SR
Whakaroa Point RR
Whakaipo Bay SR
Te Tuhi Pt
Tuhingamata 661
Tapuaeharuru Bay
Rangatira Point SR
Modern Maori Rock Carvings Accessible by boat only
Whakamoenga Pt
Boat Cruises Trout Fishing
See Map 97
Taupo Suburbs See Map 98

Western Bay
Lake Taupo (Taupomoana)

Wharenui Stm
Lake Kuratau
Rangitukua Scenic Res
Poukura Pa
Te Hapua Bay Scenic Res
Te Oineohu Pt
Karangahape Cliffs
Tangingatahi Pt
Whanganui
Waikino Scenic Res
Hingarae Scenic Res
Waihaha
Kakaho
Tihoi
Okaia Stream SR
Otaketaka Stream Scenic Res
Tutaeuaria SR
Kotukutuku Stream SR
Waihora Stream SR
Titiraupenga 1042
Arataki
Mokai
Oruanui
Te Pouwhakatutu
Maroanui 897
Pakuri SR
Puke SR
Ngamariki Hot Springs Scenic Res
Tahorakuri
Parekarangi
Golden Springs
Mihi
Wairahana
Ohaaki
Te Kopia Scenic Res
PAEROA RA
Paeroa 979
Maleme Bush SR
Atiamuri
Ohakuri
Lake Ohakuri
Puaiti Bush SR
Orakei Korako
The Hidden Valley
Geothermal Area
Waikato River
Opepe Bush Scenic & Historic Reserve
Wharekawa SR
Waimihia
Iwitahi

Lake Maraetai
Lake Whakamaru
Mangakino
Whakamaru
Kaahu SR
Tirohanga Scenic Res

To Tokoroa
To Tokoroa, Rotorua

KAIMANAWA MTNS
KAIMANAWA FOREST
Kaimanawa Road
Umukarikari 1591
Ngapukeahuanga 1439
Waipakihi Hut
Te Raketuangiangi 1605
Makorako 1726
Makokomiko 1454
Ngapuketurua 1510
Pikiawatea 1373
Ahipaepae 1193
Maungaorangi 1436
Waingakia 1617
Waingakla
Tihorea 1024
Te Iringa 1240
Kakapo
Army Road
Clements Clearing
Clements Roadend
Te Iringa
Oamaru Hut
Boyd Hut
Tussock Hut
Ahikaeaea 1242
Mangatainoka Hut
Cascade Hut
KAWEKA

To Waiouru
To Raetihi
To Taumarunui

59
49
48
43
67
21
24
30
12
13
18
17
27
6
1
5

To Rotorua   To Rotorua

8   9   10   11   12   14   13   14

Lady Knox Geyser
Waiotapu Thermal Area
Wharepaina
Reporoa
Broadlands

Wharekaunga Stm
Kaingaroa Forest
Maori Rock Drawings
Wairohia Stm
Wairapukao

Horomanga
Galatea
Fort Galatea Historical Res
Galatea Rec Res
Murupara

Kopuriki
Duckville Hut
TE UREWERA
Hikurangi 929
Rakautapu 767
NATIONAL
Manaohau
Right Branch Hut
Walkare Junction Hut
Oueari 831

PARK
Tawhiuau 1017
Midway Hut
Kanohinui 884
Hanamahihi Hut
Terangaaruamuku 901
Whakatatara 881
Paetawa Track
Pawairoto 827

RANGE
Ngaheramai Hut
Takarua Hut
Otanetea Hut
Taurawharana Hut

Okui Hut
Mangapouri Hut
Tawhiwhi Hut
Ohaua
Te Hue Track
Puketapu 993

Tikorangi 668
Te Whaiti
Taupiri 713
Mangamate

Ngaputahi
IKAWHENUA
Kopuparapara 965
Waiawa Hut
Maungapohatu
Ihutoto 1024
Maungapohatu Track
Kanohirua Hut

Minginui
Mid Okahu Hut
Sanctuary
Okahu
Papueru
Helpipi
194
Ruatahuna
Te Waiti

Te Pokapoka 737
Tuwatawata 1134
Turiohaua 1149
HUIARAU
RANGE
Raukatau 1148
Oranghikaka
Whakatakaa Hut
45

WHIRINAKI
Whakataka 1252
Whanganui Hut
Mokau Tarns Track

FOREST
Skips (Whangatawhia) Hut
Te Totara Hut
Pakiaka Hut (Parahaki)
Waiharuru Hut
Lake Track
Mokau Landing

Mangamate Hut
Moerangi Hut
Rogers Hut (Te Wairoa)
Central Waiau Hut
Marauiti Hut
Lake Waikaremoana

Central Whirinaki Hut
Mangakahika Hut
Te Waiotukapiti Hut
Waiopaoa Hut
Pukenui 1181

PARK
Upper Whirinaki Hut
Maungataniwha 1373
Lake Track
OTAUNOA RANGE
PANEKIRI RANGE
Panekiri Hut

Upper Te Hoe Hut
Central Te Hoe Hut
21

Upper Matakuhia Hut

Rangitaiki
Omeruiti 876
39
Opureke Track
Lower Matakuhia Hut
Lake Rotonuiaha

Te Ihuorurumaioterangi 763
Putete Scenic Res

Lake Pouarua
Runanga Armed Constabulary HR
Otumakiore 1112
128
Waipunga Falls Scenic Reserve
Waipunga Falls
Pohokura

Frasers Bush SR

Kaimatangi 1035
Opoto Scenic Res
Tarawera Hot Springs Scenic Reserve
Hot Springs
Tarawera

Kakariki Scenic Reserve
Manga-whitirangi SR

Panemanga 1014
AHIMANAWA RANGE
Tataraakina 1130
24
Kotemaori

Te Matai 1235
16
Turangakumu Scenic Reserve
Everetts
Boundary Stream Scenic Reserve
106
Putorino

Te Haroto
Tarapsnui 1308
Bellbird Bush Scenic Res
Boundary Stream Track
Oruahi Scenic Reserve

Mangatainoka Hot Springs
Te Puia Lodge
Makino Hut
Glentalls
Kopua 1073
MAUNGAHARURU RANGE

To Napier, Hastings   28   To Napier, Hastings   To Wairoa

map 21 NORTH ISLAND

Hawke's Bay & Gisborne

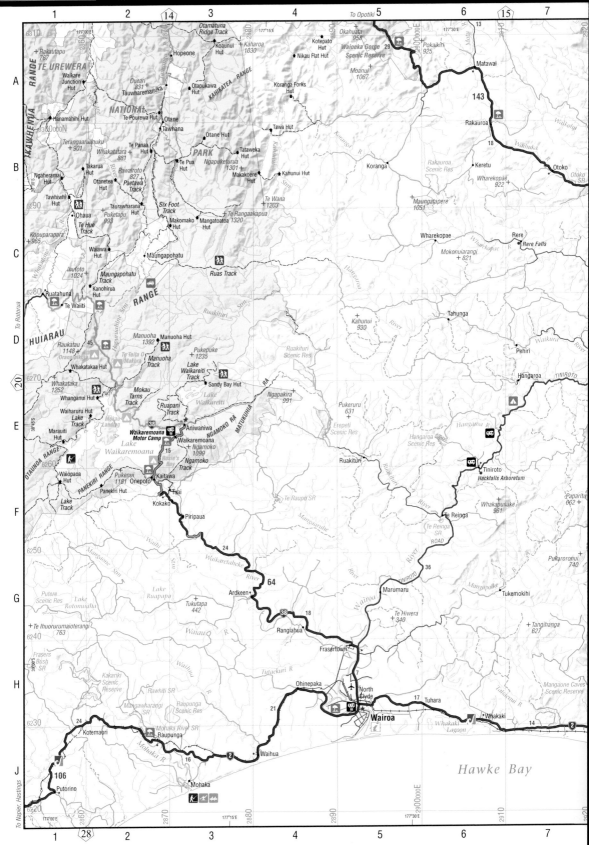

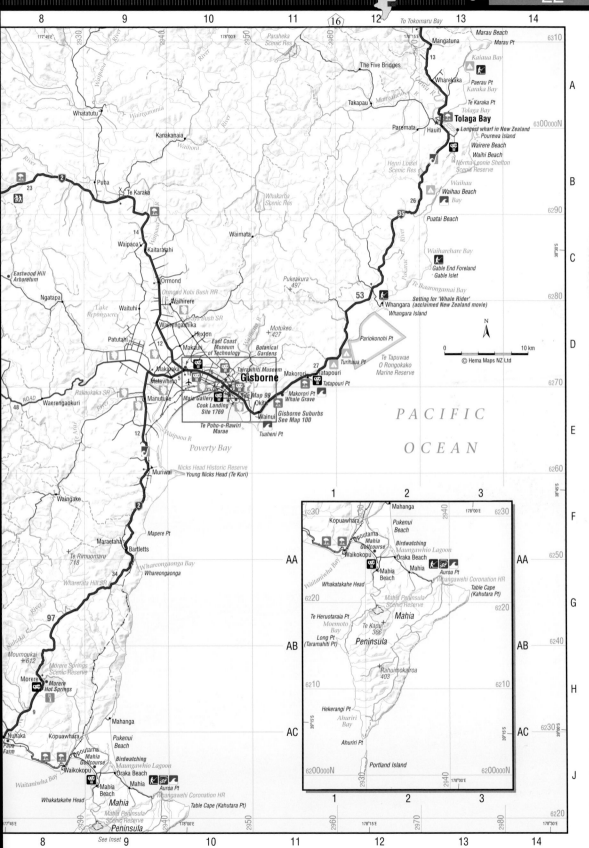

map
23
NORTH ISLAND
Taranaki & River Region

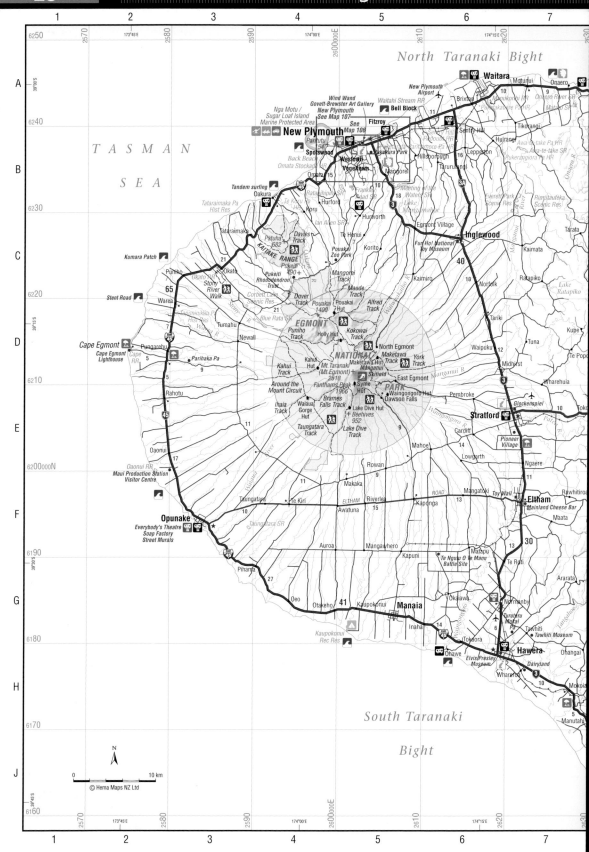

North Taranaki Bight

T A S M A N

S E A

South Taranaki

Bight

0   10 km

© Hema Maps NZ Ltd

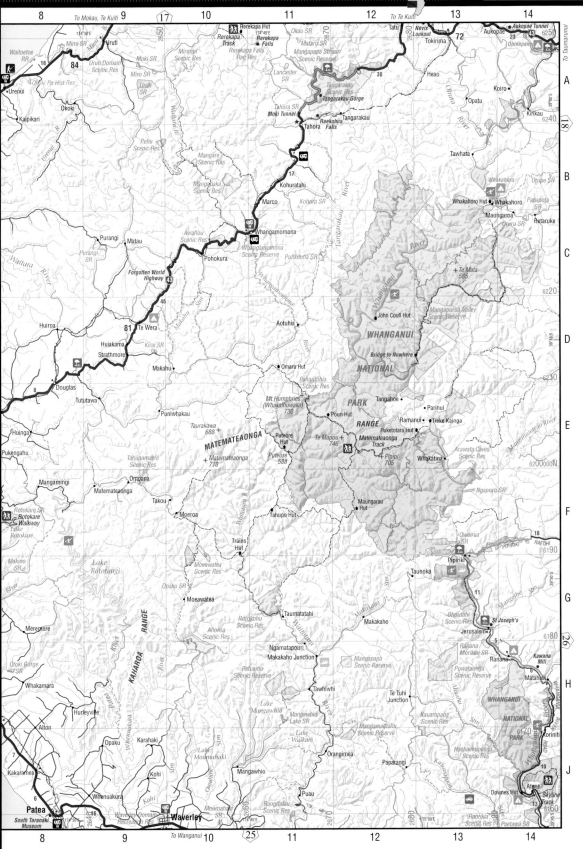

map
25
NORTH
ISLAND
South Taranaki

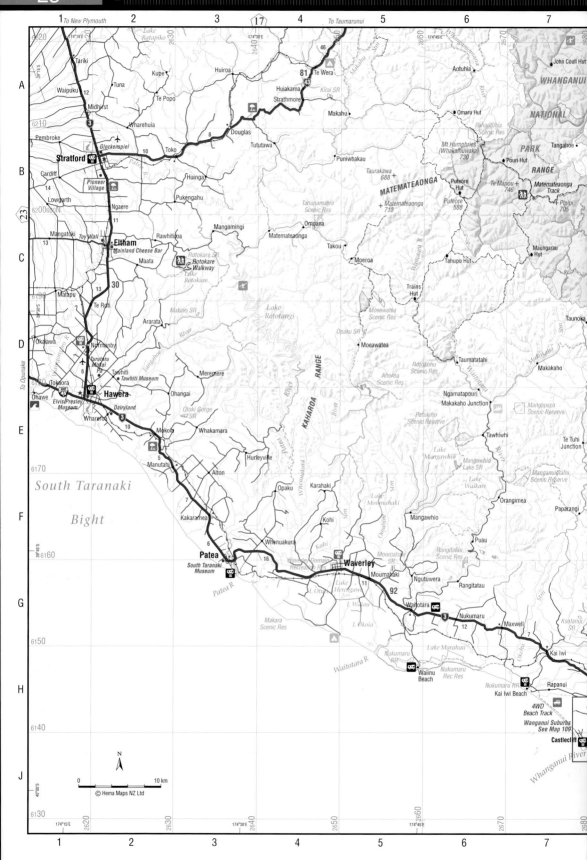

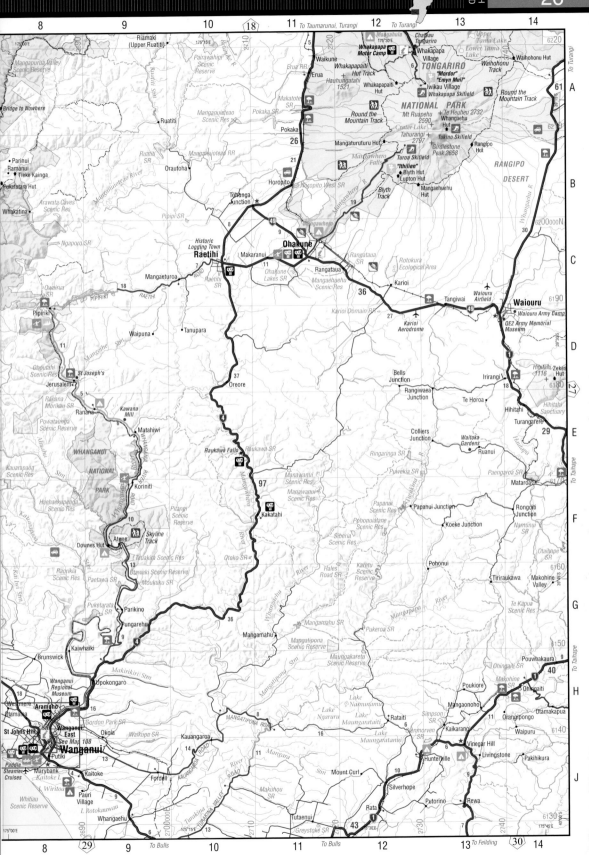

map
27
NORTH ISLAND

Napier & Hastings

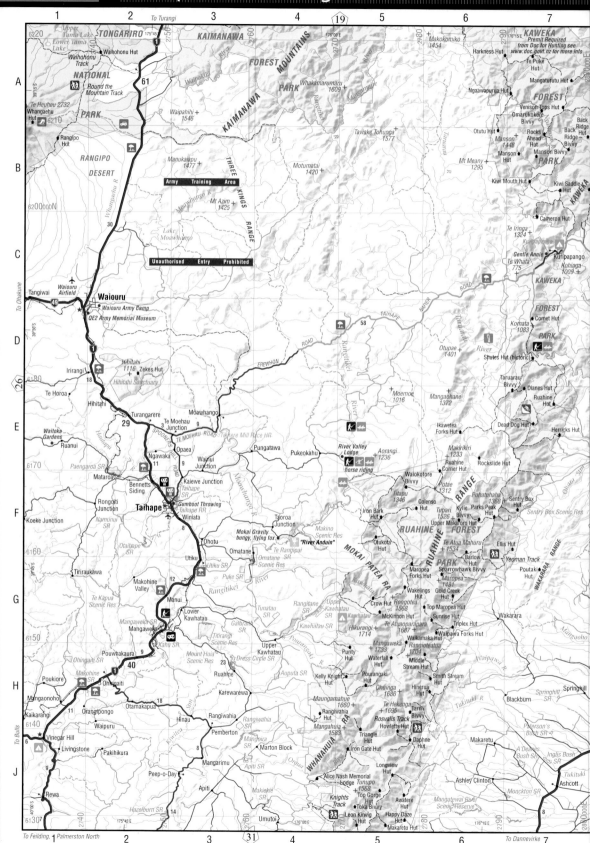

To Taupo   To Wairoa

Mangataira Hot Springs
Te Pua Lodge
Makino Hut
Middle Hill Hut
Ballard Hut
Iron Whare Hut
Kaweka Flats Bivvy
North Kaweka 1707
Dominie Hut
Black Birch Bivvy
Makahu Saddle
Studholme Hut
Saddle Hut
Mackintosh Hut
Kaweka Hut
Kaweka 1724
Puketitiri
Patoka
Fern Birch Bush Nature Res
Lawrence
Willowford
Otamauri
Sherenden
Kereru
Maraekakaho

Te Pohue Upper Mohaka Recreation Reserve
Kopua 1072
MAUNGAHARURU RA
Te Waka 1021
Te Pohue
Ohurakura
Waikoau
Kahika
Tutira
Tutira Domain RR
Lake Tutira
Tiwaewae Memorial Reserve HR
Mangapokahu Scenic Res
Waipatiki SR
Waipatiki Beach
Tangoio Falls Scenic Res
Tangoio
Tangoio Bluff
Whirinaki

Hawke Bay

PACIFIC OCEAN

Esk Kiwi Sanctuary
White Pine Bush SR
Eskdale
Heipipi Pa Hist Res
Bay View
Rissington

Napier Hastings Suburbs See Map 183

Napier
See Map 101
Art Deco Capital of the World
Hawkes Bay Museum
Tom Parker Fountain
Marineland
The National Aquarium
Ocean Spa heated saltwater pools

Westshore
Poraiti
Puketapu
Moteo
Taradale
Meeanee
Marewa
Waiohiki
Awatoto
Seahorse Farm
Omahu
Fernhill
Twyford
Pakowhai
Clive
Whakatu
Haumoana
Olive Grange Rec Res
Flaxmere
Hastings
See Map 102
Karamu
Te Awanga
Ngatarawa
Clifton
Cape Kidnappers Nature Reserve
Gannet Sanctuary
Cape Kidnappers
Bridge Pa
Sileni Estates
Longlands
Pakipaki
Pukahu
Havelock North
Splash Planet
Te Mata Peak Walkway
Te Mata Peak 399
Te Mata Peak 399

Oingo Lake
Runanga Lake

Ngaruroro River

Ocean Beach

Poukawa
Mt Erin 474
Te Hauke
Lake Poukawa
Kahuranaki 646
Waimarama
Bare Island (Motu o Kura)
Karamea (Red Island)

Tikokino
Argyll East
Pukehou
Maraetotara Gorge SR
Parkers Bush SR
Mohi Bush SR
Maraetotara Scenic Res

Ongaonga
Ruataniwha
Otane
Patangata
Elsthorpe SR
Elsthorpe
Horseshoe Lake

Waipawa
Abbotslee Historic Home
Kairakau Beach

N
0   10 km
© Hema Maps NZ Ltd

Waipukurau
To Dannevirke
To Porangahau
Mangakuri Beach

RAUKAWA RANGE
KAOKAOROA RANGE
SILVER RANGE

map
29
NORTH ISLAND
Manawatu & Horowhenua

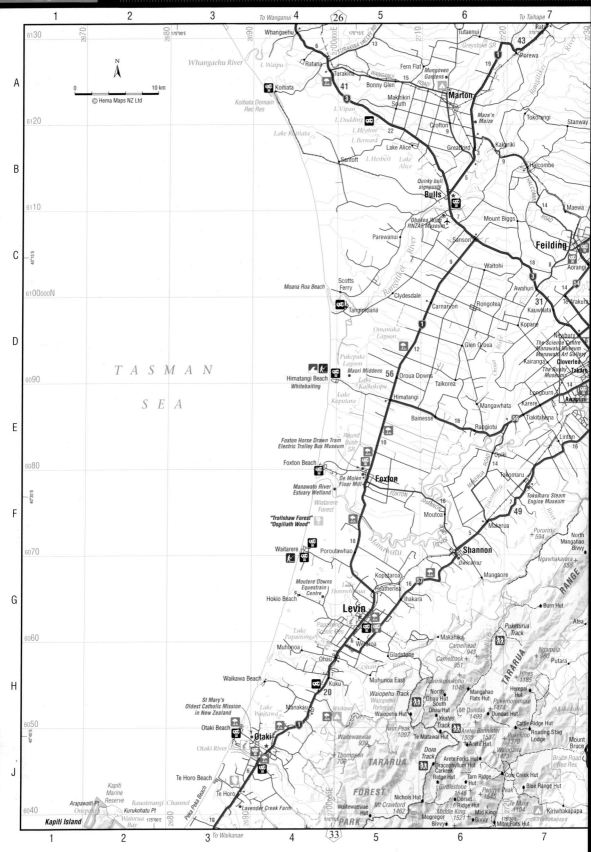

Map labels (top to bottom, left to right)

To Wanganui
26
To Taihape

A — Whangaehu, Whangaehu River, L. Waipu, Ratana, Koitiata, Turakina, WANGANUI, Fern Flat, Mungoven Gardens, Tutaenui, Rata, 43, Porewa, Greystoke SR, 19, TURAKINA VALLEY RD, 175°15'E, 13, 6, 41, Bonny Glen, Makirikiri South, Marton, Maze'n Maize, Tokorangi, Stanway

Koitiata Domain Rec Res, L. Vipan, L. Dudding, Crofton, 9, Greatford, 3, Kakariki, Halcombe, 22

B — Lake Koitiata, L. Heaton, L. Bernard, Lake Alice, Santoft, L. Herbert, Lake Alice, Quirky bull signposts, Bulls, Mount Biggs, Maewa, 5, 14

C — Ohakea World RNZAF Museum, Parewanui, Sanson, Waitohi, Feilding, Aorangi, 7, 9, 18, 8, 3

D — Moana Roa Beach, Scotts Ferry, Clydesdale, Carnarvon, Rongotea, Awahuri, 31, Te Arakura, Kauwhata, Kopane, Newbury, The Science Centre, Manawatu Museum, Manawatu Art Gallery, Kairanga, Cloverlea, The Rugby Museum, Takaro, 54, 14, Tangimoana, Pukepuke Lagoon, 12, Glen Oroua, Oroua Downs, Taikorea, 56, Omanuka Lagoon, Lake Kaikokopu, Himatangi, Mangawhata, Karere, Longburn, 14, Awapuni

E — Himatangi Beach, Whitebaiting, Maori Middens, Lake Koputara, Bainesse, Rangiotu, 56, Tiakitahuna, Linton, 16, Round Bush SR, Opiki, 14, 16, 10

F — Foxton Horse Drawn Tram Electric Trolley Bus Museum, Foxton Beach, De Molen Flour Mill, Foxton, FOXTON, Tokomaru, 49, Tokomaru Steam Engine Museum, Manawatu River Estuary Wetland, Wiatarere Forest, Moutoa, SHANNON, 16, Makerua, Pururiri 594, North Mangahao Bivvy, "Trollshaw Forest" "Osgiliath Wood", 7

G — Waitarere, Poroutawhao, 18, Koputaroa, Owlcatraz, Shannon, Mangaore, Ngawhakarara 855, RANGE, Moutere Downs Equestrian Centre, Hokio Beach, Lake Horowhenua, Heatherlea, Ihakara, 16, 57, Levin, Burn Hut, Puketurua Track, Atea

H — Papaitonga Scenic Res, Lake Papaitonga, Weraroa, 6, Makahika, Camelhead 943, Camelback 851, Ngamaia 980, Putara, Muhunoa, Ohau, Gladstone, Ohau River, TARARUA, Hines 1185, Waikawa Beach, Kuku, 20, Muhunoa East, Waiopehu Track, Waiopehu Reserve, Te Mirikohukohu 1049, North Ohau Hut, Ohau Hut South, Mangahao Flats Hut, Herepai Hut, Pukemoremore, Makakahi

J — St Mary's Oldest Catholic Mission in New Zealand, Manakau, Waiopehu Hut, Twin Peak 1097, Mt Dundas 1499, Dundas Hut, Cattle Ridge Hut, Otaki Beach, Otaki, Lake Waitawa, Waikawa River, Waitewaewae 939, Te Matawai Hut, Areta Bannister 1505 1587, Pukekino 1370, Roaring Stag Lodge, Mount Bruce, Yeates Track, Waingawa 1423, Bruce Road Rec Res, Te Horo Beach, Otaki River, Te Horo, Waiorongomai 708, Thompson 708, Dora Track, Arete Forks Hut, Dracophyllum Hut, Cook Creek Hut, Blue Range Hut, TARARUA, Carkeek Ridge Hut, Tarn Ridge Hut, Peggys Peak 1545, Kapiti Marine Reserve, Onepoto, Arapawaiti Pt, Kurukohatu Pt, Lavender Creek Farm, FOREST, Nichols Hut, Mt Crawford 1462, Girdlestone 1546, Dorset Ridge Hut, Kiriwhakapapa, Kapiti Island, Waiorua Bay, Rauoterangi Channel, Peka Peka Beach, Waitewaewae Hut, Middle King 1521, Mcgregor Bivvy, Mid King, Mitre Flats Hut, Mt Mara 1104, To Waikanae, 33, To Waikanae

© Hema Maps NZ Ltd

0   10 km

N

TASMAN SEA

RANGITIKEI RIVER, Rangitikei River, Oroua River, Manawatu River, Tokomaru River, Makerua Road, Shannon Road

8 To Taihape 9 10 11 (27) 12 13 14 To Napier

To Hastings, Napier

Mangatewai River Scenic Reserve
Knights Track
Toka Bivvy
Umutoi
Leon Kinvig Hut
Makaretu Hut
Happy Daze Hut
Utuwai
Whaingapuna 1405
Shorts Track
Ngamoko Hut
Makareki
Rakautatahi
Takapau
Piripiri Hut
Mid Pohangina Hut
Ngamoko
Waituna West
Kimbolton
RUAHINE RANGE
Takapari 1257
Cattle Creek Hut
Norsewood Pioneer Museum Trolls
Norsewood
Otawhao
Dunolly
54
RUAHINE
Standfield Hut
Kopua
Whenuahou
Beaconsfield
12
Kiwitea
Mount Richards
Komako
Te Ekaou Hut
Diggers Hut
Forks Hut
Traverse Hut
Ormondville
Makotuku
Whetukura
Cheltenham
FOREST
Numutaoroa
Tamaki
Matamau
59
Makino
61
Almadale
Almadale Scenic Res
Pohangina
Opawe Hut
Kumeti Hut
Kumeti
Ruaroa
Piripiri
Ahiweka 734
Maharahara 1095
Keretaki Hut
Ruaroa
Mangapuaka Stream SR
Saleyard Tours
Colyton
Awahou North
PARK
Dannevirke
Mangatera
Raumati
Raumai
Ross Peak 1954
Awahou South
Makirikiri
Tahoraiti
Tapapakuku
Okaihau
Tiratu
Te Uri
Taonui
Wharite Peak 920
Maharahara West
Kiritaki
Maharahara
Timber Bay
Kaitoke
Okarae
Awariki
Mangahei
Hiwinui
Oringi
Mangatoro
Ngapaeruru
Bunnythorpe
26
Ashhurst
Mangarawa
Waiaruhe
27
100000mN
Palmerston North Suburbs See Map 105
3
Woodville
Papatawa
Mangatuna
Milson
Kelvin Grove
Roslyn
Whakarongo
Hopelands
Waitahora
Motea
Toi Flat
Terrace End See Map 104
Manawatu Gorge Scenic Reserve
Woodville Domain Rec
Kumeroa
Red River Scenic Reserve
Palmerston North
Aokautere
Te Apiti Wind Farm
Waitapu 352
Waipatiki
57
Victoria Esplanade Gardens
Tarakamuku 544
Ruawhata
Ngawapurua
Haukopua Scenic Res
Weber
Turitea
14
Ballance
Mangatainoka
Kohinui
Waewaepa Scenic Reserve
Waihi Falls Scenic Res
Waihi Falls
Makomako
Marima 563
Mangahao 13
Mangamutu
Pahiatua
Tui Brewery Tower
WAEWAEPA RANGE
Ohinereiata 731
Summit 803
Coonoor
Horoeka
Waimiro
Mt Arthur 220
Nikau
Carnival Park Hall Polish Memorial
40
Ngaturi
Makuri Conservation Scenic Reserve
Waione
Kopikopiko
Marima
Te Aupapa 304
Waikuku 527
Pipinui Waterfall Scenic Res
Korora
Mt Alta 230
Waiwera
Konini
Kaitawa
PUKETOI RANGE
Puketoi
Kakariki
Hamua
Mt Heale 354
Koropeke 303
Makuri
Taraora 425
Mangatiti
Pongaroa
Akaroa
Mt Attila 353
Hukanui
Tane
Mangatiti 352
Kohiku
Nireaha
2
Rongomai
Mt Marchant 578
Hinemoa
Pori
Makuri Gorge Scenic Reserve
Haunui
Rakaunui Waihoki 440
Waihoki
Newman
Tawataia
Tiraumea
Waihoki Valley
6060
Eketahuna
Spring Hill 331
44
Rongokokako
Parkville
Flat Hill 312
Alfredton
Tiraumea River
Mara
Waiwaka
Pleckville
Mangaoranga
17
Kaiparoro
Hastwell
Mt Baker 446
Neds Hill 401
Mt York 384
Owahanga Hill 226
Mt Bruce National Wildlife Centre Bruces Hill
Mt Marsh 416
Castlehill
Owahanga
Mt Bruce 710 Scenic Res
Ihuraua
16
Maungarau 398
Omaruapakihau 300
PACIFIC
Mauriceville West
Mauriceville
Dreyers Rock
Green Hill 245
Mataikona
OCEAN
41
Mt Percy 473

8 To Masterton (34) 9 10 11 12 13 14

map
31
NORTH ISLAND
Manawatu & Wairarapa

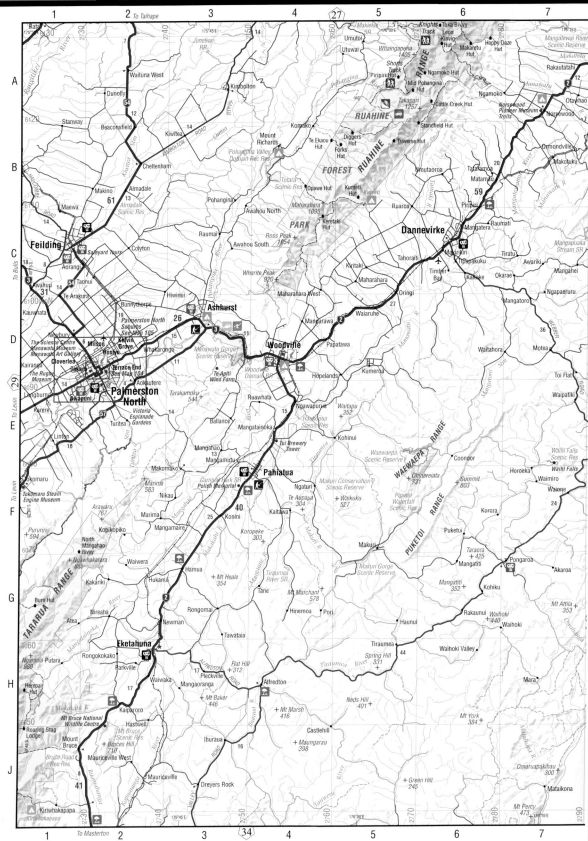

To Taihape

Ratai
Rangitikei River

Waituna West

Dunolly

Stanway

Beaconsfield

Makino

Maewa

Feilding

Aorangi

Wahupi

Te Arakura

Kauwhata

Newbury

Milson

Roslyn

Cloverlea

Takaro

Palmerston North

Awapuni

Longburn

Kerere

Linton

Okomaru

Tokomaru Steam Engine Museum

Pururiri

Kopikopiko

North Mangahao Bivvy

Ngawhakarara

Waiwera

Kakariki

Atea

Nireaha

Burn Hut

Ngamaia Putara

Herepai Hut

Roaring Stag Lodge

Mount Bruce

Eketahuna

Rongokokako

Parkville

Waiwaka

Kaiparoro

Mt Bruce National Wildlife Centre

Hastwell

Mauriceville West

Mauriceville

Kiriwhakapapa

Kimbolton

Cheltenham

Almadale

Colyton

Taonui

Hiwinui

Bunnythorpe

Palmerston North Suburbs
See Map 105

Ashhurst

Whakarongo

Kelvin Grove

Terrace End
See Map 104

Aokautere

Turitea

Victoria Esplanade Gardens

Makomako

Marima

Nikau

Marima

Mangamaire

Arawaru

Hukanui

Hamua

Rongomai

Newman

Tawataia

Flat Hill

Pleckville

Mangaoranga

Mt Baker

Ihuraua

Mauriceville West

Dreyers Rock

Mount Richards

Pohangina

Raumal

Awahou North

Awahou South

Wharite Peak
920

Maharahara West

Mangarawa

Woodville

Papatawa

Woodville Domain RR

Te Apiti Wind Farm

Manawatu Gorge Scenic Reserve

Ruawhata

Ballance

Mangatainoka

Mangahao

Mangamutu

Pahiatua

Ngaturi

Te Aupaua

Kaitawa

Konini

Koropeke

Tane

Hinemoa

Rongomai

Alfredton

Castlehill

Maungarau

Green Hill

Mataikona

Omaruapakihau

Mt Percy
473

Korako

Te Ekaou Hut

Diggers Hut

Forks Hut

Opawe Hut

Kumeti Hut

Maharahara
1095

Keretaki Hut

Ross Peak
1054

FOREST **RUAHINE**

PARK

Traverse Hut

Nmutaoroa

Ruaroa

Oringi

Kiritaki

Maharahara

Waiaruhe

Hopelands

Kumeroa

Ngawapurua

Waitapu
352

Hautoua Scenic Res

Kohinui

Waewaepa Scenic Reserve

Ohinereiata
731

Makuri Conservation Scenic Reserve

Waikuku
527

Pipinui Waterfall Scenic Res

Makuri

Makuri Gorge Scenic Reserve

Mangatiti
352

Kohiku

Tiramea

Spring Hill
331

Waihoki Valley

Neds Hill
401

Mt Marsh
416

Mt York
384

RUAHINE

RANGE

Whaingapuna
1405

Shorts Track

Piripiri Hut

Takapari
1257

Standfield Hut

Umutoi

Utuwai

Komako

Knights Track

Leon Kinvig Hut

Ngamoko Hut

Cattle Creek Hut

Mid Pohangina Hut

Toka Bivvy

Makaretu Hut

Happy Daze Hut

Rakautatahi

Ngamoko

Norsewood Pioneer Museum Trails

Norsewood

Otawhao

Dannevirke

Makirikiri

Tahoraiti

Timber Bay

Kaitoke

Okarae

Mangatera

Raumati

Tapakura

Matamau

Piripiri

Tiatoa

Tiratu

Awariki

Mangahei

Ngapaeruru

Mangatoro

Waitahora

Motea

Toi Flat

Waipatiki

Coonoor

Horoeka

Waimiro

Waione

Korora

Puketoi

Taraora
425

Mangatiti

Pongaroa

Akaroa

Rakaunui

Waihoki
440

Waihoki

Mt Attila
353

Mara

Waihoki

Ormondville

Makotuku

WAEWAEPA **RANGE**

PUKETOI **RANGE**

Haunui

Pori

To Masterton

To Levin

To Bulls

map
33
NORTH ISLAND

Wellington & South Wairarapa

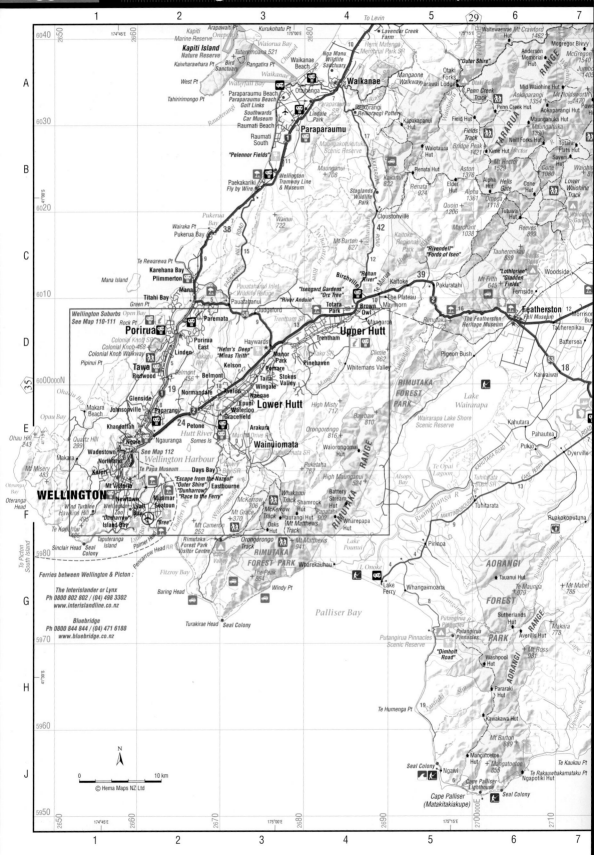

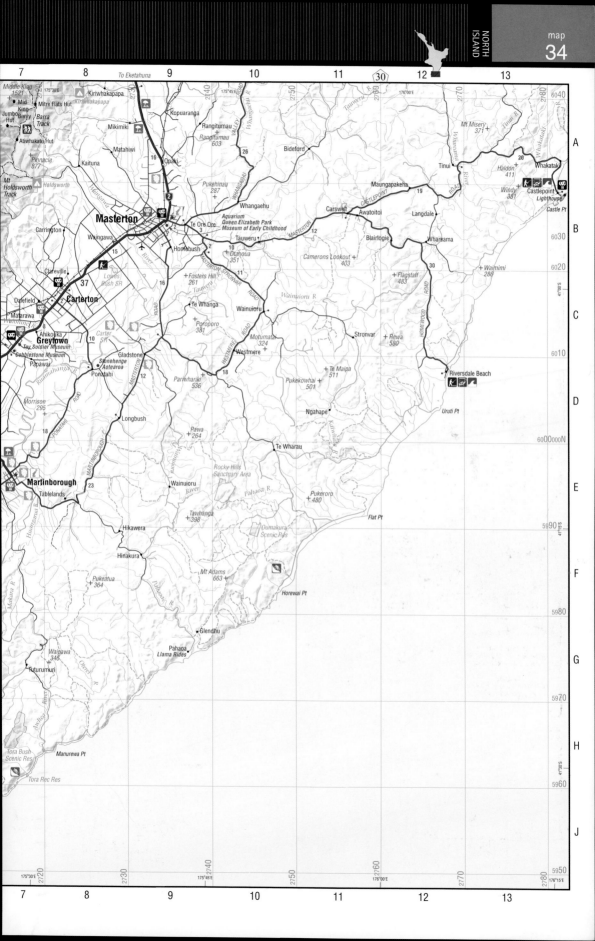

map
35
NORTH ISLAND
Cook Strait

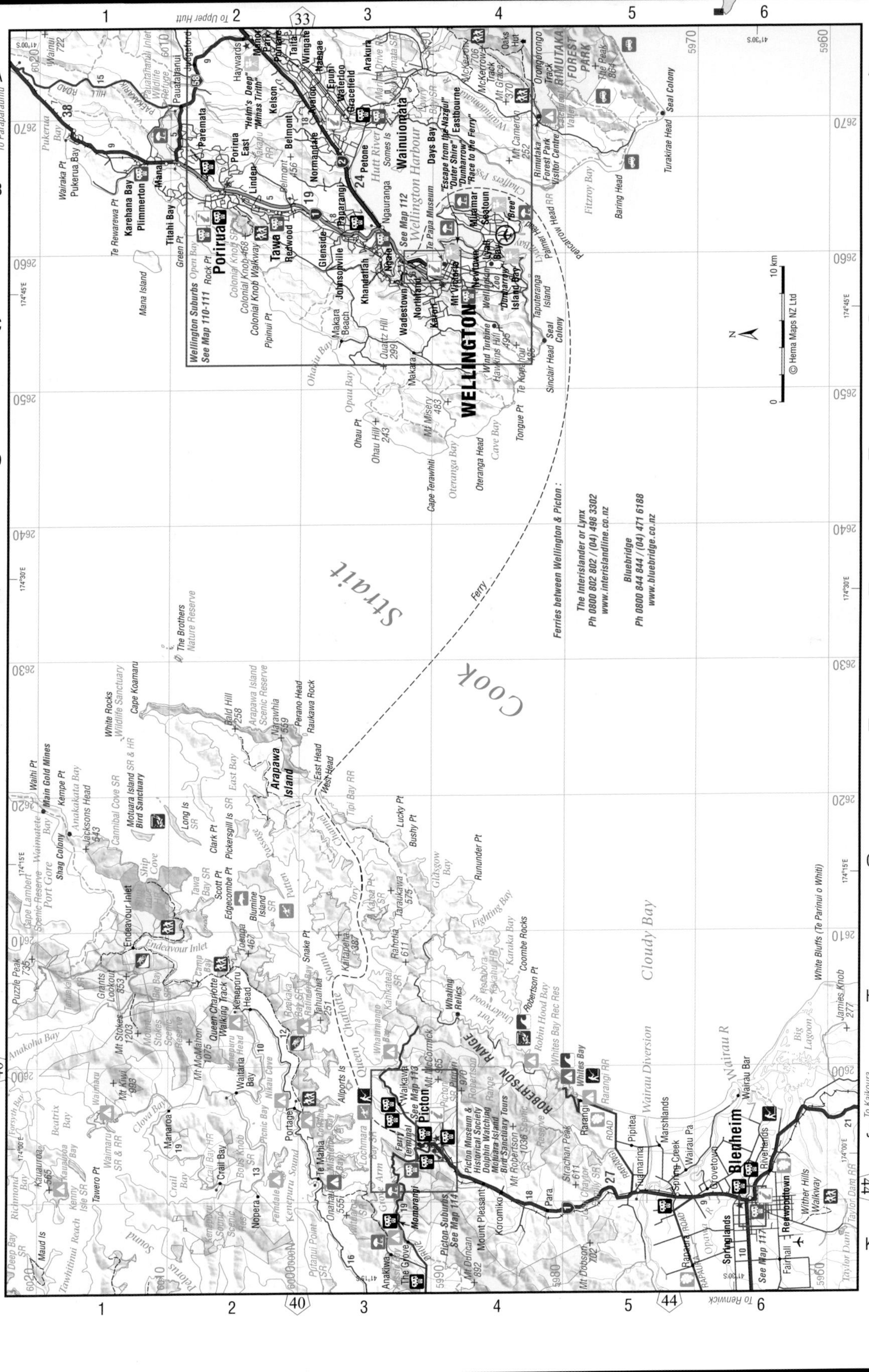

WELLINGTON

Wellington Suburbs See Map 110-111

See Map 112 Wellington Harbour

Cook Strait

Cook Strait

Ferry

Ferries between Wellington & Picton:

The Interislander or Lynx
Ph 0800 802 802 / (04) 498 3302
www.interislandline.co.nz

Bluebridge
Ph 0800 844 844 / (04) 471 6188
www.bluebridge.co.nz

Picton
Blenheim

Renwicktown
Springlands
Fairhall

Arapawa Island

Queen Charlotte Walking Track

RIMUTAKA FOREST PARK

Porirua
Paremata
Plimmerton
Mana
Titahi Bay
Tawa
Redwood

Petone
Wainuiomata
Eastbourne

Cloudy Bay

Marlborough Sounds

To Parapararumu

To Upper Hutt

To Kaikoura

To Renwick

10 km

N

© Hema Maps NZ Ltd

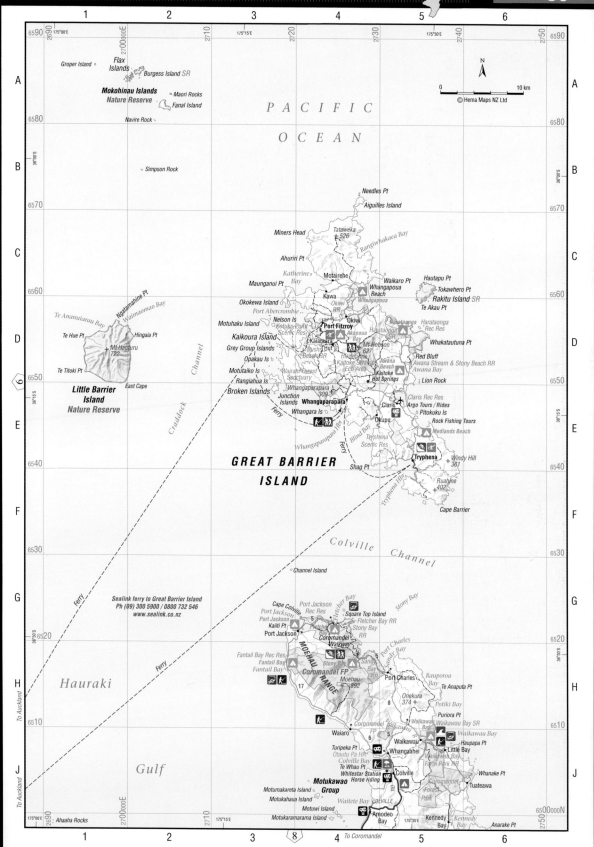

map
37
SOUTH ISLAND
Nelson

1 2 3 4 5 6 7

172°00'E 172°15'E 172°30'E 172°45'E

A

B

C

D

E

F

G

H

J

6080 6070 6060 6050 6040 6030 6020 6010 6000000N 5990

40°30'S 40°45'S 41°00'S 41°15'S

TASMAN SEA

Cape Farewell
Pillar Point Lighthouse
Wharariki Beach
Pilch Pt
Puponga
Port Puponga
Farm Pk
Nguroa Bay
Curious Cliff
Mt Lunar 239
Mt Beale 288
Te Rae
Kaihoka Pt
Kaihoka Lakes SR
Westhaven SR
Seaford
Pakawau Inlet
South Head Cone
Whanganui Inlet SR
Pakawau
22
Westhaven (Te Tai Tapu) Marine Reserve
Sharks Head
Taimatea Point
Waikato
Opou
Knuckle Hill 506
Ferntown
Paturau River
Mangarakau
Mt Burnett 641
Gibbtown
Ruataniwha Inlet
Collingwood
Kaituna Track
Milnthorpe Park Scenic Reserve
Parapara Inlet
Lake Otuhie
Mt Haidinger 629
Milnthorpe
Parapara Peninsula Historic Reserve
Anatori River
Aorere
Parapara
Kaipuke Cliffs
Macpherson Knob 500
Mt Higgins 906
Rockville
Te Anaroa Caves
Turimawiwi River
NORTH-WEST NELSON
Fosters Lookout 916
Aorere Historic Goldfields
Mt Rikopai 153
Onekaka
Anaweka River
CONSERVATION PARK
Bainham
Aorere Caves SR
Washbourne SR
Patons Rock
Kahurangi Pt
Conical Hill 162
Mt Stevens 1213
Devils Hill 240
25
Puramahoi
Kahurangi Keepers House
Pupu Springs Scenic Res
Otukoroiti Pt
Otukaro Historic Reserve
Bare Hill 762
Lookout Knob 535
Bushy Cone 612
Parapara Peak 1249
Seal Bay
Moutere R
Black Cow 606
Peter Knob 724
Pupu Springs Walking Track
Rocks Pt
MacKay Downs Hut
Percy Peak 1163
Brown Hut
Anatoki Track
The Minaret 1273
Mt Hardy 1505
Waikoropupu Springs (Pupu Springs)
Big Bay
Mt Teddy 870
Mt White 1075
"Rugged country south of Rivendell" "Eregion Hills"
The Pulpit 1247
Brown Cow 1452
Anatoki Salmon
James MacKay Hut
Gouland Downs Hut
Mt Perry 1238
Boulder Lake
Mt Christmas 1539
Steep Pt
Saxon Hut
Aorere Hut
Clark Peak 1622
Boulder Lake Hut
Paradise Peak 1549
Wekakura Pt
Kotaipapa Pt
Heaphy Track
Tubman Hill 897
Perry Saddle Hut
Heaphy Track
Mt Olympus 1519
Gladiator Peak 1450
HAUPIRI RANGE
Whakapoai Pt
Lewis Hut
Adelaide Tarn Hut
Anatoki Forks Hut
Northwest Nelson Conservation Park
Mt Gouland 1474
Mt Inaccessible 1495
Adelaide Tarn
The Needle 1563
ANATOKI RANGE
Porters Beach
Heaphy Bluff
Heaphy River
Heaphy Hut
Mt Ross 1309
Burnt Hill 1325
Anatoki Peak 1662
Drunken Sailors 1546
Devil River Peak 1784
DEVIL RANGE
Heaphy Beach
Mt Barr 1231
TASMAN
Amohia Peak 1542
KAHURANGI NATIONAL PARK
Lonely Lake Hut
Lake Stanley
Twenty Minute Beach
Heaphy Track
DOMETT
RANGE
Aorere Peak 1730
Kakapo Peak 1783
Waingaro Track
Nettle Beach
Mid Point
Twin Beach
Katipo Creek Shelter
Island Lake
Waingaro Peak 1604
Mt Snowdon 1865
SNOWDON RA
Waingaro Forks Hut
Riordans Hut
North-west Nelson Cons Park
Koura Beach
Big Rock Beach
Centre Mountain 1565
Mt Gibbs 1645
Fenella Hut
Cobb Hut
Mt Benson 1661
Mt Lockett 1621
LOCKETT RANGE
Scotts Beach
Kohaihai Bluff
Kohaihai River
Suspension Bridge & Lagoon
Mt Domett 1646
MOUNTAINS
Mt Cobb 1716
Mt Prospect 1702
Cobb Track
Sylvester Hut (Bushline)
Asbestos
Kohaihai
Kohaihai Shelter
MORGAN RANGE
Lake Cobb
Mt Ranolf 1660
Lake Sylvester
Cobb River
North Cottage
Limestone Arches
MARSHALL RANGE
Mt Mytton 1535
Trilobite Hut
Myttons Hut
Mt Hodder 1377
Caldervale
Bald Knob 1281
False Peak 1628
Mt Peel 1654
Balloon Hut
Growler Shelter (Dry Rock)
Lower Gridiron Rock Shelter
Lodestone 1462
Lake Aorere
Balloon Hill 1303
Salisbury Hut
Caves & Potholes
Flora Hut
Oparara River
Oparara
FENIAN RANGE
Tableland 1260
Gordons Pyramid 1489
Mount Arthur 1795
ARTHUR RANGE
6000000N
Karamea Centennial Museum
Roaring Lion Hut
Karamea Bend Hut
Spluegeons Shelter
Mt Arthur 1795
Winter Peak 1750
Karamea
Fenian 899
Greys Hut
Mt Garibaldi 1339
Sandy Peak 1395
The Twins 1809
Ellis Hut
Karamea River
Market Cross
Pyramid 1465
Loveridge Peak 1586
Barron Bold 1332
Umere
Arapito
Stormy 1084
The Haystack 723
Flanagans Hut
Loveridge Hut
Kongahu
Leslie - Karamea Track
Mt Olive 1445
Crow Hut
Cowins Track
Camel Back 591

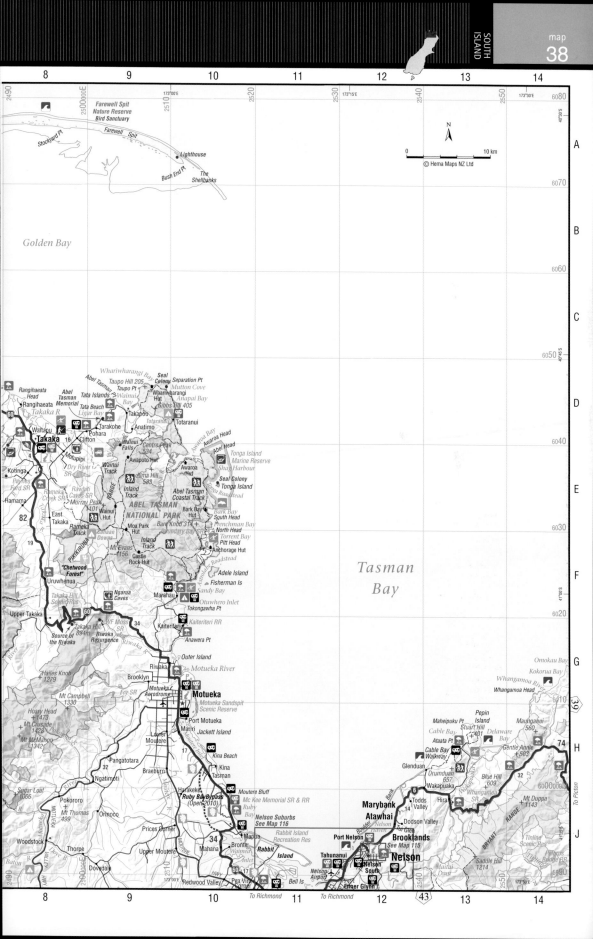

8   9   10   11   12   13   14

N

0   10 km

Golden Bay

Farewell Spit
Nature Reserve
Bird Sanctuary

Stockyard Pt

Farewell Spit

Lighthouse

Bush End Pt

The
Shellbanks

A

B

C

D

E

F

G

H

J

6080
6070
6060
6050
6040
6030
6020
6010
6000000N
5990

2490
2500000E
2510
2520
2530
2540
2550

173°00'E
173°15'E
173°30'E

40°30'S
40°45'S
41°00'S

**Tasman
Bay**

Whariwharangi Bay
Taupo Hill 205
Taupo Pt
Seal
Colony
Separation Pt
Mutton Cove
Whariwharangi
Hut
Anapai Bay
Wainui
Bay
Gibbs Hill 405
Totaranui

Rangihaeata
Head
Rangihaeata
Abel Tasman
Abel Tasman
Memorial
Tata Islands
Tata Beach
Ligar Bay
Tarakohe
Takapou
Anatimo
Totaranui

Takaka R
Waitapu
Takaka
16
Pohara
Clifton
Centre Peak
534
Awaroa Bay

Motupipi
Wainui
Falls
Awapoto Hut
Awaroa Head

Kotinga
Dry River
SR
Wainui
Track
Alma Hill
593
Awaroa
Hut
Tonga Island
Marine Reserve

60
Paynes
Ford SR
Rawhiti
Caves SR
Murray Peak
401
Inland
Track
Awaroa
Shag Harbour

Hamama
Rameka
Creek SR
Wainui
Hut
ABEL TASMAN
Seal Colony
Tonga Island

82
East
Takaka
Rameka
Track
Moa Park
Hut
NATIONAL PARK
Bark Bay
Hut
Bark Bay
South Head

19
Canaan
Downs
Mt Evans
1156
Inland
Track
Bare Knob 311
Boundary Bay
Frenchman Bay
North Head

PIKIKIRUNA
Castle
Rock Hut
Abel Tasman
Coastal Track
Torrent Bay
Pitt Head
Anchorage Hut

"Chetwood
Forest"
Uruwhenua
Ngarua
Caves
Adele Island
Fisherman Is
Sandy Bay

Takaka Hill
Scenic Res
60
Marahau
Oturwhero Inlet
Tokongawha Pt

Upper Takaka
Takaka Hill
894m
Riwaka
Resurgence
34
Kaiteriteri
Kaiteriteri RR

Source of
the Riwaka
WF Moss
SR
Anawera Pt

RANGE

Hailes Knob
1279
Riwaka
Outer Island
Motueka River

Riwaka
Brooklyn
Motueka
Aerodrome
Motueka

Mt Campbell
1330
Fry SR
Motueka Sandspit
Scenic Reserve

Hoary Head
1473
Port Motueka

Mt Crusade
1428
Mariri
Jackett Island

Mt McMahon
1342
Lower
Moutere
17
Kina Beach

Pangatotara
Kina
Tasman

Sugar Loaf
1066
Ngatimoti
Braeburn
Harakeke
Moutere Bluff
Mc Kee Memorial SR & RR

Pokororo
Mt Thomas
499
Orinoco
Ruby Bay Bypass
(Open 2010)
Ruby
Bay

Woodstock
Thorpe
Prices Corner
Upper Moutere
34
Mapua
Bronte
Waimea
Rabbit Island
Recreation Res
Nelson Suburbs
See Map 116

Baton
Dovedale
Mahana
Rabbit
Island
Waimea
Inlet
Port Nelson
See Map 115

Redwood Valley
60
Pea Vine
Corner
Bell Is
Tahunanui
Nelson
Airport
Nelson
South

To Richmond
To Richmond
Emer Glynn

Omokau Bay
Kokorua Bay
Whangamoa River
Whangamoa Head

Pepin
Island
Maheipuku Pt
Stuart Hill
401
Delaware
Bay
Maungarui
560

Cable Bay
Walkway
Ataata Pt
Gentle Annie
503
74

Glenduan
Drumduan
657
Blue Hill
609
32

Wakapuaka
Hira
Mt Duppa
1143

**Marybank
Atawhai**
6
Todds
Valley
14
Whangamoa
SR

Dodson Valley

Brooklands
Hira
Glen

Nelson
Tinline
Scenic Res

Maitai
Dam
Saddle Hill
1214

BRYANT
RANGE

To Picton

39

43

Boulder Bank

Woodman
1214

map
39
SOUTH ISLAND
Nelson & Marlborough

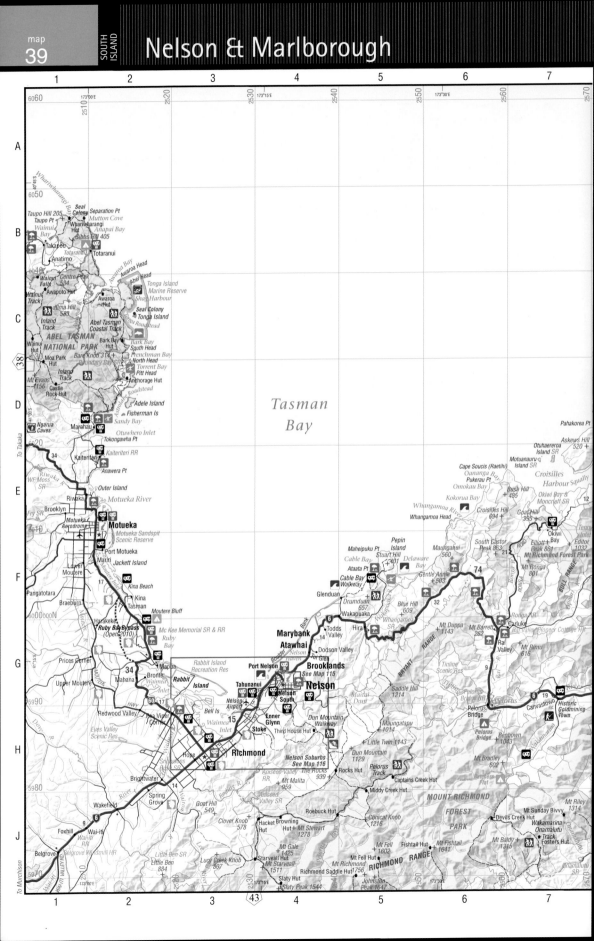

Tasman Bay

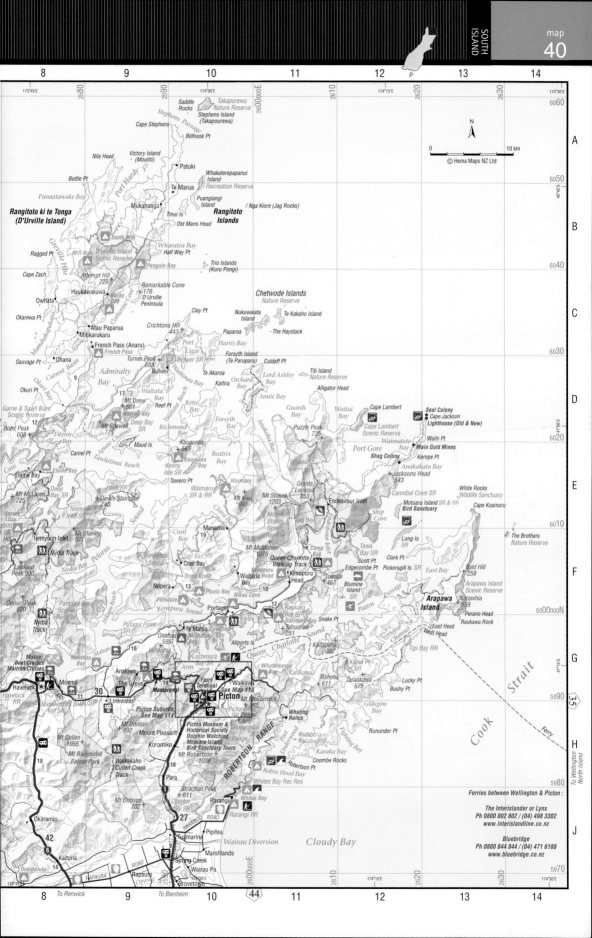

8   9   10   11   12   13   14

6060

A

Saddle
Rocks
Takaporewa
Nature Reserve
Stephens Island
(Takapourewa)
Cape Stephens
Billhook Pt

N

0   10 km

© Hema Maps NZ Ltd

Nile Head
Victory Island
(Moutiti)
Patuki
6050

Whakaterepapanui
Island
Recreation Reserve

Bottle Pt
Te Marua
Port Hardy
Puangiangi
Island
Nga Kiore (Jag Rocks)

Punaatawake Bay
Mukahanga

Rangitoto ki te Tonga
(D'Urville Island)
Tinui Is
Old Mans Head
Rangitoto
Islands

B

South Arm
Mill Arm
D'Urville Island
Scenic Reserve
Wharatea Bay
Half Way Pt

Ragged Pt
Penguin Bay
Trio Islands
(Kuru Pongi)
6040

Cape Zach
Attempt Hill
729

Haukawakawa
Jacky
Bay
Catherine Cove
+176
D'Urville
Peninsula
Remarkable Cone
Chetwode Islands
Nature Reserve

Owhata
C
Crichtons Hill
443
Clay Pt
Nukuwaiata
Island
Te Kakaho Island

Okarewa Pt
Atau Paparua
Mitikarukaru
Paparoa
The Haystack
6030

French Pass (Anaru)
French Pass
Port
Ligar
Bulwer SR
Harris Bay

Sauvage Pt
Ohana
Turner Peak
683
Bulwer
Te Akaroa
Forsyth Island
(Te Paruparu)
Culdaff Pt
Titi Island
Nature Reserve

Okuri Pt
9
Waitinau Reach
Kaitira
Lord Ashley
Bay
Orchard
Bay
Alligator Head

Garne & Savill Bays
Scenic Reserve
Admiralty
Bay
Waitata
Bay
17
Annie Bay
Waitui
Bay
Cape Lambert
D
Bobs Peak
608
12
Mt Drew
661
Reef Pt
Ketu
Bay
Guards
Bay
Puzzle Peak
735
Cape Lambert
Scenic Reserve
Seal Colony
Cape Jackson
Lighthouse (Old & New)
6020

Fitzroy
Bay
Mt Shewell
773
Deep Bay
SR
Richmond
Bay
Forsyth
Bay
Waimatete
Bay
Waihi
Main Gold Mines

Camel Pt
Maud Is
Kauauroa
565
Kauauroa
Bay
Port Gore
Shag Colony
Kempe Pt
Anakakata Bay
Jacksons Head
543

Elaine Bay
Elaine Bay
Tawhitinui Reach
Kenny
Isle SR
Beatrix
Bay
Tahuanui
Cannibal Cove SR
White Rocks
Wildlife Sanctuary

E
Deep
Bay SR
Mt McLaren
725
Devils Staircase
Tawero Pt
Waimaru
SR & RR
Waimaru
Mt Kiwi
993
Mt Stokes
1203
Grants
Lookout
853
Endeavour Inlet
Motuara Island SR & HR
Bird Sanctuary
Cape Koamaru

Harvey
Bay
Hill
Tennyson Inlet
Mt Stanley
971
Clova Bay
Mount
Stokes
Scenic
Reserve
Big Bay
Ship
Cove
6010

Nydia Track
Manaroa
Crail
Bay
Mt McMahon
1075
Camp
Long Is
SR
The Brothers
Nature Reserve

F
Lookout
Peak 900
Nydia
Bay
Nydia
Track
Crail Bay HR
Crail Bay
Bobs Knob
Queen Charlotte
Walking Track
Kenepuru
Head
Tawa
Bay SR
Scott Pt
Clark Pt
Bald Hill
258
Arapawa Island
Scenic Reserve

Opour Peak
920
Nopera
13
Picnic Bay
Waitaria
Bay
Kenepuru
Bay
Toenga
467
Edgecombe Pt
Pickersgill Is
East Bay
Narawhia
569

Nydia
Track
Paradise Bay
Scenic
Reserve
Ferndale
Kenepuru Sound
Portage
Nikau Cove
12
Ruakaka
Bay SR
Blumine
Island
SR
Patten
Passage
Arapawa
Island
6000000N
Perano Head
Raukawa Rock

Mussel
Boat Cruises
Mailron Cruises
Putanui Point
SR
Te Mahia
Cowshed
Bay
Onahau
555
Mistletoe
Bay
Allports Is
Ratimera Bay
Tahuahua
251
Snake Pt
I Kaitapeha
387
Torea
East Head
West Head
Tipi Bay RR
Raukawa
Channel
G

Havelock
Meetopu
Bay
Anakiwa
Grove
Arm
Lochmara
SR
Whatanango
Kahikatea
Rahotia
611
Kaioa Pt
SR
Lucky Pt
41°15'S
35

Moenui
The Grove
19
Momorangi
Ferry
Terminal
Waikawa
See Map 113
Taraukawa
575
Bushy Pt
Cook
Strait
5990

Linkwater
30
Mahakipawa
Hill SR
CHARLOTTE
Picton
See Map 114
Picton Suburbs,
See Map 114
Picton
Mt McCormick
465
Whaling
Relics
Glasgow
Bay
Ferry

H
18
Mt Cullen
1055
Mt Richmond
Forest Park
Waikakaho
Cullen Creek
Track
Mt Duncan
892
Mount Pleasant
Koromiko
Picton
Underway
870
Range
Robertson
Mt Robertson
1036
Scenic
Reserve
Picton Museum &
Historical Society
Dolphin Watching
Motuara Island
Bird Sanctuary Tours
Mababara
Kakaho HR
Karaka Bay
Coombe Rocks
Rununder Pt
Whites Bay Rec Res
Robertson Pt
Robin Hood Bay
ROBERTSON RANGE
5980

18
Para
1
Strachan Peak
611
J Chaytor
Emily SR
27
Rarangi
Rarangi RR
Whites Bay
Whites Bay

To Renwick
42
6
Okaramio
Mt Dobson
702
RARANGI
ROAD
J

Kaituna
14
Onamalutu
Spring Creek
Tuamarina
Marshlands
Wairau Pa
Pipitea
Wairau Diversion
Cloudy Bay
Ferries between Wellington & Picton:

The Interislander or Lynx
Ph 0800 802 802 / (04) 498 3302
www.interislandline.co.nz

Bluebridge
Ph 0800 844 844 / (04) 471 6188
www.bluebridge.co.nz

HAPAURA
Rapaura
Opawa
ROAD
Grovetown
5970

map
41
SOUTH ISLAND
Buller & Tasman

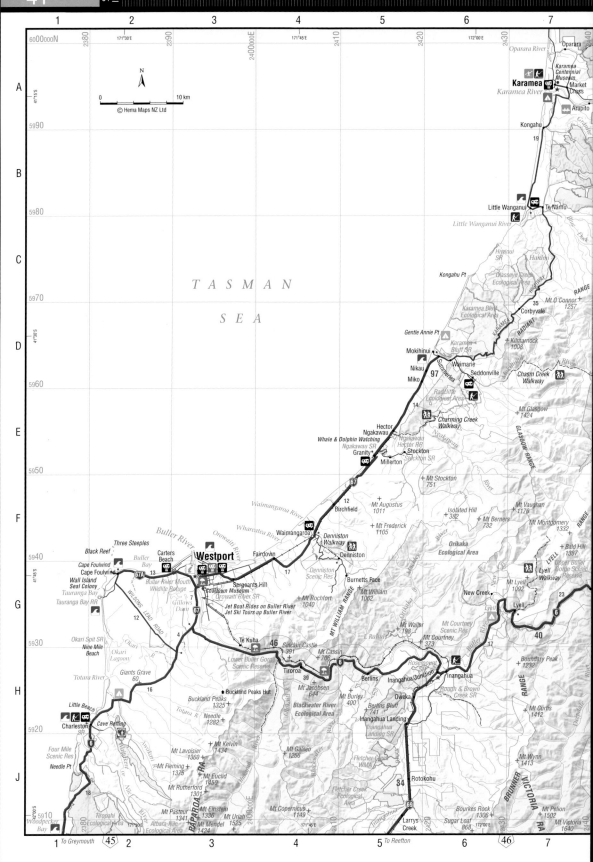

8 9 37 10 11 12 13 38 14

39

Ngatimoti 6000000N

FENNIN RANGE
Roaring Lion Hut
Earthquake Lakes
Mt Garibaldi 1339
Greys Hut
Fenian 899
Pyramid 1465
Sandy Bay Hut
Karamea Bend Hut
Splugeons Shelter
Mount Arthur Hut
Sugar Loaf 1066
Pokororo
Orinoco
Mt Thomas 499

Umere
Stormy 1084
The Haystack 723
Mt Arthur 1795
Winter Peak 1750
Ellis Hut
The Twins 1809
Barron Bold 1332
Woodstock
Thorpe
Dovedale
5990

Leslie - Karamea Track
Crow Hut
Venus Hut
Mt Olive 1445
Loveridge Peak 1586
Loveridge Hut
Camel Back 591
Stanley Brook
26

Black Rat 1000
Flanagans Hut
Cowins Track

KAHURANGI NATIONAL PARK

Kakapo Track
Mt Scarlett 1226
Kakapo Hut
Thor Hut
Mt Kendall 1702
Moonstone Lake
Mt Star 1588
Mt Sodam 1565
Thomson Hill 744
Battery Hill 262
Tapawera

Bell Town Manunui Hut Anaconda
Mt Brilliant 1422
Mt Herbert 1507
Trevor Carter Hut
Mt Luna 1630
Kiwi Saddle Hut
Mt Baldy 1542
Mt Gomorrah 1592
Gomorrah Track
Mt Jones 944
Rakau

Mt Radiant 1305
Wangapeka Taipo Biyv
Luna Hut
John Reid Hut
Mt Patriarch 1701
Chummies Track
Mararewa

Mt Johnson 1323
Mt Zetland 1413
Stag Flat Shelter
Biggs Tops 1384
Stone Hut
Gibbs Track
Old Sow 965
Tadmor
Motupiko
78
Kohatu
Belgrove
Spooners Range SR

Marris Peak 1313
Mt Allen 1510
Helicopter Flat Hut
Kiwi Track
Nugget Knob 1502
Rolling Junction Shelter
Davils Thumb 1206
12
15

Johnson Hut
Pike Peak 1487
Wangapeka Track
Courthouse Flat
Mt Norriss 531
16
Hiwipango

Mt Webb 1350
Cecil Kings Hut
Kings Creek Hut
Culliford Hill 1756
Billies Knob 1648
Mt Bell 1857
Kaka
Tuk
Pinchback 648
Korere
Golden Downs

Hurricane Hut
Boyd Hut
Branch Creek Hut
Granity Pass Hut
Conical Hill 1202
6
5960

Mt Snodgrass 1091
Haystack Hut
Lake Jeanette
MARINO MOUNTAINS
Mt Owen 1875
Sunrise Peak 1585
"Dimrill Dale"
Kaka Scenic Res

Mokihinui Forks Hut
The Needle 1438
Larrikin Creek Hut
Mt Baigent 1419
Mt Misery 1383
The Haystack 1526
Atapo

Goat Creek Hut
Poor Pete's Hut
McConchies Hut
Trent Peak 1446
Ben Murray 1440
Clark Knob 654
21
Gordons Knob 1592
GORDON RA

Mokihinui Forks Ecological Area
Glenhope
28
Rainy River SR
Kerr Hill 725
16
43

Lake Matiri Hut
Rain Peak 1320
Puke 803
Mt Hope 1244
Kawatiri Junction
Kawatiri Walkway
Kikiwa
5950

New Zealand's Longest Newton Swingbridge
Owen River
Owen Junction
Kawatiri
Howard Junction
Nestor 852
Beebys Hut
Beebys Knob 1442

Mt Newton 1360
6
Owen River SR
Gowanbridge
Gowan River SR
Top House SR
F

New Zealand Kayak School
45
Mt Murchison 1470
Glenhope Scenic Reserve
Porika Knob 850
63
25
Tophouse

Matiri Hut 745
20
Beeres Rock 831
Lake Rotoroa
Howard
14

Fern Flat
Four Rivers Plain
Matiri SR
Noels Peak 1053
Saint Arnaud
5940

Ariki
Longford
Mangles Valley
Longford
Mt Harte 1135
Twins 1152
Rotoroa
BRAEBURN
Botoiti Nature Recovery Project
Kerr Bay
6
G

Sphinx 725
Murchison
Tutaki 953
Mt Baring 1127
West Bay
St Arnaud Track
17

Mt Brown 863
Glengarry
Blue Rock 880
Tutaki
Mt Cotton 1256
Speargrass Track
Bushline Hut
Lake Head Track
5930

Mt Allman 1061
Historic Gold Mining Sites
Six Mile
Mt Robert Skifield
Speargrass Hut
Coldwater Hut
Lakehead Hut
Rainbow Valley Skifield

Minehaha
65
Shenandoah
Shenandoah Scenic Reserve
Six Mile Walkway & Track
Tiraumea Track
NELSON LAKES NATIONAL PARK
Rotoroa Track
Howard Track
Lake Angelus
Lakeside Track
Mt McRae 1878
Dip Flat
H

Paenga
28
Historic Gold Mining Sites
Tiraumea Hut
Mt Hutton 1400
D'Urville Hut
Sabine Hut
Mt Cedric 1532
Angelus Hut
Cascade Track
Peanter Peak 1880

Old Man of the Buller 1155
Three Peaks 1086
Mt Misery 1601
Hopeless Hut

Mailman 920
Burnt Spur
Mount Mistery Hut
Mt Hopeless 2278
The Camel 1889

Mt Mantell 1606
D'Rourke 936
Thomson 1270
Jameson Ridge Track
Mole Hut
Mole Tops 1651
Cupola Hut
John Tait Hut
Connors Creek Hut
Elise Peak 1823
J

Matakitaki
Murty 711
Mole Track
Morgan Hut
Mt Windward 1966
Mt Cupola 2260
Cotterell Peak 2106
Mt Cashel 1594

71
Upper Matakitaki
Mt Oliver 772
Baldy 1431
Mt Watson 1871
West Sabine Hut
Travers - Sabine Track
Mt Travers 2338
Upper Travers Hut
Mt Chittenden 2205
5910

8 To Springs Junction 9 10 11 47 12 13 14

To Nelson
To Blenheim
To Springs Junction

map
43
SOUTH ISLAND
Marlborough

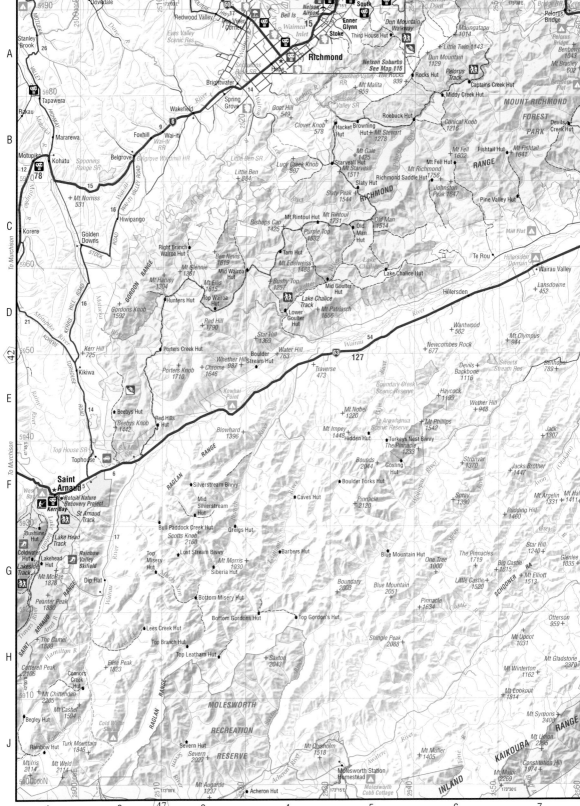

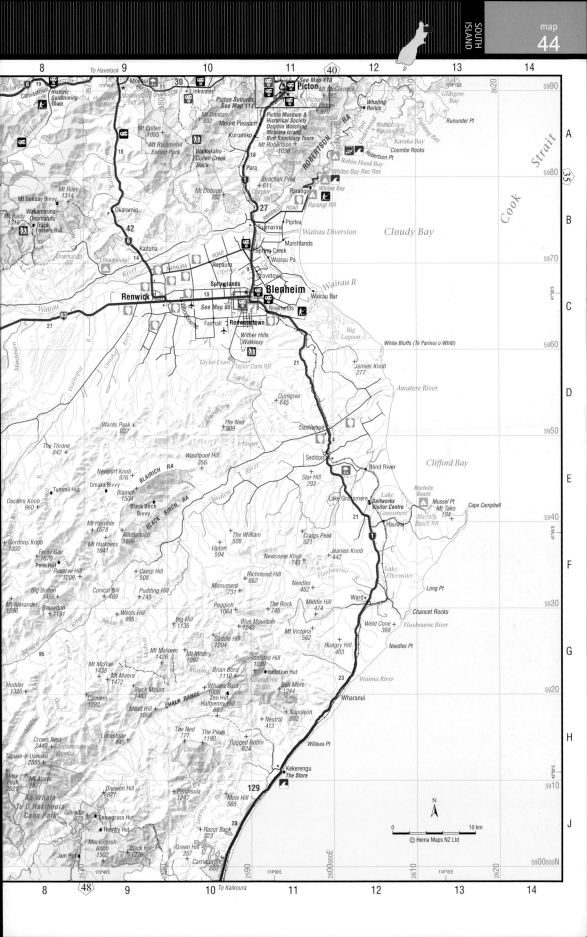

map
45
SOUTH ISLAND
Central West Coast

To Westport

© Hema Maps NZ Ltd

0   10 km

N

TASMAN SEA

PAPAROA NATIONAL PARK

PAPAROA RANGE

Woodpecker Bay
Seal Is
Kaipakati Pt
Tiromoana
Pahautane
Motukutuku Pt
Meybille Bay
Irimahuwheri Bay
Perpendicular Pt
Te Miko SR
Te Miko Glass Bead Studio
Te Miko
Punakaiki
Dolomite Pt
Pancake Rocks & Blowhole
Razorback Pt
Punakaiki River Scenic Reserve
Waikori
Pakiroa Beach
Langridge SR

Mt Pasteur 1341
Mt Einstein 1336
Mt Uriah 1525
Tiropahi Ecological Area
Altara-Nile Ecological Area
Mt Mendel 1424
Mt Faraday 1485
Mt Curie 1345
Mt Micawber 1475
Mt Priestley 1392
Mt Dewar 1431
The Pinnacle 1365
Mt Epping 1440
Mt Lodge 1447
Mt Ramsay 1406
Mt Beeche 1265
Mt Bovis 1252
Mt Wise 1292
Mt McHardy 1271
Lone Hand 947
Mt Johnston 1241
White Knight 1224
Mt Pecksniff 1306
Mt Marshall 1276
Sexton Ecological Area
Hawera 1190

Barrytown
Croesus Track
Mt Ryall 1220
Mt Anderson 1070
Seventeen Mile Bluff
Marconi Hill 1178
Croesus Knob 1204
Croesus Top Hut
Craigieburn
Fourteen Mile Bluff
Mt Saint Patrick 1082
Roaring Meg Ecological Area
Moonlight Eco Area
Slaty Creek
Totara Flat
Twelve Mile Bluff
Greigs
Mt George 320
Mt Leitch 1153
Mt Watson 1102
Roa
Atarau
Raupo
Kaka Hill 272
Ikes Peak 637
Rewanui
Blackball
Matai
Anaura
Rapahoe
Mt Davy 1012
Blackball RR
Tui Kaiwai Scenic Res
Ngakere
Point Elizabeth
Point Elizabeth Walkway
Dunollie
Paparoa Peak 850
Ngahere
Red Jacks
Nelson Creek
Nelsoir Creek Rec Res
Runanga
Rapahoe Range SR
See Map 118
Coal Creek SR
Brunner
Stillwater
Kamaka
Notown
Deadman Eco Area
Lake Hochstetter
Cobden
Grey River (Mawheraui)
Greymouth
Jade Boulder Gallery
Monteith's Brewing Company
Taylorville
Brunner Mine HR
Dobson
Bywash Pakihi Ecological Area
Karoro
Omoto
Kaiata
Boddytown
Onototu SR
Kokiri
South Beach
Card Creek Ecological Area
Mt Fox 385
Kaimata
Dees Creek Ecological Area
Paroa
Arararoi SR
Kakawau 447
Arnold River SR
Kotuku
Rutherglen
Shantytown
Historic Gold Town
Bell Hill
Gladstone
Camerons
Marsden
Dunganville
Aratika
Kiwi House Conservation Park
Moana
Ruru
Bell Hill SR
Bell Hill 839
Taramakau River
Kumara Junction
Te Kinga
Kangaroo Lake
Lady Lake Scenic Reserve
Lady Lake
Granite Hill 1156
Chesterfield
Greenstone Ecological Area
Lake Brunner
Greenstone (Pounamu)
Drakes Hill 187
Mitchells
Whitestone SR
Cooked River SR
Rotomanu
Awatuna
Kumara
Seddon House HR
Dillmanstown
Three Mile Hill 330
Lake Brunner Lodge
Castle Hill 1067
Mt Te Kinga 1204
Mosquito Hill
Kaihinu
Stafford
Goldsborough (Waimea)
Three Mile Hill
Hohonu Scenic Res
Mt Te Kinga Scenic Reserve
Camp Creek Hut
Jacko Flat Hut
Houhou
Arahura
Taramakau
Hohonu
Mt French 1305
Ben Claddagh 1295
Taft Tor 1283
Lake Poerua
Poerua
KAIMATA RANGE
Glow Worm Grotto
Westland Waterworld
Hokitika
Blue Spur
Eco World
National Kiwi Centre
Jade Greenstone Artisans
Mt Smart 1246
Hohonu Range
Inchbonnie
Mt Alexander 1958
Mt Howe 1660
ALEXANDER RANGE
Hokitika River
Southside RR
Humphreys
Kaniere Reservoir
Mt Bruce Murray 1356
Mt Treacey 1356
Orangipuku River SR
Rocky Point SR
The Avenue SR
Jacksons
Takutai
Arthurstown
Kaniere
Turiwhate
Mt Turiwhate 1368
Wainihinihi
Mt McInerney 1137
Dillons Homestead Hut
Kellys Hill 1394
Aickens
Mananui
Rimu
Woodstock
Tunnel Hill 209
Island Hill (Tumuaki) 1003
Griffin Creek Hut
Rocky Creek Hut
Dillon Hut
Carroll Hut
AICKEN RANGE
Mahinapua Creek Rail Bridge HR
Overlook Hill 169
Conical Hill 764
Milltown
Mt Griffin 1438
Mt Kerr 1516
Top Olderog 1569
Scottys Bivvy
KELLY RANGE
BALD RANGE
Goat Hill 1656
Otira
Ruatapu
Lake Mahinapua
Lake Mahinapua Scenic Reserve
Lake Mahinapua
Lake Kaniere
Hans Bay
Lake Kaniere SR
Wainihinihi
Tuhua 1125
Mt Olson 1603
TARA TAMA RANGE
Tara Tama 1854

8 41 9 To Inangahua 10 11 12 To Murchison 13 42 14

Mt Copernicus 1149
Mt Steele 1291
Mt Stevenson 1414
Mt Raoulia 1362
Te Wharau Wildlife Management Area
Te Wharau Eco Area
Cronadun
Larrys Creek
Sugar Loaf 868
Bourkes Rock 1306
Conical Hill 1047
Kirwans Track
Mt Pelion 1502
Mt Victoria 1640
Mt Ralph 1543
Mt Rutland 1315
Walter Peak Scenic Reserve
Mt Oliver 772
Upper Matakitaki
Baldy 1431
Nardoo 1449

A

Capleston
Reefton
Waitahu
Reefton Courthouse Historic Res
Kirwans Hill
Kirwans Hut
Montgomerie River
Wheel Creek Hut
Mt Crosscut 1613
Creighton Peak 1582
Warwick Junction
Granite Pinnacle 926
Emily Peaks 2031
Nardoo Hut
17
71
Burnbrae

Taipoiti
Blacks Point
Crushington
Mai Mai SR
Maimai
Montgomerie Hut
VICTORIA
FOREST
RANGE
Maruia
Mt Cann 1693
Burn Creek Hut

B

Hinau
Progress Junction
Stab Hut Creek
Globe Hill 680
Mt Albert 1547
Ivess Peak 1749
Top Waitahu Bivvy
Maruia War Memorial RR
Woolley River SR
Maruia
65
Fyfe Peak 1610
Mid Glenroy Hut
Mt Burn 2145
Mt Maling 2127
Bobs Hut

Mawheraiti SR
Merrijigs
7
Quigleys Track
Mt Ross 1516
Klondyke Track
Lake Stream Bivvy
Woolley River
18
Victoria Forest Park
Mt Burn

C

Waimaunga
Hukarere
Blackwater
Big River
Big River Hut
Waiuta-Big River Track
45
Mt Penneal 1487
Mt Haast 1587
Mt Hunter 1552
Mt Kemp 1637
Blackwater Scenic Res
Baldy 1329
Lake Daniell
Manson Nicholls Memorial Hut
Pell Stream Hut
Lewis Pass
Saint James Walkway
Ada Pass Hut
Cannibal Gorge Hut

Ikamatua
Waipuna
Nobles
Mount Harata Ecological Area
Bald Hill 1191
Hukawai
Waiuta
Mt Gore 1488
Mt Beckman 1588
Mt Puttick 1623
Mt Alexander 1282
Springs Junction
15
Mt Mueller 1630
Scenic Reserve
FREYBERG RANGE
Mt Freyberg 1817
Zampa 1710

D

Ahaura Terraces Ecological Area
Mt Harata 1385
Conical Hill 1602
Granville Wildlife Management Area
Clarke
Pinnacle 1500
Lake Christabel Track
Maruia Springs Thermal Resort
Maruia Springs
6
Discovery Peak 1661
Lewis Trovatore Pass 1737

Hochstetter Wildlife M/A
Jim's Flat Hut
Flagstaff Eco Area
Ahaura-Kopara Scenic Reserve
Mt Rameses 1453
Turpentine 1368
State Slip Hill 1447
Lake Christabel
Lake Christabel Hut
Mt Hatless 1660
Brass Monkey Bivvy
Mt Technical 1870
Norma 1722
Lucretia Hut
The Grand Duchess 1703
Mt Lucia 1711
Rokeby Hut
7
16
Boyle Flat

E

The Pyramid 1341
Mt Elliot 1379
Mt Hochstetter 1575
Mid Robinson Hut
Top Robinson Hut
Mt Boscawen 1780
Upper Nina Bivvy
Mt Barron 1806
Devils Den Bivvy
Mt Carrington 1743
Nina Hut
Mt Quail 1653
Doubtless Hut
Sylvia Flat Hot Springs
Boyle Village
Lewis Pass
Lake Sumner Forest Park
Faust 1710
Saint James Walkway
47

F

Nancy's Clearing Ecological Area
Mt Novaro 1567
Slaty Creek Hut
Mt Lakeman 1782
Le Man
Doubtful Hut
Mt Murray 1611
Mons Sex Millia 1835
Garnet Peak 1776
Mt Garfield 1676
Engineers Camp
10
82

G

Lake Ahaura
Haupiri
Kopara
Eldon Coates Scenic Res
Mt Ranunculus 1419
Mt Newcombe 1337
Mt Ajax 1834
Lake Sumner Forest Park
Top Hope Hut
Saint Jacob's Hut
Hope Shelter Hut
DOUBTFUL RANGE
Lake Sumner Forest Park
To Hammer Springs

Lake Haupiri
Mt Mason 1269
Mt O'Shanessy 1462
Lake Morgan
L. Morgan Hut
Mt Fraser 1386
Waikiti Hut
Tutaekuri Hut
Tutaekuri River
THE NELSON TOPS
Hope Kiwi Hut
Neschacker Hill 1525
Mt Skiddaw 1673
Scaw Fell 1636

Cone Creek Hut
Mt Elizabeth 1750
Mt Stapp 1703
Mt Tuke 1723
Mackenzie Hut
Mackenzie Bivvy
Three Mile Stream Hut
Niggerhead 1395
Macs Knob 1435
Harper Pass Track
Mt Emerson 1834
Harper Pass
Mt Edison 1790
Mt Pan 1545
WYE RANGE

H

Top Crooked Hut
SOUTHERN
Elizabeth Hut
Mt Monotis 1574
Mid Trent Hut
Top Trent Hut / Lagoon Hut
Mt Wilson 1543
Mt Drake 1426
Cameron Hut
ALPS
Hurunui Hot Springs
Hurunui No. 3 Hut
Hurunui Hut
Lake Marion
Lake Sumner
Mt Longfellow 1901
Evangaline Bivvy
Jollie Brook Hut
Glenrae Bivvy
Jollie Brook 1528
Gabriel Hut

RANGE
Kiwi Hut
Mt Dixon 1556
Harper Pass Bivvy
Locke Stream Hut
Mt Byrne 1448
Howitt Peak 1699
Blake Peak 1623
Taipuni Peak 1245
Terrible Knob
CRAWFORD RANGE
Loch Katrine
Loch Katrine Rec Reserve
L. Jason
Lake Sheppard
Cold Stream Hut
Glenrae Hut 1421

J

Harper Pass Track
Lake Kaurapataka
Pfeifer Bivvy
Mt Pfeifer 1704
Koropuku Hut
ARTHUR'S PASS NP
DAMPIER RANGE
Mt Wikinson 1430
Townsend Hut
Harper Pass 1245
Taipuni Peak
Lookout Peak 1647
Upper South Branch Hut
Lake Sumner Forest Park
Stony Stream Hut
Lake Taylor
Lake Taylor
ORONOKO RANGE
Cherry Tree Hill 980
Mt Catherine 804
Ben Cliberick

Mt Tarapuhi 1605
Mt McRae 1753
Mt Koeti 1786
Minchin Bivvy
Poulter Bivvy
Mt Scarface
Mt Morrison 1720
Mt Row 1673
Candlesticks Bivvy
Mt Crossley 1980
POULTER RANGE
North Branch
Mt Miza 1464

8 52 9 10 11 12 13 53 14

map
47
SOUTH ISLAND
Kaikoura & Hurunui

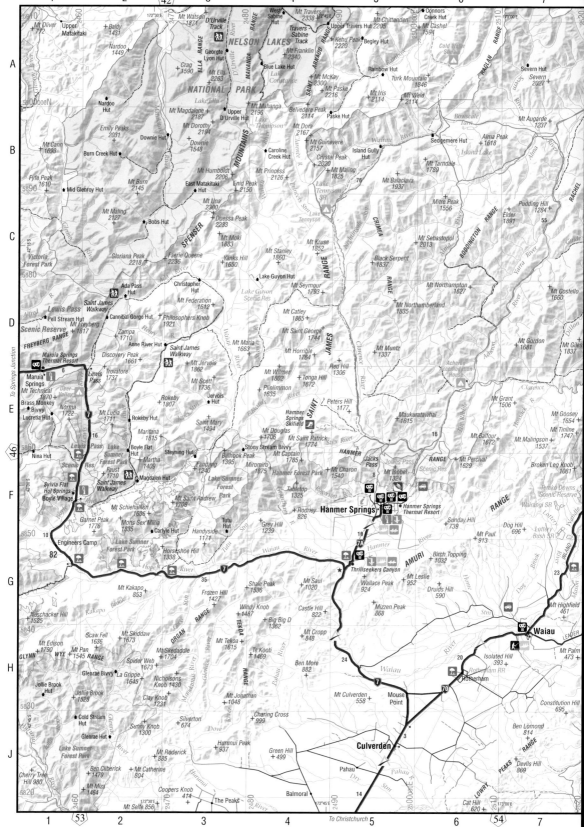

8 43 9 10 11 12 13 44 14

A
B
C
D
E
F
G
H
J

To Blenheim

Mt Chisholm 1518
Molesworth Station Homestead
Molesworth Cobb Cottage
Acheron Hut
Awatere River
Mt Muller 1405
Saint Bernard 2256
Mt Major 2269
KAIKOURA
Carters Knob 1566
RANGE
Mt Lookout 1814
Mt Symons 2408
Mt Union 2295
Ka Whata Tu'O Rakihouia Cons Park
Constitution Hill 1974
Mithe Peak 2621
Mt Alarm 2877
Division Hill 671
Peninsula Scenic Reserve
Clarence Bedad Scenic Reserve
Mole Hill 565
Razor Back
Gibraltar 675
Snowgrass Hut
Hornby Hut
Jam Hut
Mackintosh Knob 1502
Black Hill 1276
Green Hill 357
Carrion Hill 220
Pigeon Hill 292

Barefell 1928
MOLESWORTH
RECREATION
RESERVE
INLAND
RANGE
Turks Head 1958
Little Benledi 1042
Beattie 1582
The Clock Face 1091
Lake Tennyson
Wood River
Mt Jackson 1524
The Observatory 894
Seymour Hut
Red Hill 1022
Dubious Bivvy
Red Hill 822
Limestone Hill 1320
Mustering Hill 765
Goose Flat Hut
Bluff Hill 910
Fidgit Bivvy
Te ao Whekere 2590
HAYDOCK RANGE
Haycocks Bivvy
Tarahaka 2283
Devils Lookout 886
Middle Hill 902
Clarence
Waipapa Bay
Okiwi Bay

Dillon Cone 2173
Palmer Hut
Palmer 1989
Willows Hut
Ka Whata Tu O Rakihouia Conservation Park
Limestone Hut
Bluff Damp Hut
Snowflake 1870
Mt Saunders 2146
Mount Uwerau Nature Reserve
Manakau 2608
Mount Manakau SR
Barratts Bivvy
Mt Stace 1167
Uwerau 2213
Hapuku Hut
Kaitoa 723
Pudi Pudi SR
Mt Alexander 1197
Batty 1195
Patutu 1162
Balance Rock
Jacobs Ladder 662
Rangataua 537
Rakautara
Nins Bin (crayfish)
Te Ikawhataroa
KAIKOURA
Okiwi Bay SR
Paparoa Point
Paparoa Point SR
Ohau Point Seals
Half Moon Bay SR
Half Moon Bay

The Beacon 1355
Mt Ross 1570
Palmer Bivvy
Alfred Hut
Devils Lookout 1265
Mt Horrible 1568
Warder 1481
Tentpoles Hut
Cairn 1716
Kahutara Bivvy
Mt Clear 1444
Mt Arthur 1525
Black Hill 994
Swyncombe 826
Gables End
Kowhai Hut
Mt Fyffe 1592
Mt Fyffe Hut
Humpback 1160
Mt Fyffe 1602
Mount Fyffe Scenic Res
Lavendyl Lavender Farm
Hapuku SR
Mangamaunu
Hapuku
Hapuku River

Dog Hill 1312
Mt Terako 1742
Snowden Scenic Reserve
Mt Lyford Skifield
SEAWARD
70
55
INLAND
Rangamahoe 327
Lake Rotorua
Kahutara R
Maori Leap Caves
Kaikoura
Nga Niho Pa HR
South Bay
Pt Kean
Kaikoura Wildlife Refuge
Kaikoura Peninsula Walkway

Mt Peter 993
Mt Cookson 866
Mt Stewart 938
Flax Hill 557
Ngaroma Scenic Res
Armchair 755
Monument 825
Peketa
Rileys Hill 473
Pinnacle Rock Nature Res
Rileys Lookout (Panau Island) NR
Scenic Reserve
Pohio te atua 845
Goose Bay
Otumatu Rock Rock Art
Goose Bay-Omihi Scenic Reserve
Oaro RR
Oaro
Pukaroro Rock
Spy Glass Point (Piripaua)
Atia Pt
South Bay
Seal Colony
Whale Watching
Bird Watching
Dolphin Swimming
Seal Snorkelling
Sea Kayaking
Glass Bottom Boat Rides

Maori Chief Peak 681
Peaked Hill 807
18
1
68
Mt Guardian 404
Hundalee
Claverley
Conway River
Conway River RR
Conway Flat
Haumuri Bluffs

PACIFIC
OCEAN

Solomons Throne 360
Skull Peak 489
Ferniehurst
29
17
Hawkswood
Mt Wilson 649
HAWKSWOOD RANGE

The Wart 505
Mt Emily 242
Mt Parnassus 697
Parnassus
Spotswood
Dead Mans Hill 605
Medina R

Mt Styche 446
Mt Ward 335
Phoebe
Leamington
16
Mata Kopae Lagoon RR
Caverhill
Waiau Rivermouth SR
Waiau River Mouth RR
Waiau River

Mt Ellen 418
Mt Crombie 240
Mina
Cheviot
Cheviot Museum
Cheviot RR
Mt Beautiful 423
Shag Rock SR
Shag Rock

Tormore 446
Nonoti
54
To Christchurch

N
0 10 km
© Hema Maps NZ Ltd

map
49
SOUTH ISLAND
Glacier Country

N

0   10 km

© Hema Maps NZ Ltd

T A S M A N

S E A

Wanganui River
Wanganui Heads
Oneone WMA
Poerua River

Saltwater Lagoon
Scenic Reserve

Saltwater
Ecological
Area

Abut Head
Scenic Res

Abut Head
Whataroa River

White Heron
Nesting Site
Waitaiti Bluff
Commissioner Pt

Waitangiroto NR

Waitangiroto
Nature Reserve

Rotokino

The Exi
SR

Scenic
Res

Mt Bird
3457

Okarito Lagoon

Okarito

Kohuamarua Bluff
Kohuamarua
573

Three Mile Beach
Blanchards Bluff

Okarito Forks
Okarito Forks
Ecological Area

Five Mile Beach

Waiho River

Three Mile
Lagoon

Five Mile
Lagoon

Waiho Beach
Omoeroa Bluff

Sandfly Beach

**WESTLAND
TAI POUTINI
NATIONAL PARK**

Alpine Lake
(Ata Puai)

Lake
Mapourika

Otto
MacDonalds

The Forks

Lake
Wahapo

6

Tours to White
Heron Sanctuary
Whataroa

Kotuku Gallery

14

Ralfes Knob 411

Mt Price
1033

Fardowner Peak
1655

Salmon
& Trout

Waitangitaona
Scenic Res

18

Gunn Peak
1753

Stan's
Hut

Mt Cloher
1689

Moonlight
Beach

Omoeroa Hill
684

Tatare

Canavans Knob
249

Scenic Flights
Glacier Hiking

**Franz Josef
Glacier**

Hukawai Glacier Centre &
Indoor Ice Climbing Wall

Mt Downe
2002

McFetrick Peak
2188

Seal Colony
Gillespies Pt (Kohaihai)
Gillespies Beach

Galway Pt

Lake
Mueller

24

BURSTER

RANGE

Mt Burster
1395

"Lighting of
the Beacons"

Junction
Peak 2219

Mt Park
2312

Otorokua Pt

Old Gold Mining
Settlement

Lake
Matheson

L Gault

Glacier views
Ebenezer Peak
1338

Mt Gunn 1261

Castle
Rocks Hut

Almer
Hut

Thelma Peak 2087

Whymper Peak
2343

Roderick Peak
2343

Cook River
Cook Bluff

Fox
River

Scotchmans Bluff
Karangarua Bluff

Fox Glacier

Mt Mitchell
1623

Mt Moltke
1987

Mt Roon
2231

Zurbriggen

Mackay
Rocks Hut

Drummond
Peak 2514

Mt Elie De Beaumont
3109

Karangarua River

Ohinetamatea

Mt Fox
1021

Mt Anderegg
1935

Col

Matenga
Peak 2665

Mt Walter 2905

VICTORIA RANGE

Chancellor
Hut

Mt Halcombe
2659

Centennial
Hut

Minarets
3031

Mt Green
2837

Mt Aylmer
2699

Tasman
3070

Hunt
Beach

The Sugar Loaf
160

Karangarua

Glacier views

Lookout

**FOX
GLACIER**

Chancellor
Dome 2004

Mt Garnier
2266

Mt Du Fresne
2266

Sam Peak
1827

Pioneer
Hut

Mt Barnicoat
2800

Conway Peak 2899

Douglas Peak

De La Beche
Hut

De La
Beche

Mt Darwin
2952

Mt Turnbull
2265

Kelman
Hut

Haeckel Peak
2965

Makawhio Pt
Jacobs River SR

Makawhio River
(Jacobs River)
Sandy Beach

Jacobs River

20

Karangarua
Bridge SR

Ngataus Knob
1211

COPLAND RANGE

Ryan Peak
1939

Lyttle Peak
2240

Shiels Peak
2055

WESTLAND

TAI POUTINI

NATIONAL PARK

BALFOUR RANGE

Belmont

Mt Haidinger
3070

Mt Tasman 3497

Mt Dampier
3440

Plateau
Hut

Haast
Hut

AORAKI / MOUNT COOK

Mt Chudleigh
2966

Mt Hutton
2822

Bruce
Bay

L Kini

58

Toaroha
Creek SR

Mt Myers
1697

Copland
Track

Mt Copland
2326

La Perouse
3078

Aoraki / Mt Cook
3754

Empress
Hut

Anzac Peaks
2528

Mt Johnson 2692

Mt Hamilton

Haast
2219

Onslow Hut
(Steffan
Memorial Hut)

To Haast

59

NAVIGATOR RANGE

NATIONAL PARK

2240

169°45'E

2250

2260

170°00'E

2270

2280

170°15'E

2290

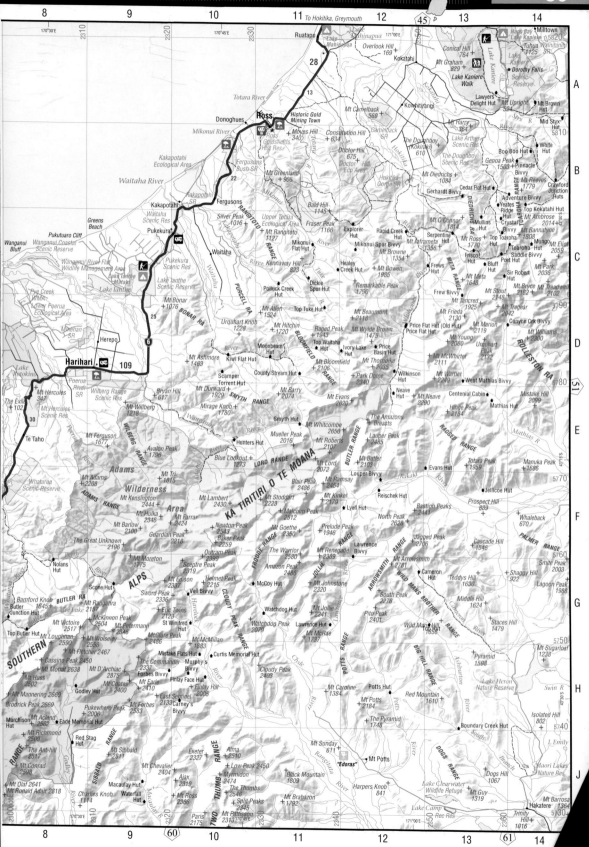

map
51
SOUTH ISLAND
Arthur's Pass

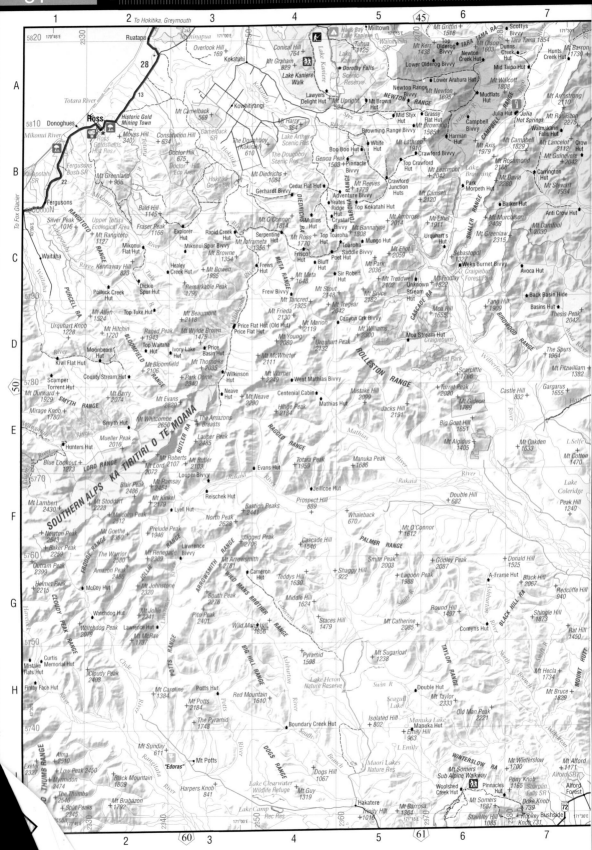

To Greymouth

8 9 10 11 46 12 13 14

ARTHUR'S PASS

© Hema Maps NZ Ltd

10 km

A

Otira
Goat Hill 1656
Lookout
Mt Pfeifer 1704
Korbpuku Hut
Mt Taraphui 1605
Mt McRae 1753
Mt Scarface
Poulter Bivvy
Mt Morrison 1720
Candlesticks Bivvy
DAMPIER
Mt Crossley 1980
Esk Head 1864
Virginia Peak 986
Mt Stuart 1906
Mt Russel 1868
Otehake Hut
Worsley Bivvy
Green Hill Hut
Poulter Hut
Trust / Poulter Hut
RANGE
Mt Turnbull 2024
Ant Stream Bivvy
Dampier Corner 1630
Phipps Peak 1965
Mt Franklin 2145
Goat Pass Hut
Mt Hunt 1825
Poulter Hut 1583
Ranger Bivvy
Shingle Hill 1804
Ant Stream Hut
Esk Bivvy
Anderson's Hut
Upper Deception Hut
Falling Mountain 1901
Castle Hill 1545
Casey Hut
Bull Creek Hut
Mt Meehan 1150

B

Arthur's Pass
Avalanche Creek Shelter
Temple Basin Skifield
Mt Oates 2041
East Hawdon Bivvy
Hawdon Hut
Forest Peak 1470
Lochinvar Hut
Big Flora 1242
Townshend Huts
Black Rock 1714
Mt Whatno 1396
Gola Peak 1285
Mt Bealey 1836
Arthur's Pass Museum
Mingha Bivvy
Mt Aicken 1659
Edwards Hut
NATIONAL PARK
Brown Hill 1216
Gray Hill 1845
Little Flora 1035
Block Hill 1297
Mt Williams 1718
Dome 1945
Woolshed Hill 1428
Andrews Track
Andrews Shelter
Peveril Peak 1755
Mt White 1741
Little Peveril 784
Turnbull Bivvy
Puketeraki 1623
Youngman Stream Hut
Lilburne 405
Spring Hill 1292

C

Greyneys
Klondyke Corner
Bealey Hotel 73
Bealey Spur
Binser Saddle Track
Sugar Loaf 1359
Cass
L Sarah
Mt Binser 1860
Lake Letitia
Mt Pember 1714
Tarn Hut
Pancake Hill 1338
Okuku Hill 1143
Bealey Spur Hut 27
Bealey Hut
Mt Misery 1765
Mt Bruce 1630
Lake Grasmere
Scenic Res & Wildlife Refuge
Lake Pearson
Whale Hill 871
Retreat Hill 1000

D

Lagoon Saddle A Frame Hut
Mid Hill 1831
Stag Hill 1639
Packard Peak 2066
Craigieburn Forest Park
Baldy Hill 1834
Lake Pearson
Wildlife Refuge
Lake Hawdon
Craigieburn
Chest Peak 1936
Blackwater Lake
Puketeraki Bivvy
Ashley Hill 1016
Pinchgut Hut
West Harper Hut
Hamilton Peak 1922
Craigieburn Skifield
Mt Manson 1859
Purple Hill 1680
Lake Marymere
Mt Rosa 1032
Whistler
Bob's Camp Bivvy
Mt Thomas 1023
Hamilton Hut
Mt Cockayne 1874
Broken River Skifield
Craigieburn Shelter
Broken Hill 1486
Avoca
Mt Storm 1254
Lees Valley
Mt Richardson 1047
Blowhard Track
Richardson Track
Ladbrooks Hill 1030

E

Mt Cheeseman 2031
Mt Olympus 2094
Mt Cheeseman Skifield
Mt Izard 2019
Flock Hill 998
Broken River Hut
Avoca Homestead
Bold Hill 1286
Staircase
Black Hill 1335
Lower Salmon Creek Bivvy
Black Hill Hut
Wharfedale Hut
Fosters Hill 1094
Wharfedale Track
Mt Oxford 1364
Mt Richardson 1047
Ashley Gorge
Glentui
Ashley
Summerhill
Mt Olympus Skifield
Mt Ida 1695
L Catherine
Mt Cloudsley 2107
Leith Hill 1384
Lance McCaskill Nat Res
Castle Hill Village
Prebble Hill 902
Korowai Torlesse
Otarama Peak 1963
Paterson Hill 1113
Mt Torlesse 1961
Wilson Hill 872
View Hill SR
Coopers Creek
Oxford
Bennetts
Cadeton
Horrellville

F

Mt Hennah 1109
Mt Enys 2194
Knuckles 1316
Porter Heights Skifield
Mt Plenty 1459
Castle Hill Peak 1998
Foggy Peak 1741
Caesars Hut
Kowai Bush
Lords Bush SR
Yummy Homemade Food Cafe
View Hill 419
View Hill
Gammans Creek
The Warren
Red Hill 1641
Mt Lyndon 1489
Ice Skating
Lake Lyndon
Rabbit Hill 1198
Springfield
Rockford
Kowai Pass RR
Bexley
Oxford Domain RR
SOUTH
EYRE

G

Mt Georgina 944
Korowai Torlesse Tussocklands Park
Ben More 1655
Russell Range
Benmore Hut
Hawkins River
Annat
Waddington
Racecourse Hill
Burnt Hill 368
Eyrewell Forest
Lake Coleridge
Mt Barker 896
Big Ben 1416
Russells Flat
Sheffield
Abners Head 579
Kimberley
Courtenay
Waimakariri River

H

Steepface Hill 1876
Rakaia River
Snowdon HR
Quartz Hill 790
High Peak 968
Golgotha 475
Flagpole 897
Cairn Hill 500
Whitecliffs
Homebush
Hawkins
Darfield
Kimberley RR
Courtenay RR
Kirwee RR
Halkett
Mt Hutt 2185
South Peak 2081
Mount Hutt Skifield
Terrace Downs High Country Resort golf course
Rakaia Gorge Walkway
Round Top 894
Mt Misery 666
South Malvern
Coalgate
Glentunnel
Glentunnel Rec Res
Darfield
Kirwee
Aylesbury
Charing Cross

J

Mount Hutt
Windwhistle
Glenroy
Hororata
Hororata River
Greendale
Transit Of Venus Historic Apse
Burnham
Mount Hutt Methven Airfield
Methven
Highbank
Te Pirita
Norwood Selwyn
To Ashburton
To Christchurch

8 9 10 11 62 12 13 14
To Ashburton

map
53
SOUTH ISLAND
Central Canterbury

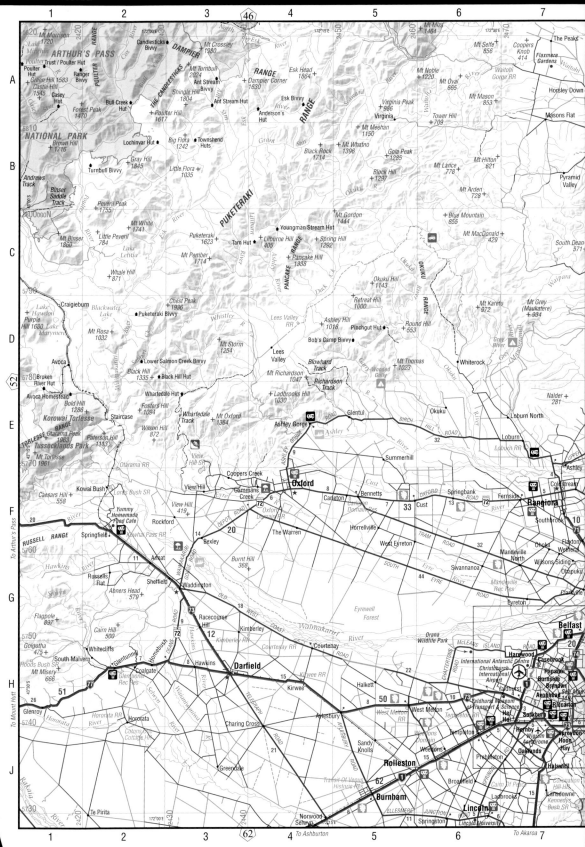

PACIFIC

OCEAN

Pegasus

Bay

To Culverden
To Kaikoura
To Kaikoura

Balmoral
Medbury
Hurunui River
Hurunui
Cat Hill 620
Mt Jon 477
Tormore 446
Nonoti
Domett
Cheviot
Cheviot Museum
Cheviot RR
Shag Rock SR
Shag Rock
Gore Bay SR
Gore Bay
Port Robinson RR
Cathedral Cliffs
Port Robinson
Point Gibson
Manuka Bay SR
Port Robinson Walkway
Hurunui Mouth
Hurunui River

Lowry Peaks Ra
Ben Lomond 480
Mt Alexander 748
Mt Percy 536
Mt Percy
Pendle Hill 529
Blythe
Blythe Valley
Napenape SR
Napenape

Hawarden RR
Hawarden
Castle Hill 539
Scargill
Greta Valley Walkway
Greta
56
Neds Farewell 337
Mt Pleasant 251

Maori Cave Art
Weka Pass Hist Res
Waikari
Mt Donald 491
Moores Hill North 289
Moores Hill South 442
Greta Valley
Spye

Weka Pass
Weka Pass Historic Railway
North Dean 573
Middle Dean 565
Omihi
Centre Hill 558
Vulcan 411
Motunau Beach RR
Motunau Beach
Motunau Island Nature Reserve

Waipara
Mt Cass 525
Tiromoana SR

Glasnevin
Broomfield
Greneys Road
Tiromoana SR

Amberley Domain Res
Amberley
Waipara River
Amberley Beach Rec Res
Amberley Beach
Leithfield
Kowai River
Baldairn
Leithfield Beach
Sefton
Saltwater Creek
Ashworths Spit
Ashley River
Waikuku Beach
Waikuku RR
Waikuku
Tuhaitara Coastal Reserve
Tutae Patu Wildlife Reserve
Woodend
Woodend Beach
Tuhaitara Coastal Reserve
Pegasus Bay Walkway
Kaiapoi
The Pines Beach
Kairaki
Waimakariri River
Brooklands
Stewarts Gully
Kainga
Brooklands Lagoon
Spencerville
Spencer Park
Christchurch Suburbs See Map 120
Chaneys
Ouruhia
Rottle Lake Forest
Marshland
Parklands
Redwood
Burwood
Waimairi Beach
Shirley
St Albans
Avonside
Aranui
New Brighton
CHRISTCHURCH
Linwood
Addington
Southshore
Woolston
Opawa
Redcliffs
Casmere
Mt Pleasant
Sumner Head
Heathcote Valley
Sumner
Mt Pleasant 499
Taylors Mistake
Godley Head
Christchurch Gondola
Cass Bay
Lyttelton Whakaraupo
Adderley Head SR
Governors Bay
Ohinetahi
Allandale
Diamond Harbour
Mt Evans 703
Purau
Charteris Bay
Quail Is
Port Levy
Puari
Wakaroa Pt
Whitehead Bay
Pigeon Bay
Menzies Bay
Otohuao Head
Little Akaloa Bay
Long Lookout Pt
Zig Zag 318

© Hema Maps NZ Ltd

N

0   10 km

map
55
SOUTH ISLAND
Ashburton & Christchurch

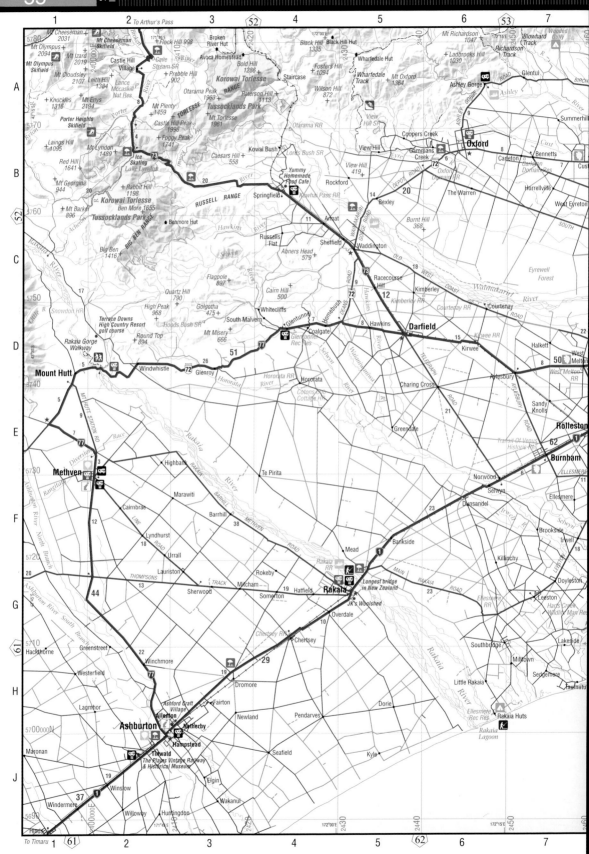

map
57
SOUTH ISLAND
Southern West Coast

N

0 10 km

© Hema Maps NZ Ltd

T A S M A N

S E A

Open Bay Islands
Wildlife Sanctuary
Taumaka Is

Mussel Pt

Hannahs Clearing

Jackson Bay

Penguins & Seals
Smoothwater Pt
Smoothwater Bay
Jackson Head
Jackson Bay
Waiatoto River
Waiatoto
Gill Hill 106

Neils Beach
Stafford Bay
Stafford Hut
Mt McLean 671
Lake Nisson

Cascade Pt
Teer Hill 340
Arawhata
Clarke Hill 631
Mt Ellery 793
Mt Watney 1503

Cascade River
Mt Iota 146
STAFFORD RANGE
Mt Alpha 826
Lake Ellery
Mt Heveldt 1416
Lake Greaney

Halfway Bluff
Watson Bluff
Barn Bay
Martyr
Mt Beta 983

Cascade Bay
Steep Head 494
Mt Eggeling 1136
Smiths Ponds
Mt Jackson 1189
Mt Duncan 1753
Mt Clio 1910

Sandrock Bluff
Browne Island
Mt Delta 1161
Lake Clarke
Mt Lindsay 1181
Lake Leeb
Rosy Peak 2093
DRAKE

Bonar Knob
Spoon Hut
Mt Theta 1137
Distal 1420
Collyer 1643
Baal 945
Sombre Peak 2040

Rocky Pt
Gorge Islands
Gorge River Hut
Martyr Hill 1031
Dagon 1683
Datamos 1816
Flanagans Summit 2044
Pegasus Peak 2160

Longridge Pt
Mt Malcolm 718
Staircase Mountain 1660
Lucifer 1751
HAAST RANGE
Fingals Head 1986
Munro Peak 2374

MALCOLM RANGE
Junction Hill 1012
Theta Tarn
Mt Richards 1450
Tararua Peak 1579
RANGE
Mt.Bel 1618
Hyperia 1780
Canon Peak 2149
Mt Ragan 2254

Mt Raddle 1297
Bald Mountain 1547
Mt Nob 1279
Mt Barry 1374

Mt Beck 1083
OLIVINE
Mt Barry 1374
MOUNT ASPIRING NATIONAL PARK

Awarua Pt
Mt McKenzie 981
Pyke Big Bay Track
Telescope Hill 1117
Joe Peak 1927
The Pommel 1154
Snowden 1543
Corner Post 1832
Moonraker 2054
Mt Taurus 2009

Big Bay
Big Bay Hut
The Knoll 407
RED HILLS RANGE
Alfred Peak 1781
Spike 2126
Pickelhaube 2265
Glacier Dome 2367

Three Mile Beach
Penguin Rock
Waiuna Lagoon
Beacon 1531
Battlement Peak 1605
Red Mountain 1705
Toreador Peak 1951
Buncombe 1918
Tyler 1976
Eros 2230
Mt Ionia 2266
Turks Head 1831
Colin Todd Hut
Stargazer 2352
Rolling Pin 2249
Fastness Peak 2383
Sisyphus Peak 1859

To Fox Glacier

169°00'E 169°15'E 169°30'E

8 9 10 11 12 13 14

Sandy Beach
Heretaniwha Pt
Bruce Bay
I. Kini
Mt Jacob 1334
Bruce Bay
Mahitahi SR
Mahitahi
Bannock Brae 1245
Mt Hermann 1815
Mt Stratford 1977
Titira Head
Paringa River
Buttress Pt
Mt Arthur 421
Awataikato Pt
Piakatu Pt
Mt Gates 381
Paringa Hill 616
Hunt Hill 781
Mt Baird 1409
Mt Douglas 1189
Mt Reynolds 1591
22
123
Argentum 1236
Mt Hawkins 2205
STRACHAN RANGE
Otumotu Pt
Monro Beach Penguins
Moeraki HR
Lake Rasselas
Fish Hill 409
Lake Paringa Scenic Res
Salmon Farm
Ward Hill 544
Paringa Bridge SR
Mt Paterson 1925
Mathers Peak 2299
Knights Point Lookout
Moeraki Hill 843
Lake Paringa
Lake Paringa
Mariners Peak 1535
Mt Millington 1898
Mt Gorden 1880
Mt Jack 2343
Seal Pt
Lake Moeraki
Mt Kinnaird 1227
Power Knob 1508
Tunnel Creek Hut
Mt McCullaugh 2266
Otoko Lake
Adiantum Bluff
Lake Moeraki Scenic Reserve
Blue River (Blowfly) Hut
Horseshoe Flat Hut
Middle Head Hut
Mt Hooker 2640
Mt Gow 1860
Tauperikaka Pt
Bald Hill 850
Mt Docherty 836
Mt Clarke 1379
Rainytop 1606
Plover Crag 1746
Eureka 1815
The Outpost 1654
Waita River
32
Law Hill 890
Maori Saddle Hut
Coppermine Ck
Creek Hut
Haast Paringa Track
Mt Smith 1278
Mt Stephenson 1821
Law Peak 1980
Monro Peak 2044
Mt Solution 1710
SOLUTION RANGE
Creswicke Flat Hut
Haast River
Tawharekiri Lakes
Mt Swindle 1588
Roaring Billy Hut
Mt Macfarlane 2057
Shattered Peak 2080
Low Spur 1865
Clarkes Mound 1105
Mt McKenzie 2156
Haast Beach
Mosquito Hill
Thomas River Hut
Deelaw 1187
Mt Thomas 1422
Mt Cuttance 1436
Birch Knob 1022
Mt Wilson 2113
59
Haast
Scenic Boat Cruises
Mt Browne 244
THOMAS RANGE
MATAKETAKE RANGE
Wills Peak 2140
Mt Maitland 2280
Mt Strauchon 2391
Okuru River
Okuru SR
Mt Marks 1495
Rough Ridge 1508
Macpherson Knob 1553
Lake Barra
The Joker 1805
The Pivot 1562
Mt Awkward 1963
Shingle Top 2117
Hassing Peak 2110
Anita Peak 2380
Okuru
Mt Webster 1595
Mt Campbell 1829
Mt Abrupt 1649
The Deuce 1579
Pleasant Flat
Mt Ramsay 1645
Mt Bull 1810
Mt Holdsworth 2219
The Woolsack 1521
Mt Warren 1792
Mt Eggeling 1618
Mt Nerger 1909
The Rampart 1543
Mt Diomede 1860
Flat Top 1537
Stewart Knob 1367
BEALEY RANGE
Mt Enderby 2338
Forbes Hut
Mt Huxley 2505
BROWNING RANGE
Mt Selborne 1864
Mt Victor 1925
Mt Action 1710
Lindsay Peak 1803
Gates of Haast
Wills Hut
Mt Brewster 2515
Mt Tole 2203
Mt Ferguson 2062
Mid Flat Hut
Mt Harris 1864
Howe Knob 1568
Mt Franklin 1862
Citheron 1800
Mt Burke 1775
The Keystone 1795
The Blister 1537
Brewster Hut
Mt Armstrong 2174
Mt Wyn-Irwin 2244
Top Hut
Souter Peak 2035
Mt Actor 1839
Eyetooth 1934
Mt Dana 1612
Mt Cross 1523
Mt Kaye 1998
Ferguson Hut
Mt Calvin 2375
Hagens Hut
Mt Maitland 2249
Mt Ruera 1847
Misty Peak 1930
Mt Bertha 1692
Mt Cameron 1774
Mt Barth 2456
The Watt 1708
Young Peak 1920
Mt Stuart 1860
Castle Hill 1634
27
Tent Peak 2089
Bull Flat Hut
The Cairn 1530
Mt Calliope 1673
Mt Attica 1980
Mt Doris 2010
Mt Rigel 2097
Mt Peterson 2220
Mt Dispute 1952
Mt Dreadful 2020
Mt Awful 2192
Cameron Flat
Mt Birnam 1421
Shamrock Hut
Mt Stafford 2208
BARRIER RANGE
Mt Urania 1672
Trident Peak 2068
Mt Alba 2360
141
Cameron Hut
YOUNG RANGE
Mt Saint Mary 2337
Mt Tyndar 1966
Mt Achilles 1890
Grucible Lake
Young Hut
Leaning Mount 2077
Ahuriri Base Hut
Ahuriri Snowy Gorge Hut
Mercury Peak 2160
The Sentinel 1946
Mt Kuri 2141
Mt Turner 2150
Siberia Hut
Mt Broome 1954
Makarora
Mt Shrimpton 2002
Mt Patriarch 2015
Top Dingle Burn Hut
Conservation Park
Mt Castor 2518
Mt Juno 2012
Kerin Forks Hut
Mt Aeolus 2283
Mt Ernest 1878
Mt Gladwish 1861
Mt Pollux 2536
Mt Vesta 2027
6
Mt Constitution 2031
Big Hopwood Burn Hut
Mt Arnold 1978
Hideaway Bivvy
Mt Perseus 1815
KA TIRITIRI O TE MOANA
McKERROW RANGE
Puke Makariri 1858
SOUTHERN ALPS
Top Forks Hut
Mt Jumbo 1945
Mt Gilbert 1760
Mt White 1816
Triplet Mountain 2064
Cotters Hut
Birch Hill 1877
Ben Avon Scenic Res
Aspinall Peak 1908
Mt Albert 2064
Albert Burn Hut
26
Boundary Creek
Terrace Peak 2027
Mt Jones 1683
Ben Avon 1713
Boundary Creek Scenic Reserve
Camp Peaks 1789
Lake Hawea Western Shore Recreation Reserve
Bush Hut
The Rouster 1365
Snug Bay
66
To Wanaka

A B C D E F G H J

map
59
SOUTH ISLAND
Mackenzie Region

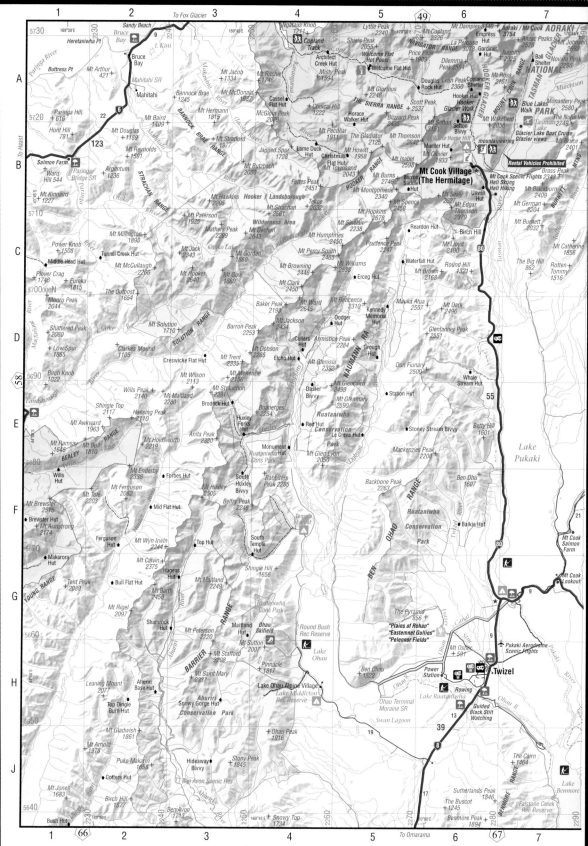

MOUNT COOK

LIEBIG RANGE

Onslow Hut (Steffan Memorial Hut)
Liebig Hut
Mt Tamaki 2444
Mt Lucia 2617
The Abbot 2630
The Abbess 2607
Mt Hutton 2822
Taranaki Peak 2302
Mt William Grant 2556
GARMMACK RANGE
HALL RANGE
Mt Radove 2430
Pikes Peak 1992
Mt Haszard 2213
Middle Gorge Hut
Mistake Peak 1921
Mt Stevenson 2330
Mt Joseph 1682

Charlies Knob 1114
Waterfall Hut
Mt Erebus 2311
Observation Hill 1689
Beuzenberg Peak 2070
Mt Hope 2086
Mt Gerald 1551
Rex Simpson Memorial Hut
Camp Stream Hut
Mt Musgrave 2251
Round Hill 1588
Round Hill Skifield
Mt Misery 2305
Sugar Loaf 1677
South Opuha Hut
TWO THUMB RANGE
SHERWOOD RANGE
Paris 2175
Split Peaks 2345
Captains Peak 2371
Mt Pattisson 2313
Mt Toby 2222
Neutral Hill 1763
Fox Peak 2330
Fox Peak Skifield
North Opuha Hut
Mt Brabazon 1792
Mt Sinclair 2065
SINCLAIR RANGE
BEN McLEOD RANGE
Rawtor 1243
Ben McLeod 1926
Phantom River
Mt Harper (Mahaanui) 1829
HARPER RANGE
Cairn Hill 1589
Grants Top 1010
Mt Catherine 1264
Mt Edith 1089
Lake Camp Rec Res
Lake Emma

Lake Alexandrina Scenic Reserve
Lake Alexandrina
Tekapo Domain
Lake Tekapo
Motuariki Is
Mt Ardmore 1989
Wee McGregor 1146
Mt Hay 1173
Dobson Peak 2095
Mt Dobson Skifield
TWO THUMB RANGE
Blue Mountain 1642
Sugar Loaf 827
Devils Peak 1587
Waihi Peak 1478
Tripps Peak 1653

Mt John Observatory
Lake Tekapo RR Ice Skating
Church of the Good Shepherd
Lake Tekapo
Mt Cox 837
Mt McDonald 780
Mt Maude 1797
Mt Edward 1916
Mt Burgess 1430
Kimbell
Three Springs Historic Woolshed
Ashwick Flat
Trentham
Mt Michael 516
Allandale
Eversley Heritage Museum
Fairlie
Heslip's Hatchery
Cattle Valley
Middle Valley
Round Hill 524
Beautiful Valley
Kakahu Hill 402
Rapuwai
Opuha
Kakahu
Opihi

MARY RANGE
Mt Mary 995
House Hill 701
Sterickers Mound 769
Burkes Pass
ALBURY RANGE
ROLLESBY RANGE
Winscombe
Pioneer Park
Maori Rock Drawings
Cricklewood
Limestone Valley
Camp Valley
Mt Gay 346
Totara Valley
Sutherlands

GRAYS HILLS
Hogget Hill 581
Mt Maggie 524
Beacon Hill 1196
GRAMPIAN MOUNTAINS
DALGETY RANGE
Mt Dalgety 1752
Chamberlain
Mount Nessing
Mt MacGregor 1018
Te Huruhuru 1591
THE HUNTERS HILLS
Mt Nessing 1601
Monavale
Mawaro
Cave
Cannington
Taiko
Cave Hill 542
Mt Horrible 388
Motukaika
Mt Nimrod (Kaumira) 1525
Mt Nimrod
Pareora River Scenic Reserve
Matata Scenic Res
Pareora SR

To Geraldine
To Timaru

N
0   10 km
© Hema Maps NZ Ltd

map
61
SOUTH ISLAND
Timaru & Ashburton

1 2 3 4 5 6 7

50
51
72

A
Mt Brabazon 1792
Hakatere
Mt Somers 1687
Duke Knob 739
Methven
Lake Camp
Rec Res
171°00'E
171°15'E
171°30'E
Trinity Hill 1016
Mt Barrosa 1364
Staveley Hill 1095
Hookey Knob 731
Bushside
Mt Sinclair 2065
Mt Harper (Mahaanui) 1829
Lake Emma
Mt Possession 1161
Woolmer Hill 700
Staveley
Ice Skating
Springburn
23
Cairn Hill 1589
Mt Tripp 1368
Buccleuch
Mount Somers
Cavendish
Mt Somers Domain
20

B
Rawtor 1243
Mt Pukanui 1145
Montalto
Valetta
Punawai
Hackthorne
Ben McLeod 1926
Mt McLeod RANGE
Hewson
Diversion
15
Anama
Westerfield
Coal Hill 1617
Mayfield
Phantom River
North Opuha Hut
Raules Gully Scenic Reserve

C
Fox Peak Skifield
North Opuha
Grants Top 1010
Mt Peel 1743
Little Mt Peel (Huatekerekere) 1311
Acland Falls
Peel Forest
Ruapuna
Ruapuna Rec Res
72
Lismore
Peel Forest Park SR
Peel Forest Walks
Maronan

D
Oari River
Mt Catherine 1264
Mt Edith 1089
Blandswood
Peel Forest
Blue Mountain 1642
Mt Frances 1025
Scotsburn Rec Res
Carew
Tripps Peak 1653
Ben Hope 1034
Orari Gorge Scenic Res
Windermere

E
Sugar Loaf 827
Devils Peak 1587
Waihi Peak 1478
Orari Gorge
Arundel
37
Hinds
Hinds RR
Lynnford
Ashwick Flat
Lake Opuha
Mt Walker 1169
Waihi Gorge Scenic Res
Waihi Gorge
Four Peaks
Woodbury
Woodbury RR
Coopers Creek
72
Ealing
18
Trentham
Hae Hae Te Moana Scenic Reserve
Te Moana
Orari Bridge
10

F
Fairlie
Eversley Heritage Museum
Mt Michael 516
Allandale
79
Cattle Valley
Middle Valley
Round Hill 524
Waitohi Hill 697
Belanger-Taylor Glass Studio
Pleasant Valley
Geraldine Downs
Geraldine
Belfield
16
Rangitata
Rangitata Island
Lowcliffe
Heslip's Hatchery
62
Gapes Valley
29
Hilton
Giant Jersey
Fellmans Chocolates
Talbot Forest Cheese
Barker Fruit Processors
Geraldine Vintage Car Machinery Museum
Caley Art Gallery / Maori Carvings
Winscombe
Chastleton 583
Beautiful Valley
Kakahu Hill 402
Kakahu Limekiln
Geraldine Flat
11
Orari
Geraldine Rec Res
Coldstream

G
Pioneer Park
Maori Rock Drawings
Rapuwai
Opuba
Kakahu
Kakahu Bush
Rangatira Valley
Te Awa
1
Obapi
Orton
Cricklewood
17
Mt Gay 346
Opihi
Upper Waitohi
Waitohi
15
Kavanagh House
Winchester
42
Clandeboye
Rangitata River
Limestone Valley
8
Camp Valley
Albury
Totara Valley
Temuka Pottery & Homeware
Temuka
Milford
Orari River
Browns Beach

H
Mt Smith 837
Tasman Smith SR
65
Cave
Monavale
Pareora SR
Sutherlands
16
Pleasant Point Museum & Railway Artisan Forge & Gallery
Pleasant Point
horseriding
Pleasant Point Rec Reserve
3
Epworth
Waiapi
Arowhenua
9
Arowhenua Pa
Orakipaoa
Milford Huts
Opihi River
Mawaro
12
Kerrytown
Waitawa
8
Richard Pearse Airport
Seadown
Waipopo
Levels Valley
11
Levels
10
Seaforth

J
Mt Nimrod (Kaumira) 1525
Matata Scenic Res
Pareora River Scenic Reserve
Taiko
Rosewill
Old Devels Homestead
Cannington
Hadlow
Puhuka
Washdyke
Washdyke Lagoon
Smithfield
Caroline Bay
See Map 121
Cave Hill 542
Claremont
Gleniti
Aigantighe Art Gallery
Centennial Park
Wallington
Timaru
Dolphin & Wildlife Cruises
Timaru Gardens
Patiti Pt
Motukaika
Mt Horrible 388
Fairview
Adair
Redruth
Scarborough
Mutu Mutu Pt
Otipua
Salisbury
Tuhawaiki Pt
Claremont West
Pareora West
To Waimate, Oamaru
To Lake Tekapo
60

1 2 3 4 5 6 7
68

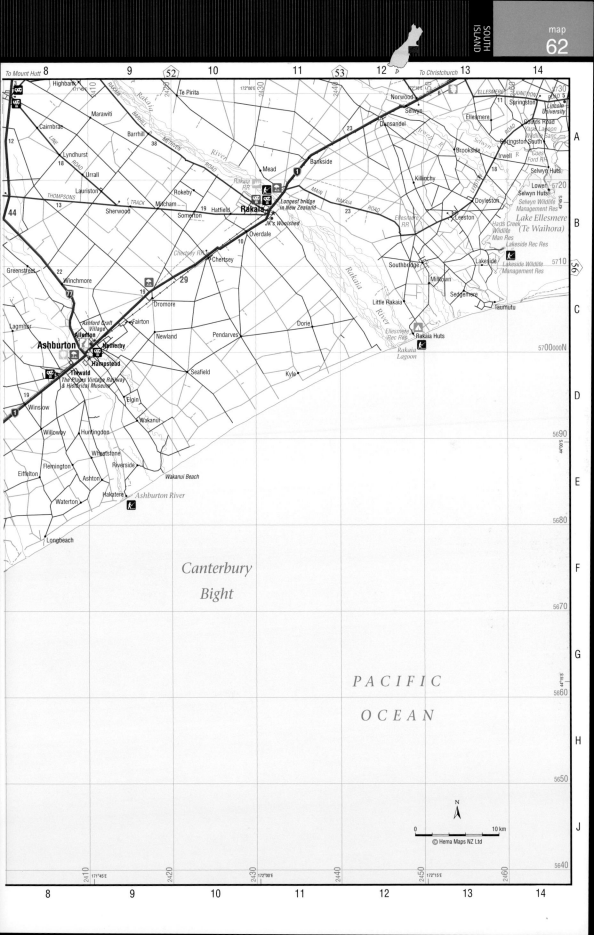

To Mount Hutt 8   9   52   10   11   53   12   To Christchurch 13   14

A

Highbank
171°45'E
2410
Rakaia
Rakaia
2420
Te Pirita
172°00'E
2430
Norwood
50
6
730
ELLESMERE JUNCTION
158
730
ROAD 5
Springston
Lincoln University

Marawiti
BARRHILL
Selwyn
Dunsandel
23
Ellesmere
Goulds Road
Yarrs Lagoon Wildlife Sanc
Springston South

Cairnbrae
River
Brookside
Irwell
Coes Ford Rd

12
Lyndhurst
ROAD
METHVEN
Barrhill
38
Killinchy
18
Selwyn Huts

18
Urrall
LINE
Mead
Bankside
1
Doyleston
Lower Selwyn Huts
5720
5729.5

THOMPSONS
Lauriston
Rakaia RR
MAIN
RAKAIA
ROAD
23
Selwyn Wildlife Management Res

B
44
13
Sherwood
TRACK
Mitcham
Rokeby
19
Hatfield
Rakaia
JK's Woolshed
Ellesmere RR
Leeston
Lake Ellesmere (Te Waihora)
Hards Creek Wildlife Man Res
Lakeside Rec Res

Somerton
Overdale
10
23
Southbridge
Lakeside
Lakeside Wildlife Management Res
5710
56

Greenstreet
22
Chertsey Rd
Chertsey
Milltown

Winchmore
19
29
Little Rakaia
Sedgemere
Taumutu

C
77
Dromore
Rakaia River
Taumutu

Lagmhor
Ashford Craft Village
Fairton
Dorie
Ellesmere Rec Res
Rakaia Huts

Ashburton
Allenton
Newland
Pendarves
Rakaia Lagoon
5700000N

Netherby
Hampstead

D
Tinwald
The Plains Vintage Railway & Historical Museum
Seafield
Kyle
5690
44°00'S

19
Winslow
Elgin

1
Willowby
Huntingdon
Wakanui

E
Eiffelton
Flemington
Wheatstone
Riverside
Wakanui Beach
5680

Ashton
Waterton
Hakatere
Ashburton River

Longbeach

F
Canterbury
Bight
5670

G
PACIFIC
5660

OCEAN

H
5650

J
N
0   10 km
© Hema Maps NZ Ltd
5640

8   9   10   11   12   13   14

2410
171°45'E
2420
2430
172°00'E
2440
2450
172°15'E
2460

map
63
SOUTH ISLAND
Northern Fiordland

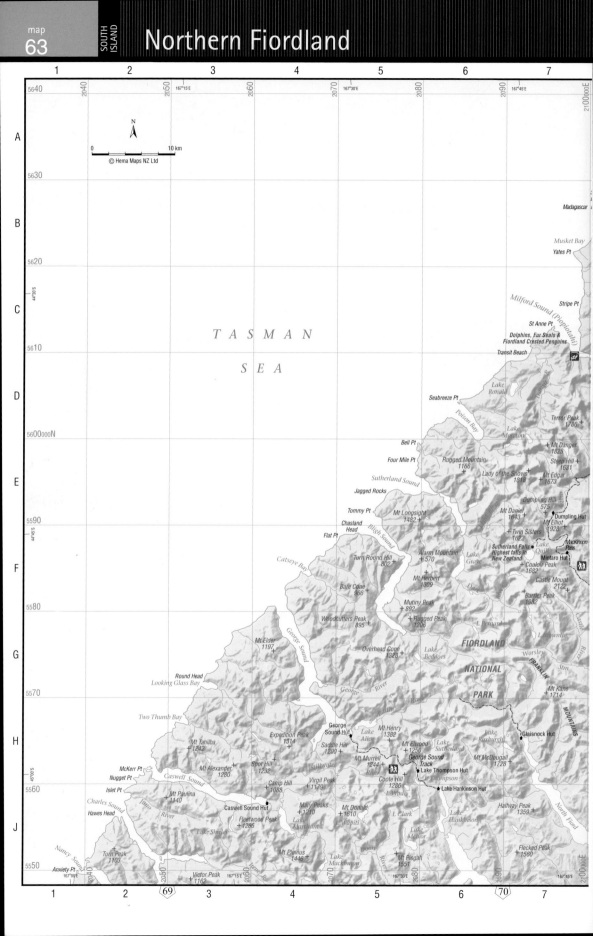

N

0   10 km

© Hema Maps NZ Ltd

TASMAN

SEA

Madagascar

Musket Bay
Yates Pt

Milford Sound (Piopiotahi)
Stripe Pt
St Anne Pt
Dolphins, Fur Seals &
Fiordland Crested Penguins
Transit Beach

Lake Ronald

Seabreeze Pt
Poison Bay
Lake Marion
Terror Peak 1786

Bell Pt
Mt Danger 1825
Four Mile Pt
Steep Hill 1631
Rugged Mountain 1166
Lady of the Snows 1818
Mt Edgar 1673
Sutherland Sound
Jagged Rocks
Dumpling Hill 575
Mt Daniel 1643
Dumpling Hut
Tommy Pt
Mt Longsight 1482
Mt Elliot 1928
Chasland Head
Twin Sisters 1622
Flat Pt
Bligh Sound
Sutherland Falls
Highest falls in
New Zealand
Lake Quill
MacKinnon Pass
Alarm Mountain 570
Lake Grave
Mintaro Hut
Catseye Bay
Turn Round Hill 802
Couloir Peak 1682
Mt Herbert 1309
Castle Mount 2122
Bare Cone 966
Barrier Peak 1982
Mutiny Peak 892
Woodcutters Peak 895
Rugged Peak 1206
L Bernard
L Browne
George Sound
Overhead Cone 1328
Lake Beddoes
FIORDLAND
Worsley Stm
Mt Elder 1197
NATIONAL
FRANKLIN
Round Head
Looking Glass Bay
George River
PARK
Mt Kane 1714
Two Thumb Bay
MOUNTAINS
George Sound Hut
Lake Alice
Mt Henry 1392
Expedition Peak 1314
Lake Roxburgh
Glaisnock Hut
Mt Tahiba 1242
Saddle Hill 1200
Mt Elwood 1250
Lake Sutherland
McKerr Pt
Mt Alexander 1280
Spot Hill 1232
Mt Murrell 1244
George Sound Track
Mt McDougall 1728
Nugget Pt
Caswell Sound
Stillwater
Lake Thompson Hut
Islet Pt
Camp Hill 1088
Virgil Peak 1179
Coote Hill 1286
Thompson
Lake Hankinson Hut
Charles Sound
Mt Paulina 1140
L Wade
Hawes Head
Iano River
Caswell Sound Hut
Misty Peaks 1210
Mt Donald 1610
L Clark
Lake Hankinson
Halfway Peak 1359
Fleetwood Peak 1286
Wapiti
Nancy Sound
Lake Shirley
Lake Marchant
Lake Michor
Flecked Peak 1560
Turn Peak 1103
Mt Pluvius 1446
Mt Pisgah 1551
Anxiety Pt
Victor Peak 1162
Lake Mackinnon
North Fiord

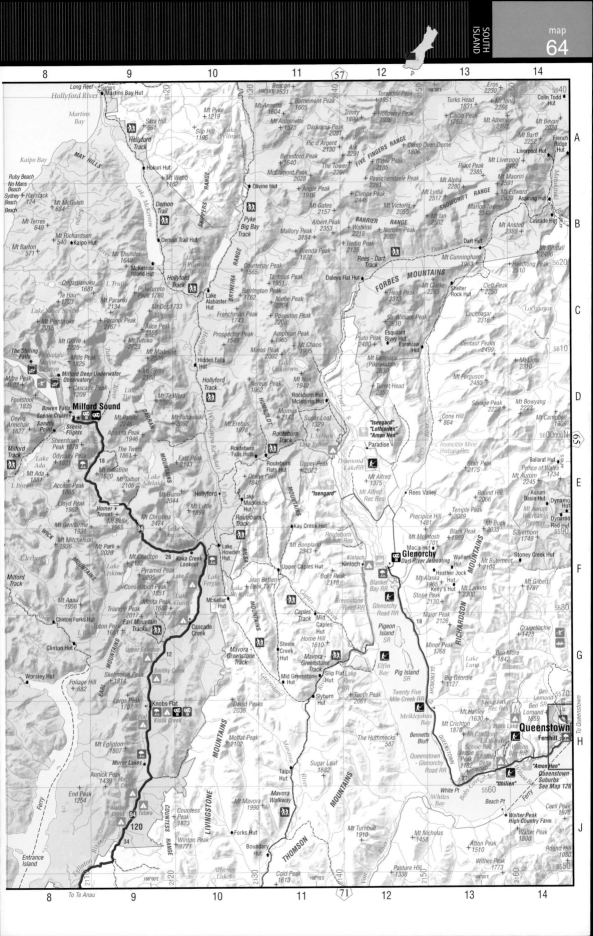

map
65
SOUTH ISLAND
Queenstown, Wanaka & Central Otago

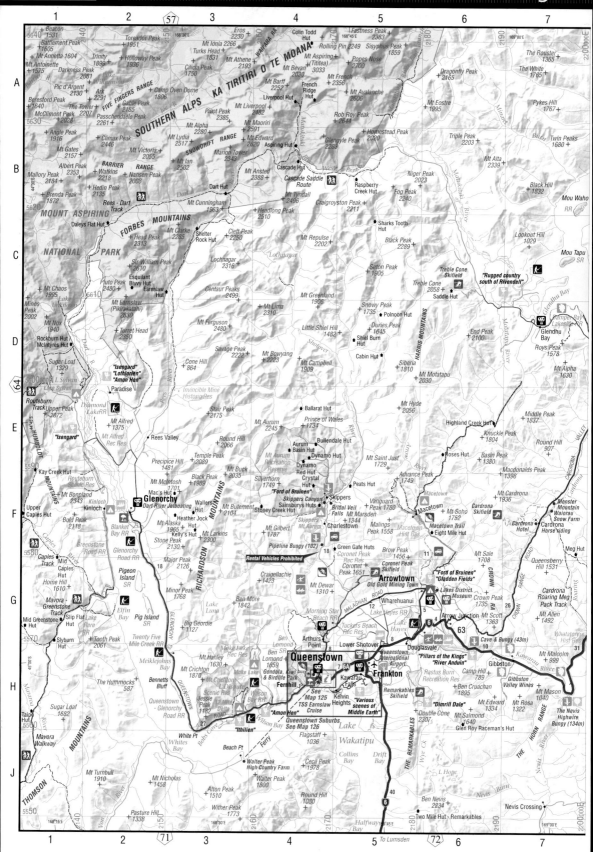

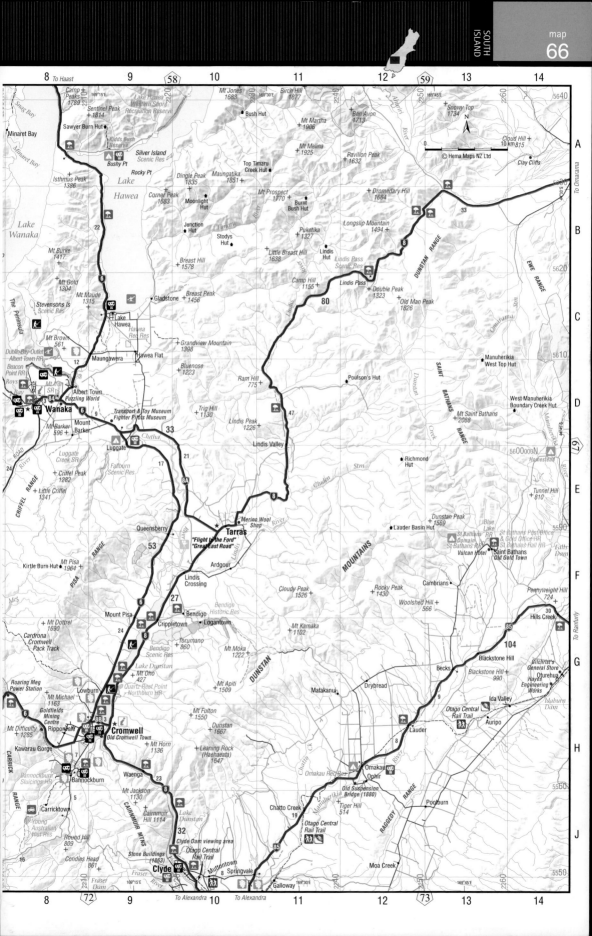

map
67
SOUTH ISLAND
Southern Canterbury & Northern Otago

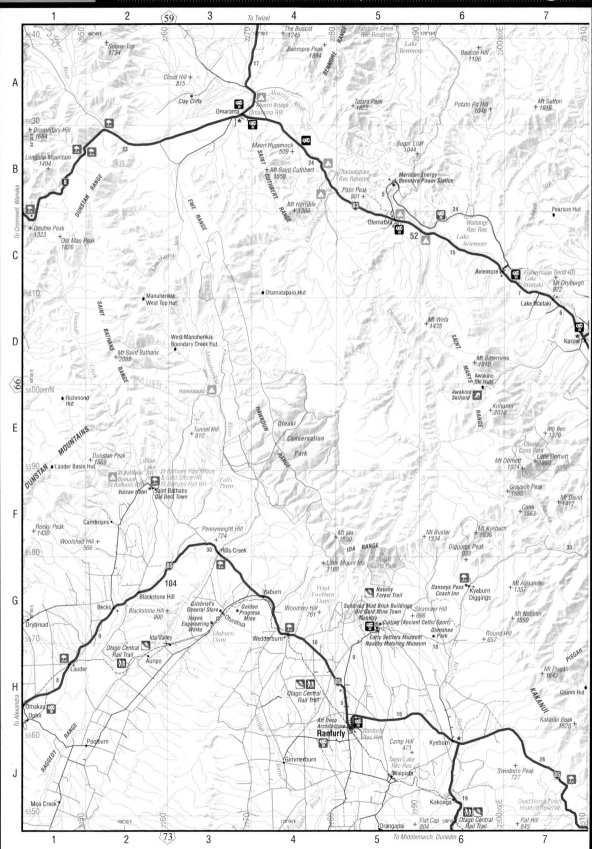

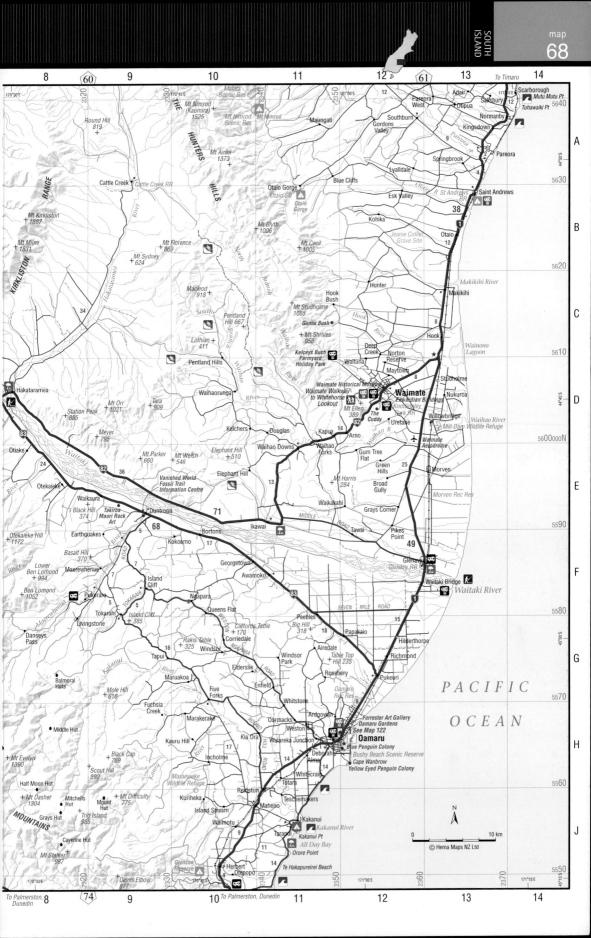

To Timaru

8 60 9 10 11 12 61 13 14

Scarborough
Mutu Mutu Pt
Tuhawaiki Pt
5640
Adair
Pareora West
Salisbury
Normanby
12
Southburn
Gordons Valley
Kingsdown
9
Maungati
Opiua
Pareora R
Springbrook
Pareora
5630
Round Hill
819
Mt Nimrod (Kaumira)
1525
Mt Nimrod
Scenic Res
Mt Nimrod
Matata Scenic Res
Lyalldale
Otaio R
St Andrews RR
Saint Andrews
Mt Airini
1373
Blue Cliffs
Otaio Gorge
Otaio SR
Esk Valley
38
Cattle Creek
Cattle Creek RR
Otaio Gorge
Kohika
1
Otaio
5620
Mt Kirkliston
1887
Mt Blyth
1006
Jeanie Collier
Grave Site
12
Mt Milne
1831
Mt Florence
869
Mt Cecil
1005
Hunter
Makikihi River
Makikihi
KIRKLISTON
Mt Sydney
624
Macleod
918
Mt Studholme
1085
Hook
Bush
8
5610
34
Pentland Hill
667
Gunns Bush
Mt Shrives
958
Hook
Hook River
Lothian
411
Kelceys Bush
Farmyard
Holiday Park
Deep
Creek
Norton
Reserve
Studholme
Wainono
Lagoon
Pentland Hills
Waituna
Maytown
8
Hakataramea
Waihaorunga
Waimate Historical Museum
Waimate Walkway
to Whitehorse
Lookout
Waimate
Edwardian Buildings
Knottingley
Park RR
Nukuroa
5600000N
Station Peak
885
Mt Orr
1021
Tara
909
Kelchers
Mt Ellen
389
The
Cuddy
Uretane
Willowbridge
Waihao River
Mill Dam Wildlife Refuge
Otiake
Meyer
795
Douglas
Kapua
14
Arno
Waihao R
Waimate
Aerodrome
83
24
Mt Parker
660
Mt Welsh
546
Elephant Hill
510
Waihao Downs
Waihao
Forks
Gum Tree
Flat
Morven
Waitaki
82
36
Elephant Hill
Green
Hills
5590
Otekaieke
Vanished World
Fossil Trail
Information Centre
13
Mt Harris
284
Broad
Gully
25
Morven Rec Res
Waikaura
Takiroa
Maori Rock
Art
Duntroon
Ikawai
Waikakahi
MIDDLE
ROAD
Otekaieke Hill
1172
Earthquakes
71
Bortons
Grays Corner
Black Hill
374
Kokoamo
17
Tawai
Pikes
Point
49
Basalt Hill
370
5
Georgetown
Glenavy
Glenavy RR
Lower
Ben Lomond
994
Maerewhenua
7
Awamoko
83
Waitaki Bridge
Waitaki River
Ben Lomond
1052
Pukerau
Island
Cliff
Ngapara
1
SEVEN
MILE
ROAD
5580
Tokarahi
Island Cliff
385
Queens Flat
Peebles
Big Hill
318
Papakaio
15
Livingstone
Cliffords Table
170
Corriedale
18
Hilderthorpe
Danseys
Pass
Rakis Table
325
Windsor
Airedale
Table Top
Hill 235
Richmond
5570
Tapui
16
Windsor
Park
Rosebery
Pukeuri
Balmoral
Huts
Maruakoa
Elderslie
Five
Forks
Oamaru
Rac Res
PACIFIC
Mole Hill
616
Enfield
OCEAN
Fuchsia
Creek
Whitstone
Ardgowan
Forrester Art Gallery
Oamaru Gardens
See Map 122
Middle Hut
Marakerake
Cormacks
Weston
5560
Kauru Hill
Kia Ora
Waiareka Junction
Oamaru
Blue Penguin Colony
Bushy Beach Scenic Reserve
Cape Wanbrow
Yellow Eyed Penguin Colony
Incholme
17
Deborah
Alma
Mt Evelyn
1390
14
Whitecraig
Half Moon Hut
Maraeweka
Wildlife Refuge
Redstone
Totara
5550
Mt Dasher
1304
Mitchells
Hut
Mt Difficulty
775
Kuriheka
Teschemakers
Grays Hut
Mount
Hut
Island Stream
Maheno
Scout Hill
892
Kakanui
Trig Island
985
Waimotu
Kakanui
Kakanui River
N
Cayenne Hut
9
Tarapo
Kakanui Pt
All Day Bay
MOUNTAINS
11
Orore Point
Mt Stalker
987
Te Hakapureirei Beach
0   10 km
Glencoe
Reserve
14
Devils Elbow
877
Herbert
Otepopo
© Hema Maps NZ Ltd

170°30'E 2320 170°45'E 2330 171°00'E 2350 171°15'E

To Palmerston,
Dunedin
8 74 9 10 To Palmerston, Dunedin 11 12 13 14

map
69
SOUTH ISLAND
Central Fiordland

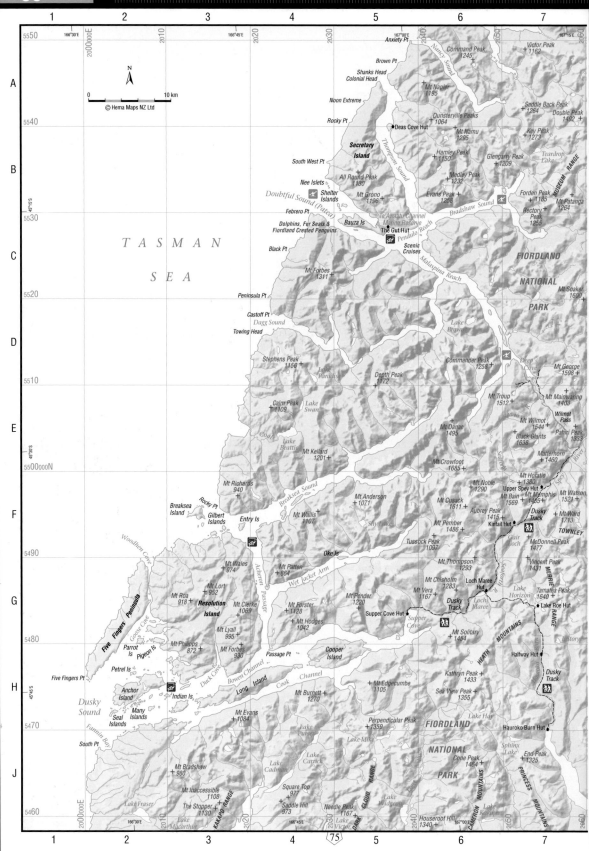

N

0   10 km

TASMAN SEA

Doubtful Sound (Patea)

Secretary Island

Anxiety Pt
Brown Pt
Shanks Head   Colonial Head
Noon Extreme
Rocky Pt
South West Pt
Nee Islets
Shelter Islands
Febrero Pt
Dolphins, Fur Seals &
Fiordland Crested Penguins
Black Pt
Bauza Is
The Gut Hut
Scenic Cruises

Command Peak
+1245
Victor Peak
+1162
Mt Napier
+1195
Dunsterville Peaks
+1064
Saddle Back Peak
+1264
Double Peak
+1492
Mt Namu
+1295
Key Peak
+1273
Deas Cove Hut
Hamley Peak
+1150
Glengarry Peak
+1209
Teardrop Lake
All Round Peak
130
Medley Peak
+1232
Mt Grono
+1196
Evans Peak
+1258
Forden Peak
+1185
Mt Patanga
+1264
Te Awaatu Channel
Marine Reserve
Rectory Peak
+1255

Thompson Sound
Bradshaw Sound
MUSEUM RANGE

Mt Forbes
+1311
Pendulo Reach
Malaspina Reach

FIORDLAND

Peninsula Pt
NATIONAL
Mt Soaker
+1600

Castoff Pt
Dagg Sound
Towing Head
PARK

Stephens Peak
+1156
Lake Paradise
Depth Peak
+1172
Commander Peak
+1258
Deep Cove
Mt George
+1598

Calm Peak
+1109
Lake Swan
Mt Troup
+1512
Mt Mainwaring
+1403
Wilmot Pass

Coal
Lake Beattie
Mt Wilmot
+1544
Pahiri Peak
+1333
Mt Danae
+1495
Black Giants
+1638
Mt Kellard
+1201
Matterhorn
+1460

Mt Crowfoot
+1685
Seaforth River

Mt Richards
940
Breaksea Sound
Mt Noble
+1290
Mt Horatio
+1380
Mt Watson
+1521
Upper Spey Hut
Mt Memphis
+1405

Breaksea Island
Rocky Pt
Gilbert Islands
Entry Is
Mt Anderson
+1071
Mt Cusack
+1611
Mt Bain
+1569
Mt Ward
+1713
Aubrey Peak
+1415
TOWNLEY
Mt Wallis
+1107
Shyt Lake
Mt Pember
+1486
Kintail Hut
Dusky Track

Tussock Peak
+1097
Gair Loch
McDonnell Peak
+1477

Oke Is
Acheron Passage
Wet Jacket Arm
Mt Thompson
+1293
Vincent Peak
+1431

Mt Wales
+874
Mt Patten
+864
Mt Chisholm
+1283
Loch Maree Hut
Lake Horizon
Tamatea Peak
+1640
MERRIE RANGE

Mt Lort
+952
Mt Pender
+1220
Mt Vera
+1167
Dusky Track
Loch Maree
Lake Roe Hut

Mt Roa
918
Resolution Island
Mt Clerke
+1069
Mt Forster
+1128
Supper Cove Hut
Supper Cove
HEATH MOUNTAINS

Five Fingers Peninsula
Mt Lyall
995
Mt Hodges
+1042
Mt Solitary
+1454

Goose Cove
Mt Philipps
872
Mt Forbes
930
Passage Pt
Cooper Island
Mt Edgecumbe
1105
Kathryn Peak
+1433
Halfway Hut

Parrot Is
Pigeon Is
Duck Cove
Bowen Channel
Passage Pt
Sea View Peak
+1355
Dusky Track

Five Fingers Pt
Petrel Is
Anchor Island
Indian Is
Mt Burnett
+1270
Mt Edgecumbe
Lake Hay
Hauroko Burn Hut

Dusky Sound
Seal Islands
Many Islands
Long Island
Cook Channel
Mt Evans
+1084
Perpendicular Peak
+1359
FIORDLAND

South Pt
Fannin Bay
Lake Purser
Lake Mike
NATIONAL
Sphinx Lake
Cone Peak
+1464
End Peak
+1325

Mt Bradshaw
980
Lake Carrick
Lake Cadman
PARK
Square Top
977
CLOUD RANGE
DARK RANGE
CAMERON MOUNTAINS
Lake Kakapo
PRINCESS MOUNTAINS

Mt Inaccessible
1108
The Stopper
+1130
Saddle Hill
973
Needle Peak
973
Houseroot Hill
+1340
Lake Fraser
Lake Macarthur
KAKAPO RANGE

45°15'S
45°30'S
45°45'S

166°30'E
166°45'E
167°00'E
167°15'E

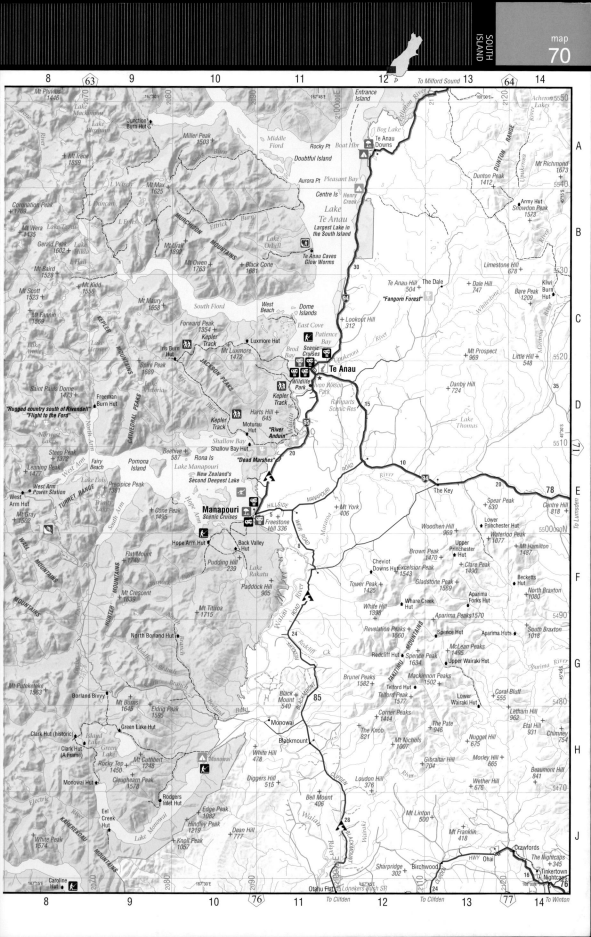

map
71
SOUTH ISLAND
Southland & Central Otago

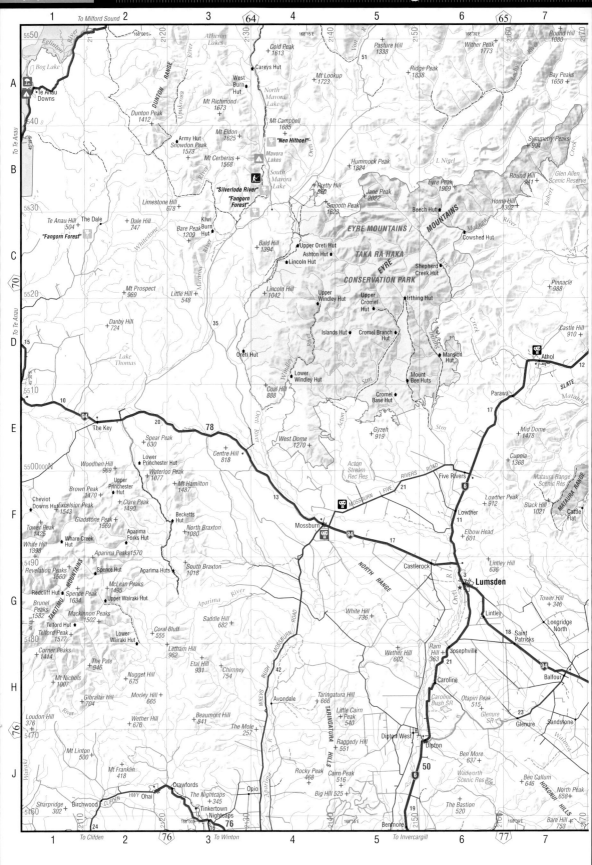

To Milford Sound

5550

Eglinton River   21

168°00'E   2120   Atheron Lakes   2130   168°15'E   2140   2150   168°30'E   2160   2170

Bog Lake

A

Te Anau Downs

To Te Anau

540   0

DUNTON RANGE

Upukerora

River

Dunton Peak 1412 +

Cold Peak 1613 +

Careys Hut

West Burn Hut

Mt Lookup 1723 +

North Mavora Lake

Mt Campbell 1685 +

"Nen Hithoel"

Pasture Hill 1338 +

Ridge Peak 1838 +

Round Hill 1080 +

Wither Peak 1773 +

Bay Peaks 1650 +

Symmetry Peaks + 904

Robert

Creek

Mt Richmond 1673 +

Army Hut Snowdon Peak 1573 +

Mt Eldon 1625 +

Mt Cerberus + 1568

Mavora Lakes

455192

B

5530

Limestone Hill 678 +

River

South Mavora Lake

"Silverlode River"

"Fangorn Forest"

Pretty Hill 860 +

Smooth Peak 1623 +

Hummock Peak + 1824

Jane Peak 2022 +

L Nigel

Eyre Peak 1969 +

Beech Hut

MOUNTAINS

Home Hill 1302 +

Round Hill 911 +

Glen Allen Scenic Reserve

C

Te Anau Hill 504 +

The Dale

"Fangorn Forest"

Dale Hill 747 +

Kiwi Burn Hut

Bare Peak 1209 +

Whitestone

River

Bald Hill 1394 +

Upper Oreti Hut

Ashton Hut

Lincoln Hut

Mataura

River

Gowshed Hut

EYRE MOUNTAINS / TAKA RA HAKA

EYRE

CONSERVATION PARK

Shepherd Creek Hut

Pinnacle + 988

To Te Anau

70

5520

Mt Prospect + 969

Little Hill + 548

Lincoln Hill 1042 +

Upper Windley Hut

Upper Cromel Hut

Irthing Hut

Castle Hill 910 +

D

15

Danby Hill 724 +

35

Mnbura

River

Islands Hut

Cromel Branch Hut

Mansion Hut

Athol

SLATE

12

Lake Thomas

Oreti Hut

Oreti

River

Lower Windley Hut

Windley

Stm

Mount Bee Huts

Mataura

Parawa

5510

10

Coal Hill 888 +

Cromel Base Hut

17

E

The Key

94

20

78

Spear Peak + 630

Centre Hill 818

West Dome 1270 +

Gyzeh + 919

Acton

Stm

Mid Dome + 1478

Cupola + 1368

Mataura Range Scenic Res

5500000N

Woodhen Hill 969 +

Lower Princhester Hut

Waterloo Peak 1077

Mt Hamilton 1487 +

Acton Stream Rec Res

RIVERS   ROAD

Five Rivers

Lowther Peak + 912

Black Hill 1021 +

MATAURA RANGE

Cattle Flat

F

Brown Peak 1470 +

Excelsior Peak 1543

Cheviot Downs Hut

Gladstone Peak 1569 +

Upper Princhester Hut

Clare Peak 1490

Aparima Forks Hut

Becketts Hut

North Braxton + 1080

13

MOSSBURN   FIVE

21

Mossburn

6

Lowther

11

Elbow Head + 601

5490

Tower Peak 1425 +

White Hill 1398 +

Whare Creek Hut

Aparima Peaks 1570

94

17

G

Revelation Peaks 1560

Redcliff Hut

Spence Peak 1634

Brunel Peaks 1582 +

TAKITIMU   MOUNTAINS

Spence Hut

McLean Peaks 1495 +

Upper Wairaki Hut

South Braxton 1018

Aparima   River

Aparima Huts

NORTH   RANGE

Oreti   R

Castlerock

Lintley Hill 636 +

Lumsden

3

Tower Hill + 346

Longridge North

Mackinnon Peaks 1502 +

Telford Hut

Telford Peak 1577 +

Lower Wairaki Hut

Coral Bluff 555 +

Saddle Hill 682 +

Letham Hill 962 +

White Hill 736 +

Lintley

Saint Patricks

18

94

Balfour

5480

Corner Peaks + 1414

The Pate + 946

Nugget Hill + 675

Etal Hill 931 +

Chimney 754 +

WREYS

BUSH

42

MOSSBURN

ROAD

Ram Hill 363 +

Josephville

21

Caroline

Otapiri Peak 515 +

Glenure SR

23

Sandstone

H

Mt Nichols + 1007

Gibraltar Hill + 704

Morley Hill + 665

Beaumont Hill 841 +

Avondale

The Mole 257 +

Taringatura Hill + 666

Little Cairn + Peak 540

Caroline Bush SR

Wether Hill 602 +

Glenure

76

5470

Loudon Hill 376 +

River

Mt Linton 500 +

Wether Hill 676 +

TARINGATURA

HILLS

Raggedy Hill 551 +

Dipton West

Dipton

Ben More 637 +

Wadworth Scenic Res

Ben Callum + 646

North Peak 658 +

HOKONUI   HILLS

J

5460

Sharpridge 302 +

Birchwood

CLIFDEN

HWY

Ohai

Mt Franklin 418 +

Crawfords

The Nightcaps + 345

Tinkertown Nightcaps

Opio

Aparima   R

Rocky Peak 468 +

Cairn Peak 516 +

Big Hill 525 +

6

50

Benmore

The Bastion 520 +

Bare Hill 753 +

2110   24   2120   168°00'E   2130   76   2140   168°15'E   2150   19   2160   168°30'E   2170

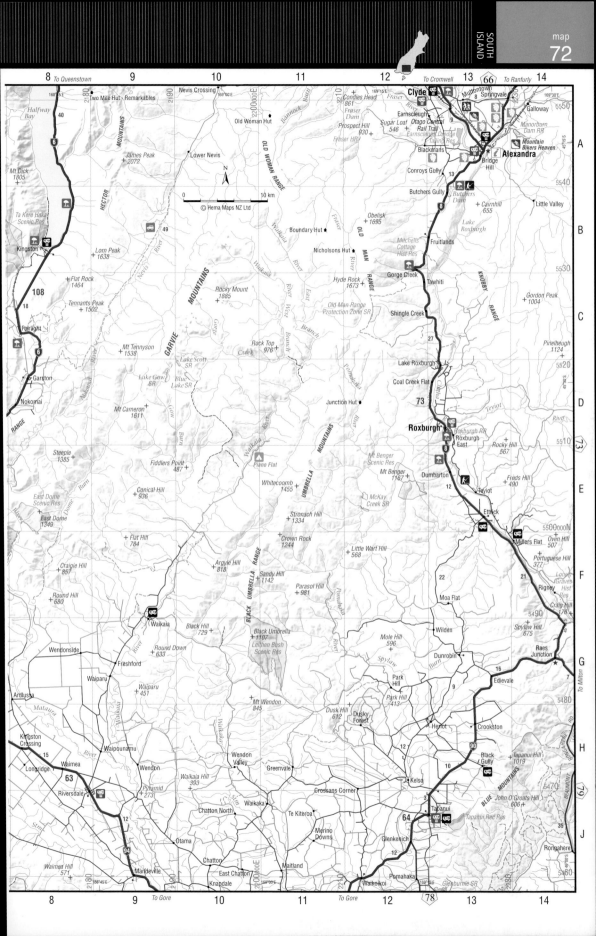

map
73
SOUTH ISLAND

Central Otago & Dunedin

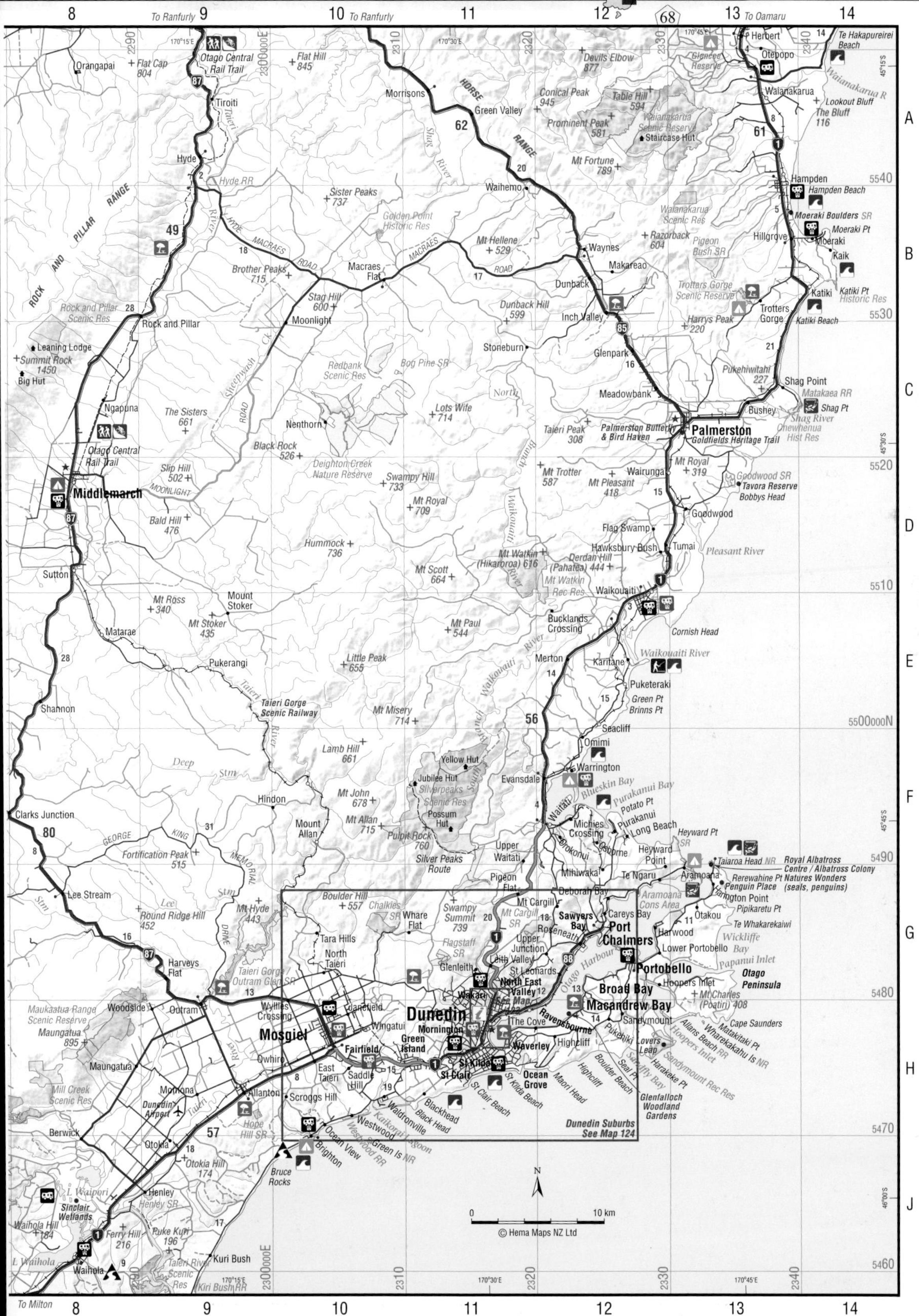

To Ranfurly To Ranfurly To Oamaru

Map grid columns: 8 9 10 11 12 13 14

Map grid rows (right margin): A B C D E F G H J

5540 5530 5520 5510 5500000N 5490 5480 5470 5460

Orangapai
Flat Cap 804
Otago Central Rail Trail
Flat Hill 845
Morrisons
Green Valley
Devils Elbow 877
Gigpeek Reserve
To Herbert
Otepopo
Te Hakapureirei Beach
Waianakarua R
Lookout Bluff
The Bluff 116
Tiroiti
Conical Peak 945
Prominent Peak 581
Table Hill 594
Hyde
Hyde RR
Sister Peaks 737
Waihemo
Mt Fortune 789
Staircase Hut
Waianakarua Scenic Reserve
Hampden
Hampden Beach
Moeraki Boulders SR
49
Golden Point Historic Res
Mt Hellene 529
Waynes
Waianakarua Scenic Res
Moeraki Pt
Moeraki
Hillgrove
Brother Peaks 715
Macraes Flat
Dunback
Makareao
Pigeon Bush SR
Razorback 604
Kaik
Katiki Pt Historic Res
Stag Hill 600
Moonlight
Dunback Hill 599
Inch Valley
85
Harrys Peak 220
Trotters Gorge
Trotters Gorge Scenic Reserve
Katiki
Katiki Beach
Rock and Pillar Scenic Res
Rock and Pillar
Stoneburn
Glenpark
Pukehiwitahi 227
Shag Point
Matakaea RR
Shag Pt
Leaning Lodge
Summit Rock 1450
Big Hut
Redbank Scenic Res
Bog Pine SR
Meadowbank
Bushey
Chewhenua Hist Res
Ngapuna
Otago Central Rail Trail
The Sisters 661
Lots Wife 714
North
Taieri Peak 308
Palmerston Butterfly & Bird Haven
Palmerston
Goldfields Heritage Trail
Middlemarch
Nenthorn
Black Rock 526
Deighton Creek Nature Reserve
Mt Trotter 587
Wairunga
Mt Royal 319
Goodwood SR
Tavora Reserve
Bobbys Head
Slip Hill 502
Bald Hill 476
Swampy Hill 733
Mt Pleasant 418
15
Goodwood
Sutton
Hummock 736
Mt Royal 709
Flag Swamp
Mt Scott 664
Mt Watkin (Hikaroroa) 616
Derdan Hill (Pahatea) 444
Tumai
Pleasant River
Mt Ross 340
Mount Stoker
Mt Stoker 435
Little Peak 655
Mt Paul 544
Mt Watkin Rec Res
Waikouaiti
Matarae
Pukerangi
Mt Misery 714
Bucklands Crossing
Cornish Head
Shannon
56
Merton
Karitane
Puketeraki
Green Pt
Brinns Pt
Lamb Hill 661
Mt John 678
Seacliff
Hindon
Yellow Hut
Jubilee Hut
Silverpeaks Scenic Res
Possum Hut
Evansdale
Omimi
Warrington
Clarks Junction
80
Mt Allan 715
Pulpit Rock 760
Silver Peaks Route
Waitati
Blueskin Bay
Purakanui Bay
Potato Pt
Purakanui
Long Beach
Heyward Pt
Lee Stream
Fortification Peak 515
Mt Hyde 443
Michies Crossing
Osborne
Heyward Point
Royal Albatross Centre / Albatross Colony
Taiaroa Head NR
Rerewahine Pt Natures Wonders
Penguin Place (seals, penguins)
Round Ridge Hill 452
Boulder Hill 557
Chalkies
Whare Flat
Upper Waitati
Mihiwaka
Te Ngaru
Aramoana
Aramoana Cons Area
Pipikaretu Pt
Harveys Flat
Tara Hills
North Taieri
Swampy Summit 739
Mt Cargill
Pigeon Flat
Deborah Bay
Sawyers Bay
Port Chalmers
Otakou
Te Whakarekaiwi
Wickliffe Bay
Woodside
Maukaatua Range Scenic Reserve
Maungatua 895
Wyllies Crossing
Outram
Taieri Gorge Outram Glen SR
Glenfield
Flagstaff SR
Leith Valley
St Leonards
Roseneath
Upper Junction
88
North East Valley
Harwood
Lower Portobello
Portobello
Hoopers Inlet
Mt Charles (Poatiri) 408
Otago Peninsula
Papamui Inlet
Mosgiel
Wingatui
Clarkfield
Dunedin
Mornington
Green Island
Wakari
Waverley
The Cove
Ravensbourne
Broad Bay
Macandrew Bay
Sandymount
Cape Saunders
Mill Creek Scenic Res
Maungatua
Momona
Saddle Hill
Fairfield
St Clair
Ocean Grove
Highcliff
Pukehiki
Allanton
Scroggs Hill
East Taieri
St Kilda
Maori Head
Sandfly Bay
Wharekakahu Is NR
Berwick
Dunedin Airport
57
Hope Hill SR
Owhiro
Waldronville
Blackhead
Black Head
St Kilda Beach
St Clair Beach
Boulder Beach
Seal Point
Allans Beach
Sandymount Rec Res
Hoopers Bay
Dunedin Suburbs See Map 124
Otokia
Green Is NR
Westwood
Ocean View
Brighton
Westwood
Waihola Hill 184
Sinclair Wetlands
Henley
Henley SR
Puke Kuri 196
Bruce Rocks
Glenfalloch Woodland Gardens
Ferry Hill 216
Taieri River Scenic Res
Kuri Bush
Kiri Bush RR
N
0   10 km
© Hema Maps NZ Ltd
Waihola
L Waihola
Qtokia
Otokia Hill 174

map
75
SOUTH ISLAND
Southern Fiordland

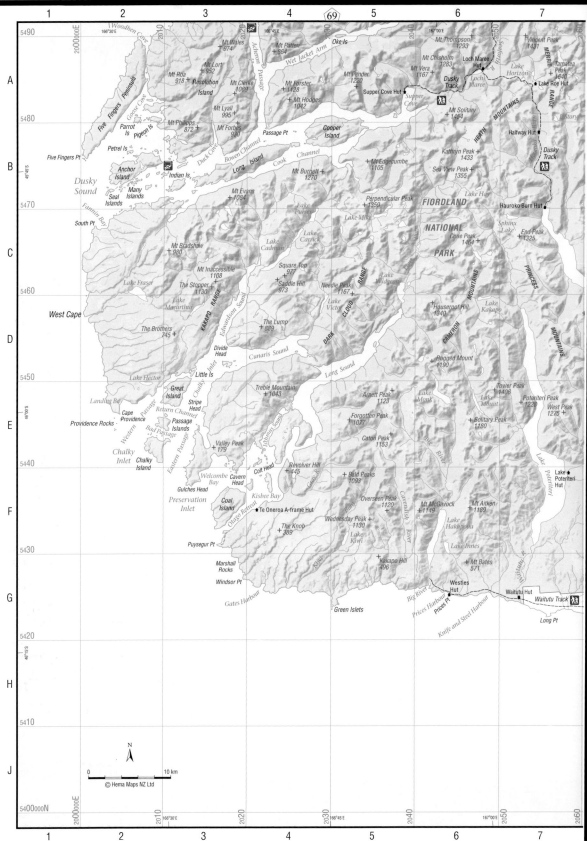

A

B

C

D

E

F

G

H

J

N

0   10 km

© Hema Maps NZ Ltd

5490
5480
5470
5460
5450
5440
5430
5420
5410
5400000N

2000000E
166°30'E
2010
2020
166°45'E
2030
2040
167°00'E
2050
2060

45°45'S
46°00'S
46°15'S

Woodhen Cove
Mt Wales 974
Mt Patten 864
Oke Is
Mt Thompson 1293
Vincent Peak 1431
Acheron Passage
Wet Jacket Arm
Mt Chisholm 1283
Loch Maree Hut
Tamatea Peak 1640
Mt Lort 952
Mt Roa 918
Resolution Island
Mt Clerke 1069
Mt Forster 1128
Mt Pender 1220
Mt Vera 1167
Dusky Track
Lake Horizon
Lake Roe Hut
Supper Cove Hut
Supper Cove
Mt Solitary 1454
Five Fingers Peninsula
Goose Cove
Mt Lyall 995
Mt Hodges 1042
HEATH
MOUNTAINS
Halfway Hut
Parrot Is
Pigeon Is
Mt Philipps 872
Mt Forbes 930
Passage Pt
Cooper Island
Kathryn Peak 1433
Dusky Track
Petrel Is
Duck Cove
Bowen Channel
Long Island
Cook Channel
Sea View Peak 1355
Story
Five Fingers Pt
Mt Burnett 1270
Lake Hay
Anchor Island
Indian Is
Mt Edgecumbe 1105
FIORDLAND
Haunoko Burn Hut
Dusky Sound
Seal Islands
Many Islands
Mt Evans 1084
Perpendicular Peak 1359
Lake Mike
NATIONAL
Sphinx Lake
Fanny Bay
Lake Purser
Lake Carrick
Cone Peak 1464
End Peak 1325
South Pt
Mt Bradshaw 980
Lake Cadman
Square Top 977
PARK
Mt Inaccessible 1108
Saddle Hill 973
Needle Peak 1167
Lake Widgeon
Houseroot Hill 1340
Lake Kakapo
Lake Fraser
The Stopper 1130
Lake Macarthur
KAKAPO RANGE
Lake Victor
CLOUD RANGE
CAMERON MOUNTAINS
MOUNTAINS
West Cape
The Brothers 745
Edwardson Sound
The Lump 889
DARK
Rugged Mount 1190
PRINCESS
Divide Head
Cunaris Sound
Long Sound
Lake Hector
Little Is
Treble Mountain 1043
Arnett Peak 1123
Lake Monk
Tower Peak 1406
Poteriteri Peak 1228
Great Island
Stripe Head
Lake Mouat
West Peak 1275
Landing Bay
Return Channel
Passage Islands
Forgotten Peak 1077
Solitary Peak 1180
Cape Providence
Providence Rocks
Bad Passage
Valley Peak 179
Caton Peak 1153
Big River
Lake Poteriteri
Chalky Inlet
Chalky Island
Eastern Passage
Western Passage
Colt Head
Revolver Hill 445
Bald Peaks 1093
Lake Poteriteri Hut
Welcombe Bay
Cavern Head
Kisbee Bay
Cavendish River
Overseen Peak 1120
Mt McGavock 1149
Mt Aitken 1189
Gulches Head
Coal Island
Te Oneroa A-frame Hut
Wednesday Peak 1130
Lake Hakapoa
Preservation Inlet
The Knob 389
Lake Kiwi
Lake Innes
Puysegur Pt
Kakapo Hill 496
Mt Bates 571
Waimatu R
Marshall Rocks
Windsor Pt
Westies Hut
Waitutu Hut
Gates Harbour
Green Islets
Big River
Prices Harbour
Prices Pt
Waitutu Track
Knife and Steel Harbour
Long Pt

1 2 3 4 5 6 7

8 9 10 11 To Te Anau 12 13 14

167°15'E 2070 167°30'E Mt Titiroa 2090 167°45'E 168°00'E 5490
1715

A

Townley Mountains
Redcliff River
North Borland Hut
Hunter Mountains
Middle Branch
Waiau River
Borland Road
Redcliff Ck
24
White Hill +1398
Revelation Peaks +1560
Aparima Peaks 1570
Spence Hut
Aparima Huts
South Braxton 1018
Redcliff Hut
Spence Peak 1634
McLean Peaks +1495
Upper Wairaki Hut
Mt Puteketeke 1563
Borland Bivvy
Mt Burns 1645
Eldrig Peak 1595
Green Lake Hut
Brunel Peaks 1582
Mackinnon Peaks +1502
Telford Hut
Telford Peak 1577
Lower Wairaki Hut
Coral Bluff +555
Letham Hill 962

B

Clark Hut (historic)
Island Lake
Clark Hut (A Frame)
Rocky Top 1450
Mt Cuthbert 1248
Green Lake
Cleughearn Peak 1578
Monowai Hut
Rodgers Inlet Hut
Black Mount 540
BLACKMOUNT
85
Monowai
Blackmount
Corner Peaks +1414
The Pate 946
The Knob 821
Mt Nichols +1007
Gibraltar Hill +704
Nugget Hill +675
Etal Hill 931
Morley Hill +665
Chimney 754
Beaumont Hill 841

Kaherekoau Mountains
Electric
Eel Creek Hut
Lake Monowai
Monowai
White Hill 478
Diggers Hill 515
Bell Mount 406
Loudon Hill 376
Mt Linton 500
Wether Hill +676
5470

C

White Peak 1574
Edge Peak 1082
Hindley Peak 1219
Dean Hill 777
Knoll Peak 1057
28
Waiau River
Wairaki River
Mt Franklin 418
5480
71

Caroline Hut
Caroline Peak 1704
Oblong Hill 996
Sharpridge 302
Birchwood
Ohai
Crawfords
The Nightcaps +345
Tinkertown
Nightcaps
76

D

Albert Edward Peak +1554
Alexander Peak 1504
Helena Peak 1380
Mary Is
Lake Hauroko
New Zealand's Deepest Lake
Tuatapere Hump Ridge Track
Thicket Burn
Goldie Hill 410
Lindsay Ecological Area
Lonekars Bush SR
Otahu Flat
Otahu SR
Eastern Bush
Feldwick
Twinlaw 551
24
Woodlaw 513
16
Wairio Hill 330
Wairio
Woodlaw

E

Teal Bay Hut
Helmet Hill +606
White Hill +248
Suspension Bridge (1899)
Clifden
Clifden Dolan
7
14
Oraka River
Orawia
Pukemaori
Merrivale
Raymonds Gap
Waikouro
Scotts Gap
Aparima
Otautau
5440

The Hump +1067
Masons Hill 250
Tuatapere Scenic Res
Piko Piko
99
Happy Valley
Ferndunlaw 621
Otautau SR

F

Dave Barlow's Hut
Southern Coastal Track
Port Craig School Hut
Mussel Beach
Thwaites Reserve
Papatotara
Tuatapere
Te Tua
20
Te Waewae
Bald Hill 804
Longwood Range
Pourakino Valley
Ermedale
Ringway
5430
77

G

Wairaurahiri Hut
Waitutu River
Sand Hill Pt Hist Res
Te Waewae Bay
Waihoaka
62
Stucks Hill +139
Martin's Hut
Pourakino Scenic Res
Gummies Bush
Waipango
5420

H

Waiau River
Orepuki
Gemstones on beach
Monkey Island
Pahia Pt
Pahia Hill +227
Pahia Hill SR
Cosy Nook Fishing Village
17
99
Falls Creek SR
Round Hill 260
Pahia
Ruahine
Wakaputa
Old Man Rock
Lake George
Wakaputa Pt
Kawakaputa Bay
Round Hill
Turnbull's (Big Dam) Hut
Longwood
Tihaka
Colac Bay (Oraka)
Colac Bay (Oraka)
Oraka Pt
Pig Island (Matau) SR
Riverton
New Windsor
11
5410

J

Rarotoka Island (Centre Island)

5400000N

167°15'E 2070 2080 167°30'E 2090 2100000E 167°45'E 2110 2120 168°00'E

8 9 10 11 12 13 14

map
77
SOUTH ISLAND
Southland

STEWART ISLAND
(RAKIURA)

RAKIURA
NATIONAL PARK

Foveaux Strait

Invercargill

Bluff

Riverton

Winton

Stewart Island Ferry Services
Ph 0800 000 511 / (03) 212 7660
www.stewartislandnz.co.nz

Southland Museum & Art Gallery
Invercargill Airport
Invercargill Suburbs
See Map 128

Oldest Town in the South Island
Taramea Bay
The Rocks

Bluff Harbour
Oysters
Ocean Beach
The Bluff (Motupohue) 265
Bluff Hill Reserve
Stirling Pt
Motupohue SR
Lookout Pt

To Halfmoon Bay (Oban)
Stewart Island

To Ohai
To Lumsden
To Clifton

map
79
SOUTH ISLAND
Coastal Otago

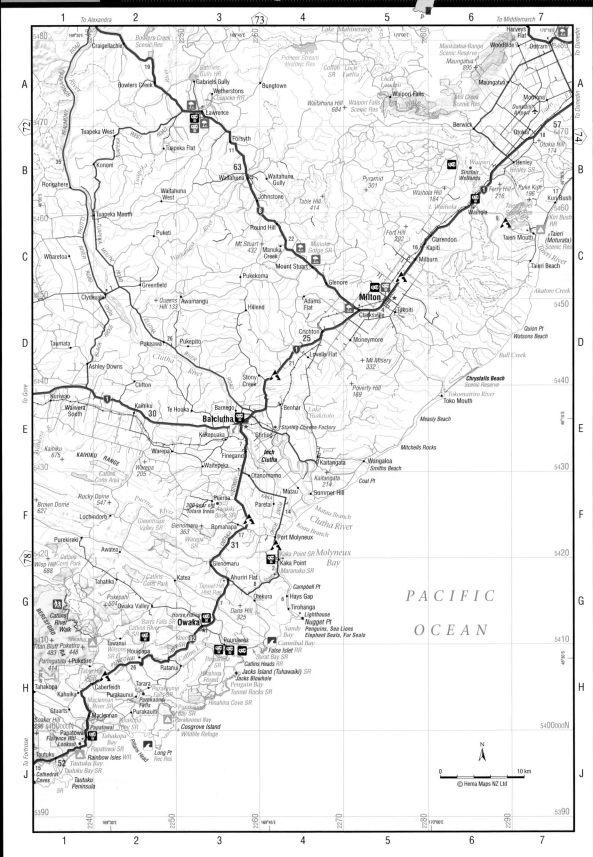

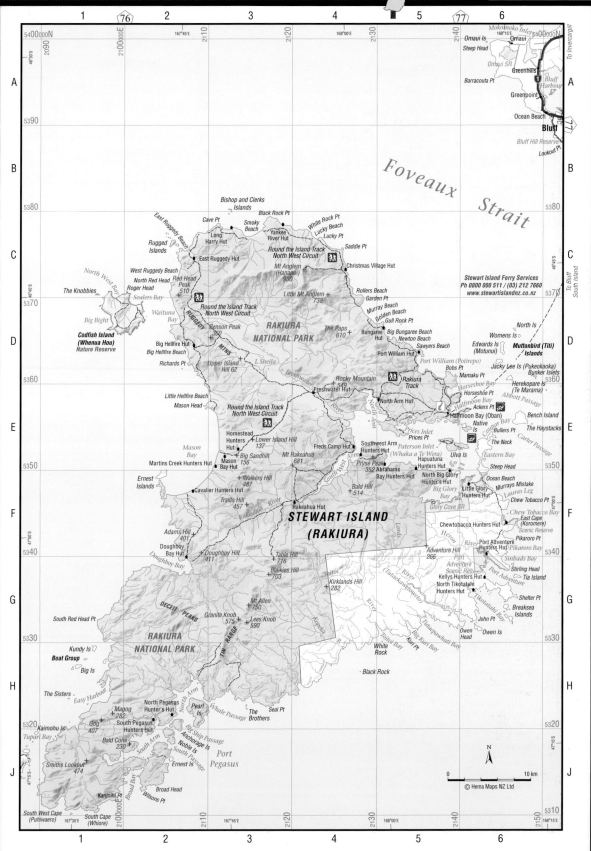

Stewart Island (Rakiura)

Foveaux Strait

Stewart Island Ferry Services
Ph 0800 000 511 / (03) 212 7660
www.stewartislandnz.co.nz

RAKIURA NATIONAL PARK

STEWART ISLAND
(RAKIURA)

RAKIURA
NATIONAL PARK

Codfish Island
(Whenua Hou)
Nature Reserve

Muttonbird (Titi)
Islands

0   10 km

© Hema Maps NZ Ltd

City and Suburbs legend

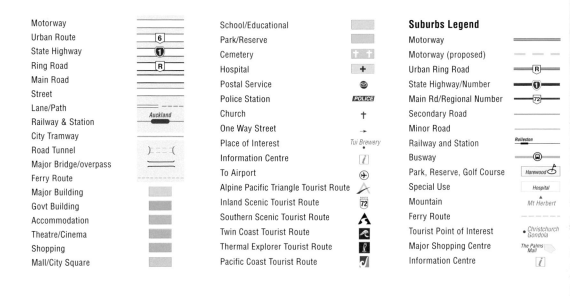

Motorway	
Urban Route	6
State Highway	1
Ring Road	R
Main Road	
Street	
Lane/Path	
Railway & Station	Auckland
City Tramway	
Road Tunnel	
Major Bridge/overpass	
Ferry Route	
Major Building	
Govt Building	
Accommodation	
Theatre/Cinema	
Shopping	
Mall/City Square	

School/Educational	
Park/Reserve	
Cemetery	† †
Hospital	✚
Postal Service	✉
Police Station	POLICE
Church	†
One Way Street	→
Place of Interest	Tui Brewery
Information Centre	𝒊
To Airport	✈
Alpine Pacific Triangle Tourist Route	
Inland Scenic Tourist Route	72
Southern Scenic Tourist Route	
Twin Coast Tourist Route	
Thermal Explorer Tourist Route	
Pacific Coast Tourist Route	

Suburbs Legend

Motorway	
Motorway (proposed)	
Urban Ring Road	R
State Highway/Number	1
Main Rd/Regional Number	72
Secondary Road	
Minor Road	
Railway and Station	Rolleston
Busway	
Park, Reserve, Golf Course	Harewood
Special Use	Hospital
Mountain	Mt Herbert
Ferry Route	
Tourist Point of Interest	Christchurch Gondola
Major Shopping Centre	The Palms Mall
Information Centre	𝒊

map 81 Bay of Islands *For touring map see map 4* **map 82** Russell **map 83** Paihia (below

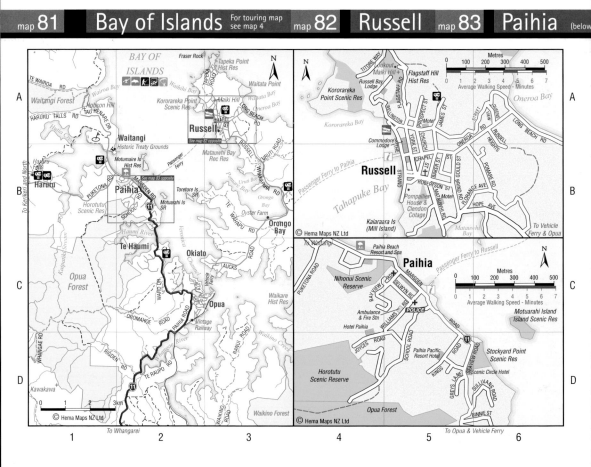

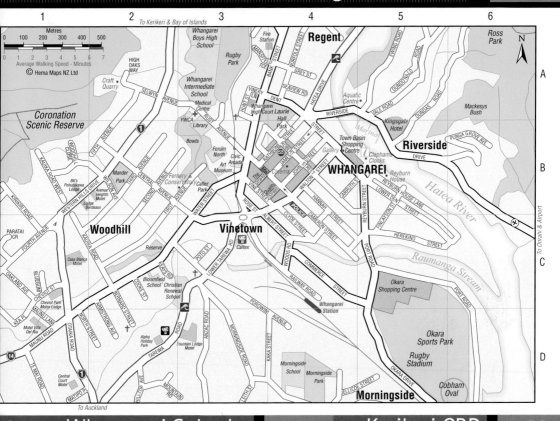

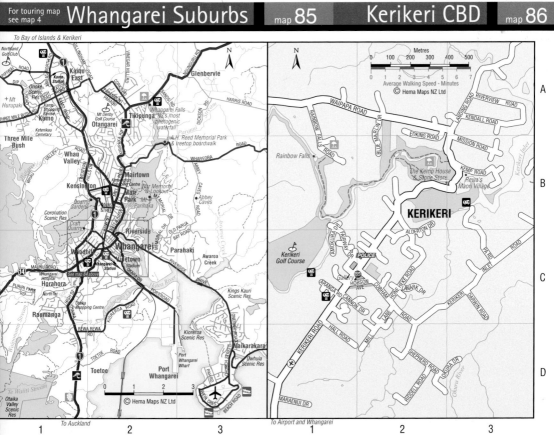

map
87
Auckland CBD

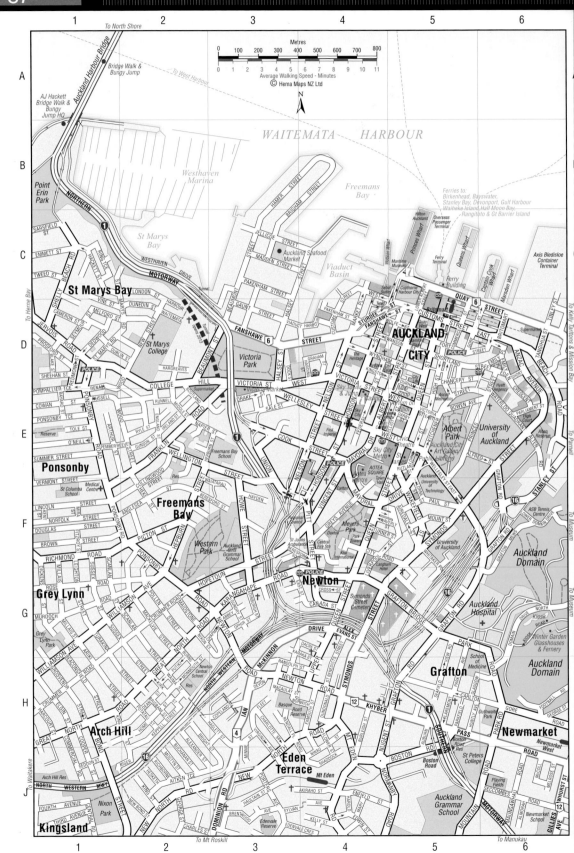

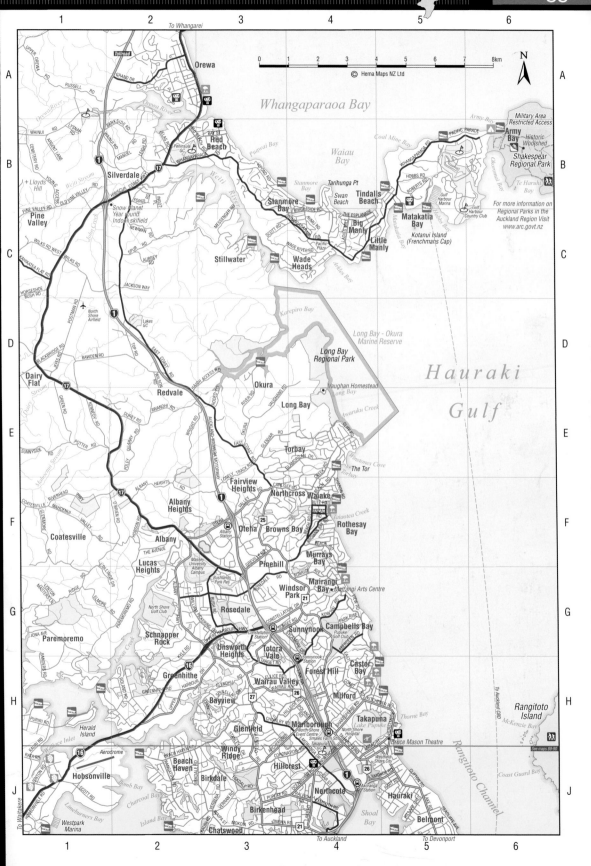

To Whangarei

Whangaparaoa Bay

0   1   2   3   4   5   6   7   8km
© Hema Maps NZ Ltd

N

Orewa

UPPER OREWA RD
GRAND DR
RUSSELL RD
WAINUI
LYSNAR RD
ARGENT LANE
CEMETERY RD
BANK SIDE RD
WAINUI RD
MANUEL
LEIGH RD
Red Beach
Peninsula GC
BAY ST
WHANGAPARAOA

Waiau Bay

Tollroad

Silverdale

+ Lloyds Hill
YOUNG ACCESS
OLD PINE VALLEY
HIBISCUS COAST
FORGE
IMPOT
Snow Planet
Year round
Indoor skifield
NEWMAN
MESSENGER RD
SPUR RD
AUBREY RD

Pine Valley
PINE VALLEY RD
WILKS RD WEST
WILKS RD
KAHIKATEA FLAT RD

Stanmore Bay
Stanmore Bay
BRIGHTSIDE RD
RIMU RD
SCOTT RD

Tarihunga Pt
Swan Beach
Big Manly
Little Manly
Pacific Plaza
THE ESPLANADE

Tindalls Beach
ROBERTS RD
HOBBS RD

Matakatia Bay

Army Bay

Military Area
Restricted Access
Army Bay
PACIFIC PARADE
Historic Woolshed
Shakespear Regional Park
Okoromai Bay
Te Haruhi Bay

Gulf Harbour Marina
Gulf Harbour Country Club

For more information on
Regional Parks in the
Auckland Region Visit
www.arc.govt.nz

Stillwater

HORSESHOE BUSH RD
BLACKBRIDGE RD
GREEN RD
BAWDEN RD
TOP RD
EAST COAST RD
WILSON RD
HAIGH ACCESS RD

Dairy Flat

Redvale
AWANOHI RD
DUREY RD
KENNEDY RD

North Shore Airfield
Lakes GC
POSTMAN RD

Wade Heads
WADE RIVER RD
Pacific
WELTI RIVER

Ardes Bay

Karepiro Bay

Long Bay - Okura
Marine Reserve

Long Bay Regional Park

Okura

Long Bay

Vaughan Homestead
Long Bay
Awaruku Creek

Haraki Gulf

SUNNYSIDE
POTTER RD
FOLEY
QUARRY RD

Coatesville
COATESVILLE
RIVERHEAD
MAHOENUI
GLENMORE
VALLEY
RIDGE RD
O'BRIEN RD

Albany Heights
ALBANY HEIGHTS RD
LONELY TRACK RD

Fairview Heights
Northcross
VALLEY RD

Torbay
UPTON RD
GLENVAR RD
DEEP CREEK RD
The Tor
Torbay
Waiake
BUTE RD

Albany
THE AVENUE
OTEHA
Albany Station
Oteha
Browns Bay
Taiaotea Creek

Rothesay Bay
BEACH RD

Lucas Heights
Massey University
Albany Campus
Bushlands Park Res

Pinehill
Murrays Bay

Mairangi Bay
Mairangi Arts Centre

Windsor Park
21
STIRRUP
SUNRISE AVE
KONINI

Paremoremo
IONA AVE
SANDFORD RD
PARKMEMORE RD
ELMORE RD
LINTON
MASTERS RD

North Shore Golf Club

Rosedale
CONSTELLATION RD

Schnapper Rock
KYLE RD

Sunnynook
Sunnynook Station
Campbells Bay
Pupuke Golf Club

Castor Bay

Greenhithe
GREENHITHE RD
GLENDHU RD
Unsworth Heights
Totara Vale
TARGET RD
ALICE RD

Herald Island
PURIRI RD

Forrest Hill
Milford
Thorne Bay

Wairau Valley
27
26

Bayview
SPINELLA RD

Auckland CBD
To Auckland CBD

Rangitoto Island
McKenzie Bay

See maps 89-90

Hobsonville
16
Aerodrome
RATA RD
KAURI RD

Westpark Marina
Limeburners Bay
Bomb Bay

Beach Haven
BEACH HAVEN RD

Windy Ridge
COLONATION

Glenfield
CHIVALRY RD
GLENFIELD RD

Marlborough
North Shore Event Centre
Smales Farm
North Shore Hospital

Takapuna
Lake Pupuke
Bruce Mason Theatre
Westfield Shore City

Birkdale
Hillcrest
PUPUKE RD

Northcote
1
26
Akoranga Station
Haraki

Birkenhead
21
ONEWA RD

Chatswood
Island Bay
Charcoal Bay

Belmont

Shoal Bay

Rangitoto Channel

Coast Guard Bay

To Waitakere
To Whatipu

Westpark Marina

To Auckland
To Devonport

map
89
NORTH ISLAND
West Auckland Suburbs
For touring map
see map 7

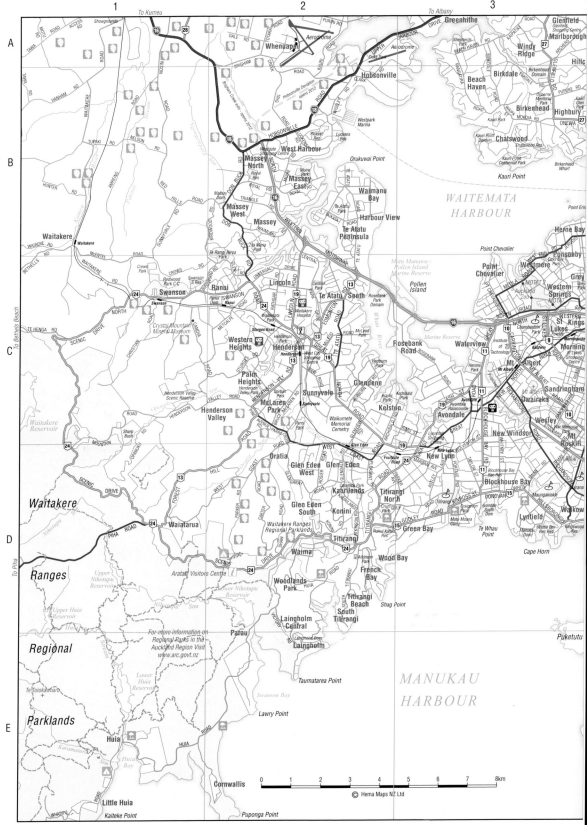

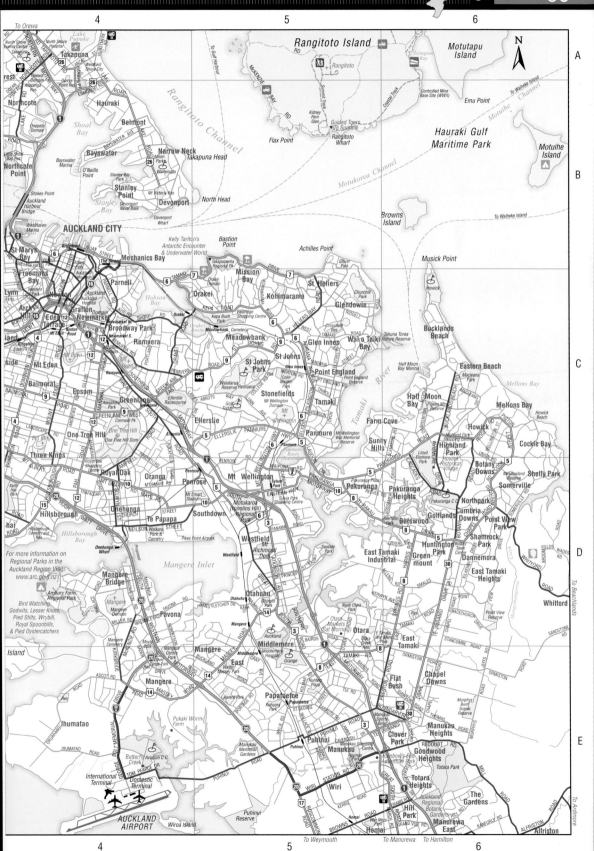

map
91
NORTH ISLAND
Hamilton CBD

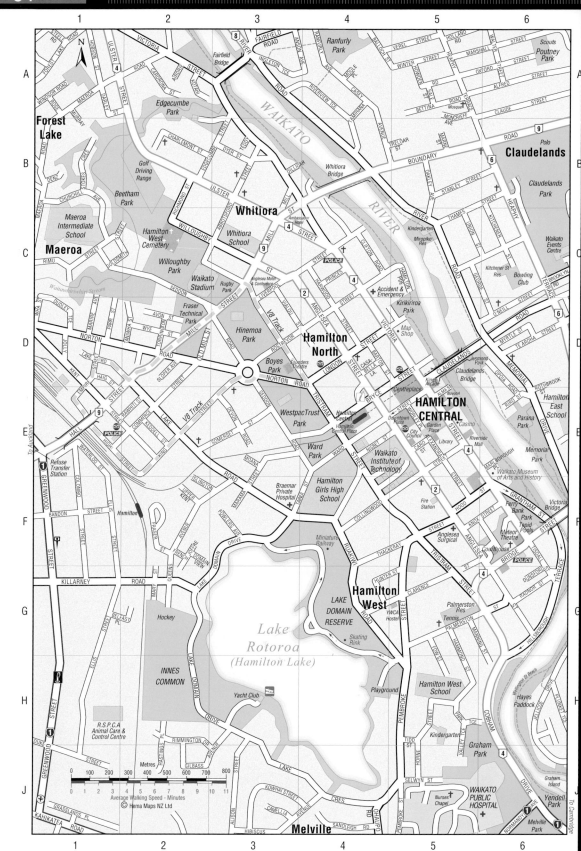

For touring map
see map 11

Hamilton Suburbs

NORTH
ISLAND

map
92

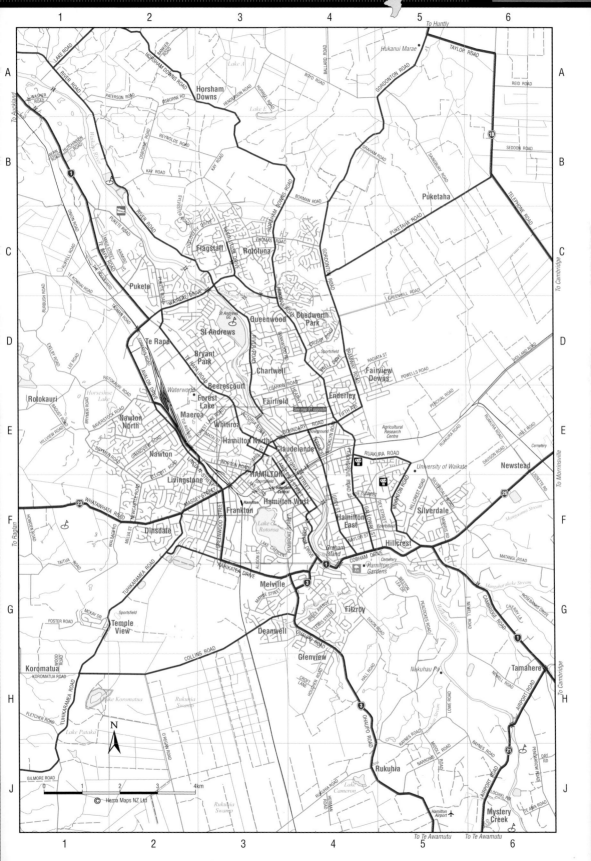

map
93
NORTH ISLAND
Tauranga CBD

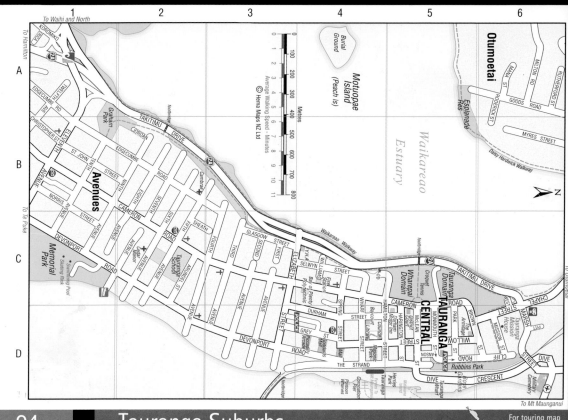

map 94
Tauranga Suburbs

For touring map
see map 13

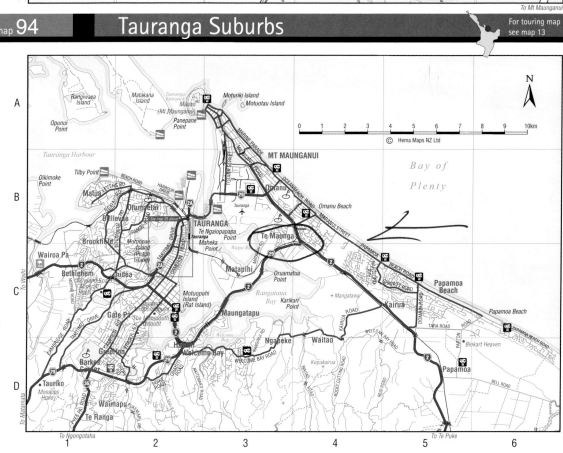

LAKE ROTORUA

To Tauranga & Whakatane

To Taupo & South

Motutara Point
Boat Ramps

Motutara Golf Course

War Memorial & Rose Gardens

Sulphur Point

Sulphur Point Wildlife Sanctuary

Rocky Point

Sulphur Flats

Thermal Area

Rugby Park

Crematorium & Cemetery

Fenton Park

The Bath House
Sportsdrome

Polynesian Spa

Lakefront

OHUWHATA DRIVE

QUEENS DRIVE

Museum of Art & History

Blue Baths

Bowling Club

Government Gardens

Millennium Rotorua

AMOHAU PL

HINEMARU STREET

AMOHAU STREET

Arawa Park Racecourse

Putt Putt

Leisure Island

TE NGAE RD

WHITE STREET

SALA STREET

HILDA ST

MARGUERITA

PEACE ST

MAIDA VALE ST

Where Arohia Hospital

Queen Elizabeth Hospital

Progress Hall

Convention Centre

POLICE

Courthouse

Tourism Library

Grand Hotel

Nomad Backpackers

Toko St

TI STREET

Four Canoes

Timura Suites

EASON ST

UNION ST

FENTON

LYTTON STREET

Glenholme

WHAKAUE STREET

PUKAKI STREET

RANGIURU STREET

ARAWA STREET

HAUPAPA STREET

Map Shop

Rotorua Central Mall

ROTORUA CENTRAL

TUTANEKAI STREET

AMOHAU STREET

VICTORIA STREET

HEREWINI ST

RUIHI ST

TOKO ST

ROAD

SEDDON STREET

CARNOT STREET

GREY STREET

ROBERTSON STREET

HOLLAND STREET

TILSLEY STREET

SUMNER STREET

KOWHAI STREET

MCLEAN STREET

Rotorua Hospital (King George V)

Rotorua Primary School

RANOLF STREET

PUKUATUA STREET

HINEMOA STREET

ERUERA STREET

AMOHIA STREET

PERERIKA ST

PRETORIA ST

KING STREET

MALFROY

St Marys School

WALLACE STREET

CRES

Glenholme School

TOTARA ST

HIGH ST

Kuirau Park
Free Thermal Area

Aquarium

Miniature Railway

To Hamilton & North

To Tirau

Metres / Average Walking Speed – Minutes

© Hema Maps NZ Ltd

For touring map see map 13

To Ngongotaha

To Whakatane

Lake Rotorua

Whakia Stream

Rainbow Springs & Farm

Rainbow Springs

Kawaha Point

Kawaha Point

Ngunguru Point

Rotokawa

Te Ngae Road

Rotorua Airport

Ngongotaha

Selwyn Heights

Koutu

Hannahs Bay

Holdens Bay

Lake Rotokawa

Gondola & Luge Rides

Hinemoa Point

Holdens Bay

Hannahs Bay

Pleasant Heights

Western Heights

Ohinemutu

See map 95 above

Motutara Point

GORDON RD

CLAYTON ROAD

OLD TAUPO ROAD

LAKE ROAD

Mangakakahi

Kuirau Park

PUKUATUA STREET

Rotorua Museum

Orchid Gardens

Bath House

Rocky Point

Owhata

Pukehangi

PUKEHANGI RD

Utuhina

MALFROY RD

RANOLF ST

FENTON ST

Ngapuna

MOREY STREET

Fordlands

SUNSET RD

DEVON ST WEST

Hillcrest

Tamaki Tours

TE NGAE ROAD

Sunnybrook

Pomare

DEVON ST

Glenholme

Fenton Park

Lynmore

TARAWERA ROAD

Matipo Heights

Sportsfield

SALA ST

Redwood Grove

Springfield

PUKEHANGI RD

DYERS RD

HEMO RD

TOKORANGI PA ROAD

Opawhero Hill

Whakarewarewa Village

Te Puia & Pohutu Geyser

Whakarewarewa

Whakarewarewa Forest

Ngatautara

Tangatarua

To Taupo

0 1 2 3 4 5km

© Hema Maps NZ Ltd

map
97

NORTH
ISLAND

Taupo CBD

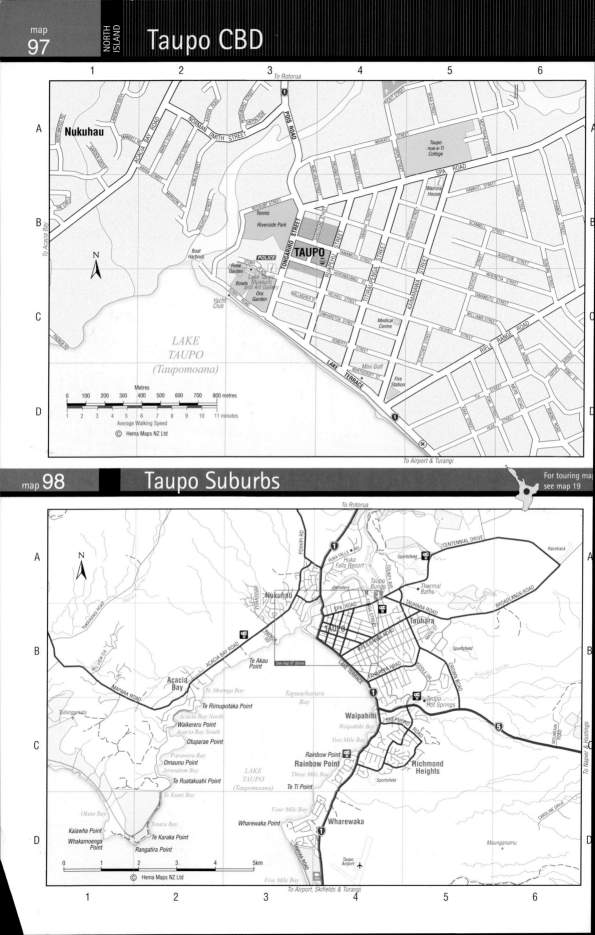

map 98

Taupo Suburbs

For touring map
see map 19

Map 97 labels:

1 2 3 4 5 6

To Rotorua

A

Nukuhau

NORMAN SMITH STREET
ACACIA BAY ROAD
POIS ROAD
WAIKATO STREET
SPA ROAD

Taupo
nua-a-Ti
College

Wairora
House

RAWHITI STREET

B

To Acacia Bay

N

REDOUBT STREET
Tennis
Riverside Park

TONGARIRO STREET

TAUPO

RUAPEHU
TITIRAUPENGA STREET
TAMAMUTU STREET
HOROMATANGI ST

SCANNELL STREET
LAUGHTON STREET
WHERETIA STREET

Boat
Harbour

Rose
Garden
Lake Taupo
Museum
and Art Gallery
Ora
Garden
POLICE
STORY

Bowls

GALLAGHER ST
HEUHEU STREET

KAIMANAWA
TAMAMUTU STREET

WILLIAMS STREET

C

Yacht
Club

LOWHARETOA STREET

ROBERTS STREET

Medical
Centre

HEUHEU STREET

RIFLE RANGE ROAD

*LAKE
TAUPO
(Taupomoana)*

Mini Golf
WORTHCROFT ST

Fire
Station

LAKE TERRACE

Metres
0 100 200 300 400 500 600 700 800 metres
1 2 3 4 5 6 7 8 9 10 11 minutes
Average Walking Speed
© Hema Maps NZ Ltd

D

To Airport & Turangi

Map 98 labels:

1 2 3 4 5 6

To Rotorua

A

N

POIHIPI RD
HUKA FALLS RD
Huka
Falls Resort
Sportsfield
CENTENNIAL DRIVE
Racetrack

JARDEN VILLE
Nukuhau
Cemetery
Taupo
Bungy
COUNTY AVE
Thermal
Baths
BROADLANDS ROAD

B

TITIRAUPENGA ROAD
HILLVIEW DR
MAPARA ROAD
ACACIA BAY ROAD
RAPIDS RD
SPA ROAD

TAUPO

Tauhara
MATA ST
TAUHARA ROAD

Te Akau
Point
See map 97 above

RIFLE RANGE ROAD
LAKE TERRACE
TE HEUHEU ROAD
Sportsfield
CROWN ROAD
MIDDLE DR
Waipahihi Stream

**Acacia
Bay**

Te Moenga Bay
*Tapuaeharuru
Bay*

KAIAPATA ROAD
Taupo
Hot Springs
5

Te Rimupotaka Point

C

Tuhingamata
Acacia Bay North
Waikereru Point
Acacia Bay South
Otuparae Point

Waipahihi
Waipahihi Bay
SHEPHERD RD

To Napier & Hastings

Parawera Bay
Omaunu Point
Jerusalem Bay

Two Mile Bay

Rainbow Point
Rainbow Point

*LAKE
TAUPO
(Taupomoana)*

**Richmond
Heights**

Te Ruatakuahi Point

Three Mile Bay
Sportsfield

Te Kumi Bay

Te Ti Point

Okuta Bay
Totara Bay
Kaiawha Point
Whakamoenga
Point
Te Karaka Point
Rangatira Point

Wharewaka Point

Four Mile Bay

Wharewaka

TAHUNA ROAD
KAROA ROAD

Taupo
Airport

Maunganamu

CAROLINE DRIVE

D

0 1 2 3 4 5km
© Hema Maps NZ Ltd

Five Mile Bay
To Airport, Skifields & Turangi

1 2 3 4 5 6

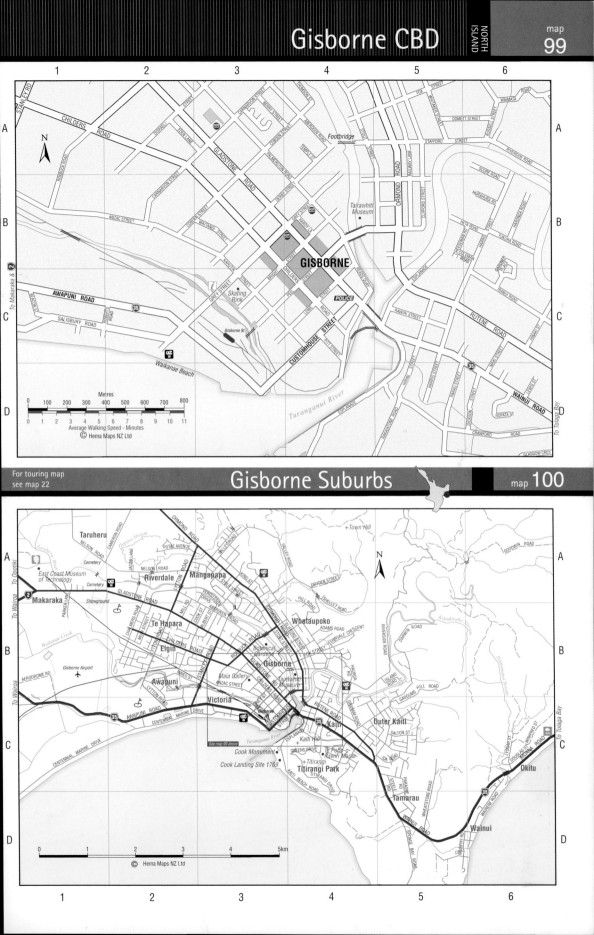

GISBORNE

POLICE

Tairawhiti Museum

Footbridge

Skating Rink

Waikanae Beach

Gisborne St

Turanganui River

To Makaraka & 2

To Tolaga Bay

Metres
0 100 200 300 400 500 600 700 800
0 1 2 3 4 5 6 7 8 9 10 11
Average Walking Speed - Minutes
© Hema Maps NZ Ltd

Taruheru

Mangapapa

Riverdale

East Coast Museum of Technology

Makaraka

Te Hapara

Elgin

Awapuni

Victoria

Whataupoko

Botanical Gardens

Gisborne

Tairawhiti Museum

Maia Gallery

Kaiti

Outer Kaiti

Kaiti Hill

Cook Monument

Cook Landing Site 1769

Titirangi Park

Tamarau

Wainui

Okitu

Town Hill

See map 99 above

Turanganui River

Te Poho-o-Rawiri Marae

Gisborne Airport

Showground

To Opotiki

To Wairoa

To Tolaga Bay

0 1 2 3 4 5km
© Hema Maps NZ Ltd

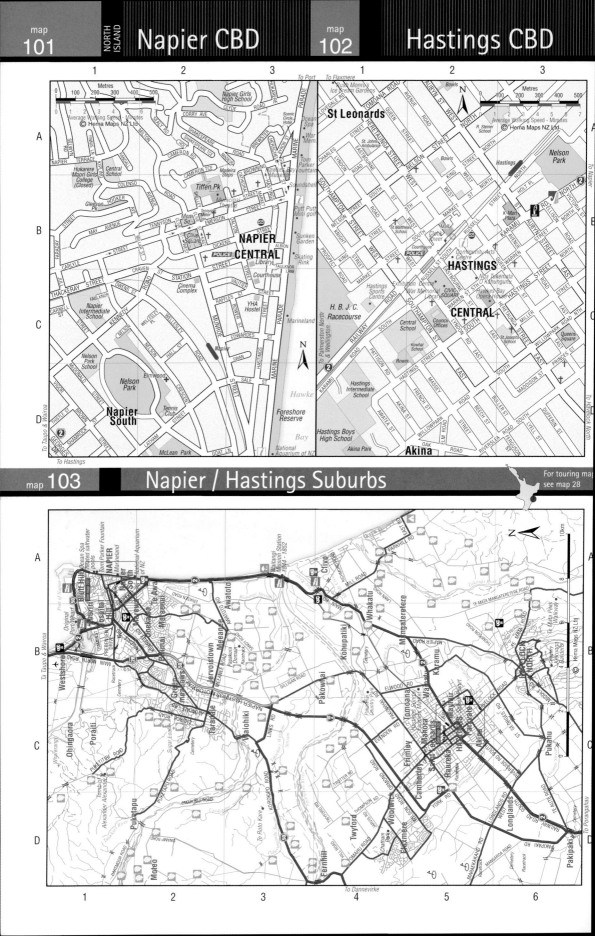

map
101

NORTH ISLAND

Napier CBD

map
102

Hastings CBD

map 103

Napier / Hastings Suburbs

For touring map
see map 28

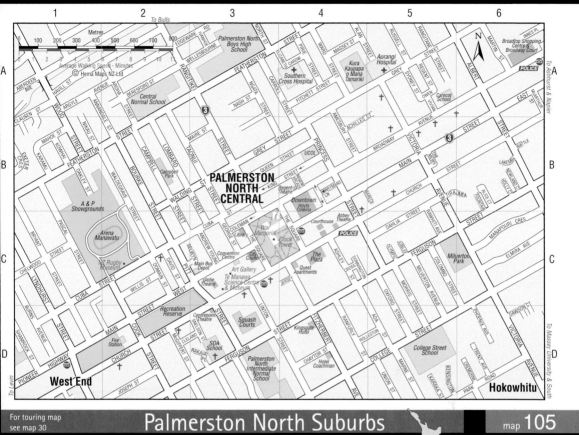

PALMERSTON NORTH CENTRAL

West End

Hokowhitu

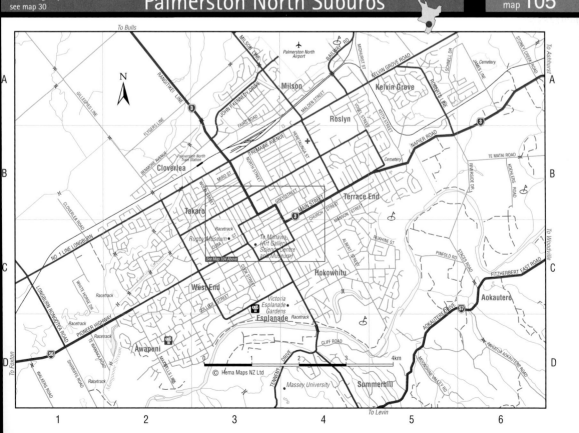

© Hema Maps NZ Ltd

map 106 NORTH ISLAND

New Plymouth CBD

map 107   New Plymouth Suburbs

For touring map see map 23

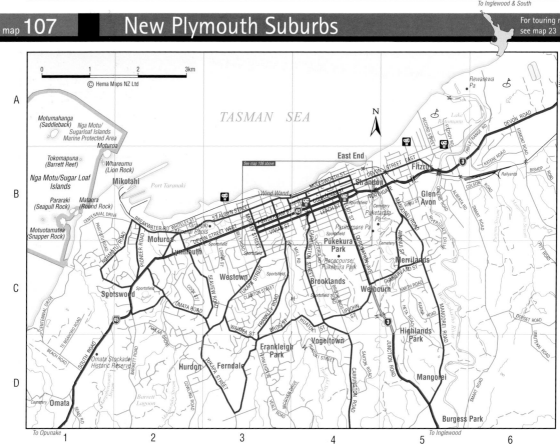

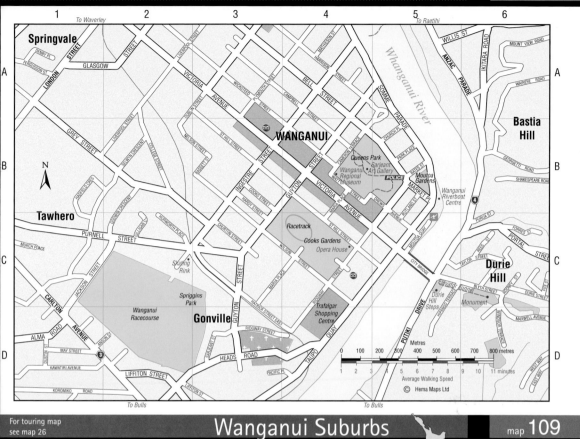

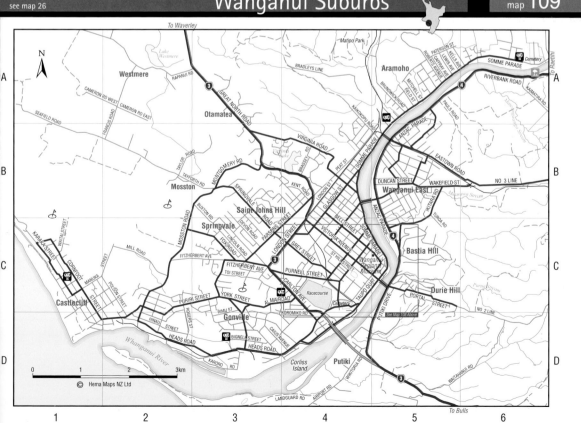

map
110
NORTH ISLAND
Wellington Suburbs
For touring ma
see map 33

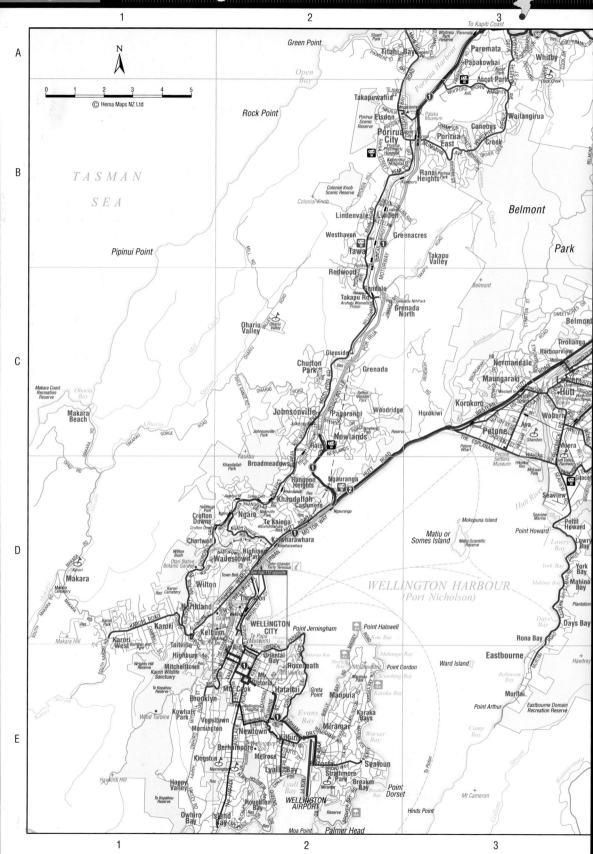

© Hema Maps NZ Ltd

0 1 2 3 4 5

N

To Kapiti Coast

A

Green Point

Stuart Park

Titahi Bay

Paremata

Papakowhai

Whitby

Rock Point

Takapuwahia

Ascot Park

Open Bay

Elsdon

Waitangirua

Porirua City

Porirua East

Cannons Creek

Pataka Museum

B

TASMAN SEA

Colonial Knob Scenic Reserve

Colonial Knob

Rangi Heights

Belmont

Pipinui Point

Lindenvale

Linden

Greenacres

Westhaven

Tawa

Takapu Valley

Park

Redwood

Belmont

Sandale

Takapu Rd

Ohariu Valley

Grenada North

Belmont

Ohariu Valley

Glenside

C

Makara Coast Recreation Reserve

Churton Park

Grenada

Tirohanga

Harbourview

Makara Beach

Johnsonville

Paparangi

Woodridge

Normandale

Maungaraki

Horokiwi

Korokoro

Lower Hutt

Ohariu Bay

Johnsonville Park

Newlands

Woburn

Broadmeadows

Ngauranga

Waiwhetu

Ava

Petone

Moera

Khandallah Park

Rangoon Heights

Matiu or Somes Island

Petone Wharf

Seaview

Khandallah

Cashmere

Seaview Marina

Crofton Downs

Ngaio

Te Kainga

Mokopuna Island

Point Howard

Chartwell

Kaiwharawhara

Lowry Bay

York Bay

D

Makara

Wilton Bush

Highland

Wadestown

Mahina Bay

Otari Native Botanic Garden

Inter-Islander Ferry Terminal

WELLINGTON HARBOUR (Port Nicholson)

Days Bay

Karori Cemetery

Wilton

Town Belt

Karori

Northland

Thorndon

Days Bay

Karori West

Kelburn

Point Jerningham

Rona Bay

Taitville

WELLINGTON CITY

Point Halswell

Eastbourne

Highbury

Te Papa Museum

Oriental Bay

Kau Bay

Mitchelltown

Aro

Roseneath

Point Gordon

Ward Island

Wrights Hill Reserve

Mt Victoria

Point Arthur

Eastbourne Domain Recreation Reserve

Karori Wildlife Sanctuary

Hataitai

Muritai

Te Kopahou Reserve

Mt Cook

Maupuia

Karaka Bay

Brooklyn

Worser Bay

Camp Bay

Kowhai Park

Vogeltown

Evans Bay

Miramar

Karaka Bays

Wind Turbine

Mornington

Newtown

Kilbirnie

Seatoun

E

Berhampore

Melrose

Strathmore Park

Kingston

Mt Cameron

Happy Valley

Lyall Bay

Breaker Bay

Point Dorset

Te Kopahou Reserve

Hawkins Hill

Houghton Bay

WELLINGTON AIRPORT

Hinds Point

Owhiro Bay

Island Bay

Moa Point

Palmer Head

Wellington CBD | map 112

map
113
SOUTH ISLAND
Picton CBD

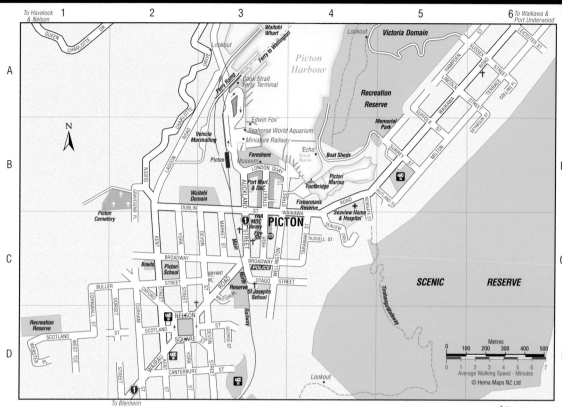

map 114
Picton Suburbs

For touring map
see map 40

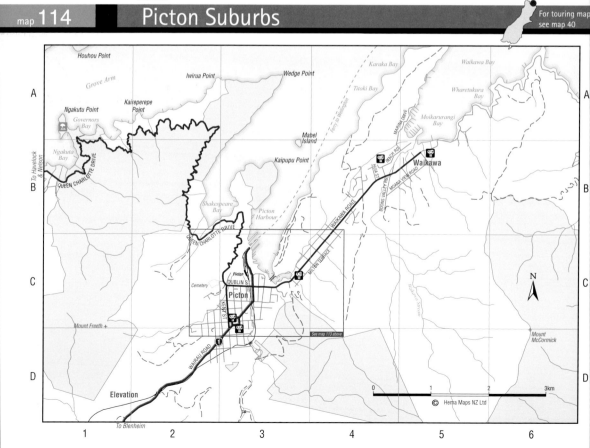

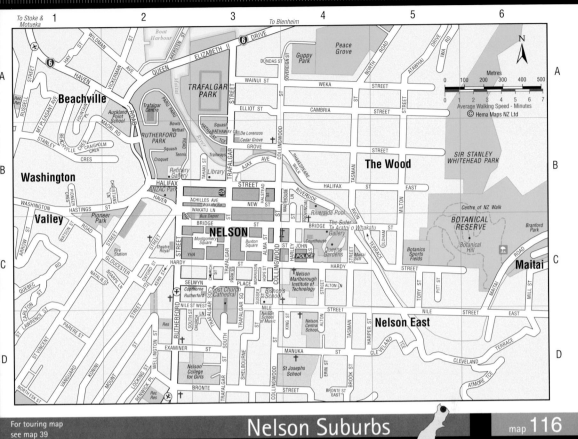

Nelson Suburbs

map 116

For touring map
see map 39

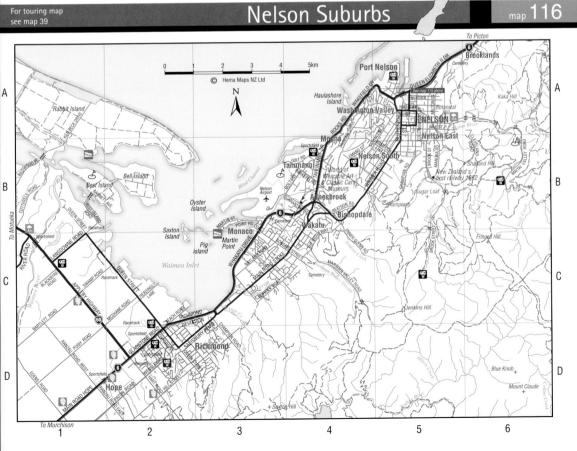

map
117
SOUTH ISLAND

Blenheim CBD

For touring map
see map 44

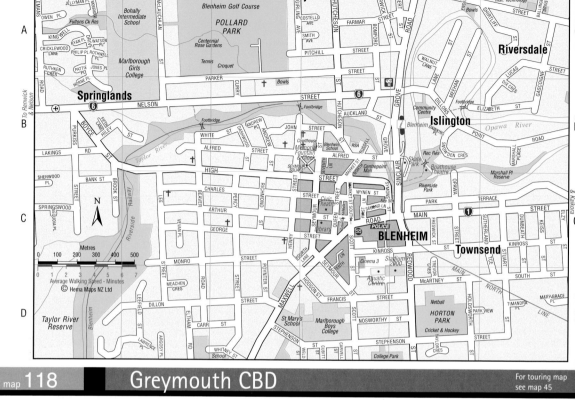

map 118

Greymouth CBD

For touring map
see map 45

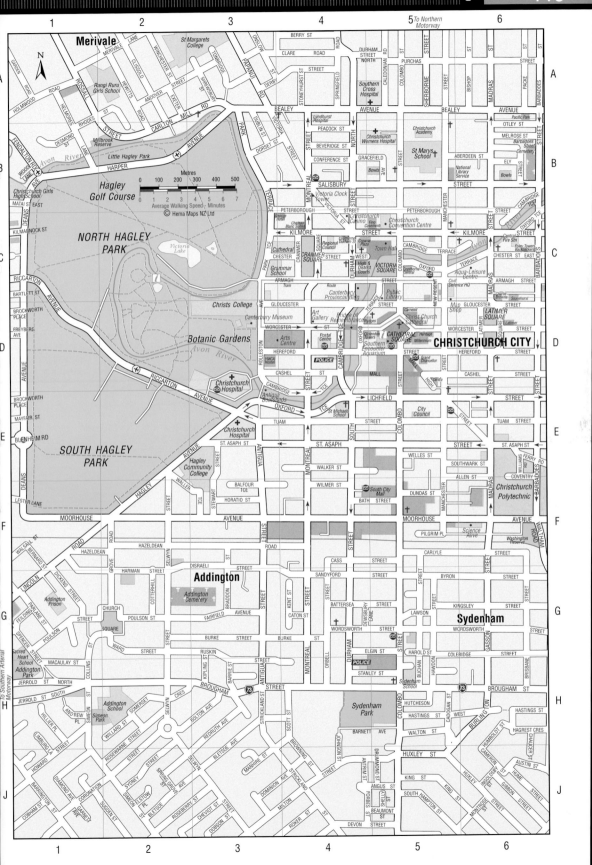

map
120
SOUTH ISLAND
Christchurch Suburbs
For touring m
see map 54

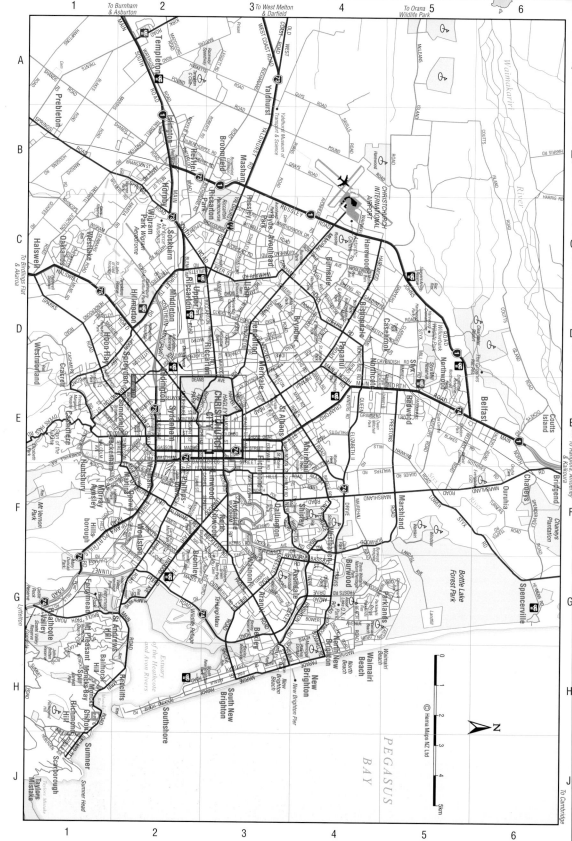

For touring map
see map 61

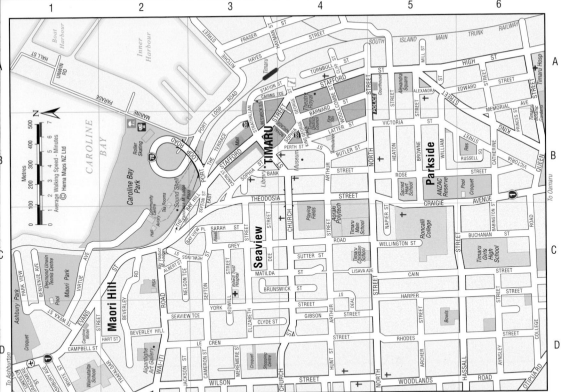

For touring map
see map 68

Oamaru CBD

map 122

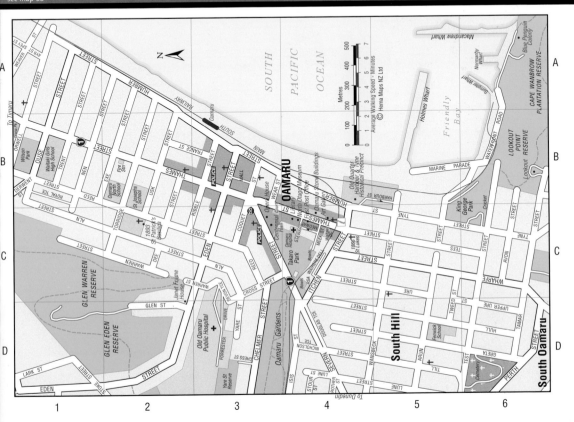

map
123
SOUTH ISLAND
Dunedin CBD

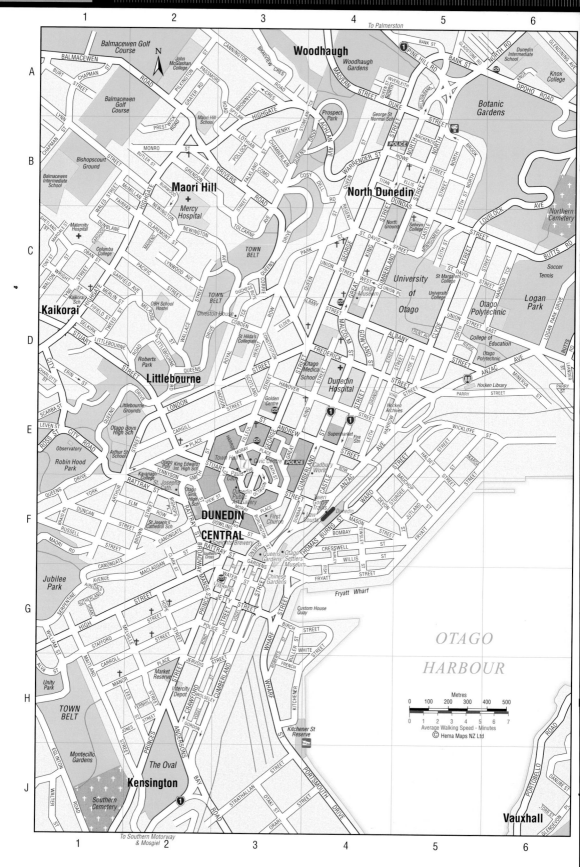

For touring map
see map 74

© Hema Maps NZ Ltd

N

Pacific Ocean

8km
7
6
5
4
3
2
1
0

A B C D E F G H J

Place labels:

Deborah Acheron Point
Rocky Point
Goldie Point
Careys Bay
Port Chalmers
NZ Marine Studies Centre
Quarantine Island/ St Martin Island
Kamau Taurua & The Westpac Aquarium
Goat Island/ Rakiriri
Pudding Island
Portobello
Harbour Cone
Styles Creek
Larnach Castle
Sandymount
Sandfly Bay
Seal Point Road
Seal Point
Roseneath
Sawyers Bay
Kilgours Point
Grassy Point
Curles Point
Company Bay
Macandrew Bay
Pukehiki
Patons Hill
Historical Site
BLUESKIN ROAD
RESERVOIR RD
UPPER JUNCTION RD
Collinswood
Glenfalloch Woodland Gardens
Highcliff
HIGHCLIFF ROAD
Highcliff Hill
Maori Head
Bird Island
Mount Martin
Mount Cutten
Mount Cargill
MOUNT CARGILL RD
Mindies Hollows
Bittars Peak
Martins Hill
McGregors Hill
Burkes
Ravensbourne
Challis
The Cove
Monument
Shiel Hill
Maori Head
Ocean Grove
KAITEMATA ROAD
To Palmerston
Pigeon Flat
Pigeon Hill
Upper Junction
Normanby
Mount Mera
Balmwin Street Signal Hill
Black Jacks Point
Burns Point
Waverley
Anderson Bay
Tainui
Lawyers Head
Monument
Cemetery
White Island
Swampy Summit
Flagstaff
Pine Hill
Liberton
North East Valley
Mt Grey
DUNEDIN
Vauxhall
St Clair
Forbury
Leith Valley
MALVERN ST
Glenleith
Woodhaugh
Maori Hill
North Dunedin
Dalmore
Belleknowes
Kensington
Mornington
St Kilda
Forbury
PRINCES STREET
Helensburgh
Halfway Bush
Wakari
Kaikorai
Brockville
Bradford
Belleknowes
Caversham
South Dunedin
Corstorphine
Concord
Blackhead
Green Island
Burnside
Black Head
Whare Flat
Waiora
Chalkies Scenic Reserve
White Hill Cairn
Powder Hill
McCallums Creek
Abbotts Hill
THREE MILE HILL ROAD
SILVERSTREAM VALLEY ROAD
Abbotsford
Sunnyvale
Waldronville
Westwood
Boulder Hill
Tara Hills
North Taieri
PUDDLE ALLEY
Janefield
WINGATUI RD
Wingatui
Fairfield
Saddle Hill
Chain Hills
Ocean View
FACTORY ROAD
HAZLETT ROAD
GLADSTONE RD
MAIN ROAD
Wyllies Crossing
MOSGIEL
East Taieri
Brighton
Scroggs Hill
Fairfield
RICCARTON ROAD WEST
GLADFIELD RD
MAIN SOUTH RD
Owhiro
To Middlemarch
To Milton
To Milton & Airport

map
125
SOUTH ISLAND

Queenstown CBD

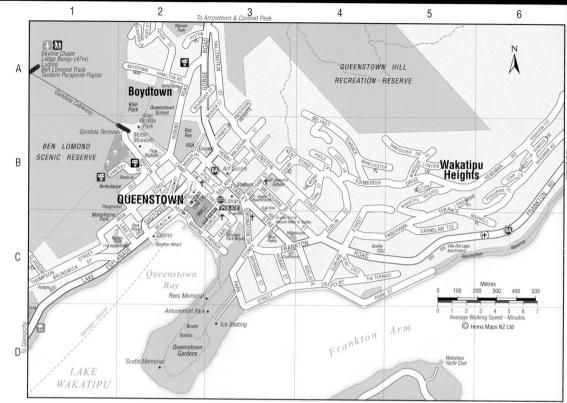

map 126

Queenstown Suburbs

For touring m
see map 65

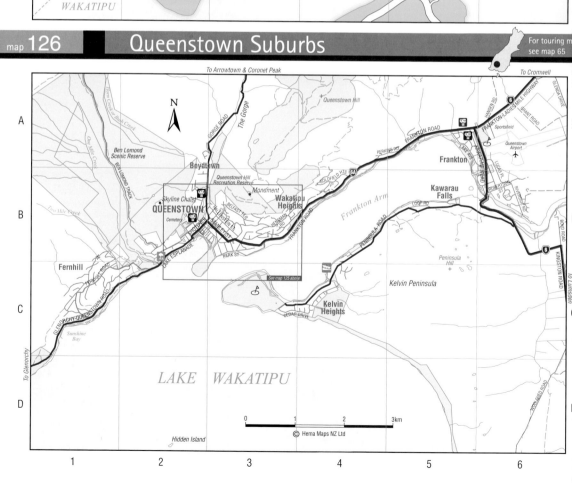

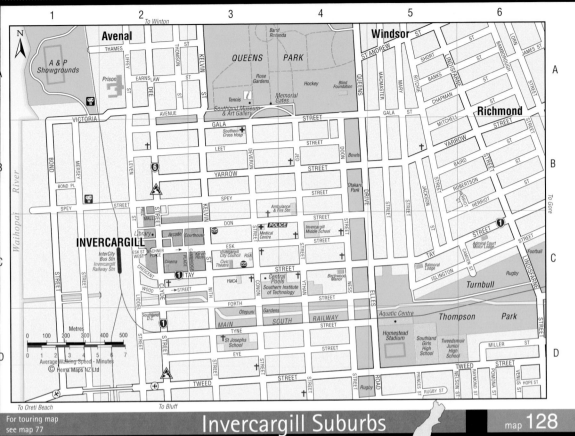

For touring map
see map 77

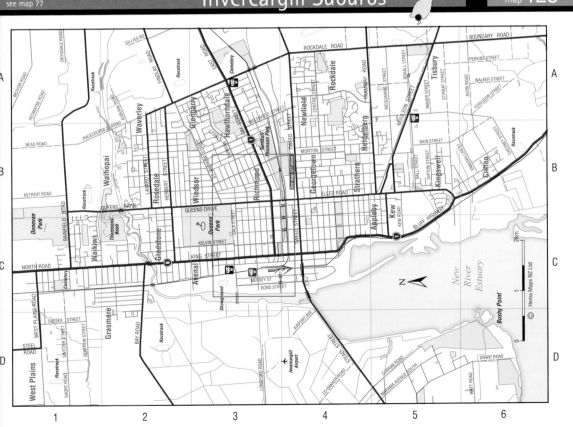

Kingston, South Island Photo: Michelle Bignell

International dump station/waste disposal signs for black and grey waste water.

 Motorhome Park / Caravan Park with Dump Station (Wastewater Disposal Site)

 Motorhome Dump Station (Wastewater Disposal Site)

The disposal of waste from the sink, shower (grey) and toilet (black) is to be made at dump station/waste disposal sites. The locations listed here refer to most of the symbols shown on the maps. There may be a charge for using a dump station at some camping grounds, unless you are staying there. Some dump stations on septic tanks may limit their availability during peak times.
Under no circumstances is it acceptable to dispose of wastewater in rubbish disposal facilities.
For more information see Ministry of Tourism brochure: Finding a dump station in NZ

For more information on campsites, caravan parks and motorhome parks see Hema Maps'
NZ Motorhome & Camping Atlas.

Motorhome Park/Caravan Park with dump station (wastewater disposal site)

NORTH ISLAND

Far North

Pukenui Holiday Park (1 F5) – Lamb Rd, Pukenui; 45km north of Kaitaia; Opposite Pukenui School: (09) 409 8803
Wagener Holiday Motor Camp (Houhora Heads Motor Camp) (1 F5) – On Houhora Heads Rd, Houhora; Opposite Wagener Museum: (09) 409 8564
Norfolk Campervan Park (1 H6) – Cnr SH1 & SH10; 300m from Awanui: (09) 406 7515
The Park Top 10 Ninety Mile Beach (1 H4) – West Coast Rd, Waipapakauri;18km north of Kaitaia: (09) 406 7298
Kaitaia Holiday Park (1 J6) – Adjacent SH1 at the south end of Kaitaia: (09) 408 1212
Ahipara Backpackers & Motor Camp (1 J5) – Takahe St, Ahipara: (09) 409 4864
Whatuwhiwhi Top 10 Holiday Park (2 F7) – 17 Whatuwhiwhi Rd, Karikari Peninsula; RD 3, Kaitaia: (09) 408 7202
Hihi Beach Holiday Camp (2 G9) – 58 Hihi Rd, Mangonui: (09) 406 0307
Whangaroa Harbour Holiday Park (2 H10) – Whangaroa Harbour, Kaeo: (09) 405 0306
Matauri Bay Holiday Park (2 H12) – Matauri Bay, Whangaroa: (09) 405 0525
Tauranga Bay Holiday Park (2 H11) – Tauranga Bay, Whangaroa; 17.5km from Kaeo: (09) 405 0436
Kerikeri Top 10 Holiday Park (4 A8) – Aranga Drive, 500m south of town centre; Opposite BP Service Station, Kerikeri: (09) 407 9326
Hideaway Lodge (4 A8) – Wiroa Rd, Kerikeri: (09) 407 9773
Gibby's Place (4 A8) – 331 Kerikeri Rd, Kerikeri: (09) 407 9024
Wagon Train RV Park (4 A9) – SH10, Kerikeri: (09) 407 7889
Waitangi Holiday Park (4 B9) – 21 Tahuna Rd, Waitangi: (09) 402 7866
Beachside Holiday Park (4 B10) – Opua-Paihia Rd, 2.5km south of Paihia: (09) 402 7678
Bay of Islands Holiday Park (4 B9) – Puketona Rd, Paihia: (09) 402 7646
Haruru Falls Resort, 'Panorama' (4 B9) – Old Wharf Rd, Haruru Falls; 5 min from Paihia: (09) 402 7525
Twin Pines Holiday Park (4 B9) – Puketona Rd, RD 1, Paihia: (09) 402 7322
Russell Top 10 Holiday Park (4 B10) – Long Beach Rd, Russell: (09) 403 7826
Orongo Bay Holiday Park (4 B10) – 5960 Russell Rd: (09) 403 7704
Taupo Bay Camping Ground (2 G10) – 1070 Taupo Bay Rd: (09) 406 0315
Millenium Nocturnal Glowworm & Ostrich Park (2J7) – Fairburn Road, Katia: (027) 896 816

Northland

Dargaville Holiday Park (3 J7) – 10 Onslow St, Dargaville: (09) 439 8296
Dargaville Campervan Park (3 J7) – 18 Gladstone St, Dargaville: (09) 439 8479
Kauri Coast Top 10 Holiday Park (3 G6) – Trounson Park Rd, Kaihu: (09) 439 0621
Baylys Beach Holiday Park (3 J6) – 22-24 Seaview Rd; 800m from beach: (09) 439 6349
Matakohe Top 10 Holiday Park (5 B5) – Church Rd, Matakohe: (09) 431 6431

Paparoa Motor Camp (5 B6) – Cnr SH12 & Pahi Rd, Paparoa: (09) 431 6515
Pahi Beach Motor Camp (5 B6) – Enter Pahi Domain and drive through to public toilets on right of wharf, Pahi: (09) 431 7322
Kellys Bay Reserve (5 D5) – Dale Rd, Kellys Bay, Pouto Peninsula: (09) 439 4204
Pakiri Beach Holiday Park (6 D10) – Pakiri River Rd, RD 2 Wellsford, Pakiri: (09) 422 6199
Tutukaka Holiday Park (4 E13) – Matapour Rd, Tutukaka: (09) 434 3938
Kamo Springs Holiday Park (4 F11) – On SH1, Whangarei: (09) 435 1208
Whangarei Top 10 Holiday Park (4 G11) – 24 Mair St, Kensington, Whangarei: (09) 437 6856
Whangarei Falls Holiday Park (85 A2) – 12 Ngunguru Rd Glenbervie: (09) 437 0609
Alpha Motel & Holiday Park (4 F11) – 34 Tarewa Rd, Whangarei: (09) 438 6600
Blue Heron Holiday Park (4 G12) – 85-87 Scott Rd, off Whangarei Heads Rd; Heading towards Parua Bay: (09) 436 2293
Treasure Island Trailer Park (4 G13) – Pataua South: (09) 436 2390
Ruakaka Reserve Motor Camp (4 J13) – 21 Beach Rd, Ruakaka: (09) 432 7590
Camp Waipu Cove (6 A8) – Cove Rd, Waipu Cove: (09) 432 0410
Waipu Cove Cottages & Camp (6 A8) – 685 Cove Rd, Waipu Cove: (09) 432 0851
Whangateau Holiday Park (6 D10) – 559 Leigh Rd, Whangateau: (09) 422 6305
Sheepworld Caravan Park (6 E9) – SH1, Warkworth: (09) 425 9962
Martin's Bay Holiday Park (6 E10) – 287 Martins Bay Rd, Sandspit/Warkworth: (09) 425 5655

Hibiscus Coast

Pinewoods Motor Park Ltd (7 B4) – 23 Marie Ave, Red Beach: (09) 426 4526
Waiwera Holiday Park (7 A4) – 37 Waiwera Place, outside the main ablution block, Waiwera: (09) 426 5270

Auckland

Auckland North Shore Holiday Park (7 D4) – 52 Northcote Rd, Takapuna; Entrance next to Pizza Hut: (09) 418 2578
Takapuna Beach Holiday Park (7 D4) – 22 The Promenade, Takapuna: (09) 489 7909
Aquatic Park Holiday Camp (5 H7) – Cnr Parkhurst & Springs Rd, Parakai; D/S is 7m from kerb: (09) 420 8998
Avondale Motor Park (7 E4) – 46 Bollard Ave, Avondale: (09) 828 7228
Manukau Top 10 Holiday Park (7 F5) – 902 Great South Rd, Manukau: (09) 266 8016
Orewa Beach Top 10 Holiday Park (7 A4) – 265 Hibiscus Coast Hwy, S end of Orewa Beach: (09) 426 5832
Pakiri Beach Holiday Park (6 D10) – 261 Pakiri River Rd, Pakiri: (09) 422 6199
Piha Domain Motor Camp (7 E2) – 21 Seaview Rd, Piha: (09) 812 8815

Counties

South Auckland Caravan Park (7 H6) – Ararimu Rd, Ramarama: (09) 294 8903
Orere Point Top 10 Holiday Park (8 F9) – 2 Orere Point Rd, Clevedon: (09) 292 2774
Miranda Holiday Park (8 H9) – Miranda Rd, Thames: (07) 867 3205
Clarks Beach Holiday Park (7 H4) – Torkar Rd, Clarks Beach: (09) 232 1685
Sandspit Motor Camp (7 J4) – 15 Rangiwhea Rd, Waiuku; Jane Gifford Reserve: (09) 235 9913

Hauraki/Coromandel

Dickson Holiday Park (8 G11) – 3km north of Thames on Coromandel Rd: (07) 868 7308
Te Puru Holiday Park (10 B8) – 473 Thames Coast Rd, Te Puru: (07) 868 2879
The Glade Holiday Park (8 G14) – 58 Vista Paku, Pauanui Beach: (07) 864 8559
Tapu Motor Camp (8 F11) – SH25, Thames Coast: (07) 868 4837
Tapu Creek Campervan Park (8 F11) – Tapu-Coroglen Rd, Tapu: (07) 868 4560
Riverglen Holiday Park (8 F12) – Tapu Rd, Coroglen; 3.5km from Coroglen Tavern: (07) 866 3130
Papa Aroha Holiday Park (8 C10) – Colville Rd, Coromandel: (07) 866 8818
Long Bay Motor Camp (8 C11) – 3200 Long Bay Rd, Coromandel: (07) 866 8720
Shelly Beach Top 10 Holiday Park (8 C11) – 243 Colville Rd, Coromandel: (07) 866 8988
Oamaru Bay Motor Camp (8 C11) – 440 Colville Rd, Coromandel: (07) 866 8735
Colville Bay Motel & Motor Camp (8 B11) – Wharf Rd, Colville, Coromandel: (07) 866 6814
Anglers Lodge Motels & Holiday Park (8 B10) – 1446 Colville Rd, Amodeo Bay: (07) 866 8584
Coromandel Motels & Holiday Park (8 C11) – 636 Rings Rd, Coromandel: (07) 866 8830
Kuaotunu Motor Camp (8 C13) – 33 Bluff Rd, Kuaotunu: (07) 866 5628
Otama Beach Camping Ground (8 C13) – 400 Blackjack Rd, RD 2, Whitianga: (07) 866 2872
Flaxmill Bay Hideaway Camp & Cabins (8 D13) – 1031 Purangi Rd, Flaxmill Bay, Whitianga: (07) 866 2386
Mercury Bay Holiday Park (8 D13) – 121 Albert St, Whitianga: (07) 866 5579
Harbourside Holiday Park (8 D13) – 135 Albert St, Whitianga: (07) 866 5746
Mill Creek Bird & Campervan Park (8 E12) – 365 Mill Creek Rd, Whitianga: (07) 866 0166
Seabreeze Tourist Park (8 E13) – 1043 Tairua/Whitianga Rd, Whenuakite: (07) 866 3050
Hahei Holiday Resort (8 D14) – Harsant Ave, Hahei, Whitianga: (07) 866 3889
Whangamata Motor Camp (8 J14) – 104 Barbara Ave, Whangamata: (07) 865 9128
Settler's Motor Camp (8 J14) – 101 Leander Rd, Whangamata: (07) 865 8181

Waikato

Port Waikato Motor Camp (9 E1) – Maunsell Rd, Port Waikato: (09) 232 9857
Te Aroha Holiday Park (10 G10) – 217 Stanley Rd, Te Aroha: (07) 884 9567

Waihi Motor Camp (10 F10) – 6 Waitete Rd, Waihi: (07) 863 7654
Opal Hot Springs Holiday Park (12 F11) – 257 Okauia Springs Rd, Matamata: (07) 888 8198
Waingaro Hot Springs Caravan Park (9 J3) – At Ngaruawahia turn west for 24km, Waingaro: (07) 825 4761
Hamilton City Holiday Park (11 C7) – 14 Ruakura Rd, Hamilton: (07) 855 8255
Hamilton East Motor Camp (11 C7) – 61 Cameron Rd, Hamilton East: (07) 856 6220
Roadrunner Motel and Holiday Park (11 E7) – 141 Bond Rd, Te Awamutu: (07) 871 7420
Cambridge Motor Park (12 D8) – 32 Scott St, Leamington, Cambridge: (07) 827 5649
Lake Karapiro Camping & Pursuits Centre (12 D9) – Access from SH1, cross low level bridge at south end of Cambridge: (07) 827 4178
Raglan Kopua Holiday Park (11 C3) – Camp signposted from town centre: (07) 825 8283
Kawhia Beachside S-Cape (11 F3) – 225 Pouewe St, Kawhia: (07) 871 0727
Otorohanga Kiwi Town Holiday Park (11 G6) – 7 Domain Dr, Otorohanga; Adjacent to Kiwi & Native Bird Park: (07) 873 8279
Otorohanga Holiday Park (11 G6) – 20 Huiputea Drive, Otorohanga: (07) 873 7253
Kiwitown Holiday Park (11 G6) – Domain Drive, Otorohanga: (07) 837 8279
Waitomo Top 10 Holiday Park (11 H5) – Waitomo Caves Rd, Waitomo Village: (07) 878 7639
Te Kuiti Domain Motor Camp (11 J5) – Hinerangi St, Te Kuiti; Opposite Primary School: (07) 878 8966

Rotorua

Rotorua Top 10 Holiday Park (13 G4) – 1495 Pukuatua St, Rotorua: (07) 348 1886
Holdens Bay Top 10 Holiday Park & Conference Centre (13 G4) – 5-7 Stonebridge Park Drive, off Robinson Ave, Rotorua: (07) 345 9925
All Seasons Holiday Park (13 G5) – 50-58 Lee Rd, Hannahs Bay, Rotorua: 0800 422 674
Blue Lake Top 10 Holiday Park (13 H5) – 723 Tarawera Rd, On shores of Blue Lake, Rotorua: (07) 362 8120
Rotorua Lakeside Thermal Holiday Park (13 G4) – 54 Whittaker Rd, Rotorua: (07) 348 1693
Cosy Cottage International Holiday Park (13 G4) – 67 Whittaker Rd, Rotorua: (07) 348 3793
Rotorua Family Holiday Park (13 F4) – 22 Beaumonts Rd, Rotorua; Near lake shore Ngongotaha: (07) 357 4289
Affordable Willowhaven Holiday Park (13 F4) – 31 Beaumonts Rd, Ngongotaha, Rotorua: (07) 357 4092
Waiteti Trout Stream Holiday Park (13 F4) – 14 Okona Cres, Ngongotaha, Rotorua: (07) 357 5255
Rotorua Thermal Holiday Park (13 G4) – 463 Old Taupo Rd (south end), Rotorua; Adjacent to golf course: (07) 346 3140
Lake Rotoiti Lakeside Holiday Park (13 F5) – On SH33, Okere Falls: (07) 362 4860
Kea Motel & Holiday Park (12 F11) – 95 Tirau St, SH1, Putaruru: (07) 882 1590
Tokoroa Motor Camp & Backpackers (12 H12) – 22 Sloss Rd, Tokoroa: (07) 886 6642
Tongariro Holiday Park (Eivins Lodge) (19 H1) – SH47, Tongariro: (07) 386 8062

e Bretts Thermal Resort (19 D5) – 1.5km from Lake Taupo; SH5 Napier/Taupo Rd: (07) 378 8559

ake Taupo Top 10 Holiday Resort (19 D5) – 28 Centennial Dr (off Spa Rd), Taupo: (07) 378 6860

reat Lake Holiday Park (19 D5) – 406 Acacia Bay Rd, Taupo: (07) 378 5159

aupo All Seasons Holiday Park (19 D5) – 16 Rangatira St, Taupo: (07) 378 4272

asis Motel & Holiday Park (19 G2) – SH41 Tokaanu: (07) 386 8569

arklands Motor Lodge (19 G3) – Cnr Arahori St & SH1, Turangi: (07) 386 7515

lub Habitat Hotels (19 G3) – 25 Ohuanga Rd, Turangi: (07) 386 7492

urangi Cabins & Holiday Park (19 G3) – Ohuanga Rd off SH41, Turangi: (07) 386 8754

lotutere Bay Holiday Park (19 F4) – On SH1, Motutere: (07) 386 8963

/hakapapa Holiday Park (18 J13) – Tongariro National Park, Mt Ruapehu: (07) 892 3897

Bay of Plenty

Vaihi Beach Holiday Park (10 F12) – 15 Beach Rd, Waihi Beach; Adjacent to Ocean Beach: (07) 863 5504

Beachhaven Motel & Holiday Park (10 F12) – 21 Leo St, Waihi Beach: (07) 863 5505

Sea-Air Motel & Holiday Park (10 F12) – Emerton Rd, Waihi Beach South: (07) 863 5655

Athenree Hot Srpings & Holiday Park (10 F12) – 1 Athenree Rd, Athenree: (07) 863 5600

Bowentown Beach Holiday Park (10 F12) – South end of Seaforth Rd, Bowentown: (07) 863 5381

Acccommodation at Te Puna (10 J13) – Cnr Waihi Rd (SH2) & Minden Rd, Te Puna, Tauranga: (07) 552 5621

Tauranga Park (10 J13) – 9 Mayfair St, Tauranga: (07) 578 3323

Sanctuary Point (10 J13) – Between Poike Rd & Welcome Bay roundabouts, on Hamilton/Mt Maunganui; SH29 bypass, Tauranga: (07) 544 0700

Silver Birch Family Holiday Park (10 J13) – 101 Turret Rd, Tauranga: (07) 578 4603

Golden Grove Holiday Park (13 B4) – 73 Girven Rd, Mt Maunganui: (07) 575 5821

Cosy Corner Holiday Park (13 B4) – 40 Ocean Beach Rd, Mt Maunganui: (07) 575 5899

Mount Maunganui Beachside Holiday Park (13 A4) – 1 Adams Ave, Mt Maunganui; at the base of the mountain: (07) 575 4471

Papamoa Village Park (13 B5) – 267 Parton Rd, Papamoa: (07) 542 1890

Papamoa Beach Top 10 Holiday Resort (13 B5) – 535 Papamoa Beach Rd, Papamoa: (07) 572 0816

Beach Grove Holiday Park (13 B5) – 386 Papamoa Beach Rd, Papamoa: (07) 572 1337

Pacific Park Christian Holiday Camp (13 B5) – 1110 Papamoa Beach Rd, Papamoa: (07) 542 0018

Bay Views Holiday Park (13 C6) – 195 Arawa Ave, Maketu: (07) 533 2222

Eastern Bay of Plenty

Awakeri Hot Springs (14 F9) – On SH30, 16km south of Whakatane: (07) 304 9117

Whakatane Holiday Park (14 E11) – McGarvey Rd, Whakatane: (07) 308 8694

Thornton Beach Holiday Park (14 E110) – 163 Thornton Beach Rd off SH2; 14km NW of Whakatane: (07) 304 8296

Opotiki Holiday Park (14 F13) – Cnr of Grey St & Potts Ave, Opotiki: (07) 315 6050

Ohope Beach Top 10 Holiday Park (14 E12) – 367 Harbour Rd, east of Ohope: 0800 264 673

Ohiwa Holiday Park (14 F12) – 380 Ohiwa Harbour Rd, Opotiki: (07) 315 4741

Tirohanga Beach Motor Camp (15 F3) – On SH35, 7km past Opotiki: (07) 315 7942

Waihau Bay Holiday Park (16 B8) – On SH35, 3km east of Waihau Bay: (07) 325 3844

Eastland

Anaura Bay Motor Camp (16 J11) – Anaura Bay Rd, Anaura Bay: (06) 862 6380

Tolaga Bay Holiday Park (22 A13) – 167 Wharf Rd, Tolaga Bay: (06) 862 6716

Tatapouri By The Sea (22 D11) – Alongside SH35, Tatapouri: (06) 868 3269

Gisborne Showgrounds Park Motorcamp (22 D10) – 20 Main Rd, Gisborne: (06) 867 5299

Waikanae Beach Holiday Park (22 E10) – Grey St, Gisborne: (06) 867 5634

Mahia Beach Motel & Holiday Camp (22 J9) – 43 Moana Dr, Mahia Beach: (06) 837 5830

Riverside Motor Camp (21 H5) – 19 Marine Pde, Wairoa: (06) 838 6301

Waikaremoana Motor Camp (21 E2) – SH38, Lake Waikaremoana: (06) 837 3803

Hawkes Bay

Waipatiki Beach Farm Park (28 B13) – 498 Waipatiki Beach Rd, Napier: (06) 836 6075

Bay View Snapper Holiday Park (28 D12) – 8 Gill Rd, Bayview: (06) 836 7084

Affordable Westshore Holiday Park (28 D12) – 88 Meeanee Quay, Westshore, Napier: (06) 835 9456

Kennedy Park Top 10 Resort (28 D12) – Storkey St, Napier: (06) 843 9126

Bay View Van Park (28 C12) – 10 Gill Rd, Bay View: (06) 836 7084

Hastings Top 10 Holiday Park (28 F12) – 610 Windsor Ave, Hastings: (06) 878 6692

Arataki Holiday Park (28 F12) – 139 Arataki Rd, Havelock North: (06) 877 7479

Ocean Beach Camping Ground (28 G13) – Ocean Beach Rd, RD 12, Havelock North: (06) 874 7894

Clifton Beach Reserve Motor Camp (28 F13) – 495 Clifton Rd, R D 2 Hastings on east coast: (06) 875 0263

River's Edge Holiday Park (28 J9) – Harker St, Waipawa; Go to town clock, turn right travelling north: (06) 857 8976

Waipukurau Holiday Park (32 A10) – River Tce, Waipukurau off SH2, adjacent Tuki Tuki River: (06) 858 8184

Warpukurau Holiday Park (32 A10) – River Tce, Waipukurau: (06) 858 8184

Dannevirke Holiday Park (31 C6) – 29 George St, Dannevirke: (06) 374 7625

Taranaki

Seaview Holiday Park (17 D5) – SH3, between Awakino and Mokau: (06) 752 9708

Taumarunui Holiday Park (18 F11) – SH4, Manunui: (07) 895 9345

Urenui Beach Camp Ground (17 G3) – 148 Beach Rd, Urenui: (06) 752 3838

Onaero Bay Holiday Park (17 G2) – SH3, North Taranaki: (06) 752 3643

Belt Rd Seaside Holiday Park (23 B5) – 2 Belt Rd, New Plymouth: (06) 758 0228

Hookner Motor Camp Park (23 B5) – 885 Carrington Rd, New Plymouth: (06) 753 9506

New Plymouth Top 10 Holiday Park (23 B5) – 29 Princes St, New Plymouth: (06) 758 2566

Marine Park Motor Camp (17 G1) – Centennial Ave, Waitara: (06) 754 7121

Fitzroy Beach Holiday Park (23 B5) – 1D Beach St, New Plymouth: (06) 758 2870

Sentry Hill Motel & Roadhouse (23 A6) – 56 Mountain Rd (SH3A): (06) 752 0696

Oakura Beach Holiday Park (23 B4) – 2 Jans Tce, Oakura: (06) 752 7861

Opunake Beach Holiday Park (23 F3) – Beach Rd, Opunake: (06) 761 7525

Stratford Holiday Park (25 B1) – 10 Page St, Stratford: (06) 765 6440

King Edward Park Motor Camp (25 E2) – 70 Waihi Rd, Hawera; SH3, adjacent to Park & gardens: (06) 278 8544

Carlyle Beach Motor Camp (25 G3) – 9 Beach Rd, Patea: (06) 273 8620

Wanganui

Raetihi Holiday Park (26 C10) – 10 Parapara Rd, Raetihi: (06) 385 4176

Ohakune Top 10 Holiday Park (26 C11) – 5 Moore St, Ohakune: (06) 385 8561

Ruakawa Falls & YMCA Raukawa Adventure Centre (26 F11) – Parapara SH4, Kakatahi; 30km south of Raetihi & 60km north of Wanganui: (06) 342 8518

Mowhanau Camp (25 H7) – Kai Iwi Beach: (06) 342 9658

Whanganui River Top 10 Holiday Park (26 H8) – 460 Somme Pde, Aramoho, Wanganui: (06) 343 8402

Castlecliff Seaside Holiday Park (25 J7) – Cnr Karaka & Rangiora St, Wanganui; Adjacent to beach: (06) 344 2227

Bignell St Motel & Caravan Park (26 J8) – 86 Bignell St, Wanganui: (06) 344 2012

Taihape Riverview Holiday Park (27 F2) – Old Abbattoir Rd, Taihape: (06) 388 0718

Manawatu

Bridge Motor Lodge (29 B6) – 2 Bridge St, Bulls: (06) 322 0894

Feilding Holiday Park (29 C7) – 5 Arnott St, Feilding: (06) 323 5623

Koitiata Camping Ground (29 A4) – Turakina Beach Rd, Koitiata: (06) 327 3770

Palmerston North Holiday Park (30 E8) – 133 Dittmer Dr, Palmerston North; Follow southern by-pass route to or from Woodville adjacent to swimming complex: (06) 358 0349

Foxton Beach Motor Camp (29 F4) – Holben Pde, Foxton: (06) 363 8211

Waitarere Beach Motor Camp (29 F4) – 133 Park Ave, Waitarere Beach: (06) 368 8732

Hydrabad Holiday Park (29 G4) – Forest Rd, Waitarere Beach: (06) 368 4941

Levin Motor Camp (29 G5) – 38 Parker Ave, Levin: (06) 368 3549

Byron's Resort (29 J3) – 20 Tasman Rd, Otaki Beach; D/S at rear of camp: (06) 364 8119

Bridge Lodge (29 J4) – 3 Otaki Gorge Rd, Otaki: (06) 364 6667

Wairarapa

Carnival Park Campground (30 F9) – Glasgow St, Pahiatua: (06) 376 6340

Eketahuna Camping (31 H2) – Standly St, Eketahuna: (06) 375 8587

Mawley Park Motor Camp (34 B9) – 15 Oxford St, Masterton: (06) 378 6454

Castlepoint Holiday Park & Motel (34 A13) – Jetty Road. D/S on roadway into camp: (06) 372 6705

Carterton Holiday Park (34 C8) – 196-8 Belvedere Rd, Carterton; 700m from main road, SH2: (06) 379 8267

Martinborough Village Camping (34 E7) – Cnr Princess & Dublin Sts, Martinborough: (06) 306 8919

Wellington

Waikanae Christian Holiday Park (33 A4) – (aka El Rancho), 1199 Kauri Rd, Waikanae: (04) 902 6287

Lindale Motor Park (33 A3) – Ventnor Dr, Paraparaumu: (04) 298 8046

Paekakariki Holiday Park (33 B3) – 180 Wellington Rd, Paekakariki: (04) 292 8292

Camp Elsdon (33 D2) – 18 Raiha St, Porirua: (04) 237 8987

Aotea Camping Ground (33 D2) – 3 Whitford Brown Ave, Porirua: (04) 235 9599

Harcourt Holiday Park (33 C4) – 45 Akatarawa Rd, Upper Hutt; turn off SH2 just north of Caltex Service Station: (04) 526 7400

Capital Gateway Motor Lodge & Caravan Park (33 E2) – 1 Newlands Rd, Newlands: (04) 478 7812

Wellington Top 10 Holiday Park (33 E3) – 95 Hutt Park Rd, Lower Hutt: (04) 568 5913

Catchpool Valley DOC Camp Site (33 F2) – On the coast road, Wainuiomata: (04) 472 7356

SOUTH ISLAND

Marlborough

Okiwi Bay Holiday Park (39 E7) – 15 Renata Rd, Rai Valley, Okiwi Bay: (03) 576 5006

Smiths Farm Holiday Park (40 G9) – 1419 Queen Charlotte Dr, Linkwater, Picton: (03) 574 2806

Havelock Motor Camp (40 G8) – 24 Inglis St, Havelock: (03) 574 2339

Alexanders Holiday Park (40 G10) – Canterbury St, Picton: (03) 573 6378

Picton Top 10 Holiday Park (40 G10) – 70-78 Waikawa Rd, Picton: (03) 573 7212

Picton Campervan Park (40 G10) – 42 Kent St, Nelson Square, Picton: (03) 573 8875

Parklands Marina Holiday Park (40 G10) – 10 Beach Rd, Waikawa Marina, Picton: (03) 573 6343

Waikawa Bay Holiday Park (40 G10) – 5 Waimarama St, Waikawa Bay: (03) 573 7434

Momorangi Bay Holiday Park (40 G9) – Momorangi Bay, Grove Arm, Queen Charlotte Sound: (03) 520 3113

Spring Creek Holiday Park (44 B10) – Rapaura Rd: (03) 570 5893

Blenheim Bridge Top 10 Holiday Park (44 C11) – 78 Grove Rd, Blenheim: (03) 578 3667

Duncannon Holiday Park (44 C11) – St Andrews, SH1; 2km south of Blenheim: (03) 578 8193

A1 Kaikoura Motels & Caravan Park (48 E12) – 11 Beach Rd, Kaikoura; on SH1: (03) 319 5999

Kaikoura Top 10 Holiday Park (48 E12) – 34 Beach Rd, Kaikoura: (03) 319 5362

Alpine-Pacific Holiday Park (48 E12) – 69 Beach Rd, Kaikoura: 0800 692 322

Kaikoura Peketa Beach Holiday Park (48 E11) – Main South Rd, Kaikoura: (03) 319 6299

Kaikoura Coastal Campgrounds, Goose Bay (48 F11) – SH1, Kaikoura: (03) 319 5348

Cheviot Motels & Holiday Park (48 J9) – 44 Ward Rd, Cheviot: (03) 319 8607

Nelson/Tasman

Pohara Beach Top 10 Holiday Park (38 D8) – Abel Tasman Dr, Takaka, Pohara: (03) 525 9500

Totaranui DOC camping ground (38 D10) – Totaranui Rd, Abel Tasman National Park: (03) 528 8083

Abel Tasman Marahau Beach Camp (39 D2) – Franklin St, Marahau: (03) 527 8176

Kaiteriteri Beach Motor Camp (39 E2) – Sandy Bay Rd, Kaiteriteri: (03) 527 8010

Motueka Top 10 Holiday Park (39 E2) – 10 Fearon St, Motueka; north end of town: (03) 528 7189

Mapua Leisure Park (39 G2) – 33 Toru St, Mapua: (03) 540 2666

Greenwood Park (39 H3) – Cnr Lansdowne Rd & Coastal Hwy, Appleby, Richmond: (03) 544 4685

Richmond Motel & Top 10 Holiday Park (39 H3) – 29 Gladstone Rd, SH6, Richmond: (03) 544 7323

Club Waimea (39 H3) – 345 Lower Queens St, Richmond: (03) 543 9179

Maitai Valley Motor Camp (39 G4) – Maitai Valley, Nelson: (03) 548 7729

Brook Valley Holiday Park (39 H4) – Brook St, Brook Valley: (03) 548 0399

Nelson City Holiday Park (39 G4) – 230 Vanguard St, Nelson: (03) 548 1445

Tahuna Beach Holiday Park (39 G3) – 70 Beach Rd, Tahunanui, Nelson: (03) 548 5159

Quinney's Bush Camp & Caravan Park (42 C13) – SH6, Motupiko: (03) 522 4249

Gowan River Holiday Camp (42 G11) – Gowan Valley Rd: (03) 523 9921

Tapawera Settle (42 B13) – Tadmore-Motupiko Rd, Tapawera/Motueka Valley: (03) 522 4334

Kerr Bay DOC camp (42 G13) – St Arnaud; opposite kitchen shelter: (03) 521 1806

Kiwi Park Motel & Holiday Park (42 G9) – 170 Fairfax St, Murchison: (03) 523 9248

West Coast

Karamea Holiday Park (41 A7) – SH67; 3km south of Karamea: (03) 782 6758

Westport Holiday Park & Motel (41 G3) – 31-37 Domett St, Westport: (03) 789 7043

Seal Colony Top 10 Tourist Park (41 G2) – Marine Pde, Carters Beach, Westport; adjacent to beach: (03) 789 8002

The Happy Wanderer (41 G3) – 56 Russell St, Westport; by RSA carpark: (03) 789 8627

Punakaiki Beach Camp (45 B5) – SH6, Owen St, Punakaiki: (03) 731 1894

Rapahoe Beach Motor Camp (45 E4) – 10 Hawken St, Rapahoe: (03) 762 7025

Reefton Domain Camp (46 B9) – Main St, Reefton; on SH7: (03) 732 8477

Nelson Creek Domain (45 E6) – Nelson Creek; camp run jointly by DOC and local community

Central Motor Home Park (45 E4) – 117 Tainui St, Greymouth: (03) 768 4924

Jacquie Grant's Place (45 H2) – Greyhound Rd, Hokitika: 0277 556 550

Greymouth Seaside Top 10 Holiday Park (45 F4) – 2 Chesterfield St, Greymouth: 0800 867 104

South Beach Motel & Motorpark (45 F3) – 318 Main South Rd, SH6, Greymouth: (03) 762 6768

Lake Brunner Motor Camp (45 G6) – 86 Ahau St, Moana: (03) 738 0600

Lake Brunner Country Motel & Holiday Park (45 G6) – 2014 Arnold Valley Rd, Moana: (03) 738 0144

Hokitika Holiday Park (45 H2) – cnr Stafford St & Livingstone St, Hokitika: (03) 755 8172

Shining Star Beachfront Accommodation (45 H2) – SH6; north end of Hokitika: (03) 755 8921

252 Beachside Motels & Holiday Park (45 H2) – 252 Revell St, Hokitika: (03) 755 8773

Jacksons Retreat (45 J6) – SH73, Great Alpine Hwy

Rainforest Holiday Park (49 G6) – 46 Cron St, Franz Josef: (03) 752 0220

Franz Josef Mountain View Top 10 Holiday Park (49 G6) – 2902 Franz Josef Hwy, SH6, Franz Josef: (03) 752 0735

Fox Glacier Holiday Park (49 H4) – Kerrs Rd, Fox Glacier: (03) 751 0821

Fox Glacier Campervan Park (49 H4) – Sullivan Rd, Fox Glacier: (03) 751 0888

Haast Lodge (58 D9) – Marks Rd, Haast; 3km east of Haast Visitor Centre: (03) 750 0703

Haast Beach Holiday Park (58 D8) – Jackson Bay/Haast Beach Rd, Haast: 0800 843 226

Canterbury

Mountain View Top 10 Holiday Park (47 F5) – Cnr Bath St and Main St, Hanmer Springs: (03) 315 7113

Alpine Adventure Holiday Park 47 F5) – 200 Jacks Pass Rd, Hanmer Springs; 2km from village: (03) 315 7112

Hanmer River Holiday Park (47 G5) – 26 Medway Rd, Hanmer Springs: (03) 315 7111

Alpine Apartments & Campground (47 G5) – 9 Fowlers Lane, Hanmer Springs: (03) 315 7478

Pines Holiday Park (47 F5) – Jacks Pass Rd, Hanmer Springs: (03) 315 7152

Waiau Motor Camp (47 H7) – 9 Highfield St, Waiau: (03) 315 6672
Waipara Sleepers Motor Camp (54 C8) – 200m from junction of SH1 & SH7, Waipara: (03) 314 6003
Mt Lyford Lodge (48 F8) – 10 Mt Lyford Forrest Drive, RDI, Waiau: (03) 315 6446
Greta Valley Camping Ground (54 B10) – 7 Valley Rd, Greta Valley, SH1; halfway between Amberley and Cheviot: (03) 314 3340
Delhaven Motels & Caravan Park (54 D8) – 124 Carters Rd, Amberley; SH1: (03) 314 8550
Woodend Beach Holiday Park (56 B10) – 14 Beach Rd, Woodend Beach: (03) 312 7643
Waikuku Beach Holiday Park (56 B10) – 1 Domain Tce, Waikuku Beach; on SH1: (03) 312 7600
Leithfield Beach Motor Camp (56 A11) – 18 Lucas Dr, Leithfield Beach: (03) 314 8518
Rangiora Holiday Park (56 B9) – 337 Lehmans Rd, Rangiora: (03) 313 5759
Pineacres Holiday Park (56 B10) – 740 Main North Rd, Kaiapoi; on SH1: (03) 327 5022
Blue Skies (56 C10) – 12 Williams St, Kaiapoi; southern end of Old Main Rd: (03) 327 8007
Kairaki Beach Holiday Park (56 C10) – Featherstone Ave, Kaiapoi; at mouth of Waimakariri River: (03) 327 7335
Riverlands Holiday Park (56 C10) – 45 Doubledays Rd, Kaiapoi: (03) 327 5511
219 On Johns Motel & Holiday Park (56 C9) – 219 Johns Rd, Belfast: (03) 323 8640
Addington Accommodation Park (56 D9) – 47-51 Whiteleigh Ave, Addington, Christchurch: (03) 338 9770
Spencer Beach Holiday Park (54 G8) – Heyders Rd, Spencerville, Christchurch: (03) 329 8721
Amber Park (56 D9) – 308 Blenheim Rd, Riccarton, Christchurch: (03) 348 3327
Christchurch Top 10 Holiday Park (56 D9) – 39 Meadow St, Papanui, Christchurch: (03) 352 9176
Riccarton Park Holiday Park (56 D9) – 19 Main South Rd, Upper Riccarton, Christchurch: (03) 348 5690
South Brighton Motor Camp (56 D10) – 59 Halsey St, Christchurch: (03) 388 9844
All Seasons Holiday Park (56 D10) – 5 Kidbrooke St, Christchurch: (03) 384 9490
North South Holiday Park (56 D9) – Cnr Johns Rd & Sawyers Arms Rd, Harewood, Christchurch: (03) 359 5993
Alpine View Holiday Park (56 D8) – 650-678 Main South Rd, Templeton, Lincoln: (03) 349 7666
Akaroa Top 10 Holiday Park (56 G12) – 96 Morgans Rd, Banks Peninsula; off Old Coach Rd from SH75: (03) 304 7471
Duvauchelle Holiday Park (56 G12) – Seafield Rd, Duvauchelle, Banks Peninsula: (03) 304 5777
Okains Bay Motor Camp (56 F13) – Okains Bay, Banks Peninsula: (03) 304 8789
Kowai Pass Domain Camp (55 B4) – Domain Rd, Springfield; off SH73: (03) 318 4887
Glentunnel Holiday Park (55 D4) – SH77, Scenic Route 72, Homebush Rd, Glentunnel: (03) 318 2868

South Canterbury

Rakaia River Holiday Park (55 G5) – SH1, Raikaia; south end of Rakaia Bridge: (03) 302 7257
Coronation Holiday Park (55 J3) – 780 East St, Ashburton: (03) 308 6603
Abisko Lodge & Campground (55 F2) – 74 Main St, Methven: (03) 302 8875
Pudding Hill Lodge (52 J8) – SH72, Pudding Hill: (03) 302 9627
Ashburton Holiday Park (62 D8) – Tinwald Domain, Ashburton: (03) 308 6805
Grumpys Retreat N' Holiday Park (61 E5) – 7 Keen St, Orari Bridge: (03) 693 7453
Geraldine Holiday Park (61 F4) – Cnr SH79 & Hislop St, Geraldine: (03) 693 8147
Fairlie Gateway Top 10 Holiday Park (61 F1) – 10 Allandale Rd, Fairlie: (03) 685 8375
Lake Tekapo Holiday Park (60 E9) – Lakeside Dr, Lake Tekapo: (03) 680 6825
Lake Ruataniwha Holiday Park (59 H6) – Max Smith Drive, Twizel: (03) 435 0613
Omarama Holiday Park (67 A3) – 1 Omarama Ave, Omarama; junction of SH8 & SH83, closed in winter: (03) 438 9875
Ahuriri Motels (67 A3) – SH83, 5 Claycliff Dve, Omarama: (03) 438 9451
Temuka Holiday Park (61 G5) – 1 Fergusson Dr, Temuka: (03) 615 7241
Timaru Top 10 Holiday Park (61 J4) – 154a Selwyn St, Timaru: (03) 684 7690
Glenmark Motor Camp (61 J4) – 30 Beaconsfield Rd, Timaru: (03) 684 3682
Otematata Holiday Park (67 C5) – East Rd, Otematata: (03) 438 7826
Kurow Holiday Park (67 D7) – 76 Bledisloe St, Kurow; on SH83, west end of town: (03) 436 0725
Fisherman's Bend, Lake Aviemore (67 C7) – Nth side of Lake Aviemore (Oct to Apr only): (03) 689 8079
Knottingley Park (68 D12) – Waihoa Back Rd, Waimate; dump station at rear end of public toilets in camping area: (03) 689 8079
Victoria Park Camp and Cabins (68 D12) – Naylor St, Waimate: (03) 689 8079
Kelcey's Bush Farmyard Holiday Park (68 C11) – Upper Mills Rd, Waimate: (03) 689 8057
Waitaki Mouth Holiday Park (68 F13) – 305 Kaik Rd, Waitaki: (03) 431 3880
Oamaru Top 10 Holiday Park (68 H11) – Chelmer St, Oamaru; off SH1 near railway: (03) 434 7666
Hampden Beach Motor Camp (74 B13) – 2 Carlisle St, Hampden: (03) 439 4439
Moeraki Village Holiday Park (74 B14) – 114 Haven St, Moeraki: (03) 439 4759

Otago

Larchview Holiday Park (67 G5) – Swimming Dam Rd, Naseby: (03) 444 9904
Ranfurly Holiday Park (67 H5) – 8 Reade St, Ranfurly: (03) 444 9144
Blind Billy's Holiday Camp (74 D8) – Mold St, Middlemarch: (03) 464 3355
Waikouaiti Beach Motor Camp (74 E12) – 186 Beach St, Waikouaiti: (03) 465 7366
Leith Valley Touring Park (74 G11) – 103 Malvern St, Dunedin: (03) 467 9936
Dunedin Holiday Park (74 H11) – 41 Victoria Rd, St Kilda, Dunedin: (03) 455 4690
Lake Waihola Holiday Park (79 B6) – Waihola Domain: (03) 417 8908
Brighton Motor Camp (74 H10) – 1044 Brighton Rd, Brighton, Dunedin: (03) 481 1404
Aaron Lodge Holiday Park (74 H11) – 162 Kaikorai Valley Rd, Dunedin: (03) 476 4725
Portobello Village Tourist Park (74 G12) – 27 Hereweka St, Dunedin: (03) 478 0359

Clutha Valley

Lake Hawea Holiday Park (66 C9) – SH6; 500m north of Lake Hawea turn-off: (03) 443 1767
Aspiring Campervan Park (66 D8) – Studholme Rd, Wanaka: (03) 443 6603
Lake Outlet Holiday Park (66 D8) – 197 Outlet Rd, Wanaka: (03) 443 7478
Glendhu Bay Motor Camp (65 D7) – Mt Aspiring Rd, Wanaka: (03) 443 7243
Wanaka Lakeview Holiday Park (66 D8) – 212 Brownston St, Wanaka; on right just before camp: (03) 443 7883
Arrowtown Holiday Park (65 G6) – 11 Suffolk St, Arrowtown: (03) 442 1876
Glenorchy Holiday Park & Backpackers (65 F2) – 2 Oban St, Glenorchy; at the head of Lake Wakatipu: (03) 441 0303
Queenstown Top 10 Holiday Park 'Creeksyde' (65 H4) – 54 Robins Rd, Queenstown: (03) 442 9447
Shotover Top 10 Holiday Park (65 G4) – 70 Arthurs Point Rd, Queenstown: (03) 442 9306
Frankton Motor Camp (65 H5) – Yewlett Cres, Frankton; in front of Remarkables Hotel, Queenstown: (03) 442 2079
Queenstown Lake View Holiday Park (65 H4) – Breacon St, Queenstown; 150m from Gondola: (03) 442 7252
Kingston Motels & Holiday Park (72 B8) – 2 Kent St, Kingston: (03) 248 8501
Cairnmuir Camping Ground (66 H8) – 219 Cairnmuir Rd, Bannockburn: (03) 445 1956
Cromwell Top 10 Holiday Park (66 H9) – 1 Alpha St, Cromwell: (03) 445 0164
Chalets Holiday Park (66 H8) – 102 Barry Ave, Cromwell: (03) 445 1260
Alexandra Holiday Park (73 A2) – 44 Manuherikia Rd, Alexandra: (03) 448 8297
Alexandra Tourist Park (73 A2) – 31 Ngapara St, Alexandra: (03) 448 8861
Clyde Holiday & Sporting Complex (66 J10) – Whitby St, Clyde: (03) 449 2713
Balclutha Camping Ground (79 E3) – 56 Charlotte St, Balclutha: (03) 418 0088
Kaka Point Camping Ground (79 G4) – 39 Tarata St, Kaka Point; on coastal rd: (03) 412 8801
Owaka Motor Camp (79 G3) – Ryley St, Owaka: (03) 415 8728
Keswick Park Camping Ground (79 H3) – 2 Park Lane, Pounawea: (03) 419 1110
Pounawea Motor Camp (79 H3) – Park Lane, Pounawea: (03) 415 8483
Gold Park Motor Camp (79 A3) – Harrington St, Lawrence: (03) 485 9850
Curio Bay Camping Ground (78 H11) – 601 Waikawa-Curio Bay Rd, Curio Bay: (03) 246 8897
Catlins Woodstock Lodge & Camp (79 G2) – 348 Catlins Valley Rd, Owaka: (03) 415 8583
Papatowai Motor Camp (79 J1) – 2503 Papatowai Highway, Papatowai: (03) 415 8565
McLean Falls Eco Motels & Holiday Park (78 G12) – 29 Rewcastle Rd, Owaka: (03) 415 8668

Southland

Glenquoich Caravan Park (71 D7) – SH6; 1km north of Athol, beside Mataura River: (03) 248 8840
Mossburn Country Park (71 F5) – 333 Mossburn Five Rivers Rd, Mossburn: (03) 248 6313
Possum Lodge Motel & Holiday Park (70 E10) – 13 Murrell Ave, Manapouri: (03) 249 6623
Manapouri Motels & Holiday Park (70 E10) – 50 Manapouri-Te Anau Rd, Manapouri: (03) 249 6624
Te Anau Great Lakes Holiday Park (70 D11) – Cnr Luxmore Dr & Milford Rd, Te Anau: (03) 249 8538
Te Anau Top 10 Holiday Park (70 D11) – 128 Te Anau Tce & Mokonui St, Te Anau: (03) 249 7462
Te Anau Lakeview Holiday Park (70 D11) – 1 Te Anau-Manapouri Rd, Te Anau; opposite DOC Visitor Centre: (03) 249 7457
Fiordland Great Views Holiday Park (70 C11) – 129 Milford Rd, Te Anau: (03) 249 7059
Knobs Flat (64 H9) – SH94: (03) 249 9122
Tuatapere Motel (76 F12) – 73 Main St, Tuatapere: (03) 226 6250
Riverton Caravan Park (76 H14) – Hamlet St, Riverton: (03) 234 8526
Invercargill Caravan Park (77 E5) – A&P Showgrounds, 20 Victoria Ave, Invercargill: (03) 218 8787
Coachmans Inn Camp Ground (77 E5) – 705 Tay St, Invercargill; east end: (03) 217 6046
Beach Rd Holiday Park (77 F4) – Follow signs to Invercargill airport, 8km to the west: (03) 213 0400
Invercargill Top 10 Holiday Park (77 E5) – 77 McIvor Rd, Invercargill: (03) 215 9032
Amble On Inn (77 F5) – 145 Chesney St, Invercargill: (03) 216 5214
Lorneville Holiday Park (77 E5) – 352 Lorne Dancre Rd, Lorneville, Invercargill: (03) 235 8031
Bluff Camping Ground (77 G5) – Gregory St, Bluff; off SH1: (03) 212 8774
Gore Motor Camp (78 B9) – 35 Broughton St (SH1), Gore: (03) 208 4919
Dolamore Park (78 A8) – About 12km west of Gore: (03) 208 9080
Winton Golf Course & Camp (77 B4) – Sub Station Rd, Winton: (03) 236 8422

Motorhome Public dump station (wastewater disposal site)

NORTH ISLAND

Far North

Kerikeri Public D/S (4 A8) – Cobham Rd, by memorial hall, Kerikeri
Gibby's Place (4 A8) – 331 Kerikeri Rd, Kerikeri
Mangonui Public D/S (2 H8) – Beach Road, next to public toilets, 400m from SH10, Kaitaia
Omapere Public D/S (3 E3) – SH12 on harbourside next to Information Centre, opposite Opononi State School, Omapere
Kawakawa Public D/S (4 C9) – Waimio St, off SH1, on the right hand side past entrance to bowling club, Kawakawa
Kaitaia Public D/S (1 J6) – Behind Community Centre, corner of Mathews Ave and SH1, Kaitaia
Kaikohe Public D/S (3 C7) – Recreation Rd, Kaikohe; D/S on roadside at rear of Pioneer Village toilets

Northland

Dargaville Public D/S (3 J7) – Mobil Service Station on SH12 in town centre
Dargaville Public D/S (3 J7) – Caltex Service Station on SH12 in town centre
Dargaville Public D/S (3 J7) – Northern Wairoa Museum, Mt Wellesley; In public car park, Dargaville
Ngunguru Public D/S (4 F13) – Te Maika Rd, at North end of Ngunguru; Oppsite the school, near public toilets
Kamo Public D/S (4 F11) – On SH1, Lillian St, behind Fire Station, Kamo
Caltex Star Mart (4 F11) – Tarewa Rd, Whangarei
Whangarei Public D/S (4 G12) – Council Waste Water Treatment Plant; Kioreroa Rd, Whangarei
Recreational Concepts (4 F11) – 6 South End Ave, Whangarei
Waipu Public D/S (6 A8) – Langs Beach, next to public toilet, Waipu
Warkworth Public D/S (6 E10) – Kowahi Park, cnr of SH1 & Sandspit, Warkworth
Warkworth Hire Centre (6 E10) – D/S just inside main gate, Warkworth

Hibiscus Coast

Orewa Public D/S (6 G10) – South end of Orewa by KFC, Orewa
Whangaparaoa Public D/S (6 H10) – Gulf Harbour adjacent to public toilet by public boat ramp, Whangaparaoa

Auckland

Shelly Beach (7 A1) – Kaipara Harbour, Helensville; Beside public toilet
Waitakere Public D/S (7 D2) – McLeod Rd extension, Te Atatu South, fenced area in McLeod Pk opposite Riverglade Parkway road
Claris Landfill D/S (36 E5) – Gray Rd, Great Barrier Island
Manukau Mobil SS (7 F5) – Wiri Station Road, Manukau
Te Arai Point Public D/S (6 C9) – Beside public toilets, Te Arai
Wellsford Public D/S (6 D8) – Centenial Park, off SH1, Wellsford
Maraetai Public D/S (7 E7) – 188 Maraetai Dve, bowling club, Maraetai

Counties

Waharau Public D/S (8 G9) – Opposite Waharau Regional Park, Kaiaua Coast
Pukekohe Public D/S (7 H5) – Franklin Rd, Pukekohe; 400m past sports stadium
Tuakau Public D/S (7 J6) – In St Stephens Drive, Tuakau, opposite Police Station
Drury Public D/S (7 H5) – Tui St, behind shops, Pukekohe
Waiuku Public D/S (7 J4) – Jane Gifford Reserve, on bypass road to Manukau Heads, on right.

Hauraki/Coromandel

Ngatea Public D/S (8 J11) – On SH2 in village centre near public hall
Stuart Moore Motors BP Service Station (8 H11) – Thames, turn into Bank Street opposite the Toyota factory, East corner of parking area
Coromandel Public Dump Station (8 C11) – Wharf Road Scenic Reserve, Coromandel; Turn left towards Long Bay, 300m over bridge, near public toilets
Whitianga Public D/S (8 D13) – At rubbish station at Tin Town opposite airport
Pauanui Public D/S (8 F14) – Pleasant Point Boat Ramp (off Vista Paku) –
Whangamata Public D/S (8 J14) – Whangamata Domain, Whangamata; Turn off Port Rd into Aicken Rd, at public toilets
Waihi Public D/S (10 F10) – In Victoria Park, Waihi on SH2; Near public toilets in the park
Paeroa Public D/S (10 E9) – Marshall St, Paeroa; Near public toilet and information centre
Paeroa RV Centre (10 E9) – Coronation Rd, Paeroa
Tairua Public D/S (10 A11) – 175 Beach Road, Tairua
Cooks Beach Public D/S (8 D13) – Next to public toilets, Cooks Beach

Waikato

Te Kauwhata Public D/S (9 F5) – Turn off Mahi Rd into Domain in township
Te Aroha Public D/S (10 G9) – Next to public toilets on Lawrence St
Matamata Public D/S (12 C11) – On SH27, turn off Broadway into Hetana St; Near public toilets
Ngaruawahia Public D/S (9 J4) – In Waikato Esplanade Domain (The Point); On riverbank between Rowing Club & Railway bridge
Tirau Public D/S (12 E11) – Near public toilets down service lane from SH1, behind OK Tirau Motel
Te Awamutu Public D/S (11 E7) – On SH3, at Mobil Service Station at north end of town
Hamilton Public D/S (11 C6) – SH1, Lincoln St, entrance near model railway, Hamilton
Raglan Public D/S (11 C3) – Raglan Club, 22 Bow St, Raglan

Rotorua

Rotorua Public D/S (13 G4) – Entrance to Wastewater Treatment Plant, Te Ngae Rd
Tokoroa Public D/S (12 H12) – Whakauru St, Tokoroa; Next to sewerage treatment station
Wairakei BP Service Station & Truck Stop (19 C5) – On SH1 opposite hotel; D/S in parking area at the rear on left side
Kinloch Marina D/S (19 D4) – In Marina Car Park, Kinloch
Taupo Public D/S (19 D5) – 2 Mile Bay Boat Ramp, Taupo; 5 km south on SH1, next to public toilet
Tokaanu Public D/S (19 G3) – At boat ramp
Putaruru Public D/S (12 F11) – Market St. Heading south on SH1, first left turn after roundabout.

Bay of Plenty

Katikati Public D/S (10 G11) – North side of Katikati shopping centre turn off SH2 into roadway beside the A&P showgrounds
Mt Maunganui Shell Service Station (13 B4) – Hewletts Rd, Mt Maunganui on main route to Tauranga via Harbour Bridge
Tauranga BP Service Station (13 B3) – Chapel St end of Waihi-Mt Maunganui Expressway via Harbour Bridge, Tauranga
Te Puke Public D/S (13 C5) – Situated at public toilets
Tauranga Public D/S (10 J13, 94 D2) – Maleme Rd, can be reached from Oropi Rd or Cameron Rd, close to transfer station, Tauranga
Omokoroa Public D/S (10 H12) – Omokoroa Beach at west end of Peninsula in Omokoroa Domain Car and Trailer Park, Omokoroa
Omokoroa Public D/S (10 J12) – 1.9km from SH2 opposite Fire Station, turn left into road to main pump station 200m.
Mt Maunganui Public D/S (10 J14, 13 B4, 94 B3) – Tauranga Airport. Take first road on right past 'Classic Flyers NZ' Building.

Eastern Bay of Plenty

Kawerau Public D/S (14 G8) – Behind Bowling Club opposite information centre, town centre
Whakatane Public D/S (14 E10) – Caltex Service Station, Commerce St, next to fire station
Ohope Public D/S (14 E11) – Situated at public toilets, half-way along beach before bridge; In Maraetotara Reserve with play equipment;
Waiotahi Beach Public D/S (14 F13) – Waiotahi Beach Domain; On SH35 at public toilets
Opotiki BP Service Station (14 F13) – Cnr Bridges St & Church St; Past the last diesel pump
Murupara Public D/S (20 B11) – Behind BP Station, Pine Dr; off SH38, Murupara
Omaio Public D/S (15 D5) – Omaio Domain, off SH35
Te Kaha School House Bay (15 C6) – New toilet block, Te Kaha

Eastland

Gisborne Mobil Service Station (22 D10) – 49 Wainui Rd, Gisborne; East end of main road across bridge
Gisborne BP Service Station (22 D10) – Corner Ormond Rd & Sheridan St, Gisborne
Te Araroa Public D/S (16 B12) – Transfer Stn, 26 Te Arawapaia Rd, Te Araroa
Gisborne Public D/S (22 D10, 100 C3, 99 C2) – Hallrite Plumbing and Gasfitting Yard, 71 Awapuni Rd, Gisborne

Hawkes Bay

Napier Public D/S (28 D12) – Marine Parade by Ellison
Napier Public D/S (28 D12) – 104 Latham St, Napier; Beside Council Sewerage Pump Station
Clive BP S/S (28 E12) – Main Rd, Clive
Hastings BP S/S (28 F11) – Stortford Lodge; Corner Maraekakaho Rd & Heretaunga St
Waipawa Public D/S (28 J9) – 1 High St, Waipawa
Takapau Public D/S (16 F11) – 15 Nang St, Takapau

Taranaki

New Plymouth Public D/S, Mobil Service Station (23 B5) – Corner Leach & Eliot Streets
New Plymouth Public D/S, BP Service Station (23 B5) – 71 Powderham St, New Plymouth
Opunake Public D/S (23 F3) – Beach Rd, Opunake
Whangamomona Domain (24 C11) – 32 Whangamomona Rd
Normanby Public D/S (25 D1) – On Main Hwy, North of Hawera, Normanby
Aotea Park Public D/S (25 F4) – Cnr of Chester St & SH3, Waverley
Opunake Public D/S (23 F3) – Corner Napier and King Sts, Opunake

Wanganui

Taihape Public D/S (27 F2) – Linnet St, Taihape
Wanganui Public D/S (26 J8, 109 C3) – Springvale Park, London St, Wanganui
Ohakune Public D/S (26 C11) – Ohakune Club, 72 Goldfinch Ave, Ohakune
Taihape BP Connection (27 F2) – 80-88 Hautapu St, Taihape

Manawatu

Feilding BP Express Service Station (29 C7) – Corner Kimbolton Rd & Aorangi St next to KFC
Feilding Sewerage Treatment Plant (29 C7) – Kawa Kawa Rd Feilding; Past abattoir & Manfield Racetrack, on LHS down long drive, turn right at end of drive
Ashhurst Public D/S (30 D9) – Ashhurst Domain, SH3, Ashhurst
Palmerston North Caltex Service Station (29 E7) – Cnr Fitzherbert Ave & College St
Palmerston North Public D/S, Totara Rd Wastewater Plant (29 E4) – Behind Racecourse, Palmerston North
Foxton Public D/S (29 F5) – Inside the entrance to Victoria Park off Victoria St
Levin Public D/S (29 G5) – Sheffield St, Levin
Otaki Public D/S (29 J4) – Riverbank Rd, Otaki; Off SH1 just north of the Otaki River bridge

Wairarapa

Pongaroa Public D/S (30 G13) – Behind public toilets on SH52; not good van access
Woodville Public D/S (30 D10) – Swimming pool area, Normanby Rd, Woodville
Mawley Park (34 B9) – 15 Oxford St, Masterton; On bank of Waipoua River
Greytown Public D/S (34 C7) – At Arbor Reserve, Greytown; Rest/picnic area on SH2 opposite Kuranui college
Martinborough Public D/S (34 E7) – West end of Dublin St, Martinborough; Close to Motor Camp & swimming pool
Carterton Public D/S (34 C7) – Dalefield Rd, Carterton

Wellington

Upper Hutt Public D/S (33 D4, 111 B5) – On SH2 (River Rd), Upper Hutt; 500m north of Moonshine Bridge at Rest Area sign, beside toilets on gravel road by river
Tawa Public D/S (33 D2) – Tawa Swimming Pool, Davis St; D/S opposite pool entrance
Wellington Public D/S (33 F1) – 25 Urlic St, Plimmerton
Wellington Public D/S (33 F1, 110 D2) – Ngauranga Gorge, Hutt Rd, Wellington
Paraparaumu Public D/S (33 B4) – Mobil Service Station, corner SH1 and Kapiti Rd, Paraparaumu
Porirua Public D/S (33 D2) – Prosser St, Porirua
Lower Hutt Public D/S (33 E3, 110 D3) – Seaview Marina, Port Road, Lower Hutt

SOUTH ISLAND

Marlborough

Blenheim Public D/S (44 C10) – Mobil Service Station, Cnr of Grove Rd and Nelson St, Blenheim
Kaikoura BP Service Station (48 E12) – on SH1; north side of Kaikoura
Picton D/S (35 J3, 40 G10, 44 A11, 113 C3) – Challenge Service Station, Corner Wairau Rd and Kent St, Picton
Kaikoura Public D/S (48 E12) – South Bay Domain, Kaikoura

Nelson/Tasman

Collingwood Public D/S (37 C7) – At entry to Collingwood Motor Camp, at car park beside information centre
Takaka Mobil Service Station (38 E8) – Cnr Commercial St & Motupipi Rd, Takaka
Takaka Public D/S (38 E8) – Takaka Information Centre in the car park
Motueka Public D/S (38 G10) – Follow sign from High St into Tudor St to Hickmott Pl
Richmond Public D/S (43 A4) – Jubilee Park, Gladstone Rd, Richmond
Nelson Public D/S (38 J11) – Mobil Tahunanui, 28 Tahunanui Dr, Nelson
Nelson Public D/S (38 J12) – BP Truck Stop, Hay St, Port Nelson
Murchison Public D/S (42 G9) – On SH6 by entry to TNL Freight Yard, between Mobil Service Station and Matakitaki Bridge
Murchison Public D/S (42 G9) – Mobil Service Station, SH6, Murchison; on back fence past the truck diesel pump

West Coast

Greymouth Public D/S (45 F4) – Caltex S/S Tainui St, Greymouth
Hokitika Public D/S (45 H2) – SH6; north end of town, 1km from centre, adjacent to sewage ponds in large laybys on either side of road
Goldfields Tourist Centre (50 A11) – Ross; beside public toilet on roadside
Glacier Motors Mobil Service Station (49 G6) – Franz Josef, on SH6
Haast Public D/S (58 D9) – 3km from junction of SH6 & Jackson Bay Rd, Haast
DOC camp site, rest area (58 E12) – On SH6; 45km east of Haast beside the river, in front of toilet block, Pleasant Flat
Westport Public D/S (41 G3) – New World car park, Palmerston St, Westport
Nelson Creek Public D/S (45 E6) – Nelson Creek Domain, Nelson Creek
Blackball Public D/S (45 D5) – Adjacent to Sports Domain
Runanga Public D/S (45 E4) – Runanga Workingmen's Club, corner of Pitt and McGowan Sts, Runanga
Ross Goldfields Information and Heritage Centre (50 B11, 51 B2) – 4 Aylmer St, Ross
Greymouth Public D/S (45 F3) – New World car park, cnr High and Marlborough St
Greymouth Public D/S (45 F3) – Cobden Bridge rest area, north side of bridge

Canterbury

Cheviot Public D/S (48 J9) – Centre of village, accessed from service lane (key at Mobil service station)
Waikari Public D/S (54 B8) – in domain, Princess St; signposted off SH7 at Waikari (Key held by Mary Booker, 20 Princes St or Roger Mander, 18 Princes St)
Oxford Public D/S (53 F4) – High St, Oxford; approximately 800m from the cnr of Oxford Rd & Main St
Amberley Public D/S (54 D8) – Mobil S/S Carters Rd, Amberley
Kaiapoi Public D/S (54 G8, 56 C10) – Charles St, Kaiapoi
Rangiora Public D/S (53 F7, 56 B9) 22 Railway Rd, Rangiora

Christchurch

Christchurch Public D/S (53 F3, 56 D9, 119 C5, 120 E4) – Styx Mill Transfer Station, off SH1 between Belfast and Redwood, Christchurch)
Styx Mill Rd Transfer Station (53 H7) – Off SH1 between Belfast & Redwood, Christchurch; enter transfer station drive to kiosk and ask to use D/S
A & P Showgrounds (53 J6) – Curletts Rd, Christchurch; between motorway corridor and Lincoln/Halswell Rd intersection
Lincoln Club (53 J6) – 24 Edward St, Lincoln
Templeton Public D/S (56 D8) – at information kiosk; off SH1
Rolleston BP Service Station (56 E8) – Rolleston

South Canterbury

Washdyke Public D/S (61 J5) – Allied Truck Stop site, Sheffield St, Timaru
Fairlie Public D/S (60 F12, 61 F1) – Gladstone Grand Hotel, 43 Main St, Fairlie
Lake Tekapo Public D/S 2 (60 E9) – On road in Lake Drive, follow Motor Camp sign for 200m.
Rakaia Public D/S (55 G5) – Rolleston St, Rakaia; off SH1, beside public toilet
Rakaia Gorge Public D/S (55 D2) – SH72; at public toilet, north side of river
Methven Public D/S (55 F1) – Mobil Service Station (Methven Motor Services), Hall St, Methven
Lake Tekapo Public D/S 1 (60 E9) – Tekapo village; on roadside, 400m from village centre on SH8 towards Fairlie
Twizel Public D/S (59 H6) – Turn off SH8 to town centre, adjacent to Shell Service Station
Timaru Public D/S (61 J4) – Follow truck by-pass route off Marine Pde to Caroline Bay; adjacent to toilet and carpark by rollerskating rink
St Andrews Domain (68 B13) – Main South Rd, St Andrews; 250m south
Lake Aviemore (67 C6) – North side of Waitaki Lakes; closed May to Oct
Waitangi Bay (67 C7) – Waitaki Lakes; closed May to Oct
Gillies Caltex Service Station (68 H11) – Thames St, Oamaru

Otago

DK Auto Shell Service Station (74 E12) – Waikouaiti; at rear
Warrington Public D/S (74 F12) – Warrington Domain; off SH1 at Evansdale, follow signs to beach, at public toilet
Mosgiel Public D/S (74 H10) – BP Service Station, 77 Gordon Rd, Mosgiel
BP Dunedin North (74 H11) – one way system, south near gardens
Dunedin Shell Service Station (74 H11) – turn off SH1 for Andersons Bay Rd, adjacent to Old Gas Works between Hillside St & McBride St
Dunedin Shell Service Station (74 H11) – Kaikorai Valley Rd, Kaikorai Valley; off SH1, 3km
Fleetwood Motors (74 H10) – Shell Service Station, SH1, Fairfield Straight
Ranfurly Public D/S (67 H5) – Intersection of Northland and Charlemont St, off SH85, Ranfurly
Dunedin Public D/S (74 H11) – BP Truck Stop, 867 Cumberland St, Dunedin

Clutha Valley

Boundary Creek Reserve (DOC camp site) (58 J10) – Approximately 20km south of Makarora, 12km on Haast side of the Neck
Kidds Bush Reserve (DOC camp site) (66 A9) – Hunter Valley Rd, Lake Hawea
Arrowtown Public D/S (65 G6) – Behind the Lake Districts Museum at the public toilets
Queenstown BP Connect Public D/S (65 H4) – Cnr SH6 & Frankton Rd, Queenstown
Caltex Service Station (66 H8) – Village centre, Cromwell
Caltex Service Station (72 A13) – 50 Centennial Ave, Alexandra
Council Depot (72 D13) – Teviot St, Roxburgh; close to motorcamp
Lawrence Public D/S (79 A3) – SH8; on west side of town beside rest area
Clinton Public D/S (78 C13) – On the roadside adjacent to park, from SH1 turn at BP Service Station and War Memorial
Albion Cricket Club (66 D9) – SH6, Main Rd, Luggate
Omakau Public D/S (66 H12, 67 H1) – Omakau Recreation Reserve, 13 Alton St, Omakau
Cromwell Public D/S (66 H9) – BP Service Station, Sargood Drive
Queenstown Public D/S (65 H5, 125 B2, 126 B2) – Cemetery Rd
Clyde (66 J10) – Clyde Recreation Reserve, 7 Whitby St.
Tapanui Public D/S (73 J2) – Bushy Hill St.

Southland

Milford Sound Public D/S (64 D9) – In car park
Knobs Flat Public D/S (64 H9) – SH 94, Te Anau, Council operated
Te Anau Public D/S (70 C11) – Lake Front Dr, Te Anau; at boat harbour, adjacent to public toilets
Manapouri Public D/S (70 E11) – Hillside Rd, Manapouri
Otautau Public D/S (76 F14) – At public toilet, behind Plunket Rooms in Hulme St, just off Main St
Riverton BP Service Station (77 E2) – Bay Rd, towards Riverton Rocks
Invercargill Public D/S (77 E5) – Rockgas Invercargill, 20 Spey St, Invercargill
Riversdale Service Station (72 J9) – SH94, Riversdale
Gore Public D/S (78 B9) – Gore A&P Showgrounds; down first entry
Gore Public D/S (78 B9) – Richmond Rd, Gore; at kerbside, 750m upstream from SH1 Bridge and Trout Monument
Winton Public D/S (77 B4) – SH6; behind Mobil Service Station, Winton
Tokanui Shop (78 G9) – Southern Scenic Route through Catlins (old SH92), Tokanui

A

1849 Dansey Pass Hotel - Kyeburn Diggings 67 G6
Abbotsford 124 F5
Abbotslee Historic Home - Waipawa 28 J9
Abel Tasman Coastal Track - Great Walk 38 E10 39 C2
Abel Tasman Memorial 38 D9
Abel Tasman National Park 38 E9 39 C1
Acacia Bay 19 D5
Acheron Hut 43 J4 48 B8
Acheron Lakes 64 J10 70 A14 71 A3
Acland Falls 61 C5
Ada Pass Hut 46 D14 47 D2
Adair 61 J4 68 A13
Adams Flat 79 C4
Adams Wilderness Area 50 F9
Addington 53 H7 56 D9 119 G3 120 D2
Adelaide Tarn 37 F6
Adelaide Tarn Hut 37 F6
Adele Island 38 F10 39 D2
Agrodome - Rotorua 13 F4
Ahaura 45 D6
Ahikiwi 3 G6
Ahikouka 34 C7
Ahipara 1 J5 3 A1
Ahititi 17 F4
Ahuriri 103 B1
Ahuriri Base Hut 58 H13 59 H2
Ahuriri Conservation Park 58 H14 59 H3
Ahuriri Flat 79 G3
Ahuroa 6 F9
Aickens 45 J7
Aiguilles Island 36 B4
Airedale 68 G11
Airim Basin Hut 64 E14 65 E4
Aka Aka 7 J4 9 D1
Akaroa, NI 30 G13 31 G7
Akaroa, SI 56 G12
Akarua 111 D4
Akatere 2 G9
Akerama 4 D10
Akina 102 D2 103 C5
Akitio 32 G8
Albany Heights 6 J9 7 C3 88 F2
Albany Village 88 F2
Albert Town 66 D8
Albury 60 G13 61 G2
Aldermen Islands 10 A13
Alexandra 72 A13 73 A2
Alford Forest 51 J7
Alfred Track 23 D5
Alfredton 30 H10 31 H4
Alfriston 7 F6 9 A3 90 E6
Algies Bay 6 F10
Alicetown 110 C3
Allandale 60 F12 61 F1
Allanton 74 H9
Allendale 54 J8 56 F10
Allenton 55 H2 62 C8
Allports Island 35 J3 40 G10
Alma 68 H11
Almadale 30 B8 31 B2
Almer Hut 49 H6
Alpha Hut 33 B6
Alpine Lake / Ata Puai 49 F5
Alton 24 H8 25 E3
Amberley 54 D8
Amberley Beach 54 D9 56 A11
Amodeo Bay 8 B10 36 J4
Amuri Skifield 47 E4
Anakiwa 35 K3 40 G9
Anama 61 B6
Anatimo 38 D9 39 B1
Anatoki Forks Hut 37 F6
Anatoki Track 37 E6
Anawhata 7 E2
Anchor Island 69 H2 75 B2
Anchorage Hut 38 F10 39 D2
Anchorage Island 80 H2
Ancient Kauri Kingdom - Awanui 1 H6
Anderson Memorial Hut 33 A6
Andersons Bay 124 D4
Anderson's Hut 52 A13 53 A4
Andrews Track 52 B10 53 B1
Angelus Hut 42 H12
Aniwaniwa 21 E3
Annat 52 G11 53 G2 55 C4
Anne River Hut 47 D3
Annesbrook 116 B4

Ant Stream Hut 52 A12 53 A3
Anti Crow Hut 51 C7
Aokautere 30 D8 31 D2 105 C6
Aongatete 10 H12 12 A13 13 A2
Aoraki/Mt Cook 59 B6
Aoraki/Mt Cook National Park 49 J6 59 A7
Aorangi (East Cape, NI) 16 F10
Aorangi (Manawatu) 29 C7 31 C1
Aorangi Forest Park 33 G6
Aorere 37 C6
Aorere Historic Goldfields 37 C6
Aorere Hut 37 E5
Aoroa 4 J8 5 A3
Aotea 11 E2
Aotuhia 24 D11 25 A6
Apanui 14 F13 15 F2
Aparima 76 E14 77 B2
Aparima Forks Hut 70 F13 71 F2 76 A13
Aparima Huts 70 G14 71 G3 76 A14
Apata 10 H12 12 A13 13 A2
Apiti 27 J3
Apiti Hut 14 J10
Aponga 4 F9
Apotu 4 F11
Appleby 128 C5
Aputerewa 2 H8
Arahiwi 12 F13 13 F2
Arahura 45 H2
Arakura 33 E3 35 A3
Aramiro 11 D4
Aramoana, NI 32 B12
Aramoana, SI 74 G13
Aramoho 26 H8 109 A5
Aranga 3 G5
Aranga Beach 3 G5
Aranui 54 H8 56 D10 120 G3
Arapae 18 A9
Arapaoa 5 C5
Araparera 6 F8 7 A2
Arapawa Island 35 G2 40 F12
Arapito 37 J2 41 A7
Arapohue 4 J8 5 A3
Arapuni 12 F10
Ararata 23 G7 25 D2
Ararimu 7 H7 9 C4
Ararua 5 A5
Arataki 19 B3
Aratapu 5 A3
Aratiatia 19 C6
Aratika 45 G6
Aratoro 18 B10
Arawhata 57 F6
Arch Hill 87 H1 90 C4
Archway Islands 37 A7
Ardgour 66 F10
Ardgowan 68 H11
Ardkeen 21 G3
Ardlussa 72 G8
Ardmore 7 F6 9 A3
Ardmore Airport 7 F6 9 A3
Arero 16 J11
Arete Forks Hut 29 J6
Argyll East 28 H9
Aria 18 B8
Ariki 42 G8
Army Bay 88 B6
Arno 68 D12
Aroha Island 2 K13 4 A9
Arohena 12 G9
Around the Mount Circuit 23 E4
Arowhenua 61 H5
Arowhenua Pa 61 H5
Arrow Junction 65 G6
Arrowtown 65 G6
Arthur's Pass 52 B8
Arthur's Pass National Park 52 A10 53 A1
Arthurs Point 65 G4
Arthurstown 45 J2
Arthurton 78 B11
Arundel 61 D5
Ashburton 55 H2 62 C8
Ashcott 27 J7
Ashers 77 F7
Ashhurst 30 D9 31 D3
Ashley 52 E17 56 A9
Ashley Clinton 27 J6 30 A13 31 A7
Ashley Downs 78 B13 79 D1
Ashley Gorge 52 E13 53 E4 55 A6
Ashton 62 E9
Ashton Hut 71 C4
Ashwick Flat 60 E12 61 E1
Aspiring Hut 64 B14 65 B4
Ataahua 56 G10
Atapo 42 E13

Atarau 45 D6
Atau Paparua 40 C9
Atawhai 38 J12 39 G4
Atea 29 G7 31 G1
Atene 24 J14 26 F9
Athenree 10 F12
Athenree Hot Springs 10 F12
Athol 71 D7
Atiamuri 19 A5
Atiwhakatu Hut 34 A7
Auckland 7 D4
Auckland City 87 D5
Auckland International Airport 7 F4 9 A1 90 E4
Auckland Zoo 7 D4
Aukopae 18 F9 24 A14
Aurere 2 G7
Auripo 66 H13 67 H2
Auroa 23 F4
Ava 110 C3
Avalon 33 E3 35 A3 111 C4
Avenal 127 A2 128 C3
Avenues 93 B1
Aviemore 67 C6
Avoca Hut 51 C7
Avoca, NI 4 H8
Avoca, SI 52 D10 53 D1
Avondale (Auckland) 89 C3
Avondale (Christchurch) 120 G4
Avondale (Southland) 71 H4
Avonhead 54 H8 56 D9 120 C3
Avonside 54 H8 56 D10 120 F3
Awahou 13 F4
Awahou North 30 B9 31 B3
Awahou South 30 C9 31 C3
Awahuri 29 C7 31 C1
Awaiti 10 E9
Awakaponga 14 E9
Awakeri 14 F10
Awakeri Hot Springs 14 F9
Awakeri Springs 14 F9
Awakino 17 C5
Awakino Point 4 J8
Awakino Ski Huts 67 E6
Awakino Skifield 67 E6
Awamangu 79 C3
Awamarino 11 H2
Awamoko 68 F11
Awanui (Bay of Plenty) 15 D6
Awanui (Northland) 1 H6
Awapoto Hut 38 E9 39 C1
Awapuni (Gisborne) 100 B2
Awapuni (Manawatu) 29 E7 31 E1
Awapuni (Palmerston North) 105 D2
Awariki 30 C13 31 C7
Awaroa 3 B2
Awaroa Creek 85 C3
Awaroa Hut 38 E10 39 C2
Awarua, NI 3 E7
Awarua, SI 77 F5
Awatane 11 G7
Awatea 78 D14 79 F2
Awatere 16 C12
Awatere Hut 27 J5
Awatoitoi 34 B11
Awatato 28 E12 103 A3
Awatuna, NI 23 F5
Awatuna, SI 45 H3
Awhitu 7 G3
Awhitu Central 7 G3
Aylesbury 52 H14 53 H5 55 D7

B

Back Ridge Hut 27 B7
Back River 2 H8
Back Valley Hut 70 F10
Bainesse 29 E6
Bainham 37 D6
Balaclava 124 E4
Balcairn 54 E8 56 A10
Balclutha 79 E3
Balfour 71 H7
Ballance 30 E9 31 E3
Ballarat Hut 64 E14 65 E4
Ballard Hut 28 A8
Balloon Hut 37 H6
Balmoral 90 C4
Balmoral Hill 120 H1
Balmoral Huts 68 G8
Balmoral, SI 47 J4 54 A8
Bankside 55 F5 62 A11

Bannockburn 66 H8
Bare Island / Motu o Kura 28 H13
Bark Bay Hut 38 E10 39 C2
Barker Hut 51 B6
Barkes Corner 94 B1
Barlow Hut 27 F6
Barnego 79 E3
Barra Track 34 A7
Barrhill 55 F3 62 A9
Barron Saddle Hut 59 B5
Barrys Bay 56 G12
Barrytown 45 C5
Barryville 18 B13 19 B1
Bartletts 22 F9
Basins Hut 51 D7
Bastia Hill 108 B6 109 C5
Batley 5 C6
Battersea 33 D7
Bauza Island 69 C5
Bay of Islands Airport 4 A8
Bay View (Auckland) 88 H3
Bay View (Hawkes Bay) 28 C12
Baylys Beach 3 J6
Bayswater 90 B4
Bayswater, SI 77 B2
Beach Haven 88 J2
Beachlands 7 E6
Beachville 115 A1 116 A4
Beaconsfield 30 B8 31 B2
Bealey Hut 52 C8
Bealey Spur 52 C8
Bealey Spur Hut 52 C8
Beaumont 73 G4
Beautiful Valley 60 F14 61 F3
Beckenham 120 E1
Becketts Hut 70 F14 71 F3
Becks 66 G13 67 G2
Beebys Hut 42 F14 43 E2
Beerescourt 92 E3
Belfast 54 G8 56 C10 120 E6
Belfield 61 F5
Belgrove 39 J1 42 C14 43 B2
Bell Block 23 A5
Bell Hill 45 G7
Bell Island 38 J11 39 G3 43 A4
Belknowes 124 E4
Bells Junction 26 D12
Bellvue 94 B1
Belmont (Auckland) 90 B4
Belmont (Wellington) 33 D3 35 A2 110 C3
Bench Island 80 E6
Bendigo 66 F10
Benhar 79 E4
Benio 78 A10
Benmore 71 J5 77 A4
Benmore Hut 52 G9 55 C2
Bennetts 52 F14 53 F5 55 B7
Bennetts Siding 27 F2
Benneydale 18 B11
Berhampore 110 E2
Berlins 41 H5
Berwick 74 J8 79 B6
Bethlehem 10 J13 12 B14 13 B3 94 C1
Bexley 52 F12 53 F3 55 B5 120 G3
Bideford 34 A11
Big Bay 7 F3
Big Bay Hut 57 J2
Big Hellfire Hut 80 D2
Big Island 80 H1
Big Lagoon 35 H6 44 C12
Big Manly 88 C5
Big Omaha 6 D10
Big River 46 C9
Big River Hut 46 C9
Billy Goat Track 8 G12 10 B10
Binser Saddle Track 52 C10 53 C1
Birch Hill 59 C6
Birchfield 41 F4
Birchville 33 C4
Birchwood 70 J13 71 J2 76 C13
Bird Island 77 J6
Birdlings Flat 56 H10
Birkdale 88 J2
Birkenhead 7 D4 6 J10 89 B3
Bishop and Clerks Islands 77 H1 80 B3
Bishopdale (Christchurch) 120 D4
Bishopdale (Nelson) 116 B4
Black Gully 72 H13 73 H2
Black Hill Hut 52 D11 53 D2 55 A4
Black Reef 41 F2
Black Rock 80 H4
Blackball 45 D5

Blackburn 27 H7
Blackhead, NI 32 C12
Blackhead, SI 74 H11 124 F5
Blackmans 72 A12 73 A1
Blackmount 70 H11 76 B11
Blacks Point 46 B9
Blackstone Hill 66 G13 67 G2
Blackwater 46 C8
Blackwater Lake 52 D11 53 D2
Blackwater River Ecological Area 41 H4
Blairlogie 34 B12
Blaketown 118 A2
Blandswood 61 D4
Blenheim 35 J6 44 C11 117 C4
Blind River 44 E12
Blockhouse Bay 7 E4 89 D3
Blowhard Track 52 D13 53 D4
Blue Cliffs 68 A11
Blue Lake Hut 47 A4
Blue Lake, NI 18 J14 19 J2
Blue Lake, SI 72 D10
Blue Lakes Walk 59 A7
Blue Range Hut 29 J7 31 J1
Blue River (Blowfly(Hut 58 C11
Blue Spur 45 H2
The Bluff/Motupohue 77 H5
Bluff Damp Hut 48 C10
Bluff Hill 103 A1
Bluff Hut 50 C13 51 C4
Blumine Island 35 G2 40 F12
Blyth Hut 26 B12
Blyth Track 26 B12
Blythe Valley 54 B12
Boat Group 80 H1
Bobs Hut 46 C14 47 C2
Boddytown 45 F4
Bog Inn Hut 18 C13 19 C1
Bog Lake 70 A12 71 A1
Bombay 7 H6 9 C3
Bonny Glen 29 A5
Bortons 68 F10
Botany Downs 90 D6
Bouldcott 111 C4
Boulder Lake 37 E6
Boundary Stream Track 20 J12
Bowen Falls 64 D8
Bowentown 10 F12
Bowlers Creek 73 H4 79 A2
Bowscale Tarn 47 B6
Boyd Hut 19 J6
Boydtown 125 A2 126 A2
Boyle Flat Hut 46 E14 47 E2
Boyle Village 46 F13 47 F1
Bradford 124 E4
Braeburn 38 H9 39 F1
Braigh 5 A7
Brames Falls Track 23 E4
Branch Creek Hut 42 D10
Branxholme 77 D4
Breaker Bay 110 E2
Breaksea Island 69 F3
Breaksea Islands (North Stewart Is) 77 J7
Breaksea Islands (South Stewart Is) 80 G6
Bream Islands 4 H14
Brewster Hut 58 F12 59 F1
Bridal Veil Falls, NI - Raglan 11 D3
Bridal Veil Falls, SI 65 F4
Bridge Hill 72 A13 73 A2
Bridge Pa 28 F11
Bridgend 120 F6
Brighton 74 J10 124 J6
Brightwater 39 H2 43 A3
Brixton 17 G1 23 A6
Broad Bay 74 G12
Broad Gully 68 E12
Broadfield 53 J6 56 E8
Broadlands 20 B8
Broadmeadows 110 D2
Broadway Park 90 C4
Broadwood 3 A3
Brockville 124 F3
Brodrick Hut 59 E3
Broken Hills 8 G13 10 B10
Broken Islands 36 E3
Broken River Hut 52 E10 53 E1 55 A3
Broken River Skifield 52 D9
Bromley 120 G2
Bronte 38 J10 39 G2
Brookby 7 F6 9 A3
Brookfield 94 B1
Brooklands (New Plymouth) 106 D4 107 C4
Brooklands Lagoon 54 G8 56 C10

Brooklands, SI (Christchurch) 54 G8 56 C10
Brooklands, SI (Nelson) 38 J12 39 G4
116 A6
Brooklyn 110 E1
Brooklyn, SI 38 G9 39 E1
Brookside 55 F7 62 A13
Broomfield 54 D8 120 B3
Brown Hut 37 E5
Brown Owl 33 D4 111 A4
Browne Island 57 G3
Browns 77 B5
Browns Bay 6 J10 7 C4
Browns Beach 61 G6
Browns Island 7 D5
Bruce Bay 58 A13 59 A2
Brunner 45 E5
Brunswick 26 H8
Bruntwood 12 C8
Bryant Park 92 D3
Brydone 78 C8
Brynavon 4 F13
Brynderwyn 5 B7
Brynderwyn Hills Walkway 6 B8
Bryndwr 53 H7 56 D9 120 D4
Buccleuch 61 A6
Buckland (Auckland) 7 J6 9 D3
Buckland (Waikato) 12 D10
Buckland Peaks Hut 41 H3
Bucklands Beach 7 D6 90 C6
Bucklands Crossing 74 E12
Buckleton Beach 6 E10
Bull Creek Hut 52 A11 53 A2
Bull Flat Hut 58 G13 59 G2
Bulls 29 B6
Bulwer 40 D9
Bungaree Hut 80 D5
Bungtown 73 H6 79 A4
Bunker Islets 80 D6
Bunnythorpe 30 D8 31 D2
Burgess Island 36 A2
Burgess Park 107 D5
Buried Village - Rotorua 13 H5
Burkes 124 C2
Burkes Pass 60 F11
Burn Creek Hut 46 B14 47 B2
Burn Hut 29 G7 31 G1
Burnbrae 46 A12
Burnetts Face 41 G5
Burnham 52 J14 53 J5 55 E7
Burnside (Christchurch) 53 H7 56 D9
120 C4
Burnside (Dunedin) 124 F5
Burnt Bush Hut 66 B11
Burswood 90 D6
Burwood 54 H8 56 D10 120 G4
Bush Hut 58 J12 59 J1 66 A10
Bush Siding 77 F7
Bushey 74 C13
Bushline Hut 42 H13 43 G1
Bushline Hut (Sylvester(37 G6
Bushside 51 J7 61 A6
Butchers Dam 72 B13 73 B2
Butchers Gully 72 B13 73 B2
Butler Junction Hut 50 G8

C

Caberfeidh 78 F13 79 H1
Cabin Hut 65 D5
Cable Bay 2 H8
Cable Bay Walkway 38 H13 39 F5
Cairnbrae 55 F2 62 A8
Caldervale 37 H2
Callaghans 45 H3
Camberley 103 C5
Cambrians 66 F13 67 F2
Cambridge 12 D8
Cameron Hut (Lake Sumner) 46 H10
Cameron Hut (Ruahine FP) 27 C7
Cameron Hut (Westland) 50 G12 51 G3
Camerons 45 G3
Camp Valley 60 G12 61 G1
Campbells Bay 88 G4
Cannibal Gorge Hut 46 D14 47 D2
Cannington 60 J13 61 J2
Cannons Creek 110 B3
Canvastown 39 G7 44 A8
Cape Brett Track 4 A12
Cape Foulwind 41 G2
Cape Palliser Lighthouse 33 J6
Cape Reinga 1 A1
Cape Reinga Lighthouse 1 A1

Caples Track 64 F11 65 F1
Capleston 46 A10
Captains Creek Hut 39 H5 43 A6
Cardiff 23 E6 25 B1
Cardrona 65 F7
Cardrona Cromwell Pack Track 66 G8
Cardrona Hotel 65 F7
Cardrona Roaring Meg Pack Track 65 G7
Cardrona Skifield 65 F6
Carew 61 D5
Careys Bay 74 G12 124 A1
Carkeek Hut 29 J6
Carleton 52 F14 53 F5 55 B7
Carluke 39 G7
Carlyle Hut 47 F2
Carnarvon 29 D6
Caroline 71 H6
Caroline Creek Hut 47 B4
Caroline Hut 70 J8 76 D8
Carricktown 66 J8
Carrington 34 B8
Carrington Estate Golf Course 2 F7
Carrington Hut 51 B7
Carroll Hut 45 J7
Carswell 34 B11
Carters Beach 41 G3
Carterton 34 C8
Cascade Creek 64 G10
Cascade Hut (Kaimanawa FP) 19 H5
Cascade Hut (Mt Aspiring NP) 64 B14 65 B4
Cascade Saddle Route 65 B4
Cascade Track 42 H13
Casebrook 53 H7 56 D9 120 D5
Casey Hut 52 A10 53 A1
Cashmere (Christchurch) 120 E1
Cashmere (Wellington) 110 D2
Cashmere, SI 54 J8 56 E10
Casnell Island 6 F10
Cass 52 C9
Cass Bay 54 J8 56 E10
Cass Saddle Hut 52 D9
Cassel Flat Hut 59 A4
Castle Hill Village 52 E9 55 A2
Castle Rock Hut 38 F9 39 D1
Castle Rocks Hut 49 H6
Castlecliff 25 J7 109 C1
Castlehill 30 J10 31 J4
Castlepoint 34 B13
Castlerock 71 G6
Castor Bay 6 J10 7 C4 88 H5
Cathedral Caves 78 G13 79 J1
Cathedral Cliffs - Gore Bay 54 A13
Cathedral Cove - Haihei 8 D13
Catlins Conservation Park 78 E12
Catlins Lake 79 H3
Catlins River Walk 78 E13 79 G1
Cattle Creek 68 A9
Cattle Creek Hut 30 A12 31 A6
Cattle Flat 71 F7
Cattle Ridge Hut 29 J7
Cattle Valley 60 E13 61 E2
Cavalli Islands 2 H12
Cave 60 H13 61 H2
Cavendish 61 B6
Caverhill 48 J9
Caversham 124 E4
Cayenne Hut 68 J8
Cedar Flat Hut 50 B13 51 B4
Central Te Hoe Hut 20 F11
Central Waiau Hut 20 E12
Central Whirinaki Hut 20 E10
Centre Bush 77 A4
Centre Island 70 B11
Chain Hills 124 H4
Chalky Island 75 E2
Challis 124 C4
Chamberlain 60 G12
Chancellor Hut 49 H5
Chancet Rocks 44 G12
Chaneys 54 G8 56 C10 120 F6
Chapel Downs 90 E6
Charing Cross 52 H13 53 H4 55 D6
Charleston 41 H2
Charlestown 65 F4
Charlton 78 B9
Charming Creek Walkway 41 E6
Charteris Bay 54 J8 56 F10
Chartwell (Hamilton) 92 D3
Chartwell (Wellington) 110 D1
Chaslands 78 G12
Chasm Creek Walkway 41 D7
Chatswood 88 J3

Chatto Creek 66 J11
Chatton 72 J10 78 A9
Chatton North 72 J10
Cheddar Valley 14 F12
Chedworth Park 92 D4
Cheltenham (Auckland) 90 B4
Cheltenham (Manawatu) 30 B8 31 B2
Chertsey 55 G4 62 B10
Chesterfield 45 G3
Chetwode Islands 40 C10
Cheviot 48 J9 54 A13
Cheviot Museum 48 J9 54 A13
Chorlton 56 F13
Christchurch 54 H8 56 D10
Christchurch City 119 C5 120 E4
Christchurch International Airport 53 H7
56 D9
Christmas Village Hut 77 J2 80 C4
Christopher Hut 47 D3
Chrystalls Beach 79 D6
Chummies Track 42 C11
Churchill 9 F4
Churton Park 110 C2
Clandeboye 61 G6
Claremont 61 J3
Clarence 48 B14
Clarendon 79 C6
Clareville 34 C8
Claris 36 E5
Clark Hut 70 H8 76 B8
Clarks Beach 7 G4 9 B1
Clarks Junction 74 F8
Clarksville 79 D5
Clarkville 53 G7 56 C9
Claudelands 91 B6 92 E4
Claverley 48 G10
Clay Cliffs 66 A14 67 A3
Clendon House - Rawene 3 C4
Clevedon 7 F7 9 A4
Clifden 76 D12
Clifton (Christchurch) 120 H1
Clifton (Hawkes Bay) 28 F13
Clifton, SI (Clutha) 78 B14 79 D2
Clifton, SI (Invercargill) 77 F5 128 B6
Clifton, SI (Tasman) 38 D8
Clinton 78 C12
Clinton Forks Hut 64 G8
Clive 28 E12 103 A4
Cloustonville 33 B4
Clover Park 90 E6
Cloverlea 29 D7 31 D1 105 B2
Clyde 60 J12 72 A13 73 A2
Clydesdale 29 C5
Clydevale 78 A14 79 C2
Coal Creek Flat 72 D13 73 D2
Coal Island 75 F3
Coalgate 52 H11 53 H2 55 D4
Coatesville 6 J9 7 C3 88 F1
Cobb Hut 37 G6
Cobb Reservoir 37 H7
Cobb Track 37 G6
Cobden 45 E4
Codfish Is (Whenua Hou) Nature Res 80 D1
Codfish Island (Whenuahou) 80 D1
Colac Bay/Oraka (township) 76 H13 77 E1
Cold Stream Hut 46 J13 47 J1
Coldstream (Ashburton) 61 F7
Coldstream (Waimakariri) 53 F7 56 B9
Coldwater Hut 42 H13 43 G1
Colenso Hut 27 F5
Colin Todd Hut 57 J6 64 A14 65 A4
Colliers Junction 26 E13
Collingwood 37 C7
Collinswood 124 B4
Colonial Knob Walkway 33 D2 35 B2
Colville 8 B11 36 J5
Colyton 30 C8 31 C2
Comet Hut 27 D7
Company Bay 124 B3
Concord 124 F5
Cone Hut 33 B6
Conical Hill 78 A11
Conroys Gully 72 A13 73 A2
Conway Flat 48 G10
Cooks Beach 8 D13
Coombe Rocks 35 H4 40 H11 44 A12
Coonoor 30 E12 31 E6
Cooper Island 69 H5 75 B5
Coopers Beach 2 H8
Coopers Creek (Timaru) 61 E5

Coopers Creek (Waimakariri) 52 F12 53 F3 55 B5
Cooptown 56 G11
Copland Track 49 J3 59 A4
Corbyvale 41 D7
Cormacks 68 H11
Cornwallis 7 F3 89 E2
Coroglen 8 E13
Coromandel 8 C11
Coromandel Forest Park 8 A10 36 H4 10 D10
Coromandel Walkway 8 A10 36 G4
Coronet Peak Skifield 65 G5
Corriedale 68 G10
Corstorphine 124 E5
Cosgrove Island 79 H3
Cosseys - Wairoa Track 7 G7 9 B4
Cosseys Reservoir 7 G7 9 B4
Cotters Hut 58 J13 59 J2
County Stream Hut 50 D11 51 D2
Courtenay 52 H13 53 H4 55 D6
Coutts Island 120 E6
Cove, The 74 H11 124 C4
Cow Creek Hut 29 J6
Cowes 8 D8
Cowins Track 37 J6 42 B11
Cracroft 120 D1
Craigellachie 73 H4 79 A2
Craigieburn (Buller) 45 D7
Craigieburn (Selwyn) 52 D10 53 D1
Craigieburn Conservation Park 52 C8
Craigieburn Skifield 52 D9
Crail Bay 35 J2 40 F10
Crater Lake 26 A13
Crawford Junction Huts 50 B14 51 B5
Crawfords 70 J14 71 J3 76 C14
Crichton 79 D4
Cricklewood 60 G12 61 G1
Crippletown 66 G9
Croesus Track 45 C5
Crofton 29 A6
Crofton Downs 110 D1
Cromel Base Hut 71 E5
Cromel Branch Hut 71 D5
Cromwell 66 H9
Cronadun 46 A9
Crookston 72 H13 73 H2
Crossans Corner 72 H12
Crow Hut (Arthur's Pass NP) 51 B7
Crow Hut (Kahurangi NP) 37 J5 42 A10
Crow Hut (Ruahine FP) 27 G5
Crown Hill 88 H4
Croydon 78 A9
Crucible Lake 58 G9
Crumb Hut 67 H7
Crushington 46 B9
Cullers Hut 59 D4
Culverden 47 J5
Cumbria Downs 90 D6
Cupola Hut 42 J12
Curio Bay 78 H11
Curtis Memorial Hut 50 H10 51 H1
Cust 53 F5 55 B7
Cuthill 6 J10 7 C4 88 G3

D

Dacre 77 D7
Dairy Flat 6 H9 7 B3 88 D1
Dairy Flat Airport 6 H9 7 B3
Dale, The 70 C13 71 C2
Dalefield 34 C7
Daleys Flat Hut 64 C12 65 C2
Dallington 120 F3
Dalmore 124 D3
Dannemora 90 D6
Dannevirke 30 C12 31 C6
Danseys Pass 68 G8
Daphne Hut 27 J5
Darfield 52 H12 53 H3 55 D5
Dargaville 4 J8
Dart Hut 64 B13 65 B3
Dashwood 44 D11
Davies Track 23 C4
Dawson Falls 23 E5
Days Bay 33 E2 35 B3 110 D3
Dead Dog Hut 27 E7
Deanwell 92 G3
Deas Cove Hut 69 A5
Deborah 68 H11
Deborah Bay 74 G12 124 A1
Deep Creek 68 C12

Demon Trail 64 B9
Demon Trail Hut 64 B9
Denniston 41 F5
Denniston Walkway 41 F4
Devonport 7 D5 90 B4
Diamond Harbour 54 J8 56 E10
Diamond Lake 64 E12 65 E2
Dianes Hut 27 E7
Dickie Spur Hut 50 C11 51 C2
Diggers Hut 30 B11 31 B5
Diggers Valley 1 K6 3 A2
Dillmanstown 45 H4
Dinsdale 92 F2
Dip Flat 42 H14 43 G2
Dipton 71 J6
Dipton West 71 J5
Dobson 45 E5
Dodger Hut 59 D4
Dodson Valley 38 J12 39 G4
Dog Island 77 H5
Dome Islands 70 C11
Dome Valley 6 E9
Dome Valley Forest Track 6 E9
Domett 54 A12
Donnellys Crossing 3 F5
Donoghues 50 A10 51 A1
Dora Track 29 J6
Dorie 55 H5 62 C11
Dorothy Falls 50 A14 51 A5
Dorset Ridge Hut 29 J6 33 A7
Doubtful Hut 46 F13
Doubtful Island 70 A11
Doubtful Sound 69 B4
Doubtless Hut 46 F12
Douglas Corner 13 D4
Douglas Rock Hut 59 A5
Douglas, NI 24 D8 25 A3
Douglas, SI 68 D11
Douglasvale 65 G5
Dovedale 38 J9 42 A14 43 A2
Dover Track 23 D4
Downes Hut 24 J14 26 F9
Downie Hut 47 B3
Doyleston 55 G7 62 B13
Dreyers Rock 30 J9 31 J3
Dromore 55 H3 62 C9
Drummond 77 B3
Drury 7 G6 9 B3
Drybread 66 G12 67 G1
Duckville Hut 14 J9 20 A12
Dumbarton 72 E13 73 E2
Dumpling Hut 63 E7
Dun Mountain Walkway 39 H4 43 A5
Dunback 74 B12
Dundas Hut 29 H6
Dunearn 77 A3
Dunedin 74 H11 124 D4
Dunedin Airport 74 H9 79 A7
Dunedin Central 123 F3
Dunganville 45 G5
Dunmore 9 H3 11 A4
Dunns Creek Hut 51 A7
Dunollie 45 E4
Dunolly 30 A8 31 A2
Dunrobin 72 G13 73 G2
Dunsandel 55 F6 62 A12
Duntroon 68 E9
Durie Hill 108 C6 109 C5
D'Urville Hut 42 H12
D'Urville Track 42 J11 47 A3
Dusky Forest 72 H12
Dusky Sound 69 H1 75 B1
Dusky Track 69 F7
Duvauchelle 56 G12
Dyerville 33 E7

E

Eade Memorial Hut 50 H8
Ealing 61 E6
Earl Mountain Tracks 64 G9
Earnscleugh 72 A13 73 A2
Earnslaw Hut 64 C12 65 C2
Earthquake Flat 13 H5
Earthquake Lakes 37 H5 42 A10
Earthquakes 68 F9
East Cape Lighthouse 16 C13
East Chatton 72 J10 78 A9
East Egmont 23 D5
East End 107 B4
East Gore 78 B9
East Island / Whangaokeno Island 16 C14

East Matakitaki Hut 47 B3
East Ruggedy Hut 80 C2
East Taieri 74 H10 124 H5
East Takaka 38 E8
East Tamaki 7 E5 90 D6
East Tamaki Industrial 90 D6
Eastbourne 33 F2 35 B4 110 E3
Eastern Beach 90 C6
Eastern Bush 76 D12
Echo Cliffs - Turangi 19 G3
Echolands 18 F11
Eden Terrace 87 J3 90 C4
Edendale 78 D8
Edgecumbe 14 E9
Edievale 72 G13 73 G2
Edwards Hut 52 B8
Edwards Island (Motunui) 80 D6
Egmont National Park 23 D5
Egmont Village 23 C5
Eiffelton 62 E8
Eight Mile Hut 65 F6
Eight Mile Junction 18 A9
Eketahuna 30 H8 31 H2
Elaine Bay 40 E8
Elcho Hut 59 D4
Elderslie 68 G10
Elephant Hill 68 E10
Elgin (Canterbury) 55 J3 62 D9
Elgin (Gisborne) 100 B2
Elizabeth Hut 46 H9
Ella Hut 47 A3
Ellerslie 90 C5
Ellesmere 55 F7 62 A13
Elletts Beach 7 G5 9 B2
Ellis Hut (Kahurangi NP) 37 J7 42 A12
Ellis Hut (Ruahine FP) 27 F7
Elsdon 110 B2
Elsthorpe 28 J11
Elstow 10 G9
Eltham 23 F7 25 C2
Empress Hut 49 J5 59 A6
Endeavour Inlet 35 H1 40 E11
Enderley 92 E4
Enfield 68 G11
Engineers Camp 46 G13 47 G1
Enner Glynn 38 J12 39 H4 43 A5
Entrance Island 63 J1 69 A5
Entry Island 69 H2 75 B2
Epsom 90 C4
Epuni 33 E3 35 A3 111 C4
Epworth 61 G5
Erceg Hut 59 C5
Ermedale 76 G14 77 D2
Ernest Island 80 J2
Ernest Islands 80 F2
Erua 26 A11
Esk Valley 68 B12
Eskdale 28 C11
Ettrick 72 E13 73 E2
Eureka 9 J7 12 B8
Evans Hut 50 E13 51 E4
Evansdale 74 F12
Eversley 60 F12 61 F1
Explorer Hut 50 C12 51 C3
Eyre Mountains/Taka Ra Haka Conservation Park 71 C5
Eyreton 53 G7 56 C9

F

Fairburn 2 J7
Fairdown 41 F4
Fairfax 77 C2
Fairfield (Dunedin) 74 H10 124 G4
Fairfield (Hamilton) 92 E3
Fairfield (Wellington) 111 C4
Fairhall 35 K6 44 C10
Fairlie 60 F12 61 F1
Fairlight 72 C8
Fairton 55 H3 62 C9
Fairview 61 J4
Fairview Downs 92 D4
Falls Dam 66 F14 67 F3
Fanal Island 36 A2
Farewell Spit Nature Reserve 38 A9
Farm Cove 90 C5
Farnham 117 A1
Favona 90 D4
Featherston 33 D6
Featherston Heritage Museum 33 D6
Feilding 29 C7 31 C1
Feldwick 76 D12

Fencourt 12 D8
Fendalton 120 D3
Fenella Hut 37 G6
Fenton Park 95 B6 96 D3
Ferguson Hut 58 F13 59 F2
Fergusons 50 B10 51 B1
Fern Flat, NI (Northland) 2 J8
Fern Flat, NI (Wanganui) 29 A6
Fern Flat, SI 42 G8
Ferndale (New Plymouth) 107 D3
Ferndale (Southland) 78 C9
Fernhill, NI 28 E11 103 B4
Fernhill, SI 64 H14 65 H4 126 C1
Ferniehurst 48 G9
Fernland Spa Mineral Pools - Tauranga 10 J13 12 B14 13 B3
Fernside, NI 33 C6
Fernside, SI 53 F7 56 B9
Ferntown 37 B7
Ferry landing 8 D13
Ferrymead 120 G1
Field Hut 33 A6
Fields Track 33 B6
Fife Rock 77 J5
Finegand 79 E3
Finlay Face Hut 50 H10 51 H1
Fiordland National Park 69 A7
Fisherman Island 38 F10 39 D2
Fitzroy (Hamilton) 92 G4
Fitzroy (New Plymouth) 23 A5 107 B5
Five Bridges, The 22 A12
Five Forks 68 G10
Five Mile Lagoon 49 F5
Five Rivers 71 F6
Five Roads 77 B4
Flag Swamp 74 D12
Flagstaff 92 C3
Flanagans Hut 37 J6 42 A11
Flat Bush 90 E6
Flat Island 2 G11
Flaxmere 28 F11 103 D5
Flaxton 53 F7 56 B9
Flemington, NI 32 B9
Flemington, SI 62 E8
Flora Hut 37 H7
Forbes Hut 58 F13 59 F2
Fordell 26 J9
Fordlands 96 C2
Forest Lake 91 B1 92 E2
Forks Hut 30 B11 31 B5
Forks, The 49 F6
Forsyth 73 J5 79 B3
Forsyth Island / Te Parupuru 40 D10
Fortification 78 F10
Fortrose 78 G8
Four Peaks 61 E3
Four Rivers Plain 42 G9
Fox Glacier 49 H4
Foxhill 39 J1 43 B2
Foxton 29 F5
Foxton Beach 29 E4
Frankleigh Park 107 D3
Frankton (Hamilton) 92 F3
Frankton (Queenstown) 65 H5 126 A5
Franz Josef Glacier 49 G6
Fraser Dam 66 J9 72 A12 73 A1
Frasertown 21 H5
Freds Camp Hut 80 E4
Freemans Bay 87 F2 90 C4
French Bay 89 D2
French Farm 56 G12
French Pass, SI 40 C9
French Pass, NI 12 D9
French Ridge Hut 64 A14 65 A4
Frenchmans Swamp 4 B10
Freshford 72 G9
Frews Hut 50 C13 51 C4
Frimley 103 C5
Frisco Hut 50 C13 51 C4
Fruitlands 72 B13 73 B2
Fuchsia Creek 68 H9

G

Gable Islet 22 C13
Gabriel Hut 46 H13
Gabriels Gully 73 H5 79 A3
Gair Loch 69 F7
Galatea 20 A11
Galloway 66 J11 72 A14 73 A3
Gammans Creek 52 F13 53 F4 55 B6
Gap Road 77 C4
Gapes Valley 61 F4
Gardens, The 90 E6

Gardiner Hut 59 A6
Garston 72 D8
Gate Pa 10 J13 94 C2 13 B3
Gebbies Valley 56 F9
George Sound Track 63 H5
Georgetown (Invercargill) 128 B4
Georgetown (Oamaru) 68 F10
Geraldine 61 F4
Geraldine Downs 61 F4
Geraldine Flat 61 F5
Gibbs Track 42 C11
Gibbston 65 H7
Gibbstown 37 C7
Gilbert Islands 69 F3
Gillespies Beach 49 H3
Gillows Dam 41 G3
Gimmerburn 67 J4
Gisborne 22 D10 99 B4 100 B3
Gisborne Point 13 F6
Gladfield 77 B3
Gladstone, NI (Manawatu) 29 H5
Gladstone, NI (Wellington) 34 C9
Gladstone, SI (Grey) 45 F3
Gladstone, SI (Invercargill) 128 C2
Gladstone, SI (Queenstown) 66 C9
Glasnevin 54 D8
Glen Afton 9 H3 11 A4
Glen Avon 107 B5
Glen Eden 7 E3 89 D2
Glen Eden South 89 D2
Glen Eden West 89 D2
Glen Innes 7 E5 90 C5
Glen Massey 9 H4 11 A5
Glen Murray 9 F3
Glen Oroua 29 D6
Glenavy 68 F13
Glenbervie 4 F12 85 A3
Glenbrook 7 H4 9 C1
Glenbrook Beach 7 H4 9 C1
Glencoe 77 C7
Glendale 111 D4
Glendene 89 C2
Glendhu 34 G9
Glendhu Bay 65 D7
Glendowie 90 C5
Glenduan 38 H13 39 F5
Glenfield 6 J10 7 C4 88 H3
Glengarry (Invercargill) 77 E5 128 B2
Glengarry (Tasman) 42 H8
Glenham 78 E9
Glenholme 95 D5 96 C3
Glenhope 42 E11
Gleniti 61 J4
Glenkenich 72 J12 73 J1
Glenleith 74 G11 124 E2
Glenomaru 79 G3
Glenorchy 64 F12 65 F2
Glenore 79 C4
Glenpark 74 C12
Glenrae Hut 46 J14 47 J2
Glenroy 52 H10 53 H1 55 D3
Glenside 33 E2 35 B3 110 C2
Glentui 52 E14 53 E5 55 A7
Glentunnel 52 H11 53 H2 55 D4
Glenure 71 H7
Glenvar 6 J10 7 C4 88 E3
Glenview 92 H4
Glinks Gully 5 B2
Glorit 6 F8
Goat Creek Hut 42 E8
Goat Island 6 D11
Goat Pass Hut 52 A8
Godley Hut 50 H8
Gold Creek Hut 27 G6
Golden Cross 10 E10
Golden Downs 42 D14 43 C2
Golden Springs 19 B7
Golden Stairs Walkway 3 C2
Golden Valley 10 E11
Goldsborough / Waimea 45 H3
Golflands 90 D6
Gomorrah Track 42 C11
Gonville 108 D3 109 D3
Goodwood 74 D13
Goodwood Heights 90 E6
Goose Bay 48 F10
Gordon 10 J10 12 B11
Gordons Valley 68 A12
Gordonton 9 J6 11 B7
Gore 78 B9
Gore Bay 54 A13
Gorge Creek 72 B12 73 B1

Gorge Islands 57 H2
Gorge Road 77 F7
Gouland Downs Hut 37 E4
Goulds Road 56 F8 62 A14
Governors Bay 54 J8 56 E10
Gowanbridge 42 F11
Gracefield 33 E3 35 A3 110 D3
Grafton 87 H5 90 C4
Grahams Beach 7 G3 9 B1
Granity 41 E5
Granity Pass Hut 42 D11
Grasmere 77 E5 128 D2
Grassy Flat Hut 51 A6
Grays Corner 68 E12
Grays Hut 68 J8
Great Barrier Island 36 D4
Great Island 75 E3
Great Mercury Island 8 B14
Greatford 29 B6
Green Bay 89 D3
Green Gate Huts 65 F5
Green Hills 68 E12
Green Island, SI (Dunedin) 74 H11 124 F4
Green Island, SI (Foveaux Strait) 77 J7
Green Island, SI (Pacific Ocean) 74 J10
Green Islets 75 G5
Green Lake 70 H9 76 B9
Green Lake Hut 70 H9 76 B9
Green Meadows 103 B2
Green Valley 74 A11
Greenacres 110 B2
Greendale 52 J12 53 J3 55 E5
Greenfield 78 A14 79 C2
Greenhills 77 G4 80 A6
Greenhithe 89 A2
Greenland Reservoir 73 C4
Greenlane 90 C4
Greenmount 90 D6
Greenpark 56 F9
Greenpark Huts 56 G9
Greenpoint 77 G4 80 A6
Greenstone / Pounamu 45 H4
Greenstreet 55 G2 62 B8
Greenvale 72 H11
Greerton 10 J13 12 B14 13 B3 94 D1
Greigs 45 D4
Grenada 110 C2
Grenada North 110 C2
Greneys Road 54 D8
Greta Valley 54 B10
Greta Valley Walkway 54 B10
Grey Group Islands 36 D3
Grey Lynn 7 D4 87 G1
Greymouth 45 F4 118 A4
Greys Hut 37 J3 42 A8
Greytown 33 C7
Griffin Creek Hut 45 J5
Groper Island 36 A1
Gropers Bush 77 D2
Grough Hut 59 D5
Grove Bush 77 D6
Grove, The 35 K3 40 G9
Grovetown 35 J6 40 J10 44 C11
Gulf Harbour 6 H11 7 B5
Gum Tree Flat 68 E12
Gumdiggers Park 1 G6
Gummies Bush 76 G14 77 D2
Gumtown 4 F10
Guthrie 12 J14 13 J3

H

Haast 58 D9
Haast Beach 58 D8
Haast Hut 49 J6
Haast Paringa Track 58 C10
Hackthorne 55 H1 61 C7
Hadlow 61 J4
Hagens Hut 58 G14 59 G3
Hahei 8 D14
Hairini (Bay of Plenty) 10 J13 13 B4
Hairini (Waikato) 11 E7
Hakarimata Walkway 9 H4 11 A5
Hakaru 6 B8
Hakataramea 68 D8
Hakatere (Ashburton Coast) 62 E9
Hakatere (Ashburton) 50 J14 51 J5 61 A4
Haku 11 J3 17 A7
Halcombe 29 B7 31 B1
Haldane 78 G10
Half Moon Bay 7 E6 90 C6
Half Moon Hut 68 H8

Halfmoon Bay / Oban 80 E5
Halfway Bush 124 E3
Halfway Hut 69 H7 75 B7
Halkett 52 H14 53 H5 55 D7
Halswell 53 J7 56 E9 120 C1
Hamama 38 E8
Hamilton 9 J6 11 B7 92 E3
Hamilton Airport 11 D7
Hamilton Central 91 E5
Hamilton East 92 F4
Hamilton Hut 52 D8
Hamilton North 91 D4 92 E3
Hamilton West 91 G4 92 F3
Hampden 74 A13
Hampstead 55 J3 62 D9
Hamua 30 G9 31 G3
Hamurana 13 F4
Hanamahihi Hut 20 A13 21 A1
Hangaroa 21 E7
Hangatiki 11 H6
Hanmer Conservation Park 47 F4
Hanmer Springs 47 F5
Hanmer Springs Thermal Resort 47 F5
Hannahs Bay 13 G5 96 B5
Hannahs Clearing 57 E7
Happy Daze Hut 27 J5 30 A12 31 A6
Happy Valley (Auckland) 7 H7 9 C4
Happy Valley (Wellington) 110 E1
Happy Valley, SI 76 E12
Hapuakohe Track 9 E6
Hapuku 48 D13
Harakeke 38 J10 39 G2
Harapepe 11 D5
Harbour View (Auckland) 89 B2
Harbour View (Wellington) 110 C3
Haretaunga 111 B5
Harewood 53 H7 56 D9 120 C4
Harihari 50 D9
Hariki Beach 15 C6
Harington Point 74 G13
Harini 94 D2
Harkness Hut 27 A6
Harman Hut 51 B6
Haroto Bay 11 C4
Harper Pass Track 46 H11
Harrisville 7 J6 9 D3
Haruru 4 B9 81 B1
Haruru Falls - Paihia 4 B9
Harveys Flat 74 G9 79 A7
Harwood 74 G12
Hastings 28 F11 103 C5
Hastings Central 102 B2
Hastwell 30 H8 31 H2
Hataitai 110 E2
Hatepe 19 F5
Hatfield 55 G4 62 B10
Hatfields Beach 6 G10 7 A4
Hatuma 32 A9
Hatuma Lake 32 A10
Hauiti 22 A13
Haukawakawa 40 C9
Haumoana 28 E12
Haunui 30 G11 31 G5
Hauparu Bay 13 F5
Haupiri 46 G9
Hauraki 90 B4
Hautanoa 16 G11
Hautapu 12 D8
Hautu Village 19 G3
Hauturu 11 F3
Hauwai 44 E12
Havelock 40 G8
Havelock North 28 F12 103 B6
Hawai 15 E4
Hawarden 54 B8
Hawdon Hut 52 B9
Hawea Flat 66 C9
Hawera 23 H7 25 E2
Hawkes Bay Museum - Napier 28 D12
Hawkins 52 H12 53 H3 55 D5
Hawksbury Bush 74 D12
Hawkswood 48 H9
Hawthorndale 128 B3
Hays Gap 79 G4
Haystack Hut 42 D9
Haystack, The 40 C11
Haywards 33 D3 35 A2 111 B4
Hazletts 77 D3
Healey Creek Hut 50 C11 51 C2
Heao 18 G8 24 A13
Heaphy Hut 37 F2

Heaphy Track - Great Walk 37 E3
Heathcote Valley 54 J8 56 E10 120 G1
Heatherlea 29 G5
Hector 41 E5
Heddon Bush 77 B3
Hedgehope 77 C6
Heenans Corner 77 A3
Hei Hei 53 H7 56 D9 120 B2
Heidelberg 77 E5 128 B4
Heipipi 20 D12
Helena Bay 4 C12
Helensburgh 124 E3
Helensville 6 H8 7 B2
Helicopter Flat Hut 42 C9
Hells Gate - Rotorua 13 F5
Helvetia 7 H5 9 C2
Hen and Chickens Islands 6 A10
Hen and Chickens Islands Nature Reserve
  6 A10
Henderson 7 E3 89 C2
Henderson Valley 89 C2
Henley 74 J9 79 B7
Hepburn Creek 6 F10
Herbert 68 J10 74 A13
Herbertville 32 F10
Herekino 3 B1
Herekino Forest 1 K6 3 A2
Herekopare Island / Te Marama 80 D6
Herepai Hut 29 H7 31 H1
Herepo 50 D9
Heriot 72 H13 73 H2
Herne Bay 89 B3
Herricks Hut 27 E7
Hexton 22 D10
Heyward Point 74 G12
Hicks Bay 16 B11
Hidden Falls Hut 64 D10
Highbank 52 J9 55 E2 62 A8
Highbury (Auckland) 88 J3
Highbury (Wellington) 110 E1
Highcliff 74 H12 124 B5
Highland Park 90 C6
Highland Park (Wellington) 110 D2
Highlands Park 107 C5
Hihi 2 G9
Hihitahi 26 E14 27 E2
Hikawera 34 F8
Hikuai 8 G13 10 B10
Hikumutu 18 G10
Hikurangi 4 E11
Hikutaia 8 J12 10 D9
Hikuwai 16 H11
Hilderthorpe 68 G12
Hill Park 90 E6
Hillcrest (Auckland) 88 J3
Hillcrest (Hamilton) 92 F4
Hillcrest (Rotorua) 96 C2
Hillend 79 D3
Hillersden 43 D6
Hillgrove 74 B13
Hills Creek 66 F14 67 F3
Hillsborough (Auckland) 90 D4
Hillsborough (Christchurch) 120 F2
Hillsborough, NI (Taranaki) 23 B5
Hilltop 56 G11
Hilmorton 120 D2
Hilton 61 F4
Himatangi 29 E5
Himatangi Beach 29 D4
Hinakura 34 F9
Hinau, NI 27 H3
Hinau, SI 46 B8
Hindon 74 F10
Hinds 55 J1 61 E7
Hinehopu 13 F6
Hinemoa 30 G10 31 G4
Hinerua Hut 27 H6
Hinuera 12 D11
Hira 38 J13 39 G5
Hiruharama 16 E11
Hiwinui 30 C8 31 C2
Hiwipango 42 D14 43 C2
Hoanga 4 J8
Hobsonville 7 D3 88 J1
Hodderville 12 G11
Hoe-O-Tainui 9 G7
Hohonu 45 H4
Hokianga - Kai Iwi Coastal Track 3 E3
Hokio Beach 29 G4
Hokitika 45 H2
Hokonui 77 B6
Hokowhitu 104 D6 105 C4

Hokuri Hut 64 A9
Holborn 111 B4
Holdens Bay 13 G4 96 B5
Holly Hut 23 D5
Hollyford 64 E10
Hollyford Track 64 A9
Homai 90 E5
Home Point 4 H13
Homebush, NI 34 B9
Homebush, SI 52 H11 53 H2 55 D4
Homedale 111 D4
Homer Tunnel 64 E9
Hone Heke Monument - Kaikohe 3 C7
Honeymoon Valley 2 J8
Honikiwi 11 G5
Hook 68 C13
Hook Bush 68 C11
Hooker / Landsborough Wilderness Area
   59 B4
Hooker Glacier Walk 59 A6
Hooker Hut 59 A6
Hoon Hay 53 J7 56 E9 120 D2
Hoopers Inlet 74 G12
Hope 39 H3 43 A4 116 D2
Hope Kiwi Hut 46 G12
Hope shelter 46 G13
Hopelands 30 D11 31 D5
Hopeless Hut 42 J12
Hopeone 21 A3
Hopuhopu 9 H5 11 A6
Horace Walker Hut 59 B5
Horahia 8 J11 10 D8
Horahora 85 C1
Horahora (Northland) 4 F13
Horahora (Waikato) 12 E10
Horeke 3 C5
Hornby 53 J7 56 E9 120 B2
Hornby Hut 44 J9 48 A13
Horoeka 30 F13 31 F7
Horoera 16 B13
Horohoro 12 H14 13 H3
Horokino 18 A12
Horokiwi 110 C3
Horomanga 14 J8 20 A11
Horopito 26 B11
Hororata 52 H11 53 H2 55 D4
Horotiu 9 J5 11 B6
Horrellville 52 F14 53 F5 55 B7
Horseshoe Flat Hut 58 C12
Horseshoe Lake 28 J11
Horsham Downs 9 J5 11 B6 92 A3
Horsley Down 54 A8
Hospital Hill (Napier) 103 B1
Hospital Hill (Opotiki) 14 F13 15 F2 103 B1
Hot Water Beach 8 E14
Hot Water Beach Hot Springs 8 E14
Hoteo 6 E8
Hoteo North 6 D8
Houghton Bay 110 E2
Houhora 1 E5
Houhora Heads 1 F5
Houhou 45 H2
Houipapa 78 F14 79 H2
Houpoto 15 E5
Houto 4 G9
Howard 42 G12
Howard Junction 42 F12
Howard Track 42 H12
Howick 7 E6 90 C6
Howletts Hut 27 J5
Huapai 6 J8 7 C2
Huarau 5 B6
Huia 7 F2 89 E1
Huiakama 24 D9 25 A4
Huiarua 16 G9
Huinga 24 E8 25 B3
Huirangi 17 H1 23 B6
Huiroa 24 D8 25 A3
Huka Falls - Taupo 19 D5
Huka Village 98 A4
Hukanui 30 G8 31 G2
Hukapapa 18 H11
Hukarere 46 C8
Hukatere (Northland - Far North) 1 F4
Hukatere (Northland) 5 C5
Hukawai 46 D8
Hukerenui 4 D10
Humphreys 45 J3
Hundalee 48 G10
Hungahunga 10 J10 12 B11
Hunter 68 C12
Hunterville 26 J13

Huntingdon 55 J2 62 D8
Huntington Park 90 D6
Huntly 9 G5
Hunts Creek Hut 51 A7
Huntsbury 120 F1
Hunua 7 G7 9 B4
Hunua Falls - Auckland 7 G7 9 B4
Hunua Ranges Regional Park 8 G8 9 B5
Hupara 4 C9
Hurdon 107 D2
Hurford 23 B4
Hurleyville 24 H8 25 E3
Hurricane Hut 42 D9
Hurunui 54 A9
Hurunui Hot Springs 46 H11
Hurunui Hut 46 H11
Hurunui Mouth 54 A13
Hurworth 23 C5
Hutnters Hut 50 E10 51 E1
Hutxley Forks Hut 59 E3
Hyde 74 A9
Hyde Park 120 C3

Ice Lake 50 G8
Ida Valley 66 H14 67 H3
Idaburn 67 G4
Idaburn Dam 66 G14 67 G3
Ihaia Track 23 E4
Ihakara 29 G5
Ihumatao 90 E4
Ihungia 16 G10
Ihuraua 30 J9 31 J3
Ikamatua 46 C8
Ikawai 68 E11
Ikawatea Forks Hut 27 E6
Ilam 120 D3
Inaha 23 G6
Inangahua 41 H6
Inangahua Junction 41 H6
Inangahua Landing 41 H5
Inch Clutha 79 E4
Inch Valley 74 B12
Inchbonnie 45 H6
Incholme 68 H10
Indian Island 69 H3 75 B3
Inglewood 17 J1 23 C6
Inland Track 38 E9 39 C1
Invercargill 77 E5 127 C2
Invercargill Airport 77 E4
Irirangi 26 D14 27 D2
Iris Burn Hut 70 C10
Iron Bark Hut 27 F5
Iron Gate Hut 27 J5
Iron Whare Hut 28 A8
Irwell 55 F7 62 A13
Isla Bank 77 C3
Island Bay 33 F1 35 C4 110 E2
Island Block 7 J7 9 D4
Island Cliff 68 F9
Island Gully Hut 47 B5
Island Lake (Buller) 37 G5
Island Lake (Southland) 70 H9 76 B9
Island Lake (Tasman) 47 B6
Island Stream 68 J10
Island View 10 F12
Islands Hut 71 D5
Islington (Blenheim) 117 B5
Islington (Christchurch) 120 B2
Ivory Lake Hut 50 D12 51 D3
Ivydale 3 C5
Iwikau Village 26 A13
Iwitahi 19 F7

Jackett Island 38 H10 39 F2
Jacks Blowhole 79 H3
Jacks Island / Tuhawaiki 79 H3
Jackson Bay 57 E5
Jacksons 45 J6
Jacky Lee Island / Pukeokaoka 80 D6
Jacobs River 49 J2
Jam Hut 44 J8 48 A12
James Mackay Hut 37 E3
Jameson Ridge Track 42 J11
Janefield 74 H10 124 H4
Jerusalem 24 G13 26 D8
Jervois Hut 47 E3
Jervoistown 103 B2
John Coull Hut 24 D12 25 A7
John Reid Hut 42 C11

John Tait Hut 42 J13
Johnson Hut 42 C8
Johnson Track 42 C8
Johnsonville 33 E2 35 B3 110 C2
Johnstone 73 J5 79 B3
Jollie Brook Hut 46 H13 47 H1
Josephville 71 H6
Jubilee Hut 74 F11
Judea 94 C2
Judgeford 33 D3 35 A2 111 B4
Julia Hot Springs 51 A7
Julia Hut 51 A7
Jumbo Hut 34 A7
Junction Burn Hut 70 A9
Junction Hut 66 B10
Junction Islands 36 E3

K

Ka Whata Tu o Rakihouia
   Conservation Park 48 C11
Kaawa 9 G2
Kaeo 2 J11
Kaharoa 13 E4
Kahika 28 A12
Kahikatoa 3 B5
Kahoe 2 H10
Kahotea 11 G6
Kahui Hut 23 D4
Kahui Track 23 D4
Kahuika 78 F13 79 H1
Kahunui Hut 21 B4
Kahurangi National Park 37 F5
Kahutara 33 E6
Kai Iwi 25 H7
Kai Iwi Beach 25 H7
Kaiaka 2 J8
Kaiapoi 53 G8 56 C10
Kaiata 45 F4
Kaiate Falls 13 C4
Kaiatea 4 F13
Kaiaua 8 G9 9 B6
Kaiewe Junction 27 F3
Kaihere 9 E7
Kaihiku 78 C14 79 E2
Kaihinu 45 H2
Kaihu 3 G6
Kaihu Forest 3 G7
Kaiiwi Lakes 3 H6
Kaik 74 B14
Kaikarangi 26 H13
Kaikohe 3 C7
Kaikorai 123 D1 124 E3
Kaikou 4 E8
Kaikoura 48 E12
Kaikoura Island 36 D3
Kaikoura Peninsula Walkway 48 E12
Kaimai-Mamaku Conservation Park 10 G10
   12 E12 13 E1
Kaimamaku 4 D11
Kaimanawa Forest Park 19 H4 27 A3
Kaimarama 8 E12
Kaimata, NI 17 J2 23 C7
Kaimata, SI 45 F5
Kaimaumau 1 G6
Kaimiro 23 C5
Kainga 54 G8 56 C10
Kaingaroa 1 H7
Kaingaroa Forest 20 A10
Kainui 9 H5 11 A6
Kaipaki 11 D7
Kaipara Flats 6 E8
Kaipara Flats Airfield 6 E9
Kaipara Lighthouse 5 E5
Kaiparoro 30 H8 31 H2
Kaipikari 17 G3 24 A8
Kairakau Beach 28 J12
Kairaki 54 G8 56 C10
Kairanga 29 D7 31 D1
Kairangi 12 E9
Kairara 3 G7
Kairua 13 B4 94 C5
Kaitaia 1 J6
Kaitaia Airport - Awanui 1 H6
Kaitangata 79 E4
Kaitaratahi 22 C9
Kaitawa (Hawke's Bay) 21 F2
Kaitawa (Manawatu) 30 F10 31 F4
Kaite 100 C4
Kaitemako 13 C4
Kaiteriteri 38 G10 39 E2
Kaitieke 18 H10

Kaitoke (Manawatu) 30 C12 31 C6
Kaitoke (Waikato) 8 E13
Kaitoke (Wanganui) 26 J8
Kaitoke (Wellington) 33 C5
Kaitoke Hot Springs 36 D4
Kaitoke Lake 26 J8
Kaitui 3 F5
Kaituna Lagoon 56 G9
Kaituna Track 37 B6
Kaituna Valley 56 G10
Kaituna, NI 34 A8
Kaituna, SI 40 J8 44 B9
Kaiwaiwai 33 D7
Kaiwaka 6 C8
Kaiwera 78 B10
Kaiwhaiki 26 G8
Kaiwharawhara 110 D2
Kaka 42 D12
Kaka Point 79 G4
Kakahi 18 G11
Kakahu 60 F14 61 F3
Kakahu Bush 61 F3
Kakanui, NI 6 G8 7 A2
Kakanui, SI 68 J11
Kakapo Hut 42 B9
Kakapo Track 42 B8
Kakapotahi 50 B10
Kakapuaka 79 E3
Kakaramea 24 J8 25 F3
Kakariki (Gisborne) 16 D12
Kakariki (Manawatu) 30 G8 31 G2
Kakariki (Wanganui) 29 B6
Kakatahi 26 F11
Kamahi 78 D8
Kambton 112 D5
Kamo 4 F11 85 A1
Kamo East 85 A1
Kanakanaia 22 B10
Kangaroo Lake 45 G7
Kaniere 45 J2
Kaniwhaniwha 11 D5
Kanohi 6 G8 7 A2
Kanohirua Hut 20 C14 21 C2
Kapakapanui Hut 33 A5
Kapenga 13 H4
Kapiro 2 K12 4 A8
Kapitea Reservoir 45 H4
Kapiti 79 C5
Kapiti Island 33 A3
Kapiti Island Nature Reserve 29 J2 33 A3
Kaponga 23 F5
Kapowairau 1 A2
Kapua 68 D11
Kapuka 77 F7
Kapuka South 77 F7
Kapuni 23 F5
Karahaki 24 J9 25 F4
Karaka 7 G5 9 B2
Karakariki 9 J4 11 C5
Karamea / Red Island, NI 28 H13
Karamea Bend Hut 37 J5 42 A10
Karamea Centennial Museum 37 J2 41 A7
Karamea, SI 37 J2 41 A7
Karamu (Hawke's Bay) 28 F12 103 B5
Karamu (Waikato) 11 D5
Karangahake 10 F10
Karangahake Gorge 10 F10
Karangarua 49 J3
Karapiro 12 D9
Karatia (Thoms Landing) 1 C2
Karehana Bay 33 C2 35 B1
Karekare 7 F2
Karekare Falls 7 F2
Kareponia 1 H6
Karere 29 E7 31 E1
Karetu 4 C10
Karewarewa 27 H3
Karioi 26 C12
Karioitahi 7 J3 9 D1
Karitane 74 E12
Karori 33 F1 35 C4 110 D1
Karori West 110 D1
Kororo 45 F4
Karuhiruhi 3 D4
Katea 79 G2
Katikati 10 G11
Katiki 74 B14
Katipo Creek Shelter 37 G2
Kauaeranga 8 H12 10 C9
Kauana 77 A5
Kauangaroa 26 J10
Kaukapakapa 6 H8 7 B2

Kaupokonui 23 G5
Kauri 4 F11
Kauri Flat 9 J2 11 B3
Kaurilands 89 D2
Kauroa 11 C3
Kauru Hill 68 H10
Kauwhata 29 D7 31 D1
Kawa 36 C4
Kawaha Point 96 A3
Kawakawa (Northland - Far North) 1 G7
Kawakawa (Northland) 4 C9
Kawakawa Bay 8 E8 9 A5
Kawakawa Hut 33 H6
Kawarau Falls 65 H5 126 B5
Kawarau Gorge 66 H8
Kawatiri 42 F11
Kawatiri Walkway 42 F12
Kawau Island 6 F11
Kawautahi 18 H10
Kaweka Forest Park 19 J6 27 C7
Kaweka Hut 27 B7
Kawerau 14 G8
Kawerua 3 F4
Kawhia 11 F2
Kawhia Museum 11 F2
Kawiti 4 C8
Kawiti Caves - Kawakawa 4 C9
Kekerengu 44 H11
Kelburn 110 D1
Kelchers 68 D10
Kelly Knight Hut 27 H5
Kelly Tarltons Underwater World - Auckland
    7 D5 90 B4
Kellys Bay 5 D4
Kellyville 7 J7 9 D4
Kelman Hut 49 J7
Kelso 72 H12 73 H1
Kelson 33 D3 35 A2 111 C4
Kelston 89 C2
Kelvin Grove 30 D8 31 D2 105 A5
Kelvin Heights 65 H5
Kenana 2 H9
Kenepuru Head 35 H2 40 F11
Kenepuru Sound 35 K2 40 F9
Kenmure 124 E4
Kennedy Bay 8 C11 36 J5
Kennedy Memorial Hut 59 D5
Kennington 77 E5
Kensington 123 J2
Kensington (Dunedin) 124 E4
Kensington (Whangarei) 85 B1
Kepler Track - Great Walk 70 C10
Kereone 10 J9 12 B10
Kerepehi 8 J11 10 D8
Kereru 28 F8
Kererutahi 14 F12
Kereta 8 E10
Keretu 21 B6
Kerikeri 4 A8 86 B2
Kerikeri Inlet 2 K13 4 A9
Kerin Forks Hut 58 H9
Kerosene Creek Thermal Area - Waiotapu
    13 J5
Kerrytown 61 H4
Ketetahi Hot Springs - Tongariro National
    Park 18 J13 19 J1
Ketetahi Hut 18 J13 19 J1
Kew (Dunedin) 124 E5
Kew (Invercargill) 128 B5
Key, The 70 E13 71 E2
Khandallah 33 E1 35 C3 110 D2
Kia Ora 68 H11
Kihikihi 11 F7
Kikiwa 42 F13 43 E1
Kilburnie 110 E2
Killinchy 55 G6 62 B12
Kimbell 60 E12
Kimberley 52 G12 53 G3 55 C5
Kimbolton 30 A9 31 A3
Kime Hut 33 B6
Kimihia 9 G5
Kina 38 H10 39 F2
Kings Creek Hut 42 C10
Kingsdown 68 A13
Kingseat 7 G5 9 B2
Kingsland 87 J1 89 C3 90 C4
Kingsley Heights 111 B6
Kingston (Wellington) 110 E1
Kingston Crossing 72 H8
Kingston, SI 72 B8
Kingswell 128 B5

Kinleith 12 H12 13 H1
Kinloch, NI 19 D4
Kinloch, SI 64 F12 65 F2
Kinohaku 11 G2
Kintail Hut 69 F7
Kiokio 11 G6
Kirikau 18 G9 24 A14
Kirikopuni 4 H9
Kirioke 3 D7
Kiripaka 4 F13
Kiritaki 30 C11 31 C5
Kiritaki Hut 30 C10 31 C4
Kiritehere 11 J2
Kiriwhakapapa 29 J7 31 J1 34 A8
Kirwans Track 46 A10
Kirwee 52 H13 53 H4 55 D6
Kiwi 42 D12
Kiwi Hut 46 J8
Kiwi Mouth Hut 27 B7
Kiwi Saddle Hut (Kahurangi FP) 42 C10
Kiwi Saddle Hut (Kaweka FP) 27 B7
Kiwi Track 42 C10
Kiwitahi 10 J8 12 B9
Kiwitahi Station 10 J8 12 B9
Kiwitea 30 B9 31 B3
Klondyke Track 46 C11
Knapdale 72 J10 78 A9
Knights Track 27 J4 30 A11 31 A5
Knobbies, The 80 C1
Knobs Flat 64 H9
Koaunui Hut 14 J12 15 J1 21 A3
Koeke Junction 26 F13
Kohaihai Shelter 37 G2
Kohatu 42 C13 43 B1
Kohe 3 B2
Kohekohe 7 H3
Kohi 24 J9 25 F4
Kohika 68 B12
Kohiku 30 G12 31 G6
Kohinui 30 E11 31 E5
Kohukohu 3 C5
Kohumaru 2 J9
Kohupatiki 103 B4
Kohuratahi 17 H6 24 B11
Koiro 18 G9 24 A14
Koitiata 29 A4
Kokako 21 F3
Kokatahi 50 A12 51 A3
Kokiri 45 F5
Kokoamo 68 F10
Kokonga 67 J6
Kokopu 4 G10
Kokowai Track 23 D5
Komako 30 B10 31 B4
Komakorau 9 H5 11 A6
Komata 10 E9
Komata Reefs 10 E10
Komokoriki 6 F8
Kongahu 37 J2 41 A7
Konini (Auckland) 89 D2
Konini (Manawatu) 30 F9 31 F3
Kononi 73 J4 79 B2
Kopaki 18 A10
Kopane 29 D7
Kopara 46 G8
Kopikopiko 30 F8 31 F2
Kopu 8 H11 10 C8
Kopua 30 B14 32 B8
Kopuarahi 8 J11 10 D8
Kopuaranga 34 A9
Kopuawhara 22 J8 22 AA1
Kopuku 8 J8 9 D5
Kopuriki 14 J9 20 A12
Koputaroa 29 G5
Korakonui 12 G8
Koranga 21 B5
Koranga Forks Hut 21 A4
Korapuki Island 8 B14
Koremoa 5 B3
Korere 42 D13 43 C1
Koriniti 24 J14 26 F9
Korito 23 C5
Korokoro 110 C3
Koromatua 11 C6 92 H1
Koromiko 35 J4 40 H10 44 A11
Koropuku Hut 46 J8 52 A9
Korora 30 F12 31 F6
Korowai/Torlesse Tussocklands Park 52 E10
    52 F9
Koru 23 B4
Kotare 17 F5

Kotemaori 20 J13 21 J1
Kotepato Hut 14 J13 15 J2 21 A4
Kotinga 38 E8
Kotuku 45 F6
Kourawhero 6 F9
Koutu (Kauri Coast) 3 D3
Koutu (Rotorua) 13 G4 96 B2
Kowai Bush 52 F11 53 F2 55 B4
Kowhai Park 110 E1
Kowhitirangi 50 A12 51 A3
Kuaotunu 8 C13
Kuku 29 H4
Kukumoa 14 F13 15 F2
Kukupa 56 F12
Kumara 45 G4
Kumara Junction 45 G3
Kumara Reservoir 45 H4
Kumeroa 30 D11 31 D5
Kumeti Hut 30 B11 31 B5
Kumeu 6 J8 7 C2
Kundy Island 80 H1
Kupe 23 D7 25 A2
Kuranui 10 H8 12 A9
Kuratau 19 F3
Kuratau Junction 18 F14 19 F2
Kuri Bush 74 J9 79 B7
Kuriheka 68 J10
Kuripapango 27 C7
Kuriwao 78 C13 79 E1
Kurow 67 D7
Kutarere 14 F12 15 F1
Kyeburn 67 J6
Kyeburn Diggings 67 G6
Kyle 55 J5 62 D11

L

Ladbrooks 53 J7 56 E9
Lady Barkly 77 B4
Lady Knox Geyser - Waiotapu 13 J5 20 A8
Lady Lake 45 G7
Lagmhor 55 H2 62 C8
Laingholm 7 F3 89 E2
Laingholm Central 89 D2
Lairdvale 18 F10
Lake Ada 64 E8
Lake Adelaide 64 E9
Lake Agnes 64 C9
Lake Ahaura 46 F8
Lake Alabaster/Wawahi Waka 64 B10
Lake Alabaster Hut 64 C10
Lake Alexandrina 60 D9
Lake Alice, NI 29 B5
Lake Alice, NI (locality) 29 B5
Lake Alice, SI 63 H5
Lake Angelus 42 H12
Lake Aniwhenua 14 J9
Lake Annie 70 C8
Lake Aorere 37 G4
Lake Arapuni 12 G10
Lake Aratiatia 19 C6
Lake Areare 9 H5 11 A6
Lake Atiamuri 12 J13 13 J2 19 A5
Lake Aviemore 67 C6
Lake Barfoot 37 H4
Lake Barra 58 E11
Lake Beattie 69 E4
Lake Beddoes 63 G5
Lake Benmore 67 A5
Lake Bernard, NI 29 B5
Lake Bernard, SI 63 G6
Lake Bloxham 70 A9
Lake Brown 64 E8
Lake Browne 69 D6
Lake Browning 51 B6
Lake Brownlee 63 G7
Lake Brunner 45 G6
Lake Brunton 78 H9
Lake Cadman 69 J4 75 C4
Lake Camp 50 J13 51 J4 60 A13 61 A3
Lake Carrick 69 J4 75 C4
Lake Catherine 52 E8 55 A1
Lake Chalice 43 D5
Lake Chalice Track 43 D4
Lake Christabel 46 E12
Lake Christabel Hut 46 E12
Lake Christabel Track 46 E12
Lake Clark 63 J5
Lake Clearwater 50 J13 51 J4
Lake Cobb 37 G5
Lake Coleridge 51 F7
Lake Coleridge (locality) 52 G8

Lake Constance 47 A4
Lake Daniell 46 D13
Lake Dispute 64 H13 65 H3
Lake Dive Hut 23 E5
Lake Dive Track 23 E5
Lake Douglas 58 E9
Lake Dudding 29 A5
Lake Duncan 70 B8
Lake Dunstan 66 H9
Lake Ella 47 A3
Lake Ellery 57 F6
Lake Ellesmere / Te Waihora 56 G8
Lake Elmer 37 G4
Lake Elterwater 44 F12
Lake Emily 50 J14 51 J5
Lake Emma 50 J13 51 J4 60 A13 61 A3
Lake Erskine 64 F9
Lake Eyles 70 B9
Lake Fergus 64 F10
Lake Ferry 33 G4
Lake Forsyth 56 G10
Lake Fraser 69 J2 75 C2
Lake Gault 49 H4
Lake George 76 H13 77 E1
Lake Gow 72 D9
Lake Grasmere 52 C10
Lake Grassmere 44 E12
Lake Grassmere (locality) 44 E12
Lake Grave 63 F6
Lake Greaney 57 F7
Lake Gunn 64 F10
Lake Guyon 47 D4
Lake Guyon Hut 47 C4
Lake Hakanoa 9 G5
Lake Hakapoua 75 F6
Lake Half 1 E4
Lake Hall 70 B8
Lake Hankinson 63 J6
Lake Hankinson Hut 63 J6
Lake Hanlon 41 C7
Lake Harihari 11 G2
Lake Haupiri 46 G8
Lake Hauroko - New Zealand's deepest lake
    76 D8
Lake Hawdon 52 D10 53 D1
Lake Hawea 66 A9
Lake Hawea (locality) 66 C9
Lake Hay 69 H6 75 B6
Lake Hayes 65 G5
Lake Head Hut 42 H13 43 G1
Lake Head Track 42 H13 43 G1
Lake Heaton 29 B5
Lake Hector 75 E2
Lake Herbert 29 B5
Lake Herengawe 25 G5
Lake Heron 50 H14 51 H5
Lake Herries 70 C9
Lake Hilda 70 B9
Lake Hochstetter 45 E7
Lake Hope 65 J6
Lake Horizon 69 G7 75 A7
Lake Horowhenua 29 G5
Lake Howden Hut 64 F10
Lake Humuhumu 5 D5
Lake Ianthe 50 C9
Lake Iceberg 64 F8
Lake Innes 75 F6
Lake Jasper 44 E11
Lake Jeanette 42 D9
Lake Jewell 37 H4
Lake Kaiiwi 3 H5
Lake Kaikokopu 29 E5
Lake Kakapo 69 J6 75 D6
Lake Kaniere 50 A13 51 A4
Lake Kaniere Walk 50 A13 51 A4
Lake Kanono 5 E5
Lake Karaka 5 D4
Lake Karapiro 12 E9
Lake Kaurapataka 46 J8
Lake Kereta 5 G6
Lake Kimihia 9 G5
Lake Kini 49 J1 58 A13 59 A2
Lake Kiwi 75 F5
Lake Koitiata 29 B4
Lake Koputara 29 E5
Lake Kuratau 18 F14 19 F2
Lake Kuwakatai 5 G6
Lake Leeb 57 G6
Lake Letitia 52 C11 53 C2
Lake Lockett 37 G6
Lake Lois 70 E8
Lake Luna 64 G13 65 G3
Lake Lyndon 52 F9 55 B2

Lake Macarthur 69 J3 75 D3
Lake Mackinnon 63 J4 70 A8
Lake Mahinapua 45 J1 50 A11 51 A2
Lake Mahinerangi 73 G7 79 A5
Lake Man 46 F12
Lake Mangakaware 11 D6
Lake Mangawhio 24 H11 25 E6
Lake Manuwai 2 K11 3 A7
Lake Mapourika 49 F6
Lake Maraetai 12 J11 19 A3
Lake Marahau 25 H6
Lake Maratoto 11 D7
Lake Marchant 63 J4
Lake Marian 64 E10
Lake Marina 42 C8
Lake Marion 46 H12
Lake Marymere 52 D10 53 D1
Lake Mason 46 J12
Lake Matahina 14 G9
Lake Matheson 49 H4
Lake Matiri 42 F9
Lake Matiri Hut 42 F9
Lake Maungarataiti 26 H12
Lake Maungaratanui 26 H12
Lake McIvor 63 J5
Lake McKellar 64 F10
Lake McKerrow 64 B9
Lake McRae 48 B9
Lake Middleton 59 H4
Lake Mike 69 J5 75 C5
Lake Minchin 46 J9 52 A10 53 A1
Lake Moananui 12 H11
Lake Moawhango 26 C14 27 C2
Lake Moeraki 58 B11
Lake Moeraki (locality) 58 B10
Lake Mokeno 5 E4
Lake Monk 75 E6
Lake Monowai 70 J9 76 C9
Lake Morehurehu 1 D4
Lake Moreton 63 E7
Lake Morgan 46 H8
Lake Mouat 75 E6
Lake Moumahaki 24 J10 25 F5
Lake Mudgie 45 H4
Lake Mueller 49 H4
Lake Namunamu 26 H12
Lake Never-never 64 C8
Lake Ngaroto 11 E7
Lake Ngaruru 26 H11
Lake Ngatu 1 H5
Lake Nigel 71 B6
Lake Nisson 57 F7
Lake Norwest 70 D8
Lake Ohakuri 19 A6
Lake Ohau 59 H4
Lake Ohau Alpine Village 59 H4
Lake Ohia (locality) 1 H7
Lake Okareka 13 G5
Lake Okareka (locality) 13 G5
Lake Okataina 13 G5
Lake Okoia 25 G5
Lake Omapere 3 B7
Lake Omapere (locality) 3 B7
Lake Onoke 33 G4
Lake Onslow 73 D4
Lake Orbell 70 B11
Lake Otamangakau 18 G13 19 G1
Lake Otamatearoa 7 J3 9 D1
Lake Ototoa 5 F6
Lake Otuhie 37 C5
Lake Oturi 25 G4
Lake Owhareiti 4 C8
Lake Papaitonga 29 G4
Lake Paradise 69 D4
Lake Parangi 11 E2
Lake Paringa 58 B11
Lake Paringa (locality) 58 B12 59 B1
Lake Pearson 52 D10
Lake Perrine 42 D8
Lake Phyllis 42 C8
Lake Poerua 45 H6
Lake Pokorua 7 H3
Lake Poteriteri 75 E7
Lake Poteriteri Hut 75 F7
Lake Pourua 20 G8
Lake Poukawa 28 G10
Lake Pounui 33 F4
Lake Pukaki 59 F7
Lake Pupuke 6 J10 7 D4
Lake Purser 69 J4 75 C4
Lake Quill 63 F7
Lake Rahui 41 G5

Lake Rakatu 70 F10
Lake Rasselas 58 B11
Lake Ratapiko 17 J2 23 C7 25 A2
Lake Repongaere 22 D9
Lake Rerewhakaaitu 13 J6
Lake Roe Hut 69 G7 75 A7
Lake Ronald 63 D7
Lake Ross 64 G9
Lake Rotoaira 18 H14 19 H2
Lake Rotoehu 13 F7
Lake Rotoiti, NI 13 F6
Lake Rotoiti, SI 42 G13 43 F1
Lake Rotokakahi 13 H5
Lake Rotokare 24 F8 25 C3
Lake Rotokauri 9 J5 11 B6
Lake Rotokauwau 26 J9
Lake Rotokawa 19 C6
Lake Rotoma 13 F7
Lake Rotoma (locality) 13 F7
Lake Rotomahana 13 H6
Lake Rotongaro 9 F4
Lake Rotonuiaha 20 G14 21 G2
Lake Rotopounamu 19 H2
Lake Rotorangi 24 G9 25 D4
Lake Rotoroa, NI (Northland) 1 H5
Lake Rotoroa, NI (Waikato) 11 C7
Lake Rotoroa, SI 42 H12
Lake Rotorua, NI 13 F4
Lake Rotorua, SI 48 E11
Lake Rototuna 5 D4
Lake Roxburgh (Central Otago) 72 C13
   73 C2
Lake Roxburgh (locality) 72 D13 73 D2
Lake Roxburgh (Southland) 63 H7
Lake Ruapapa 21 G3
Lake Ruataniwha 59 H6
Lake Sarah 52 C10
Lake Scott 72 D10
Lake Selfe 51 E7
Lake Serpentine 11 E7
Lake Sheila 80 D3
Lake Sheppard 46 J12
Lake Shirley 63 J3
Lake Stanley 37 H6
Lake Story 69 G7 75 A7
Lake Sumner 46 H12
Lake Sumner Conservation Park 46 F14
   47 F2
Lake Sutherland 63 H6
Lake Swan 69 E4
Lake Sylvan 64 D11 65 D1
Lake Sylvester 37 G6
Lake Taeore 1 D4
Lake Taharoa (Northland) 3 H5
Lake Taharoa (Waikato) 11 G2
Lake Tarawera 13 H6
Lake Tauanui 3 D7
Lake Taupo / Taupomoana 19 E4
Lake Taylor 46 J12
Lake Te Anau 70 A11
Lake Te Au 70 B8
Lake Te Kahika 1 C4
Lake Tekapo 60 D10
Lake Tekapo (locality) 60 E9
Lake Tennyson 47 C4
Lake Thomas 75 E2
Lake Thompson (Southland) 63 H5
Lake Thompson (Tasman) 47 B4
Lake Tikitapu 13 H5
Lake Track 20 E13 21 E1
Lake Truth 64 C9
Lake Tuakitoto 79 E4
Lake Turner 64 D9
Lake Tutira 28 A12
Lake Unknown 64 D11 65 D1
Lake Victor 69 J4 75 D4
Lake Victoria 70 D9
Lake Vipan 29 A5
Lake Waahi 9 G4
Lake Wade 63 J5
Lake Wahakari 1 D3
Lake Wahapo 49 F6
Lake Waiau 25 G5
Lake Waihola 74 J8 79 B6
Lake Waikare (Taranaki) 24 J11 25 F6
Lake Waikare (Waikato) 9 F5
Lake Waikareiti 21 E3
Lake Waikareiti Track 21 D3
Lake Waikaremoana 20 E14 21 E2

Lake Waikere 3 G5
Lake Waimimiha 1 J5
Lake Waipapa 12 J10
Lake Waiparera 1 G5
Lake Waipori 74 J8 79 B6
Lake Waipu 29 A4
Lake Wairarapa 33 E5
Lake Waitaki 67 C7
Lake Waitaki (locality) 67 D7
Lake Waitawa 29 H4
Lake Wakatipu 64 H14 65 H4
Lake Wanaka 66 B8
Lake Wapiti 63 J5
Lake Whakamaru 19 A4
Lake Whakaneke 5 E4
Lake Whangape 9 F4
Lake Widgeon 69 J5 75 C5
Lake Williamson 64 A12 65 A2
Lake Wilmot 64 A10
Lake Wiritoa 26 J8
Lake Wisely 70 A9
Lakeside 55 G7 62 B13
Lakeside Track 42 H13 43 G1
Langdale 34 B12
Langs Beach 6 A8
Lansdowne 53 J7 56 E9
Larrikin Creek Hut 42 D9
Larrys Creek 41 J5 46 A9
Lauder 66 H12 67 H1
Lauriston 55 G3 62 B9
Lawrence 73 H5 79 A3
Lawrence Hut 50 G11 51 G2
Lawyers Delight Hut 50 A13 51 A4
Le Bons Bay 56 G13
Le Crens Hut 59 E5
Leamington, NI 12 D8
Leamington, SI 48 J8
Lee Flat 73 G7
Lee Stream 74 G8
Lees Valley 52 D13 53 D4
Leeston 55 G7 62 B13
Leigh 6 D11
Leith Valley 74 G11 124 D2
Leithfield 54 E8 56 A10
Leithfield Beach 54 E8 56 A10
Leon Kinvig Hut 27 J5 30 A12 31 A6
Lepperton 17 H1 23 B6
Leslie - Karamea Track 37 J5 42 A10
Levels 61 H4
Levels Valley 61 H3
Levin 29 G5
Lewis Hut 37 F2
Lewis Pass Scenic Res 46 D13 47 D1
Liberton 124 D3
Lichfield 12 F11
Liebig Hut 60 A8
Limehills 77 A4
Limestone Downs 9 F1
Limestone Valley 60 G12 61 G1
Lincoln 89 C2
Lincoln University 53 J6 56 F8 62 A14
Lincoln, SI 53 J6 56 F8
Linden 33 D2 35 B2 110 B2
Lindenvale 110 B2
Lindis Crossing 66 F10
Lindis Hut 66 B11
Lindis Valley 66 D11
Linkwater 40 G9 44 A10
Lintley 71 G6
Linton 29 E7 31 E1
Linwood 54 H8 56 D10 120 F3
Lismore 61 D6
Little Akaloa 56 F12
Little Barrier Island 6 C13 36 D1
Little Barrier Island Nature Reserve 6 C13
   36 D1
Little Bay 8 B11 36 J5
Little Huia 7 F2 89 E1
Little Island 75 D3
Little Manly 88 C5
Little Rakaia 55 H6 62 C12
Little River 56 G11
Little Valley 72 B14 73 B3
Little Waihi 13 C6
Little Wanganui 41 B7
Littlebourne 123 D2
Liverpool Hut 64 A14 65 A4
Livingstone (Hamilton) 92 F2
Livingstone (Wanganui, NI) 26 J13 27 J1
Livingstone, SI 68 G8
Loburn 53 E7 56 A9
Loburn North 53 E7 56 A9

Loch Katrine 46 H12
Loch Loudon 73 H7 79 A5
Loch Luella 73 H7 79 A5
Loch Maree 69 G6 75 A6
Loch Maree Hut 69 G6 75 A6
Loch Norrie 6 H8 7 B2
Lochiel 77 C4
Lochindorb 78 D14 79 F2
Lochinvar Hut 52 B11 53 B2
Lochnagar 64 C14 65 C4
Locke Stream Hut 46 J9
Logantown 66 G10
Lonely Lake Hut 37 F6
Long Bay 6 H10 7 B4 88 E4
Long Beach 74 F12
Long Harry Hut 77 J1 80 C3
Long Island (Marlborough) 35 G2 40 F12
Long Island (Southland) 69 H3 75 B3
Long Range Lake 32 B12
Longbeach 62 F8
Longburn 29 E7 31 E1
Longbush, NI 34 D8
Longbush, SI 77 E6
Longford 42 G9
Longlands 28 F11 103 D6
Longridge 72 H8
Longridge North 71 G7
Longview Hut 27 J5
Longwood 76 H14 77 E2
Lorneville 77 E5
Lovells Flat 79 D4
Loveridge Hut 37 J6 42 A11
Lowburn 66 G9
Lowcliffe 61 F7
Lower Arahura Hut 51 A6
Lower Goulter Hut 43 D4
Lower Hutt 33 E3 35 A3 110 C3
Lower Kaimai 12 C13 13 C2
Lower Kawhatau 27 G3
Lower Matakuhia Hut 20 G10
Lower Moutere 38 H9 39 F1
Lower Nevis 72 A10
Lower Portobello 74 G12
Lower Princhester Hut 70 E13 71 E2
Lower Selwyn Huts 55 G8 62 B14
Lower Shotover 65 H5
Lower Tama Lake 19 J1   26 A13 27 A1
Lower Waihou 3 C3
Lower Waiohine Track 33 B7
Lower Wairaki Hut 70 H13 71 H2 76 B13
Lower Windley Hut 71 D4
Lowgarth 23 E6 25 B1
Lowry Bay 33 E3 35 A3 110 C3
Lowther 71 F6
Lucretia Hut 46 E13 47 E1
Luggate 66 D9
Lumsden 71 G6
Luna Hut 42 C9
Luxmoore Hut 70 C10
Lyall Bay 33 F2 35 B4 110 E2
Lyalldale 68 A12
Lyell 41 G7
Lyell Hut 50 F12 51 F3
Lyell Walkway 41 G7
Lyndhurst 55 F2 62 A8
Lynfield 89 D3
Lynmore 13 G4 96 C5
Lynmouth 107 C2
Lynnford 61 E7
Lyttelton 54 J8 56 E10
Lyttelton Harbour/Whakaraupo 54 J9

M

Maata 23 F7 25 C2
Mabel Bush 77 D6
Macandrew Bay 74 H12 124 B3
Macetown 65 F5
Mackaytown 10 F10
Mackenzie Hut 46 H10
Mackford 17 D5
Mackintosh Hut 28 B8
Maclennan 78 F13 79 H1
Macraes Flat 74 B10
Maerewhenua 68 F9
Maeroa 91 C1 92 E2
Maewa 29 C7 31 C1
Magdalen Hut 46 F14 47 F2
Mahakirau 8 E12
Mahana 38 J10 39 G2
Mahanga 22 H9 22 AA2
Maharahara 30 C11 31 C5
Maharahara West 30 C10 31 C4

Maharakeke 32 A9
Maheno 68 J10
Mahia 22 J9 22 AA2
Mahia Beach 22 J9 22 AA2
Mahina Bay 110 D3
Mahinepua 2 H11
Mahitahi 58 A13 59 A2
Mahoe 23 E6
Mahoenui 17 B7
Mahora (Bay of Plenty) 16 E12
Mahora (Hastings) 103 C5
Mahurangi 6 F10
Mahurangi West 6 F10 7 A4
Mahuta (Northland) 5 A2
Mahuta (Waikato) 9 G4 11 A5
Maia 124 C3
Maihiihi 11 H7
Maimai 46 B8
Maioro 7 J4 9 D1
Maioro Sands 9 E1
Mairangi Bay 6 J10 7 C4
Mairehau 120 E4
Mairetahi 5 G7
Mairoa 11 J4
Mairtown 85 B2
Maitahi 3 H6
Maitai 115 C6
Maitai Dam 38 J13 39 G5 43 A6
Maitland 72 J11 78 A10
Makahika 29 G6
Makahu 24 D10 25 A5
Makahu Saddle Hut 28 B8
Makaka (Taranaki) 23 F5
Makaka (Waikato) 11 D2
Makakaho 24 G12 25 D7
Makakaho Junction 24 H11 25 E6
Makakoere Hut 21 B4
Makara 33 E1 35 C3 110 D1
Makara Beach 33 E1 35 C3 110 C1
Makaraka 22 D10 100 A1
Makaranui 26 C11
Makarau 6 G8 7 A2
Makareao 74 B12
Makaretu 27 J6 30 A13 31 A7
Makaretu Hut 27 J5 30 A12 31 A6
Makarewa 77 D5
Makarewa Junction 77 D5
Makarora 58 H10
Makarora Hut 58 G12 59 G1
Makauri 22 D10
Makerua 29 F6
Maketawa Track 23 D5
Maketu 13 C6
Maketu Pa 11 F2
Makikihi 68 C13
Makino 30 B8 31 B2
Makirikiri 30 C12 31 C6
Makirikiri South 29 A5
Makohine Valley 26 G14 27 G2
Makomako (Manawatu) 30 F9 31 F3
Makomako (Waikato) 11 E3
Makomako Hut 21 C3
Makorori 22 D11
Makotuku 30 B13 31 B7
Makuri 30 F11 31 F5
Mamaku 12 F14 13 F3
Mamaranui 3 H6
Mana 33 C2 35 B1
Mana Island 33 C1 35 C1
Manaia (Taranaki) 23 G5
Manaia (Waikato) 8 D11
Manakau 29 H4
Mananui 45 J1
Manaohou Right Branch Hut 20 A13
Manapouri 70 E10
Manaroa 35 J2 40 F10
Manawahe 13 F7
Manawaora 4 B11
Manawaru 10 H10 12 A11
Manawatawhi/Great Island (75 E3)
Manawatu Art Gallery - Palmerston North
30 D8 31 D2
Manawatu Museum - Palmerston North
30 D8 31 D2
Manawatu River Estuary Wetland 29 F4
Mandeville 72 J9 78 A8
Mandeville North 53 G7 56 C9
Mangaehuehu Hut 26 B12
Mangaeturoa 26 C10
Mangahao 30 E9 31 E3
Mangahao Flats Hut 29 H6
Mangahei 30 C13 31 C7
Mangahouhou 18 G13 19 G1

Mangaiti 10 G9
Mangakahika Hut 20 F11
Mangakahu Valley 18 D11
Mangakakakahi 96 C2
Mangakino 12 J11 19 A3
Mangakino Track 10 G10
Mangakirikiri Hut 3 C5
Mangakura 6 F8
Mangakuri Beach 28 J12 32 A13
Mangamahu 26 G11
Mangamaire 30 F9 31 F3
Mangamako Hut 14 J9
Mangamate Hut 20 E11
Mangamaunu 48 D13
Mangamingi 24 F8 25 C3
Mangamuka 2 K9 3 A5
Mangamuka Bridge 3 A5
Mangamuka Gorge Walkway 2 K7 3 A3
Mangamutu 30 E9 31 E3
Manganui Skifield - Mt Taranaki / Mt Egmont
23 D5
Manganuku Hut 15 J3
Mangaohae 11 J3
Mangaokewa 18 A11
Mangaone Walkway 33 A5
Mangaonoho 26 H13 27 H1
Mangaoranga 30 H9 31 H3
Mangaorapa 32 D9
Mangaore 29 G6
Mangaorongo 11 G7
Mangaotaki 17 A7
Mangapa 2 J9 3 A5
Mangapai 4 H11
Mangapakeha 34 B12
Mangapapa 100 A3
Mangaparo 18 F8
Mangapehi 18 B11
Mangapiko 11 E6
Mangapiko Valley 9 F6
Mangapouri Hut 20 C12
Mangarakau 37 B5
Mangarawa 30 D10 31 D4
Mangarimu 27 J3
Mangaroa 33 D4
Mangaroa Valley 111 B6
Mangatainoka 30 E10 31 E4
Mangatainoka Hot Springs - Tarawera 20 J8
28 A8
Mangatainoka Hut 19 J7
Mangataiore 2 J8 3 A4
Mangatangi 8 H8 9 C5
Mangatangi Reservoir 8 G8 9 B5
Mangatara 3 J7
Mangataraire 3 C6
Mangatarata 8 J10 9 D7
Mangatawhiri 7 H7 9 C4
Mangatea 11 J5
Mangateparu 10 H8 12 A9
Mangatepopo Hut 18 J13 19 J1
Mangatera 30 C12 31 C6
Mangateretere 28 F12 103 B4
Mangati 11 F5
Mangatiti 30 G12 31 G6
Mangatoatoa Hut 21 C3
Mangatoetoe 2 J7
Mangatoetoe Hut 33 J5
Mangatoi 13 D4
Mangatoki 23 F6 25 C1
Mangatoro 30 D13 31 D7
Mangatu 3 F5
Mangatuna (Gisborne) 16 J11 22 A13
Mangatuna (Manawatu) 30 D14 32 D8
Mangatupoto 18 D10
Mangaturutu Hut 27 A7
Mangaturuturu Hut 26 B12
Mangatutara Hut 15 E7
Mangatutu 12 H8
Mangawara 9 G5
Mangaweka 27 G2
Mangawhai Cliffs Walkway 6 B9
Mangawhai Golf Course 6 B9
Mangawhai Heads 6 B9
Mangawhai Point 6 B9
Mangawhata 29 E6
Mangawhere 3 J7
Mangawhero (Northland) 3 D4
Mangawhero (Taranaki) 23 F5
Mangawhero (Waikato) 11 H6
Mangawhero Hut 20 A12
Mangawhio 24 J10 25 F9
Mangere 7 F5 9 A2 90 E4
Mangere Bridge 90 D4
Mangere East 90 E5

Mangitaipa 3 A4
Mangles Valley 42 G9
Mangonui 2 H8
Mangonui Whaling Museum 2 G8
Mangorei 23 B5 107 D5
Mangorei Track 23 C4
Mangungu 3 C5
Mangungu Mission House 3 C5
Maniatutu 13 D6
Manoeka 13 C5
Manor Park 33 D3 35 A2 111 B4
Manorburn Reservoir 73 B4
Mansion Hut 71 D6
Manson Hut 27 B7
Manson Nicholls Memorial Hut 46 D13
Mansons Siding 18 H11
Manui 27 G2
Manuka Creek 79 C4
Manuka Lake 51 H5
Manukau - Auckland 7 F5 9 A2 90 E5
Manukau - Northland 3 A2
Manukau Heights 90 E6
Manunui 18 F11
Manuoha Track 20 D14 21 D2
Manurewa 7 F5 9 A2
Manurewa East 90 E6
Manutahi 23 H7 25 E2
Manutuke 22 E9
Many Islands 69 H2 75 B2
Maori Hill (Dunedin) 123 B2 124 D3
Maori Hill (Timaru) 121 D2
Maori Lakes 50 J14 51 J5
Maori Rocks 36 A2
Maoribank 111 A6
Mapau 5 B4
Mapiu 18 C10
Mapua 38 J10 39 G2
Mara 30 H13 31 H7
Maraehara 16 D12
Maraekakaho 28 F10
Maraenui 103 B2
Maraeroa (Northland) 3 B5
Maraeroa (Waikato) 18 B13
Maraetaha 22 F9
Maraetai (Auckland) 7 E7
Maraetai (Waikato) 12 J10
Marahau 38 F10 39 D2
Marakerake 68 H10
Maramarua 8 J8 9 D5
Mararewa 42 C13 43 B1
Maratoto 8 J13 10 E10
Marauiti Hut 20 E13 21 E1
Marawiti 55 F3 62 A9
Marco 17 H6 24 B11
Mareretu 5 A6
Marewa 28 D12 103 B2
Marima 30 F8 31 F2
Mariri 38 H10 39 F2
Market Cross 37 J2 41 A7
Marlborough 88 H3
Marlborough Forest 3 F6
Marlow 4 E10
Marohemo 5 B6
Marokopa 11 H2
Marokopa Falls 11 H3
Maromaku 4 D10
Maronan 55 J1 61 D7
Maropea Forks Hut 27 G5
Maropiu 3 H6
Marsden 45 G4
Marsden Bay 4 H13
Marsden Point Oil Refinery 4 H13
Marshland 54 H8 56 D10 120 F5
Marshlands 35 J5 40 J10 44 B11
Martha Gold & Silver Mine - Waihi 10 E11
Martinborough 34 E7
Marton 29 A6
Marton Block 27 J4
Marua 4 E12
Maruakoa 68 G10
Maruia 46 B12
Maruia Springs 46 E13 47 E1
Maruia Springs Thermal Resort 46 E13
47 E1
Marumaru 21 G5
Mary Island 76 D9
Marybank, NI 26 J8
Marybank, SI 38 J12 39 G4
Maryhill 124 E4
Masham 120 B3
Mason Bay Hut 80 E3
Masons Flat 53 A7

Massey 7 D3 89 B2
Massey East 89 B2
Massey North 89 B2
Massey West 89 B2
Masterton 34 B9
Mata (Northland - Far North) 3 B4
Mata (Northland) 4 H12
Matahanea 14 G13 15 G2
Matahapa 14 G12 15 G1
Matahi 14 J11
Matahina 14 G9
Matahiwi (Wanganui) 24 H14 26 E9
Matahiwi (Wellington) 34 A8
Matahuru 9 F6
Matai, NI 12 C11
Matai, SI 45 D6
Mataikona 30 J13 31 J7
Matakana 6 E10
Matakana Island 10 H13 12 A14 13 A3
94 A2
Matakanui 66 G11
Matakatia Bay 88 C5
Matakawau 7 G3
Matakitaki 42 J9
Matakohe 5 B5
Matamata 12 C11
Matamata Aerodrome 10 J10 12 B11
Matamau 30 B12 31 B6
Matangi 12 C8
Matangirau 2 H11
Matapihi 13 B4 94 C3
Matapouri 4 E13
Matapu 23 F6 25 C1
Matarae 74 E8
Matarangi 8 C12
Mataraua 3 E6
Mataraua Forest 3 E5
Matarawa 34 C7
Matariki 42 C12
Mataroa 26 F14 27 F2
Matata 14 D9
Matatoki 8 H12 10 C9
Matau, NI 17 J4 24 C9
Matau, SI 79 F4
Mataura 78 C9
Mataura Island 78 E8
Matauri Bay 2 H12
Matawai 21 A6
Matawaia 4 D8
Matawhera 3 C4
Matawhero 22 D10
Matea 20 E9
Matemateaonga 24 F9 25 C4
Matemateaonga Track 24 E12 25 B7
Matiere 18 E9
Matihetihe 3 C2
Matingarahi 8 F9 9 A6
Matipo Heights 96 D2
Matira 9 G2 11 A3
Matua 94 B1
Maud Island 35 K1 40 E9
Maude Track 23 C5
Mauao/Mt Maunganui 94 A2
Mauku 7 H5 9 C2
Maungahuka hut 33 A6
Maungakaramea 4 H10
Maungapohatu 20 C14 21 C2
Maungapohatu Track 20 C14 21 C2
Maungaraki 110 C3
Maungarau Hut 24 F12 25 C7
Maungaroa 18 J9 24 C14
Maungatapere 4 G10
Maungatapu 13 B4 94 C3
Maungatautari 12 E9
Maungati 68 A11
Maungatua 74 H8 79 A6
Maungaturoto 5 B7
Maungawera 66 C9
Maungawhio Lagoon 22 J9 22 AA2
Maunu 4 G11
Maupuia 110 E2
Mauriceville 30 J8 31 J2
Mauriceville West 30 J8 31 J2
Mavora - Greenstone Track 64 G10
Mavora Walkway 64 J11 65 J1
Mawaro 60 H13 61 H2
Mawheraiti 46 C8
Maxwell 25 G6
Mayfair 103 C5
Mayfield 117 A3
Mayfield (Ashburton) 61 C6

Maymorn 33 D4 111 A6
Mayor Island / Tuhua 10 E13
Maytown 68 D12
McConchies Hut 42 E9
McCoy Hut 50 G10 51 G1
McKellar Hut 64 F10
McKerrow Island Hut 64 B9
McKerrow Track 33 F3 35 A4
McKinnon Hut 27 G5
McLaren Falls - Tauranga 12 C13 13 C2
McLaren Park 89 C2
McLean Falls (SI) 78 G12
McLeod Bay 4 H13
McNab 78 A9
Mead 55 F5 62 A11
Meadowbank 90 C5
Meadowbank, SI 74 C12
Mechanics Bay 90 B4
Medbury 54 A8
Meeanee 28 E12 103 B2
Meg Hut 65 F7
Mellons Bay 90 C6
Melrose 110 E2
Melville 91 J4 92 G3
Menzies Ferry 78 D8
Mercer 7 J7 9 D4
Meremere (Taranaki) 24 G8 25 D3
Meremere (Waikato) 7 J7 9 E4
Meringa 18 F12
Merino Downs 72 J11
Merita 2 F7
Merivale 119 A1 120 D3
Mermaid Pods - Matapouri 4 E13
Merrijigs 46 C9
Merrilands 107 C5
Merrivale 76 E13
Merton 74 E12
Methven 52 J9 55 F2 62 A8
Michies Crossing 74 F12
Mid Flat Hut 58 F13 59 F2
Mid Glenroy Hut 46 B13 47 B1
Mid Goulter Hut 43 D4
Mid Greenstone Hut 64 G11 65 G1
Mid Okahu Hut 20 D12
Mid Pohangina Hut 30 A11 31 A5
Mid Robinson Hut 46 F11
Mid Styx Hut 50 A14 51 A5
Mid Taipo Hut 51 A7
Mid Trent Hut 46 H9
Mid Waiohine Hut 33 A7
Mid Wairoa Hut 43 D4
Middle Head Hut 58 C12 59 C1
Middle Hill Hut 28 A8
Middle Hut 68 H8
Middle Stream Hut 27 H6
Middle Valley 60 F13 61 F2
Middlemarch 74 D8
Middlemore 90 D5
Middleton 120 D2
Middy Creek Hut 39 J5 43 B6
Midhirst 23 D6 25 A1
Midway Hut 20 B12
Mihi 19 B7
Mihiwaka 74 G12
Mikimiki 34 A9
Miko 41 D5
Mikonui Flat Hut 50 C11 51 C2
Mikotahi 107 B2
Milburn 79 C5
Milford Huts 61 H5
Milford Sound (Piopiotahi) 63 C7
Milford Sound (locality) 64 D8
Milford Track - Great Walk 64 E8
Milford, NI 6 J10 7 C4
Milford, SI 61 G5
Mill Creek 8 E12
Mill Road 77 E5
Millers Flat 72 F14 73 F3
Millerton 41 E5
Milltown (Selwyn) 55 H7 62 C13
Milltown (Westland) 45 J4 50 A14 51 A5
Milnthorpe 37 C7
Milson 30 D8 31 D2 105 A4
Milton 79 C5
Mimihau 78 D9
Mina 48 J8
Minaret Bay 66 A8
Minden 10 J12 12 B13 13 B2
Minehaha 42 H8
Minginui 20 D11
Mintaro Hut 63 F7
Miramar 33 F2 35 B4 110 E2

Miranda 8 H9 9 C6
Miranda Hot Springs 8 H9 9 C6
Mirror Lakes 64 H9
Mission Bay 7 D5 90 C5
Mission Bush 7 H4 9 C1
Mistake Flats Hut 50 H10 51 H1
Mitcham 55 G3 62 B9
Mitchells 45 H5
Mitchells Hut 68 J8
Mitchelltown 110 E1
Mitikarukaru 40 C8
Mitimiti 3 C2
Mititai 5 A3
Mitre Flats Hut 29 J6 34 A7
Moa Creek 66 J12 67 J1 73 A4
Moa Flat 72 F13 73 F2
Moa Park Hut 38 F9 39 D1
Moana (Nelson) 116 B4
Moana (Westland) 45 G6
Moana Roa Beach 29 C5
Moawhango 27 E3
Moeatoa 11 J2
Moeawatea 24 G10 25 D5
Moehau 3 D5
Moengawahine 4 F9
Moenui 40 G8 44 A9
Moera 110 C3
Moeraki 74 B14
Moeraki Boulders 74 B13
Moerangi (Waikato) 11 E4
Moerangi (Wanganui) 18 F13 19 F1
Moerangi Hut 20 E11
Moerewa 4 C9
Moeroa 24 F10 25 C5
Moewhare 4 H11
Mohaka 21 J3
Mohuiti 3 B4
Moirs Hill Walkway 6 F9
Mokai 19 B4
Mokaikai Scenic Reserve 1 B3
Mokau (Northland) 4 C12
Mokau (Waikato) 17 D5
Mokau Tarns Track 20 E14 21 E2
Mokauiti 18 C9
Moke Lake 64 H14 65 H4
Mokihinui 41 D6
Mokihinui Forks Ecological Area 42 E8
Mokihinui Forks Hut 42 D8
**Mokohinau Islands (Flax Islands) Nature
 Reserve** 36 A2
Mokohinau Islands / Flax Islands 36 A2
Mokoia 23 H7 25 E2
Mokoia Island 13 F4
Mokoreta 78 E10
Mokotua 77 F7
Mole Hut 42 J11
Mole Track 42 J11
Molesworth Recreation Reserve 48 B8
Momona 74 H9 79 A7
Monaco 116 C3
Monavale, NI 12 D8
Monavale, SI 60 H12 61 H1
Moncks Bay 120 H1
Moncks Spur 120 H1
Moneymore 79 D5
Monowai 70 H11 76 B11
Monowai Hut 70 H9 76 B9
Montalto 61 B5
Montgomerie Hut 46 B10
Monument Hut 59 E4
Moonbeam Hut 50 D11 51 D2
Moonlight 74 C10
Moonlight Hut 66 B10
Moonstone Lake 42 B10
Morere 22 H8
Morere Hot Springs 22 H8
Morgan Hut 42 J12
Morningside (Auckland) 89 C3
Morningside (Whangarei) 84 D5
Mornington 110 E1
Mornington (Dunedin) 74 H11 124 E4
Morrinsville 10 H8 12 A9
Morrisons 74 A11
Morrisons Bush 33 D7
Morton Mains 77 D7
Morven 68 E13
Mosgiel 74 H10 124 J4
Mossburn 71 F4
Mosston 109 B2
Motairehe 36 C4
Motakotako 11 D3
Motatau 4 D9
Motea 30 D13 31 D7

Moteo 28 D11 103 D2
Motiti Island 13 A6
Motu 15 J4
Motu Rimu 77 F5
Motuanauru Island 39 E7
Motuara Island 35 G1 40 E12
Motuariki Island 60 D10
Motuarohia Island 4 A10
Motueka 38 G10 39 E2
Motueka Aerodrome 38 G9 39 E1
Motuhaku Island 13 A7
Motuhaku Island / Schooner Rocks 13 A7
Motuhina Island 16 J11
Motuihe Island 7 D6 90 B6
Motukahaua Island 8 B10 36 J4
Motukaika 60 J14 61 J3
Motukaraka 3 C4
Motukaramarama Island 8 C10 36 J4
Motukarara 56 G9
Motukauri 3 C3
Motukawaiti Island 2 H12
Motukawanui Island 2 H12
Motukawao Group 8 C10 36 J4
Motuketekete Island 6 F11
Motukiekie Island 4 A11
Motukiore 3 C5
Motumakareta Island 8 B10 36 J4
Motumaoho 10 J7 12 B8
Motunau Beach 54 C11
Motunau Island / Plate Island, NI 13 B7
Motunau Island, SI 54 C11
Motunui 17 G2 23 A7
Motuoapa 19 G3
Motuora Island 6 F11 7 A5
Motuoroi Island 16 J11
Motuoruhi Island 8 C10
Motupapa Island 2 K13 4 A9
Motupiko 42 C13 43 B1
Motupipi 38 E8
Moturau Hut 70 D10
Moturekareka Island 6 F11
Moturoa 107 B2
Moturoa Island (Northland - Far North) 1 E7
Moturoa Islands 1 E7
Moturua Island (Northland) 4 A10
Moturua Island (Waikato) 8 C10
Motutaiko Island (Auckland) 36 D3
Motutaiko Island (Taupo) 19 F4
Motutangi 1 F5
Motutangi Swamp 1 F5
Motutapere Island 8 D10
Motutapu Island 6 J12 7 C6 90 A6
Motutapu Island Recreation Reserve 6 J12
 7 C6
Motutere 19 F4
Motuti 3 C3
Mototoa 3 D3
Motuwi Island 8 B10 36 J4
Mou Tapu 65 C7
Mou Waho 65 B7
Moumahaki 25 G5
Moumoukai 8 G8 9 B5
Mount Albert 7 E4
Mt Albert 89 C3
Mount Allan 74 F10
Mt Arthur Hut 37 H7 42 A12
Mount Aspiring National Park 57 H7
Mount Auckland Walkway 6 F8
Mount Barker 66 D8
Mount Bee Huts 71 D5
Mount Biggs 29 C7
Mount Brown Hut 50 A14 51 A5
Mount Bruce 29 J7 31 J1
**Mount Bruce National Wildlife Centre -
 Eketahuna** 30 H8 31 H2
Mount Cargill 74 G12 124 B1
Mount Cheeseman Skifield 52 D9
Mt Cook (Wellington) 110 E2 112 E5
Mount Cook / Aoraki, SI 59 B6
Mount Cook / Aoraki National Park 49 J6
 59 A7
Mount Curl 26 J12
Mount Eden 7 E4 90 C4
Mt Eggeling 57 G4
Mount Herbert Walkway 56 F10
Mount Holdsworth Track 34 A7
Mount Hut 68 J9
Mount Hutt 52 H8 55 D1
Mount Hutt Methven Airfield 52 J8
Mount Hutt Skifield 52 J8
Mount Lyford Skifield 48 F8
Mt Marua 111 A6
Mount Matthews Track 33 F3

Mount Maunganui 13 A4 94 B3
Mount Nessing 60 H12 61 H1
Mount Olympus 37 E5
Mount Olympus Skifield 52 E8 55 A1
Mount Owen 42 D11
Mount Parahaki 4 G12
Mount Pisa 66 F9
Mount Pleasant 54 J8 56 E10 120 G1
Mount Pleasant (Marlborough) 35 J4 40 H10
 44 A11
Mount Pleasant (mountain) 54 J8 56 E10
Mount Potts 50 J12 51 J3
Mount Richards 30 B10 31 B4
Mount Richmond Conservation Park 39 F7
 40 H8 43 B7 44 A9
Mount Robert Skifield 42 H13 43 G1
Mount Roskill 7 E4
Mt Roskill 89 C3
Mount Somers 61 A6
Mount Stoker 74 E9
Mount Stuart 79 C4
Mount Victoria 33 F1 35 C4 110 E2 112 E6
Mount Wellington 7 E5 90 D5
Mount Wesley 3 J7
Mountain House Hut 33 A7
Mourea 13 F5
Mouse Point 47 H5
Moutahiauru Island 16 G12
Moutoa 29 F6
Moutohora 15 J4
Moutohora Island 14 D10
Moutoki Island 14 D10
Mud Spa - Rotorua 13 F5
Mudflats Hut 51 A6
Mueller Hut 59 B6
Muhunoa 29 H4
Muhunoa East 29 H5
Mukahanga 40 B9
Mullins Hut 50 C13 51 C4
Mungo Hut 50 C14 51 C5
Mungoven Gardens - Marton 29 A6
Murchison 42 G9
Murchison Hut 49 H7
Muritai 110 E3
Muriwai 22 H9
Muriwai Beach 7 D1
Murray Aynsley 120 F2
Murray Bay 88 F4
Murupara 20 B11
Musselburgh 124 D4
Muttontown 66 J10 72 A13 73 A2
Myross Bush 77 E5
Mystery Creek 11 D7
Myttons Hut 37 H6**

N

Naenae 33 E3 35 A3 111 C4
Naike 9 G3
Napenape 54 B13
Napier 28 D12 103 A1
Napier Central 101 B3
Napier South 101 D1 103 A1
Narrow Neck 90 B4
Naseby 67 G5
National Aquarium - Napier 28 D12
National Park 18 J11
Native Island 80 E6
Naumai 5 B3
Nawton 92 E2
Nawton North 92 E2
Neave Hut 50 E12 51 E3
Neavesville 8 H13 10 C10
Nee Islets 69 B4
Neill Forks Hut 33 B6
Neils Beach 57 E6
Nelson 38 J12 39 G4 115 C3 116 A5
Nelson Airport 38 J11 39 H3 43 A4
Nelson Creek 45 E6
Nelson East 115 D5 116 B5
Nelson Island 36 D3
Nelson Lakes National Park 47 A3
Nelson South 38 J12 39 G4 43 A5 116 B4
Nenthorn 74 C10
Ness Valley 8 F8 9 A5
Netherby, NI 9 H6 11 A7
Netherby, SI 55 H3 62 C9
Netherton 10 E9
Nevis Crossing 65 J7 72 A10
New Brighton 54 H8 56 D10 120 H4
New Creek 41 G6

New Lynn 7 E4 89 D3
New Plymouth 23 B5 106 B3
New Windsor 89 C3
New Windsor, SI 76 H14 77 E2
Newall 23 D3
Newbury 29 D7 31 D1
Newfield 128 A4
Newland 55 H3 62 C9
Newlands 110 C2
Newman 30 G8 31 G2
Newmarket 87 H6 90 C4
Newstead 11 C7 92 E6
Newton 87 G4 90 C4
Newton Creek Hut 51 A6
Newton Flat 42 G8
Newtown 33 F1 35 C4 110 E2
Nga Kiore / Jag Rocks 40 B10
Nga Manu Wildlife Sanctuary - Waikanae
    33 A4
Nga Motu/Sugar Loaf Islands 23 B5
Ngaawapurua Hut 27 A7
Ngaere 23 E7 25 B2
Ngahape (Waikato) 11 G7
Ngahape (Wellington) 34 D11
Ngaheramai Hut 20 B13 21 B1
Ngahere 45 E6
Ngahinapouri 11 D6
Ngaio 33 E1 35 C3 110 D2
Ngaiotonga 4 B11
Ngaiotonga - Russell Forest Track 4 C11
Ngakawau 41 E5
Ngakonui 18 E11
Ngakuru 13 J3
Ngamatapouri 24 H11 25 E6
Ngamoko 30 A12 31 A6
Ngamoko Hut 30 A12 31 A6
Ngamoko Track 21 E3
Ngapaenga 11 J3
Ngapaeruru 30 C13 31 C7
Ngapara 68 F10
Ngapeke 13 B4 94 D3
Ngapipito 4 C8
Ngapuhi 3 D7
Ngapuke 18 F11
Ngapuna (Otago) 74 C8
Ngapuna (Rotorua) 96 C4
Ngaputahi 20 C12
Ngararatunua 4 F11
Ngarimu Bay 8 G11 10 B8
Ngaroma 12 J9
Ngaroto 11 E7
Ngarua 10 J9 12 B10
Ngaruawahia 9 H5 11 A6
Ngataki 1 E4
Ngatamahine 18 B9
Ngatapa 22 D8
Ngatea 8 J11 10 D8
Ngatimoti 38 H9 42 A14
Ngatira 12 F12 13 F1
Ngatiwhetu 1 D3
Ngaturi 30 F10 31 F4
Ngauranga 33 E2 35 B3 110 D2
Ngawaka 27 E2
Ngawapurua 30 E10 31 E4
Ngawaro 12 E14 13 E3
Ngawha 3 C7
Ngawha Springs - Kaikohe 3 C7
Ngawi 33 J5
Ngongotaha 13 F4
Ngongotaha Valley 12 G14 13 G3
Ngunguru 4 F13
Ngutunui 11 F5
Ngutuwera 25 G5
Niagara 78 G11
Niagara Falls 78 G11
Nichols Hut 29 J6 33 A7
Nightcaps 70 J14 71 J3 76 D14 77 A2
Nihoniho 18 E8
Nikau Caves - Waikaretu 9 G2
Nikau Flat Hut 21 A4
Nikau, NI 30 F9 31 F3
Nikau, SI 41 D6
Nina Hut 46 E13 47 E1
Nireaha 30 G8 31 G2
Noble Island 80 J2
Nobles 46 D8
Nokomai 72 D8
Nolans Hut 50 G8
Nonoti 48 J8 54 A12
Nopera 35 J2 40 F10
Norfolk 17 J1 23 C6
Normanby (Dunedin) 124 C2

Normanby, NI 23 G6 25 D1
Normanby, SI 68 A13
Normandale 33 E2 35 B3 110 C3
Norsewood 30 A13 31 A7
Norsewood Pioneer Museum 30 A13 31 A7
North Arm Hut 80 E5
North Cape - Northernmost point of New
    Zealand 1 A4
North Clyde 21 H5
North Dunedin 123 B4 124 D3
North East Valley 74 G11 124 D3
North Egmont 23 D5
North Harbour 88 G3
North Harbour Stadium 6 J10 7 C4
North Island 80 D6
North Linwood 120 F3
North Mavora Lake 71 A4
North New Brighton 120 H4
North River 4 J12 5 A7
North Taieri 74 G10 124 J2
Northcote (Auckland) 7 D4 88 J4
Northcote (Christchurch) 120 D4
Northcote Central 90 B4
Northcote Point 90 B4
Northcross 88 F3
Northland 33 E1 35 C3 110 D1
Northope 77 C4
North-west Nelson Conservation Park 37 C5
Northwood 120 D5
Norton Reserve 68 D12
Norwest Lakes 70 D8
Norwood 52 J13 53 J4 55 F6 62 A12
Notown 45 E6
Nuhaka 22 J8
Nukuhau 19 D5 97 A1 98 A3
Nukuhou North 14 G12
Nukumaru 25 G6
Nukuroa 68 D13
Nukutaunga Island 2 G12
Nukutawhiti 3 F7
Nukuwaiata Island 40 C11
Nydia Track 40 F8

O

Oaklands 53 J7 56 E9 120 C1
Oakleigh 4 H11
Oaks Hut 33 F3 35 A4
Oakura (Northland) 4 C12
Oakura (Taranaki) 23 B4
Oamaru 68 H12 122 B4
Oamaru Hut 19 H7
Oaonui 23 E2
Oaro 48 F11
Oban / Halfmoon Bay 80 E5
Ocean Beach, NI (Hawke's Bay) 28 G13
Ocean Beach, NI (Northland) 4 H14
Ocean Beach, SI 77 G5 80 A6
Ocean Grove 74 H11 124 C5
Ocean Spa heated saltwater pools - Napier
    28 D12
Ocean View 74 H10 124 H6
Oeo 23 G4
Ohaaki 19 B7
Ohaeawai 4 C8
Ohai 70 J13 71 J2 76 C13
Ohakea Wing RNZAF Museum - Bulls 29 C6
Ohakune 26 C11
Ohakuri 19 A5
Ohana 40 D8
Ohane Hut 20 A14 21 A2
Ohangai 23 H7 25 E2
Ohapi 61 G5
Ohapuku 54 G8 56 C10
Ohariu Valley 110 C2
Ohau 29 H5
Ohau Skifield 59 G4
Ohaua 20 C13 21 C1
Ohaupo 11 D7
Ohautira 9 J3 11 C4
Ohawe 23 H6 25 E1
Ohineakai 16 F11
Ohinemutu 13 G4 96 B3
Ohinepaka 21 H4
Ohinepanea 13 D7
Ohinetahi 54 J8 56 E10
Ohinewai 9 F5
Ohingaiti 26 H14 27 H2
Ohingaroa 103 C1
Ohiwa 14 F12 15 F1

Ohiwa Oyster Farm 14 F11
Ohoka 53 F7 56 B9
Ohope 14 E11
Ohora Hut 14 J11
Ohotu 27 F3
Ohui 8 G14 10 B11
Ohura 18 F8
Ohurakura 28 A11
Ohuri 3 C4
Oingo Lake 28 E11
Oio 18 H11
Okaeria 9 E6
Okahu (Northland - Far North) 1 J6
Okahu (Northland) 5 A4
Okahu Island 4 A11
Okahukura 18 E10
Okaiawa 23 G6 25 D1
Okaihau 3 B7
Okains Bay 56 F13
Okaka 3 B6
Okapu 11 E3
Okarae 30 C13 31 C7
Okaramio 40 J8 44 B9
Okari Lagoon 41 H2
Okarito 49 E5
Okarito Lagoon 49 E6
Okato 23 C3
Okau 17 F5
Okauia 12 C12
Okauia Pa 12 C12 13 C1
Oke Island 69 G5 75 A5
Okere Falls 13 F5
Okete 11 C4
Okiato 81 C2 4 B10
Okiore 14 H13 15 H2
Okitu 22 E11 100 C6
Okiwi 36 D4
Okiwi Bay 39 E7
Okoia 26 H9
Okokewa Island 36 D3
Okoki 17 G3 24 A8
Okoroire 12 E11
Okui Hut 20 B12
Okuku 53 E6 56 A8
Okuku Reservoir 45 J4
Okupu 36 E4
Okura 88 D3
Okura, NI 6 H10 7 B4
Okuru, SI 58 D8
Okuti Valley 56 G11
Old Man Rock 76 H12
Old Powell Hut 33 A7
Olivine Hut 64 B10
Omaha 6 E10
Omaha Flats 6 E10
Omahu (Hawke's Bay) 28 E11
Omahu (Waikato) 8 J12 10 D9
Omahuta Forest 2 K9 3 A5
Omaio 15 D5
Omakau 66 H12 67 H1
Omakere 32 A12
Omamari 3 H6
Omana 4 J9
Omana Beach 7 E7
Omanaia 3 D4
Omanawa 12 C14 13 C3
Omanawa Falls 12 D14 13 D3
Omanu 13 B4 92 B3
Omanu Beach 13 B4
Omanuka Lagoon 29 D5
Omapere 3 E3
Omarama 67 A3
Omaru Hut 24 D11 25 A6
Omarumutu 14 F14 15 F3
Omata 23 B4 107 D1
Omatane 27 F4
Omaui 77 G4 80 A6
Omaui Island 77 G4 80 A6
Omaunu 2 J10
Omiha 7 D7
Omihi 54 C9
Omimi 74 F12
Omoana 24 F9 25 C4
Omokoroa 10 J12 12 B13 13 B2
Omokoroa Beach 10 H12 12 A13 13 A2
Omori 19 F2
Omoto 45 F4
Onaero 17 G2 23 A7
One Tree Hill 7 E5 90 C4
Onehunga 7 E4 90 D4
Onekaka 37 D7
Onekawa 103 B2

Onemana 8 H14 10 C11
Onepoto 21 F2
Onepu 14 F8
Onepu Hut 14 J11
Onerahi 4 G12
Oneriri 5 D7
Oneroa 6 J13 7 D7
Onetangi 7 D7
Onewhero 7 J5 9 E2
Ongaonga 28 J8
Ongarue 18 D10
Ongaruru 16 H11
Onoke 3 C3
Onuku 56 H12
Opaea 27 E3
Opaheke 7 G6 9 B3
Opahi 4 D9
Opakau Island 36 D3
Opaki 34 A9
Opaku 24 J9 25 F4
Opal Hot Springs - Matamata 12 C12
Opape 15 F3
Opara 3 C4
Oparara 37 J2 41 A7
Oparau 11 F3
Oparure 11 J5
Opatu 18 G8 24 A13
Opawa 54 J8 56 E10 120 F2
Opawe Hut 30 B10 31 B4
Open Bay Islands 57 D7
Ophir 66 H12 67 H1
Opihi 60 G14 61 G3
Opiki 29 E6
Opio 71 J3
Opito 8 C13
Opoho 124 D3
Oponae 14 J13 15 J2
Opononi 3 D3
Oporo 77 D4
Opotiki 14 F13 15 F2
Opou 37 B7
Opouriao 14 G11
Opoutama 22 J8 22 AA1
Opouteke 3 F7
Opoutere 8 G14 10 B11
Opua 4 B10 81 C3
Opuatia 9 E3
Opuawhanga 4 D12
Opuha 60 G14 61 G3
Opunake 23 F3
Opureke Track 20 G9
Oraka Beach 22 J9 22 AA2
Orakau 12 F8
Orakei 90 C5
Orakei Korako 19 B6
Orakipaoa 61 H5
Oranga 90 D4
Orangapai 67 J5 74 A8
Orangimea 24 J11 25 F6
Orangipongo 26 H13 27 H1
Oranoa 3 F5
Oraora 3 E4
Orapiu 8 D8
Orari 61 F5
Orari Bridge 61 E5
Oratia 7 E3 89 D2
Orauta 4 C8
Orautoha 26 B10
Orawau 3 B4
Orawia 76 E12
Oreore 26 D10
Orepuki 76 G12
Orere 8 F8 9 A5
Orere Point 8 F8 9 A5
Oreti Beach 77 F4
Oreti Plains 77 B4
Orewa 6 G10 7 A4 88 A3
Oriental Bay 110 E2 112 E6
Orikaka Ecological Area 41 F6
Oringi 30 C11 31 C5
Orini 9 G6
Orinoco 38 J9 42 A14
Orira 3 B5
Ormond 22 C9
Ormondville 30 B13 31 B7
Orokonui 74 F12
Oromahoe 4 B8
Orongo 8 H11 10 C8
Orongo Bay 4 B10 81 B3
Orongorongo Track 33 F3 35 A4
Oronui Hut 16 E8
Oropi 13 D3
Orotere 2 J11

Oroua Downs 29 D5
Orton, NI 9 E4
Orton, SI 61 F6
Orua Bay 7 G3
Oruaiti 2 H9
Oruaiti Beach 16 B8
Oruaiwi 18 E12
Oruanui 19 C5
Oruatua 19 F4
Oruawharo 5 D7
Oruhia 120 F6
Oruru 2 H8
Osborne 74 F12
Ostend 7 D7
Ota Creek 78 D8
Otago Central Rail Trail 66 H13 67 H2 74 C8
Otaha 2 J12
Otahu Flat 70 J11 76 D11
Otahuhu 7 E5 90 D5
Otahuti 77 C3
Otaihanga 33 A3
Otaika 4 G11
Otaika Valley 4 G11
Otaio 68 B13
Otaio Gorge 68 B11
Otaitai Bush 77 E2
Otakairangi 4 F10
Otakeho 23 G4
Otaki 29 J4
Otaki Beach 29 J3
Otaki Forks 33 A5
Otakiri 14 E9
Otakou 74 G13
Otama, NI 8 C13
Otama, SI 72 J9
Otamakapua 26 H14 27 H2
Otamaroa 16 B8
Otamatea 26 H8 109 A3
Otamatuna Ridge Track 14 J12 15 J1 21 A3
Otamauri 28 D9
Otamita 78 A8
Otane (Bay of Plenty) 21 A2
Otane (Wairarapa) 28 J10
Otanetea Hut 20 B14 21 B2
Otangarei 85 A2
Otangaroa 2 J9
Otangiwai 18 D9
Otanomomo 79 F3
Otao 4 B9
Otapiri 77 A5
Otapiri Gorge 77 A5
Otapukawa Hut 21 A3
Otara, NI 14 F13 15 F2
Otara, NI - Auckland 7 F5 9 A2 90 D5
Otara, SI 78 H9
Otaraia 78 C10
Otaramarae 13 F5
Otarawhata Island 16 A9
Otatara 77 F4
Otaua (Northland) 3 D6
Otaua (Waikato) 7 J4 9 D1
Otautau 76 F14 77 C2
Otawhao 30 A13 31 A7
Oteaki Conservation Park 67 E4
Otehake Hut 52 A9
Otehirinaki 15 D5
Otekaieke 68 E8
Otekura 79 G3
Otematata 67 C5
Otepopo 68 J10 74 A13
Oteramika 77 E7
Otewa 11 H7
Otiake 68 E8
Otikerama 78 B10
Otipua 61 J4 68 A13
Otira 45 J7 52 A8
Otiria 4 C9
Otokia 74 J9 79 B7
Otoko 21 B7
Otoko Lake 58 C14 59 C3
Otonga 4 E11
Otoroa 2 H11
Otorohanga 11 G6
Otuhaereroa Island 39 E7
Otuhi 4 H10
Otukota Hut 27 F5
Otukou 18 H13 19 H1
Otumatu Rock 48 F11
Otunui 18 F9
Oturehua 66 G14 67 G3
Oturere Hut 18 J14 19 J2

Oturoa 13 F3
Oturu 1 J6
Otutu Hut 27 B6
Otuwhare 15 D5
Otway 10 G9
Oue 3 D4
Oueroa 32 B11
Ouruhia 54 G8 56 C10
Outer Island 38 G10 39 E2
Outer Kaiti 100 C5
Outram 74 H9 79 A7
Overdale 55 G4 62 B10
Owahanga 30 H14 32 H8
Owairaka 89 C3
Owairaka Valley 12 F8
Owaka 79 G3
Owaka Valley 78 E14 79 G2
Oware 78 D9
Oweka 41 H5
Owen Island 80 G6
Owen Junction 42 F10
Owen River 42 F10
Owhango 18 G11
Owhata, NI (Bay of Plenty) 13 G4 96 C5
Owhata, NI (Northland) 3 B1
Owhata, SI 40 C8
Owhiro Bay 110 E1
Owhiro, NI 11 G3
Owhiro, SI 74 H10 124 J5
Owhiwa 4 G13
Oxford 52 F13 53 F4 55 B6

P

Pa Island / Te puke-ki-wiataha 56 F13
Pack Horse Hut 56 F10
Paekakariki 33 B3
Paemako 18 B8
Paenga 42 J8
Paengaroa 13 D6
Paepaerahi 12 F8
Paerata 7 H5 9 C2
Paerata Ridge 14 F13 15 F2
Paerau 73 C7
Paeroa 10 E9
Paetawa Track 20 B14 21 B2
Paewhenua 12 H8
Pahaoa 34 G9
Pahau 47 J5
Pahautea 45 A5
Pahautea 33 E6
Pahi 5 C6
Pahia 76 H12
Pahiatua 30 F10 31 F4
Pahoia 10 H12 12 A13 13 A2
Pahou 14 F10
Paiaka 4 D10
Paihia 4 B10 81 B2
Pakanae 3 D3
Pakaraka 4 C8
Pakatoa Island 8 D8
Pakawau 37 B7
Pakiaka Hut (Parahaki(20 E12
Pakihi Heads Hut 15 H4
Pakihi Hut 15 H4
Pakihi Island 8 E8
Pakihikura 26 J14 27 J2
Pakipaki 28 F11 103 D6
Pakiri 6 D10
Pakotai 4 F8
Pakowhai 28 E12 103 B4
Pakuranga 7 E5 90 D5
Pakuranga Heights 90 D6
Pakuratahi 33 C5
Palm Beach 6 J13 7 D7
Palm Heights 89 C2
Palmerston 74 C13
Palmerston North 30 D8 31 D2
Palmerston North Central 104 B3
Palmerston North International Airport
    105 A4
Pamapuria 1 J7
Panaki Island 2 G12
Pancake Rocks & Blowhole - Punakaiki
    45 B5
Pandora 1 B2
Panekiri Hut 20 F14 21 F2
Panetapu 12 G8
Panguru 3 C3
Panmure 7 E5
Papaaroha 8 C10

Papakai 18 H13 19 H1
Papakaio 68 G12
Papakowhai 110 A3
Papakura 7 G6 9 B3
Papamoa 13 B5 94 D5
Papamoa Beach 13 B5 94 C5
Papanui 53 H7 56 D9 120 D4
Papanui Junction 26 F12
Paparangi - Wellington 33 E2 35 B3
Paparangi (Taranaki) 24 J12 25 F7
Paparangi (Wellington) 110 C2
Paparata 7 H7 9 C4
Paparimu 7 H7 9 C4
Paparoa 5 B6
Paparoa National Park 45 A6
Paparore 1 G6
Papatawa 30 D10 31 D4
Papatea 15 B7
Papatoetoe 7 F5 9 A2 90 E5
Papatotara 76 F11
Papatowai 78 G13 79 J1
Papawai 34 D7
Papawera 16 E11
Paponga 3 B4
Papua 3 C4
Papueru 20 D12
Para 35 K4 40 H9 44 A10
Paradise 64 D12 65 D2
Paradise Valley Springs - Rotorua 12 G14
    13 G3
Parahaka 4 J11
Parahaki 85 C3
Parahi 5 A5
Parakai 5 H7 7 B1
Parakai Hot Springs 5 H7 7 B1
Parakao 4 G8
Parakiwai 8 J14 10 D11
Paranui 2 H8
Paraoanui Pa 14 J11
Parapara, NI 2 H7
Parapara, SI 37 C7
Paraparaumu 33 A3
Paraparaumu Beach 33 A3
Pararaki Hut 33 H6
Parau 7 F3 89 E2
Parawa 71 E7
Parawai 8 H11 10 C8
Parawera 12 F8
Parekarangi 19 A7
Parekura Bay 4 B11
Paremata (East Cape) 22 B12
Paremata (Wellington) 33 D2 35 B2
Paremoremo 6 J9 7 C3 88 G1
Pareora 68 A13
Pareora West 61 J4 68 A13
Paretai 79 F4
Parewanui 29 C5
Parihaka Pa (Cape Egmont) 23 D3
Parikino 26 G9
Parinui 24 E13 26 B8
Pariokara 15 D6
Park Hill 72 G12 73 G1
Park Morpeth Hut 51 B6
Parkhurst 5 H7 7 B1
Parklands 54 H8 56 D10 120 G5
Parks Peak Hut 27 F6
Parkside 121 B5
Parkvale 103 C5
Parkville 30 H8 31 H2
Parkway 111 D4
Parnassus 48 H9
Parnell 90 C4
Paroa Bay 4 B10
Paroa, NI 14 E10
Paroa, SI 45 F3
Paroanui 2 H9
Parore 3 J7
Parrot Island 69 G2 75 A2
Parua Bay 4 G13
Paske Hut 47 B4
Passage Islands 75 E3
Patangata 28 J10
Pataua 4 G13
Patea 24 J8 25 F3
Patearoa 73 A7
Paterangi 11 E6
Patetonga 10 F7
Patoka 28 B10
Patons Rock 37 D7
Patuki 40 A10
Patumahoe 7 H5 9 C2
Paturau River 37 B5

Patutahi 22 D9
Paua 1 C3
Pauanui 8 G14 10 B11
Pauatahanui 33 D3 35 A2 111 A4
Pauri Village 26 J8
Pawarenga 3 B2
Pea Viner Corner 38 J11 39 H3 43 A4
Peaks, The 47 J3 53 A7
Pearl Island 80 H2
Peats Hut 65 F5
Peebles 68 F11
Peel Forest 61 D5
Peel Forest Walks 61 C4
Peep-o-Day 27 J3
Pegasus Bay Walkway 54 F8 56 B10
Pehiri 21 D7
Pekerau 1 H7
Peketa 48 E11
Pelorus Bridge 39 H6 43 A7
Pelorus Sound 40 F9
Pelorus Track 39 H5 43 A6
Pemberton 27 H3
Pembroke 23 E6 25 B1
Pendarves 55 H4 62 C10
Penn Creek Hut 33 A6
Penn Creek Track 33 A6
Penrose 90 D5
Pentland Hills 68 C10
Pepepe 9 H3 11 A4
Pepin Island 38 H13 39 F5
Peria (Northland) 2 J8
Peria (Waikato) 12 C10
Perry Saddle Hut 37 E4
Petone 33 E2 35 B3 110 C3
Petrel Island 69 H2 75 B2
Phillipstown 120 F2
Phoebe 48 J8
Piarere 12 E10
Pickersgill Island 35 G2 40 F12
Picton 35 J3 40 G10 44 A11 113 C3
Picton Museum & Historical Society 35 J4
    40 H10 44 A11
Pig Island (Queenstown) 64 G12 65 G2
Pig Island / Matau (Southland) 76 H14 77 E2
Pigeon Bay 56 F12
Pigeon Bush 33 D6
Pigeon Flat 74 G11 124 D1
Pigeon Island (Queenstown) 64 G12 65 G2
Pigeon Island (Southland) 69 G2 75 A2
Piha 7 E2
Pihama 23 G4
Pikes Point 68 E12
Pikiwahine 4 J10
Piko Piko 76 E12
Pikowai 14 D8
Pine Bush 78 F8
Pine Hill (Auckland) 88 F3
Pine Hill (Dunedin) 124 D2
Pine Valley 88 C1
Pinedale 12 F11
Pinehaven 33 D3 111 B5
Pines Beach, The 54 G8 56 C10
Pioneer Hut 49 J6
Piopio 18 A8
Piopiotahi Marine Res 64 D8
Pios Beach 10 F12
Pipiriki 24 G13 26 D8
Pipiroa 8 J11 10 D8
Pipitea 35 J5 40 J10 44 B11
Pipiwai 4 F9
Piriaka 18 F11
Pirimai 103 B2
Pirinoa 33 F5
Piripai 14 E10
Piripaua 21 F3
Piripiri (Manawatu) 30 B12 31 B6
Piripiri (Waikato) 11 H3
Piripiri Caves 11 H3
Pirongia 11 E6
Pirongia Forest Park 11 E4
Piropiro 18 C11
Pitokuku Island 36 E5
Plateau Hut 49 J6
Plateau, The 33 C4
Pleasant Heights 96 B1
Pleasant Point 61 H4
Pleasant Point Museum & Railway 61 H4
Pleasant Valley 61 F4
Pleckville 30 H9 31 H3
Plimmerton 33 C2 35 B1
Poerua 45 H6
Poet Hut 50 C13 51 C4
Pohangina 30 B9 31 B3

Pohara 38 D8
Pohatu Marine Reserve 56 H13
Pohatukura 16 E11
Pohokura (Hawke's Bay) 20 G9
Pohokura (Taranaki) 17 J5 24 C10
Pohonui 26 G13
Pohuehue 6 F9
Point Chevalier 89 C3
Point Elizabeth Walkway 45 E4
Point England 90 C5
Point Howard 110 D3
Point View Park 90 D6
Point Wells 6 D10
Pokaka 26 B11
Pokapu 4 C8
Pokeno 7 J6 9 D3
Pokere 4 D9
Pokororo 38 J8 42 A13
Pokuru 11 F6
Pollock 7 G3
Polluck Creek Hut 50 C11 51 C2
Polnoon Hut 65 D5
Pomahaka 72 J12 73 J1 78 A11
Pomarangai 11 J2
Pomare (Rotorua) 96 C2
Pomare (Wellington) 33 D3 35 A2 111 B4
Pomona Island 70 E9
Pompeys Pillar 56 H13
Ponatahi 34 D8
Ponga 7 G6 9 B3
Pongakawa 13 D6
Pongakawa Valley 13 D6
Pongaroa 30 G13 31 G7
Ponsonby 87 E1
Ponui Island 8 E8
Poolburn 66 J13 67 J2
Poolburn Reservoir 73 B5
Poor Pete's Hut 42 E9
Popotunoa 78 A13
Poraiti 28 D12
Porangahau 32 D10
Porati 103 C1
Porewa 29 A7
Pori 30 G10 31 G4
Porirua 33 D2 35 B2 110 B2
Porirua East 33 D2 35 B2 110 B3
Porootarao 18 B11
Poroporo 14 E10
Poroti 4 G10
Poroutawhao 29 F5
Port Albert 5 D7
Port Chalmers 74 G12
Port Charles 8 A11 36 H5
Port Craig School 76 G9
Port Fitzroy 36 D4
Port Jackson 8 A10 36 G4
Port Levy 54 J9 56 F11
Port Molyneux 79 F4
Port Motueka 38 H10 39 F2
Port Nelson 38 J12 39 G4 116 A5
Port Ohope 14 F12
Port Puponga 37 A7
Port Robinson 54 A13
Port Robinson Walkway 54 A13
Port Waikato 9 E1
Port Whangarei 4 G12 85 D2
Port William Hut 80 D5
Portage 35 J2 40 F10
Porter Heights Skifield 52 F9 55 B2
Porters Creek Hut 43 D2
Portland 4 H12
Portland Island 22 AC1
Portobello 74 G12 124 A2
Possum Hut 74 F11
Potaka 16 A10
Pouakai Hut 23 D4
Poukawa 28 G10
Poukiore 26 H13 27 H1
Poukura Pa 19 F3
Poulson's hut 66 D12
Pounawea 79 H3
Pourakino Valley 76 F13 77 C1
Pourangaki Hut 27 H5
Pourerere 32 B12
Pourewa Island 22 B13
Pouri Hut 24 E11 25 B6
Pouto Point 5 E5
Pouwhakaura 26 H14 27 H2
Prebbleton 53 J7 56 E9
Prebelton 120 A2
Price Basin Hut 50 D12 51 D3
Price Flat Hut 50 D12 51 D3

Price Flat Hut (Old Hut) 50 D12 51 D3
Prices Corner 38 J10 39 G2
Progress Junction 46 B9
Progress Valley 78 G11
Providence Rocks 75 E2
Puaha 56 G11
Puahue 12 F8
Puangiangi Island 40 B10
Puari 54 J9 56 F11
Puau 24 J11 25 F6
Puerua 79 F3
Puha 22 B9
Puhata 3 B2
Puhinui 90 E5
Puhipuhi 4 D11
Puhoi 6 G9 7 A3
Puhuka 61 J4
Pukahu 28 F11 103 C6
Pukaki Aerodrome 59 H7
Pukapuka 6 F10
Pukaroro Rock 48 F11
Pukawa 19 F2
Pukearuhe 17 F4
Pukeatua 12 F9
Pukeawa 79 D2
Pukehangi 96 C1
Pukehiki 74 H12 124 A4
Pukehina 13 C7
Pukehou 28 H10
Pukeinoi 11 F3
Pukekapia 9 G4
Pukekaroro 5 B7
Pukekawa 9 E3
Pukekohe 7 H5 9 C2
Pukekohe East 7 H6 9 C3
Pukekoma 79 C3
Pukekura Park 107 B4
Pukekura, NI 12 D8
Pukekura, SI 50 C10
Pukemaori 76 E12
Pukemiro (Northland) 3 B3
Pukemiro (Waikato) 9 H3 11 A4
Pukemoremore 12 C8
Pukemutu 77 A3
Pukengahu 24 E8 25 B3
Pukenui 1 F5
Pukeokahu 27 E4
Pukeoware 7 J4 9 D1
Pukepito 79 D3
Pukepoto 1 J6
Pukepuke Lagoon 29 D5
Pukerangi 74 E9
Pukeraro 68 F8
Pukerau 78 B10
Pukerimu 12 D8
Pukeroro 12 D8
Pukerua Bay 33 C2 35 B1
Puketaha 9 J6 11 B7 92 C5
Puketapu 28 D11 103 D1
Pukete 92 D2
Puketeraki 74 E12
Puketi Forest 2 K10 3 A6
Puketi, NI 3 A7
Puketi, SI 78 A14 79 C2
Puketiro 78 F13 79 H1
Puketitiri 28 B9
Puketoi 30 F12 31 F6
Puketona 4 B8
Puketotara 11 F6
Puketotara Hut 24 E13 26 B8
Puketui 8 G13 10 B10
Puketurua 12 F10
Puketurua Track 29 G7
Puketutu 18 A10
Puketutu Island 7 F4 9 A1
Pukeuri 68 G12
Pukio 33 E6
Punakaiki 45 B5
Punakitere 3 D6
Punakitere Valley 4 D8
Punaromia 13 H5
Punaruku 4 C12
Punawai 61 B7
Punehu 3 C3
Pungaere 2 K11 3 A7
Pungapunga 18 F11
Pungarehu (Taranaki) 23 D2
Pungarehu (Wanganui) 26 G9
Pungataua 27 E3
Puni 7 J5 9 D2
Puniho 23 C3
Puniho Track 23 D4

Puniwhakau 24 E9 25 B4
Puponga 37 A7
Pupu Springs Walking Track 37 E7
Pupuke 2 J10
Purakauiti 78 F14 79 H2
Purakanui (Dunedin) 74 F12
Purakanui Bay 74 F12
Purakaunui (Clutha) 78 F14 79 H2
Purakaunui Bay 79 H2
Purakaunui Falls 79 H2
Puramahoi 37 D7
Purangi (Taranaki) 17 J4 24 C9
Purangi (Waikato) 8 E13
Purau 54 J8 56 F10
Purekireki 78 D13 79 F1
Pureora 18 B13 19 B1
Pureora Forest Park 12 J9 18 A13 19 A1
Purerua 2 J13 4 A9
Purimu Lake 32 B9
Puriri 8 J12 10 D9
Purity Hut 27 H5
Purua 4 F10
Pururu 11 J7
Putangirua Pinnacles - Aorangi Forest Park 33 G5
Putara 29 H7 31 H1
Putaruru 12 F11
Puteore Hut 24 E11 25 B6
Putiki 26 J8
Putorino (Hawke's Bay) 20 J13 21 J1
Putorino (Wanganui) 26 J13
Puwera 4 H11
Pyes Pa 12 C14 13 C3
Pyke Big Bay Track 57 J2
Pyramid Valley 53 B7

Q

Quail Island 54 J8 56 E10
Quail Island Walkway 54 J8 56 E10
Quarry Hills 78 G10
Queen Charlotte Sound 35 J3 40 G10
Queen Charlotte Walking Track 35 H2 40 F11
Queens Flat 68 F10
Queensberry 66 F9
Queenstown 65 H4 125 B2 126 B2
Queenstown Airport 65 H5
Queenwood 92 D3
Quigleys Track 46 C9

R

Rabbit Island 38 J11 39 G3
Racecourse Hill 52 G12 53 G3 55 C5
Raekohua Falls - Tahora 17 G6 24 A11
Raes Junction 72 G14 73 G3
Raetea Forest 2 K7 3 A3
Raetihi 26 C10
Raglan 11 C3
Rahanui 11 D2
Rahiri 3 B6
Rahotu 23 E2
Rai Valley 39 G6
Rainbow Falls - Kerikeri 2 K12 4 A8
Rainbow Hut 43 J1 47 A5
Rainbow Isles 78 G13 79 J1
Rainbow Point 94 D3
Rainbow Springs 96 A2
Rainbow Springs & Farm - Rotorua 13 G4 96 A2
Rainbow Valley Skifield 42 H13 43 G1
Rainbow Warrior wreck - Cavalli Islands 2 G12
Rainbows End Adventure Park - Auckland 7 F5 9 A2
Raio 1 F5
Rakahouka 77 D6
Rakaia 55 G5 62 B11
Rakaia Gorge Walkway 52 H9 55 D2
Rakaia Huts 55 H6 62 C12
Rakaia Lagoon 55 H6 62 C12
Rakau 42 C13 43 B1
Rakaumanga 9 G4
Rakaunui (Manawatu) 30 G12 31 G6
Rakaunui (Waikato) 11 F3
Rakauroa 21 B6
Rakautao 3 D7
Rakautara 48 C13
Rakautatahi 30 A13 31 A7
Rakino Island 6 J12 7 C6
Rakitu Island 36 C5
Rakiura National Park 80 D3
Rakiura Track - Great Walk 80 D5

Ramanui 24 E13 26 B8
Ramarama 7 H6 9 C3
Rameka Track 38 E8
Ranana 24 H14 26 E9
Ranfurly 67 H5
Rangataua 26 C12
Rangatira Beach 5 G5
Rangatira Valley 61 G4
Rangi Point 3 D3
Rangiahua (Hawke's Bay) 21 G4
Rangiahua (Northland) 3 B5
Rangiahua Island 36 D3
Rangiaowhia 11 E7
Rangiatea 11 H7
Rangihaeata 38 D8
Rangiora, NI 3 C4
Rangiora, SI 53 F7 56 B9
Rangiotu 29 E6
Rangipo 19 H3
Rangipo Hut 26 B13 27 B1
Rangipu 11 C3
Rangipukea Island 8 D10
Rangiputa 1 F6
Rangiriri 9 F4
Rangitaiki 20 F8
Rangitata 61 E5
Rangitata Island 61 F6
Rangitatau 25 G6
Rangitihi 1 J7
Rangitoto 11 J6
Rangitoto Island 6 J11 7 D5 90 A5
Rangitoto Island Scenic Reserve 6 J11 7 C5
Rangitoto Islands 40 B10
Rangitoto ki te Tonga / D'Urville Island 40 B8
Rangitukia 16 D13
Rangitumau 34 A9
Rangiuru 13 C5
Rangiwaea Island 10 H13 12 A14 13 A3
Rangiwaea Junction 26 D13
Rangiwahia 27 H3
Rangiwahia Hut 27 H4
Rangoon Heights 110 D2
Rankleburn 78 A12
Ranui 11 C4 89 C2
Ranui - Auckland 7 D3
Ranui Heights 110 B3
Rapahoe 45 E4
Rapaki 54 J8 56 E10
Rapanui 25 H7
Rapaura 35 K5 40 J9 44 B10
Rapid Creek Hut 50 C12 51 C3
Rapuwai 60 F14 61 F3
Rarangi 35 J5 40 J10 44 B11
Raroa 110 C2
Raroa Track 14 H11
Rarotoka Island / Centre Island 76 J13 77 F1
Raspberry Creek Hut 65 B5
Rata 26 J12 29 A7 31 A1
Rataiti 26 H12
Ratana 29 A4
Ratanui 79 H3
Ratapiko 17 J2 23 C7
Raukawa Falls 26 E10
Raukawa Rock 35 F3 40 G13
Raukokore 16 B8
Raukumara Forest Park 16 E8
Raumai 30 C9 31 C3
Raumanga 85 C1
Raumati 30 C12 31 C6
Raumati Beach 33 A3
Raumati South 33 B3
Raupo, NI 5 B3
Raupo, SI 45 D7
Raupunga 21 J2
Raureka 103 C5
Raurimu 18 J11
Ravensbourne 74 H12 124 C3
Rawene 3 C4
Rawhia 3 B5
Rawhiti 4 A11
Rawhitiroa 23 F7 25 C2
Raymonds Gap 76 E13 77 B1
Reardon Hut 59 C5
Red Beach 6 H10 7 B4
Red Hill 7 G6 9 B3
Red Hills Hut 43 E2
Red Hut 59 E4
Red Jacks 45 E6
Red Stag Hut 50 J8
Redan 78 E9
Redcliffs 54 J8 56 E10 120 H2
Redhill 5 A2
Redruth 61 J4 68 A13
Redvale 6 H10 7 B4 88 E2
Redwood Valley 38 J10 39 H2 43 A3

Redwood, NI 33 D2 35 B2 110 C2
Redwood, SI 53 H7 56 D9 120 E5
Redwoodtown 35 K6 44 C10
Reefton 46 B9
Reena 3 C3
Rees - Dart Track 64 B12 65 B2
Rees Valley 64 E12 65 E2
Regent 84 A4
Rehia 5 A4
Rehutai 3 J7 5 A2
Reidston 68 H11
Reikorangi 33 A4
Reischek Hut 50 F12 51 F3
Remarkables Skifield 65 H6
Remarkables, The 65 J5
Remuera 7 E5 90 C4
Renata Hut 33 B5
Renown 9 G4
Renwick 44 C9
Reotahi Bay 4 H13
Repia 5 B3
Reporoa 20 A8
Reporua 16 E12
Rere 21 C7
Rere Falls - Bay of Plenty 21 C7
Rerekapa Falls 17 G6 24 A11
Rerekapa Track 17 F5 24 A10
Rerewhakaaitu 13 J6
Reservoir, The 78 H10
Resolution Island 69 G3 75 A3
Retaruke 18 J9 24 C14
Retaruke Upper 18 J10
Rewa 26 J13 27 J1
Rewanui 45 E5
Rewarewa 11 H7
Rewiti 5 J7 7 C2
Riamaki (Upper Ruatiti) 18 J10 26 A10
Riccarton 53 H7 56 D9 120 D3
Riccarton Park 120 C3
Richard Pearse Airport - near Timaru 61 H4
Richardson Track 52 E13 53 E4 55 A6
Richmond (Christchurch) 120 F3
Richmond (Invercargill) 68 G12 127 A5
128 B3
Richmond (Tasman) 39 H3 43 A4 116 D3
Richmond Downs 12 C10
Richmond Heights 98 C5
Richmond Hill 120 H1
Richmond Hut 66 E12 67 E1
Right Branch Wairoa Hut 43 C3
Rigney 72 F14 73 F3
Rileys Lookout - Panau Island 48 E11
Rimariki Island 4 C13
Rimu (Southland) 77 E6
Rimu (Westland) 45 J2
Rimutaka Forest Park 33 E5 33 F3 35 A4
Ringway 76 F14 77 C2
Riordons Hut 37 G7
Ripiro Beach 3 H5
Riponui 4 E10
Ripponvale 66 H8
Rissington 28 D10
Riverdale 100 A2
Riverhead 6 J9 7 C3
Riverlands 35 J6 44 C11
Riverlea 23 F5
Riversdale (Blenheim) 117 A6
Riversdale (Central Otago) 72 J8
Riverside Beach 34 D12
Riverside 84 B5
Riverside, SI 62 E9
Riverstone Terraces 111 A5
Riverton 76 H14 77 E2
Riwaka 38 G9 39 E1
Roa 45 D5
Roaring Lion Hut 37 H5 42 A10
Roaseneath 110 E2
Robinsons Bay 56 G12
Rock and Pillar 74 B9
Rockdale 128 A4
Rockford 52 F12 53 F3 55 B5
Rocks Hut 39 H4 43 A5
Rocks, The 77 E2
Rockville 37 C6
Rocky Creek Hut 45 J5
Rodedale 128 B2
Rodgers Inlet Hut 70 J9 76 C9
Rogers Hut (Te Wairoa) 20 E11
Rokeby 55 G4 62 B10
Rokeby Hut 46 E14 47 E2

Rolleston 53 J6 56 E8
Rolling Junction Hut 42 C11
Romahapa 79 F3
Rona Bay 110 D3
Rona Island 70 E10
Rongahere 72 J14 73 J3 79 B1
Rongoiti Junction 26 F14 27 F2
Rongokokako 30 H8 31 H2
Rongomai 30 G9 31 G3
Rongotai 110 E2
Rongotea 29 D6
Rosebank Road 89 C3
Rosebery 68 G11
Roseneath (Dunedin) 74 G12 124 B2
Rosewill 61 H4
Roslyn (Dunedin) 124 E3
Roslyn (Palmerston North) 30 D8 31 D2
105 A4
Roslyn Bush 77 E6
Ross 50 B11 51 B2
Rosvalls Track 27 H5
Rotherham 47 H6
Rothesay Bay 88 F4
Rotoehu 13 F6
Rotoiti 13 F6
Rotokakahi 3 B2
Rotokare Walkway 24 F8 25 C3
Rotokauri 9 J5 11 C6 92 E1
Rotokautuku 16 E11
Rotokawa (Bay of Plenty) 13 G5 96 A6
Rotokawa (Waikato) 19 C7
Rotokino 49 E7
Rotokohu 41 J5
Rotomahana 13 J5
Rotomanu 45 H7
Rotongaro 9 G4
Rotongata (Bay of Plenty) 13 E4
Rotongata (Waikato) 12 G9
Rotoorangi 12 E8
Rotoroa 42 G11
Rotoroa Island 8 D8
Rotoroa Track 42 H12
Rotorua 13 G4
Rotorua Airport 13 G5 96 B6
Rotorua Central 95 D3
Rotorua Museum 13 G4 96 C3
Rototuna (Northland) 5 D4
Rototuna (Waikato) 9 J6 11 B7 92 C3
Rotowaro 9 H4
Round Hill (Clutha) 73 J6 79 C4
Round Hill (Southland) 76 H13
Round Hill Skifield 60 C11
Round the Island Track North West Circuit
77 J2 80 C4
Round the Mountain Track 26 A13 27 A1
Routeburn Falls 64 E10
Routeburn Flats Hut 64 E11
Routeburn Track - Great Walk 64 D11 65 D1
Rowan 23 E5
Roxburgh 72 D13 73 D2
Roxburgh East 72 D13 73 D2
Royal Oak 90 D4
Ruahine Corner Hut 27 E6
Ruahine Forest Park 27 F5 30 A11 31 A5
Ruahine Hut 27 E7
Ruahine, NI 27 H3
Ruahine, SI 76 H12
Ruakaka 4 J13
Ruakituri 21 E5
Ruakiwi 9 J2 11 B3
Ruakokoputuna 33 F7
Ruamahunga 8 F11 10 A8
Ruanui 26 E13 27 E1
Ruapani Track 21 E2
Ruapekapeka 4 D10
Ruapuke 11 D2
Ruapuke Island 77 J6
Ruapuna 61 C5
Ruarangi 4 J11
Ruaroa (Manawatu) 30 B11 31 B5
Ruaroa (Northland) 1 J7
Ruas Track 21 C3
Ruatahuna 20 C13 21 C1
Ruatangata West 4 F10
Ruataniwha 28 J8
Ruataniwha Conservation Park 59 F6
Ruatapu 45 J1 50 A11 51 A2
Ruatiti 26 A9
Ruato 13 F6
Ruatoki North 14 G11
Ruatoria 16 E11

Ruawai 5 B4
Ruawaro 9 G4
Ruawhata 30 E10 31 E4
Rugged Islands 80 C2
Rukuhia 11 D7 92 J5
Rukuwai 4 G13
Runanga 45 E4
Runanga Lake 28 E10
Runaruna 3 B3
Runciman 7 G6 9 B3
Rurima Island 14 D10
Ruru 45 G6
Russell 4 B10 81 A3
Russell Forest 4 C11
Russells Flat 52 G11 53 G2 55 C4
Russley 120 C3
Rutherglen 45 F3
Ryal Bush 77 D4

S

Sabine Hut 42 H12
Sabine Track 42 J12
Saddle Hill 74 H10 124 H5
Saddle Hut 65 C6
Saddle Rocks 40 A10
Saies 2 H10
Sainsburys Hut 65 F4
Saint Albans 54 H8 56 D10 120 E4
Saint Andrews 68 B13
St Andrews 92 D3
St Andrews Hill 120 G2
Saint Arnaud 42 G13 43 F1
Saint Arnaud Track 42 G13 43 F1
Saint Bathans 66 F13 67 F2
Saint Clair 74 H11 124 E5
St Heliers 90 C5
St Jacob's Hut 46 G12
Saint James Walkway 46 D14 47 D2
St Johns 90 C5
Saint Johns Hill 26 H8 109 B3
St Johns Park 90 C5
Saint Kilda 74 H11 124 D5
Saint Leonards 103 C5 102 A1
Saint Leonards, SI 74 G12
St Lukes 89 C3
St Martins 120 F2
St Marys Bay 87 C1
Saint Patricks 71 H7
St Winifred Hut 50 G10
Salisbury 61 J4 68 A13
Saltwater Creek 54 E8 56 A10
Saltwater Lagoon 49 D7
Sandringham 89 C3
Sandspit 6 E10
Sandstone 71 H7
Sandy Bay Hut 21 E3
Sandy Knolls 52 J14 53 J5 55 E7
Sandymount 74 H12 124 A3
Sanson 29 C6
Santoft 29 B5
Sapphire Springs - Katikati 10 H11 12 A12
13 A1
Sawyers Bay 74 G12 124 B2
Saxon Hut 37 E4
Sayers Hut 33 B7
Scarborough (Christchurch) 120 J1
Scarborough (Timaru) 61 J5 68 A14
Scargill 54 B10
Scone Hut 50 G9
Scotsman Valley 12 C8
Scotts Gap 76 E13 77 B1
Scow Landing 4 F13
Scroggs Hill 74 H10 124 J5
Seacliff 74 E12
Seadown 61 H5
Seafield 55 J4 62 D10
Seaford 37 B7
Seaforth 61 H5
Seagrove 7 G4 9 B1
Seagull Lake 51 H5
Seal Island 45 A5
Seal Islands 69 H2 75 B2
Seal Rocks 77 J7
Seatoun 33 F2 35 B4
Seaview (Timaru) 121 C3
Seaview (Wellington) 110 D3
Seaward Downs 78 E8
Secretary Island 69 B5
Seddon 44 E11
Seddonville 41 D6

Sedgemere 55 H7 62 C13
Sefton 54 E8 56 A10
Selwyn Heights 96 B2
Selwyn Huts 56 F8 62 A14
Selwyn, NI 12 D12
Selwyn, SI 52 J13 53 J4 55 F6 62 A12
Sentry Box Hut 27 F7
Sentry Hill 17 H1 23 B6
Sergeants Hill 41 G3
Serpentine Hut 50 C13 51 C4
Shaftesbury 10 H10 12 A11
Shag Lake 3 G5
Shag Point 74 C13
Shag Rock 48 J9 54 A13
Shallow Bay Hut 70 D10
Shamrock Hut 58 G14 59 G3
Shamrock Park 90 D6
Shannon, NI 29 F6
Shannon, SI 74 E8
Shantytown 45 F4
Sharks Tooth Hut 65 C5
Sheffield 52 G12 53 G3 55 C5
Shelly Beach 5 G7 7 A1
Shelly Park 90 D6
Shelter Islands 69 B5
Shelter Rock Hut 64 C13 65 C3
Shenandoah 42 H8
Sherenden 28 D9
Sherwood 55 G3 62 B9
Shiel Burn Hut 65 D5
Shiel Hill 124 D4
Shingle Creek 72 C12 73 C1
Shirley 54 H8 56 D10 120 F4
Shoe Island / Motuhoa 10 A11
Shorts Track 30 A11 31 A5
Shutes Hut 27 D7
Shy Lake 69 F5
Siberia Hut 58 H9
Silver Island 66 A9
Silver Peaks Route 74 F11
Silverdale 88 B2
Silverdale (Auckland) 6 H10 7 B4
Silverdale (Hamilton) 92 F5
Silverhope 26 J12
Silverstream 111 B5
Simmonds Islands 1 E5
Sir Robert Hut 50 C13 51 C4
Sisters, The 80 H1
Six Foot Track 21 B2
Six Mile 42 H9
Six Mile Walkway & Track 42 H9
Skippers 65 F4
Skippers Canyon 65 F4
Skyline Track 24 J14 26 F9
Slaty Creek 45 D6
Slipper Island 10 B12
Slyburn Hut 64 G11 65 G1
Smithfield 61 J5
Smiths Ponds 57 G5
Smiths Stream Hut 27 H6
Snells Beach 6 F10
Sockburn 53 H7 56 D9 120 C2
Somerfield 120 E2
Somerton 55 G4 62 B10
Somerville 90 D6
Somes Island 33 E2 35 B3
South Bay 48 E12
South Beach 45 F4
South Dunedin 124 E4
South Head 5 F6
South Hill 122 D5
South Hillend 77 A4
South Malvern 52 H11 53 H2 55 D4
South Mavora Lake 71 B4
South New Brighton 120 H3
South Oamaru 122 D6
South Ohau Hut 29 H6
South Temple Hut 59 G4
Southbridge 55 G6 62 B12
Southbrook 53 F7 56 B9
Southburn 68 A12
Southdown 90 D5
Southern Alps / Ka Tiritiri o te Moana 58 J8
Southern Coastal Track 76 F9
Southshore 54 H8 56 D10 120 H2
Spar Bush 77 D4
Speargrass Hut 42 H12
Speargrass Track 42 G13
Spectacle Lake 6 C9
Spence Hut 70 G13 71 G2 76 A13
Spencerville 54 G8 56 C10 120 G6

Sphinx Lake 69 J7 75 C7
Sportswood 107 C2
Spotswood, NI 23 B4
Spotswood, SI 48 J9
Spreydon 53 J7 56 E9 120 D2
Spring Creek 35 J5 40 J10 44 B11
Spring Grove 39 H2 43 A3
Springbank 53 F6 56 B8
Springbrook 68 A13
Springburn 61 A6
Springdale 10 G8
Springfield (Rotorua) 96 D2
Springfield, NI 4 H12
Springfield, SI 52 F11 53 F2 55 B4
Springhill 27 H7
Springhills 77 C6
Springlands 35 K6 44 C10 117 B1
Springs Flat 4 F11
Springs Junction 46 D12
Springston 53 J6 56 F8 62 A14
Springston South 56 F8 62 A14
Springvale (Otago) 66 J10 72 A13 73 A2
Springvale (Wanganui) 108 A1 109 C3
Spye 54 B10
Square Top Island 36 G4
Stafford 45 H3
Stafford Hut 57 E5
Stag Flat Shelter 42 C9
Staglands Wildlife Park - Cloustonville 33 B4
Staircase 52 E11 53 E2 55 A4
Stanfield Hut 30 B11 31 B5
Stanley Bay 90 B4
Stanley Brook 42 B13 43 A1
Stanley Point 90 B4
Stanmore Bay 88 B3
Stanway 29 B7 31 B1
Station Hut 59 E5
Staveley 61 A6
Stephens Island / Takapourewa 40 A10
Stephenson Island 2 G11
Stevensons Island 66 C8
Stewart Island / Rakiura 77 J1 80 C3
Stewarts Gully 54 G8 56 C10
Steyning Hut 47 F3
Stillwater 88 C3
Stillwater, NI 6 H10 7 B4
Stillwater, SI 45 E5
Stirling 79 E4
Stirling Falls, The 64 D8
Stockton 41 E5
Stodys Hut 66 B10
Stoke 39 H3 43 A4
Stokes Valley 33 D3 111 C4
Stone Hut 42 C10
Stoneburn 74 C11
Stony Creek 79 D3
Stony River Walk 23 C3
Stony Stream Hut 46 J11
Strandon 107 B4
Stratford 23 E7 25 B2
Strathern 128 B4
Strathmore 24 D9 25 A4
Strathmore Park 110 E2
Streamlands 6 E9
Stronvar 34 C11
Stuarts 78 F13 79 H1
Studholme 68 D13
Studholme Saddle Hut 28 B8
Styx 120 D5
Subritsky Homestead 1 F5
Sugar Loaf Islands / Nga Motu 23 B5
Summer Hill 79 F4
Summerhill (Canterbury) 52 E14 53 E5 55 A7
Summerhill (Palmerston North) 105 D4
Summerlea 41 D6
Sumner 54 J9 56 E11 120 J1
Sundale 110 C2
Sunnybrook 96 C2
Sunnyhills 90 C5
Sunnynook 88 H4
Sunnyvale (Auckland) 89 C2
Sunnyvale (Dunedin) 124 G5
Sunrise Hut 27 G6
Supper Cove Hut 69 G5 75 A5
Surfdale 7 D7
Sutherland Falls 63 F7
Sutherlands 60 H14 61 H3
Sutton 74 D8
Swan Lagoon 59 H5

Swannanoa 53 G6 56 C8
Swanson 7 D3 89 C1
Sweetwater 1 H6
Sydenham 119 G6 120 D2
Sylvia Flat Hot Springs 46 F13 47 F1

T

Tablelands (Bay of Plenty) 14 F13 15 F2
Tablelands (Wellington) 34 E8
Tadmor 42 C12
Taemaro 2 G9
Tahaia 11 H6
Tahakopa 78 F13 79 H1
Taharoa 11 G2
Tahatika 78 E14 79 G2
Tahawai 10 G11
Taheke 3 D5
Tahekeroa 6 G9 7 A3
Tahere 4 F13
Tahora (Bay of Plenty) 14 J12
Tahora (Taranaki) 17 H6 24 B11
Tahoraiti 30 C12 31 C6
Tahorakuri 19 C7
Tahuna 10 G8
Tahunanui 38 J12 39 G4 43 A5 116 B4
Tahunga 21 D6
Tahuroa 10 J8 12 B9
Taieri Beach 79 C7
Taieri Island / Moturata 79 C7
Taieri Mouth 79 C7
Taihape 27 F2
Taiharuru 4 G14
Taihoa 12 C11
Taikirau 4 D9
Taiko 60 J14 61 J3
Taikorea 29 D6
Taingaehe 5 C4
Tainui 124 D5
Taipa 2 H8
Taipo Hut 42 C9
Taipoiti 46 B9
Taipuha 5 A6
Tairua 8 F14 10 A11
Taita 33 D3 35 A2 111 C4
Tai Tapu 56 F9
Taitville 110 E1
Taka Ra Haka Conservation Park 71 C5
Takahiwai 4 H12
Takahue 1 K7 3 A3
Takaka 38 E8
Takaka Hill 38 F8
Takamatua 56 G12
Takamore 16 E11
Takanini 7 F6 9 A3
Takapau (East Cape, NI) 16 F11
Takapau (Gisborne) 22 A12
Takapau (Manawatu) 30 A14 32 A8
Takapou 38 D9 39 B1
Takapu Rd 110 C2
Takapu Valley 110 B3
Takapuna 7 D5 90 A4
Takaputahi 15 G5
Takapuwahia 110 B2
Takaro 29 D7 31 D1 105 B3
Takatu 6 E10
Takou 24 F10 25 C5
Takou Bay 2 J12
Takurua Hut 20 B13 21 B1
Takutai 45 J2
Tamahere 11 C7 92 H6
Tamaki 7 E5 90 C5
Tamaki Maori Village - Rotorua 13 H4
Tamarau 100 D5
Tamaterau 4 G12
Tamihana 10 J10 12 B11
Tanatana 14 H11
Tane 30 G10 31 G4
Taneatua 14 F11
Tanehopuwai 11 J5 18 A9
Tanekaha 4 E11
Tangahoe 24 E12 25 B7
Tangarakau 17 G7 24 A12
Tangarakau Gorge 17 G6 24 A11
Tangihua 4 H10
Tangihua Forest 4 H10
Tangimoana 29 D5
Tangiteroria 4 H9
Tangitu 18 C10
Tangiwai 26 C13 27 C1
Tangoake 1 C3
Tangoio 28 B12

Tangowahine 4 H8
Taniwha 9 F6
Tanoa 5 C7
Tanupara 26 D10
Taonui 30 C8 31 C2
Taoroa Junction 27 F4
Taotaoroa 12 D10
Tapanui 72 J13 73 J2
Tapapa 12 E11
Tapawera 42 C13 43 B1
Tapora 5 E6
Tapu 8 F11 10 A8
Tapuhi 4 D11
Tapui 68 G9
Tapuiwahine 18 C10
Taputeranga Island 33 F1 35 C4
Tapuwae (Northland) 3 C4
Tapuwae (Waikato) 18 B11
Tara 6 B8
Tara Hills 74 G10 124 J1
Taradale 28 E12 103 C2
Tarakohe 38 D9
Taramakau 45 H4
Taramea Bay 76 H14 77 E2
Taramoa 77 E4
Taranga Island 6 A10
Taranui 68 J11
Tarara 78 F14 79 H2
Tararu 8 G11 10 B8
Tararua Forest Park 29 H7 29 J5 31 H1 33 A6
Tarata 17 J2 23 C7
Taraunui 4 G13
Tarawera 20 H9
Tarawera Hot Springs 20 H9
Tariki 23 D6 25 A1
Taringamotu 18 F10
Taringamotu Valley 18 E11
Tarn Hut (Canterbury) 52 C13 53 C4
Tarn Hut (Mt Richmond CP) 43 C4
Tarn Ridge Hut 29 J6
Taronui Bay 2 J13
Tarras 66 E10
Taruheru 100 A1
Tarukenga 12 F14 13 F3
Tarurutangi 23 B6
Tasman 38 H10 39 F2
Tasman Lake 59 B7
Tasman Saddle Hut 49 H7
Tata Islands 38 D9 39 B1
Tataiahapi Pa 14 H12
Tatapouri 22 D11
Tataraimaka 23 C3
Tataramoa 30 B12 31 B6
Tatararariki 5 A3
Tatare 49 G6
Tataweka Hut 21 B3
Tatu 17 F7 24 A12
Tatuanui 10 H8 12 A9
Tauanui Hut 33 G6
Tauhara 98 B5
Tauhei 9 H7 12 A8
Tauherenikau 33 D6
Tauhoa 6 E8
Taumaka Island 57 D7
Taumarere 4 C9
Taumaruiti 18 F10
Taumarunui 18 F10
Taumata 78 B13 79 D1
Taumatatahi 24 G11 25 D6
Taumatawhakatangihangakoauauotamatea-
  pokaiwhenuakitanatahu - New Zealand's
  longest place name 32 E10
Taumutu 55 H7 62 C13
Taungatara 23 F4
Taungatara Track 23 E4
Taunoka 24 G12 25 D7
Taupaki 7 D2
Taupiri 9 H5 11 A6
Taupo 19 D5 97 B3 98 B4
Taupo Airport 19 E5 98 D4
Taupo Bay 2 H7
Taupo Hot Springs 19 D5
Tauranga 10 J13 13 B3 94 B2
Tauranga Bay 2 H11
Tauranga Central 93 D5
Tauranga Mission House 13 C4
Tauranga Valley 2 H11
Tauranganui 7 J5 9 E2
Taurangaruru 7 J5 9 E2
Tauraroa (Northland) 4 H11
Tauraroa (Waikato) 12 H8
Taurawharona Hut 20 B14 21 B2

Taurewa 18 H13
Tauriko 10 J13 12 B14 13 B3 94 D1
Taurikura 4 H13
Tautoro 3 D7
Tautuku 78 G13 79 J1
Tauweru 34 B10
Tauwhare (Bay of Plenty) 14 J11
Tauwhare Pa 12 C8
Tauwharemanuka 21 A2
Tauwhareparae 16 J9
Tawa 33 D2 35 B2 110 B2
Tawa Hut 21 B4
Tawai 68 F12
Tawanui 78 E14 79 G2
Tawataia 30 G9 31 G3
Tawhana 21 B2
Tawharanui 6 E11
Tawharekiri Lakes 58 C9
Tawhata 18 H8 24 B13
Tawhero 108 C1
Tawhiti, NI 23 G7 25 D2
Tawhiti, SI 72 C12 73 C1
Tawhiwhi 24 H11 25 E6
Tawhiwhi Hut 20 B13 21 B1
Taylor Dam 35 K6 44 D10
Taylors Mistake 54 J9 56 E11 120 J1
Taylorville 45 E5
Te Ahuahu 3 B7
Te Akatea 9 H4 11 A5
Te Akau 9 J2 11 B3
Te Akau South 9 J2 11 B3
Te Anau 70 D11
Te Anau Downs 70 A12 71 A1
Te Anga 11 H3
Te Angiangi Marine Reserve 32 C12
Te Aputa 18 E14 19 E2
Te Arai 6 C9
Te Arai Point 6 C9
Te Arakura 29 C7 31 C1
Te Araroa 16 B12
Te Ariuru 16 H11
Te Aro 110 E2 112 E5
Te Aroha 10 G9
Te Aroha Aerodrome 10 F9
Te Aroha West 10 H10 12 A11
Te Atatu North 7 D3
Te Atatu Peninsula 89 B2
Te Atatu South 89 C2
Te Awa (Canterbury) 61 G5
Te Awa (Napier) 103 A2
Te Awaatu Channel Marine Reserve 69 C5
Te Awamutu 11 E7
Te Awanga 28 F13
Te Ekaou Hut 30 B10 31 B4
Te Hana 6 D8
Te Hapara 100 B2
Te Hapua 1 B3
Te Haroto 20 J10
Te Hauke 28 G10
Te Haumi 81 C2
Te Henga / Bethells Beach 7 E1
Te Henga Goldie Bush Walkway 7 D1
Te Henui 23 C5
Te Hihi 7 G5 9 B2
Te Hoe 9 G6
Te Horo 29 J3
Te Horo Beach 29 J3
Te Horoa 26 E13 27 E1
Te Houka 79 E3
Te Huahua 3 B4
Te Hue Track 20 C13 21 C1
Te Huia 2 J11
Te Hutewai 11 D3
Te Iringa 3 D7
Te Kaha 15 C6
Te Kainga 110 D2
Te Kakaho Island 40 C11
Te Kao 1 D3
Te Karae 3 B4
Te Karaka (Gisborne) 22 B9
Te Karaka (Northland) 3 C3
Te Kauri 9 G4
Te Kauwhata 9 E5
Te Kawa 11 F7
Te Kawa West 11 F6
Te Kinga 45 G6
Te Kiri 23 F4
Te Kiteroa 72 J11
Te Kohanga 7 J5 9 D2
Te Kopua (Bay of Plenty) 15 C6
Te Kopua (Waikato) 11 F6
Te Kopuru 5 A3
Te Koraha 11 G3

Te Kouma 8 D11
Te Koura 18 E10
Te Kowhai (Northland) 5 B4
Te Kowhai (Waikato) 9 J5 11 B6
Te Kuha 41 G3
Te Kuiti 11 J5
Te Kumi 11 J5
Te Mahia 35 J3 40 G10
Te Mahoe 14 G9
Te Maika 11 F2
Te Maire 18 G9
Te Mapara 18 A9
Te Marua, NI 33 C4
Te Marua, SI 40 B10
Te Mata (Waikato - Coromandel) 8 F11 10 A8
Te Mata (Waikato) 11 D3
Te Mata Peak Walkway 28 F12
Te Matai 13 C5
Te Matawai Hut 29 J6
Te Maunga 13 B4
Te Mawhai 11 F7
Te Miko 45 A5
Te Miro 12 C9
Te Moana 61 E3
Te Moananui 10 F9
Te Moehau Junction 27 E3
Te Motu Island 11 F2
Te Namu 41 B7
Te Ngae 13 F5
Te Ngaire 2 H11
Te Ngaru 74 G12
Te Ohaki Pa 12 C12
Te Oneone Rangatira Beach 5 G5
Te Opai Lagoon 33 F5
Te Ore Ore 34 B9
Te Pahu 11 D5
Te Paki 1 B2
Te Paki Recreation Reserve 1 B1
Te Panaa Hut 21 B2
Te Papa Museum - Wellington 33 F1 35 C4
Te Papanui Conservation Park 73 F5
Te Papapa 90 D4
Te Papatapu 11 D3
Te Peka 78 F9
Te Pirita 52 J11 53 J2 55 F4 62 A10
Te Pohue 28 A10
Te Poi 12 D12
Te Popo 23 D7 25 A2
Te Pourewa Hut 21 A2
Te Pouwhakatutu 19 C5
Te Pu 13 E4
Te Pua 5 H7 7 B1
Te Pua Hut 21 B3
Te Puhi 2 J8
Te Puia Hut 28 A8
Te Puia Lodge 20 J8 28 A8
Te Puia Springs 16 G11
Te Puia Springs - Kawhia 11 F2
Te Puia Springs Hot Pools - East Cape 16 G11
Te Puka 16 H11
Te Puke 13 C5
Te Puna 10 J13 12 B14 13 B3
Te Puninga 10 G8 12 A9
Te Puru 8 G11 10 B8
Te Rae 37 A7
Te Rahu 11 E7
Te Raina 18 E14 19 E2
Te Ranga (Bay of Plenty) 12 C14 13 D4
   13 C3 94 D1
Te Rangiita 19 F4
Te Rapa 9 J5 11 B6 92 D2
Te Rauamoa 11 F5
Te Raumauku 11 G5
Te Raupo 1 E5
Te Rerenga 8 C12
Te Rerepahupahu Falls 17 F7
Te Rore (Northland) 2 K7 3 A3
Te Rore (Waikato) 11 D6
Te Roti 23 G6 25 D1
Te Rou 43 C6
Te Tahi 11 E5
Te Taho 50 E8
Te Teko 14 F9
Te Tii 2 J13
Te Tipua 78 C8
Te Toro 7 H3 9 C1
Te Totara Hut 20 E12
Te Tua 76 F11
Te Tuhi Junction 24 H12 25 E7
Te Tumu 13 C5
Te Uku 11 C4

Te Uku Landing 11 C4
Te Urewera National Park 14 H10 20 A13
   21 A1
Te Uri 32 C8
Te Waewae 76 F11
Te Waiiti 20 D13 21 D1
Te Waimate Mission 4 B8
Te Waiotukapiti Hut 20 F12
Te Wairoa 13 H5
Te Waitere 11 G2
Te Waiti Hut 14 H14 15 H3
Te Wakatehaua Island 1 D3
Te Wera 24 D9 25 A4
Te Whaiti 20 C11
Te Whakarae 18 F10
Te Whanga 34 C9
Te Wharau (Northland) 4 J8
Te Wharau (Wellington) 34 E10
Te Whau 2 J12 4 A8
Teal Bay Hut 76 E8
Teardrop Lake 69 B7
Teddington 56 F10
Telford Hut 70 G12 71 G1 76 A12
Temple Basin Skifield 52 A8
Temple View 11 C6 92 G2
Templeton 53 J6 56 E8 120 A2
Temuka 61 G5
Tennyson Inlet 40 F8
Tentpoles Hut 48 D10
Tepene 2 H12
Terrace End 30 D8 31 D2 105 B4
Teschemakers 68 J11
Teviot 72 E13 73 E2
Thames 8 H11 10 C8
Thames North 8 H11 10 C8
The Brothers (Marlborough) 35 E2 40 F14
The Brothers (Stewart Island) 80 H3
The Hermitage 59 B6
Theta Tarn 57 H4
Third House Hut 39 H4 43 A5
Thomsons Crossing 77 C4
Thor Hut 42 B10
Thornbury 77 D3
Thorndon 110 D2 112 C5
Thornton 14 E10
Thornton Bay 8 G11 10 B8
Thorpe 38 J8 42 A13
Three Bridges 3 E6
Three Kings 90 C4
Three Mile Bush 85 B1
Three Mile Lagoon 49 F5
Three Mile Stream Hut 46 H12
Three Steeples 41 F2
Three Streams 11 C3
Thrillseekers Canyon 47 G5
Ti Point 6 D11
Ti Tree Point 32 F8
Tia Island 80 G6
Tiakitahuna 29 E7
Tihaka 76 H14 77 E2
Tihiroa 11 F6
Tihoi 18 C14 19 C2
Tikinui 5 B3
Tikipunga 4 F12
Tikitere 13 F5
Tikitiki 16 D12
Tikokino 28 H8
Tikorangi 17 G2 23 A7
Tikotiko 9 F3
Timaru 61 J5 121 B3
Timber Bay 30 C12 31 C6
Timberlea 111 A6
Timpanys 77 F6
Tindalls Beach 88 B4
Tiniroto 21 F6
Tinkertown 70 J14 71 J3 76 C14 77 A2
Tinopai 5 D6
Tinui 34 A12
Tinui Island 40 B10
Tinwald 55 J2 62 D8
Tipapakuku 30 C12 31 C6
Tipunga 85 A2
Tiratu 30 C13 31 C7
Tirau 12 E11
Tiraumea 30 H11 31 H5
Tiraumea Hut 42 H11
Tiraumea Track 42 H11
Tiriraukawa 26 G13 27 G1
Tiritiri Matangi Island 6 H11 7 B5
Tiroa 18 B12
Tirohanga (Bay of Plenty) 14 F14 15 F3
Tirohanga (Wellington) 110 C3

Tirohanga, SI 79 G4
Tirohia 10 F9
Tiroiti 74 A9
Tiromoana 45 A5
Tiroroa 41 H4
Tisbury 128 B5
Titahi Bay 33 D2 35 B2 110 A2
Titi Island 40 D11
Titirangi 7 E3 89 D2
Titirangi Beach 89 D2
Titirangi North 89 D2
Titirangi Park 100 C4
Titirangi South 89 D2
Titiroa 78 F8
Titoki 4 G9
Toa Bridge 11 H7
Toatoa (Bay of Plenty) 15 G4
Toatoa (Northland) 2 H8
Todds Valley 38 J12 39 G4
Toetoe 4 G11 85 D2
Tohunga Junction 26 B11
Toi Flat 30 D13 31 D7
Tokaanu 19 G2
Tokanui, NI 11 F7
Tokanui, SI 78 G9
Tokaora 23 G6 25 D1
Tokarahi 68 F9
Tokata 16 B12
Tokata Island 14 D10
Tokatoka 5 A3
Tokerau 13 E5
Tokerau Beach 1 F7
Tokirima 18 G8 24 A13
Toko 24 E8 25 B3
Toko Mouth 79 E6
Tokoiti 79 D5
Tokomaru 29 F7 31 F1
Tokomaru Bay 16 H11
Tokomaru Steam Engine Museum 29 F7
   31 F1
Tokorangi 29 A7
Tokoroa 12 H12
Tolaga Bay 22 A13
Tomarata 6 C9
Tomarata Lake 6 C9
Tomoana 103 C5
Tonga Island 38 E10 39 C2
Tonga Island Marine Res 38 E10 39 C2
Tongaporutu 17 E4
Tongariro 18 H13 19 H1
Tongariro Crossing 18 H13 19 H1
Tongariro National Park 18 H13 19 H1
   26 A13 27 A1
Tongariro Northern Circuit 18 J14 19 J2
   26 A14 27 A2
Top Branch Hut 43 H3
Top Butler Hut 50 G8
Top Crawford Hut 51 B5
Top Dingle Burn Hut 58 H13 59 H2
Top Forks Hut 58 H8
Top Gorge Hut 27 J5
Top Hope Hut 46 G12
Top Hut 58 F14 59 F3
Top Kokatahi Hut 50 B14 51 B5
Top Maropea Hut 27 G6
Top Robinson Hut 46 F12
Top Timaru Ck Hut 66 A11
Top Toaroha Hut 50 C13 51 C4
Top Trent Hut / Lagoon Hut 46 H9
Top Tuke Hut 50 D11 51 D2
Top Wairoa Hut 43 D3
Top Waitaha Hut 50 D11 51 D2
Tophouse 42 G14 43 F2
Topuni 6 C8
Torbay 6 J10 7 C4 88 F4
Torehape 9 E7
Torere 15 E4
Torlesse Tussocklands Park 52 E10 52 F9
Totara Flat 45 D7
Totara Heights 90 E6
Totara North 2 H10
Totara Park 33 D4 111 A6
Totara Valley 60 G14 61 G3
Totara, NI 8 H11 10 C8
Totara, SI 68 H11
Totaranui 38 D10 39 B2
Towai 4 D10
Town Basin - Whangarei 4 G12
Townsend 117 C5
Townsend Hut 46 J9
Townsend Huts 52 B12 53 B3
Travers - Sabine Track 42 J13
Traverse Hut 30 B11 31 B5

Treaty House - Waitangi 4 B9
Treble Cone Skifield 65 C6
Trentham, NI 33 D4 111 B5
Trentham, SI 60 E13 61 E2
Trevor Carter Hut 42 C9
Triangle Hut 27 H5
Trilobite Hut 37 H6
Trinity Lakes 70 E9
Trio Islands / Kuru Pongi 40 B10
Triplex Hut 27 G6
Tripp Settlement 61 E4
Trotters Gorge 74 B13
Trust/Poulter Hut 52 A10 53 A1
Tryphena 36 E5
Tuai 21 F3
Tuakau 7 J6 9 D3
Tuamarina 35 J5 40 J10 44 B11
Tuapeka Flat 73 J4 79 B2
Tuapeka Mouth 73 J4 78 A14 79 C2
Tuapeka West 73 J4 79 B2
Tuatapere 76 F11
Tuatapere Hump Ridge Track 76 E9
Tuateawa 8 B12 36 J6
Tuatini 16 H11
Tuhara 21 H6
Tuhikaramea 11 D6
Tuhipa 4 C8
Tuhitarata 33 F6
Tuhua 18 E9
Tui 42 D12
Tui Brewery Tower - Pahiatua 30 E10 31 E4
Tui Glen 38 J12 39 G4
Tukaki Marae - Te Kaha 15 C6
Tukemokihi 21 G6
Tukino Skifield - Mt Ruapehu 26 B13 27 B1
Tumahu 23 D3
Tumai 74 D12
Tumunui 13 H5
Tuna 23 D7 25 A2
Tunakotekote 18 F10
Tunnel Creek Hut 58 C13 59 C2
Tuparehuia 4 C12
Tuparoa 16 E12
Turakina 29 A4
Turangaomoana 10 J10 12 C11
Turangarere 26 E14 27 E2
Turangi 19 G3
Turitea 30 E8 31 E2
Turiwhate 45 J5
Turiwiri 4 J8
Turoa Skifield - Mt Ruapehu 26 B12
Turua 8 J11 10 D8
Tussock Creek 77 D5
Tussock Hut 19 J6
Tutaematai 4 B11
Tutaenui 26 J11 29 A6
Tutaki 42 G10
Tutamoe 3 F6
Tutekehua 3 B4
Tutira 28 A12
Tutu Hut 47 F3
Tutukaka 4 E13
Tuturau 78 C9
Tuturumuri 34 G7
Tututawa 24 E9 25 B4
Tutuwai Hut 33 C6
Tuwhakairiora Marae - Hicks Bay 16 B11
Twelve Mile Delta 64 H13 65 H3
Twin Bridges 3 F7
Twizel 59 H6
Twyford 28 E11 103 D3

U

Ulva Island 80 E5
Umawera 3 B5
Umere 37 J3 42 A8
Umutaoroa 30 B12 31 B6
Umutoi 27 J4 30 A11 31 A5
Unahi 1 H6
Underwood 77 E4
Unwin Hut 59 B6
Upokongaro 26 H9
Upokorau 2 J11
Upper Atiamuri 12 J13 13 J2
Upper Atiamuri Hot Pools 12 J13 13 J2
Upper Charlton 78 B8
Upper Cox Hut 46 J10
Upper Deception Hut 52 A8
Upper D'Urville Hut 47 B3
Upper Hutt 33 D4 111 B6
Upper Junction 74 G12 124 C2
Upper Kawhatau 27 G4
Upper Makaroro Hut 27 F6

Upper Mangatawhiri Reservoir 8 G8 9 B5
Upper Matakitaki 42 J9 46 A13 47 A1
Upper Matakuhia Hut 20 F10
Upper Moutere 38 J10 39 G2
Upper Princhester Hut 70 F13 71 F2
Upper Riccarton 120 D2
Upper South Branch Hut 46 J10
Upper Spey Hut 69 F7
Upper Takaka 38 G8
Upper Tama Lake 18 J13 19 J1 26 A13
    27 A1
Upper Te Hoe Hut 20 F11
Upper Travers Hut 42 J12 47 A4
Upper Wairaki Hut 70 G13 71 G2 76 A13
Upper Waitati 74 F11
Upper Waitohi 61 G3
Upper Whirinaki Hut 20 F10
Upper Windley Hut 71 D4
Urenui 17 G3 24 A8
Uretane 68 D12
Uretara Island 14 F12
Urquharts Bay 4 H13
Urquhart's Hut 51 C6
Urrall 55 F2 62 A8
Urungaio 3 B4
Urupukapuka Island 4 A11
Uruti 17 G4 24 A9
Uruwhenua 38 F8
Utakura 3 C6
Utiku 27 G3
Utuhina 96 C2
Utuwai 30 A11 31 A5

V

Valetta 61 B6
Vauxhall (Auckland) 90 B4
Vauxhall (Dunedin) 123 J6 124 D4
Venison Tops Hut 27 A7
Venus Hut 42 B10
Victoria 100 C3
Victoria Conservation Park 46 A12
Victoria Valley 2 J7
Victory Island / Moutiti 40 A9
View Hill 52 F12 53 F3 55 B5
Vinegar Hill 26 J13 27 J1
Vinetown 84 C3
Virginia 52 A14 53 A5
Vogeltown (New Plymouth) 23 B5 107 C4
Vogeltown (Wellington) 110 E1

W

Waddington 52 G12 53 G3 55 C5
Wade Heads 88 C4
Wadestown 33 E1 35 C3 110 D2
Waenga 66 H9
Waerenga 9 E5
Waerengaahika 22 D9
Waerengaokuri 22 E8
Waewaetorea Island 4 A11
Waharoa 10 J10 12 C11
Wai O Taiki Bay 90 C5
Waiake 88 F3
Waianakarua 74 A13
Waianiwa 77 D4
Waiapi 61 G4
Waiare 2 J11
Waiareka Junction 68 H11
Waiaririki 78 D10
Waiaro 8 B10 36 J4
Waiaruhe 30 D11 31 D5
Waiatarua 7 E3 89 D1
Waiatoto 57 E7
Waiau Beach 7 H4 9 C1
Waiau Falls - Coromandel 8 D11
Waiau Pa 7 G4 9 B1
Waiau, NI 8 D11
Waiau, SI 47 H7
Waiaua 14 F14 15 F3
Waiaua Gorge Hut 23 E4
Waiawa Hut 20 C14 21 C2
Waihaha (Northland) 4 B11
Waihaha (Waikato) 19 D2
Waihaha Hut 18 D13 19 D1
Waihao Downs 68 E11
Waihao Forks 68 D11
Waihaorunga 68 D10
Waihapa 2 J10
Waiharakeke (Waikato - Coromandel) 8 J14
    10 D11
Waiharakeke (Waikato) 11 G3

Waiharara 1 G5
Waihau Bay 16 B8
Waiheke Island 8 D8 6 J13
Waihemo 74 B11
Waihi (Bay of Plenty) 10 F11
Waihi (Waikato) 19 G2
Waihi Beach 10 F12
Waihi Falls 30 E13 31 E7
Waihi Hot Springs 18 G14 19 G2
Waihirere 22 D10
Waihoaka 76 G12
Waihohonu Hut 18 J14 19 J2 26 A14 27 A2
Waihohonu Track 18 J13 27 A1 26 A13
    27 A1
Waihoki 30 G13 31 G7
Waihoki Valley 30 H12 31 H6
Waihola 74 J8 79 B6
Waihopai 128 B2
Waihopo 1 E4
Waihou 10 H9 12 A10
Waihou Valley 3 B6
Waihua 21 J4
Waihua Hut 14 J10
Waihuahua Swamp 1 F6
Waihue 3 H7
Waihuka 2 J11
Waiinu Beach 25 H5
Wai-iti 39 J1 43 B2
Waikaia 72 G9
Waikaka 72 J11
Waikaka Valley 78 A10
Waikakahi 68 E12
Waikakaho - Cullen Creek Track 40 H9
    44 A10
Waikamaka Hut 27 G5
Waikana 78 C9
Waikanae 33 A4
Waikanae Beach 33 A4
Waikaraka 4 G12 85 D3
Waikare 4 B11
Waikare Junction Hut 20 A13 21 A1
Waikaremoana 21 E3
Waikaretu 19 G2
Waikari (Canterbury) 54 B8
Waikari (Dunedin) 124 E3
Waikato 37 B7
Waikaura 68 E9
Waikawa (Marlborough) 35 J3 40 G10
Waikawa (Southland) 78 G11
Waikawa Beach 29 H4
Waikawa Museum 78 G11
Waikawa Valley 78 F11
Waikawau (Waikato - Coromandel Coast)
    8 E11 10 A8
Waikawau (Waikato - Coromandel) 8 B11
    36 J5
Waikawau (Waikato) 17 A5
Waikeria 11 G7
Waikiekie 4 J11
Waikino 10 F10
Waikirikiri 14 H11
Waikite Valley 13 J4
Waikite Valley Hot Pools & Thermal Area
    13 J4
Waikiwi 77 E5 128 C1
Waikoau 28 A11
Waikoikoi 72 J12 78 A11
Waikokopu 22 J8 22 AA1
Waikokowai 9 G4 11 A5
Waikorea 9 G2
Waikoropupu Springs / Pupu Springs 38 E8
Waikouaiti 74 E12
Waikoukou Valley 6 J8 7 C2
Waikouro 76 E14 77 B2
Waikowhai 89 D3
Waikuku 54 F8 56 B10
Waikuku Beach 54 F8 56 B10
Waikune 18 J11 26 A11
Waima 89 D2
Waima (East Cape, NI) 16 G11
Waima (Northland) 3 D5
Waima Forest 3 D4
Waima Main Range Track 3 E5
Waima Valley 4 E13
Waimahaka 78 F8
Waimahana 19 B7
Waimahora 11 H7
Waimairi Beach 54 H8 56 D10
Waimakariri Falls Hut 51 B7
Waimamaku 3 E4
Waimana 14 G11
Waimangaroa 41 F4

Waimangu 13 J5
Waimangu Volcanic Valley 13 J5
Waimanoni 1 H6
Waimanu Bay 89 B2
Waimapu 10 J13 94 D1 13 C3
Waimarama 28 H13
Waimari Beach 120 H4
Waimarie 41 D6
Waimata (Bay of Plenty) 10 F11
Waimata (Gisborne) 22 C11
Waimate 68 D12
Waimate Aerodrome 68 D12
Waimate Historical Museum 68 D12
Waimate Island 8 C10
Waimate North 4 B8
Waimate Walkway 68 D12
Waimatenui 3 E6
Waimatua 77 F6
Waimatuku 77 D3
Waimauku 6 J8 7 C2
Waimaunga 46 C8
Waimea 72 H8
Waimiha 18 C11
Waimihia 19 E7
Waimiro 30 F13 31 F7
Waimotu 68 J10
Waimumu 78 B8
Waingake 22 F8
Waingarara 14 F11
Waingaro 9 J3 11 B4
Waingaro Forks Hut 37 G7
Waingaro Hot Springs 9 J3 11 B4
Waingaro Track 37 F7
Waingawa 34 B8
Wainihinihi 45 J5
Wainoni (Auckland) 88 H2
Wainoni (Christchurch) 120 G3
Wainono Lagoon 68 C13
Wainui Falls - Abel Tasman National Park
    38 E9 39 C1
Wainui Hut 38 E9 39 C1
Wainui Junction (Manawatu) 27 E3
Wainui Junction (Northland) 1 J5 3 A1
Wainui Track 38 E9
Wainui, NI (Bay of Plenty) 14 F11
Wainui, NI (Gisborne) 22 E11 100 D6
Wainui, NI (Northland - Far North) 2 H11
Wainui, NI (Northland) 6 H9 7 B3
Wainui, SI 56 G12
Wainuiomata 33 E3 35 A3 111 D4
Wainuioru (Wellington) 34 C10 34 E9
Waioeka Gorge Scenic Reserve 14 H13
    15 H2
Waioeka Pa 14 G13 15 G2
Waiohau 14 H9
Waiohiki 28 E11 103 C3
Waiomatatini 16 D12
Waiomio 4 C9
Waiomu 8 F11 10 A8
Waione 30 F13 31 F7
Waioneke 5 G6
Waiopaoa Hut 20 F13 21 F1
Waiopehu Hut 29 H5
Waiopehu Track 29 H5
Waiorongomai 10 G10 12 A11
Waiorore 15 C6
Waiotahi 14 F12 15 F1
Waiotahi Beach 14 F13 15 F2
Waiotahi Marae 14 F12 15 F1
Waiotahi Valley 14 G12 15 G1
Waiotama 4 H9
Waiotapu 13 J5
Wai-o-tapu Thermal Area 13 J5 20 A8
Waiotauru Hut 33 B5
Waiotehue 3 A2
Waiotemarama 3 E4
Waiotira 4 J10
Waiotu 4 E11
Waiouru 26 D14 27 D2
Waipa Valley 18 A11
Waipa Village 13 G4
Waipahi 78 B11
Waipahihi 19 D5 98 C4
Waipaipai 4 E13
Waipakihi Hut 19 J4
Waipango 76 G14 77 D2
Waipaoa 22 J7
Waipapa (Northland) 2 K12 4 A8
Waipapa (Waikato) 12 J10
Waipapakauri 1 H6
Waipapakauri Beach 1 H5
Waipara 54 C9

Waiparera 3 D3 4 G13
Waiparu 72 G9
Waipatiki 30 E13 31 E7
Waipatiki Beach 28 B13
Waipatu 103 B5
Waipawa 28 J9
Waipiata 67 J5
Waipipi 7 H3 9 C1
Waipiro Bay 16 G11
Waipopo 61 H5
Waipori Falls 73 H7 79 A5
Waipoua Forest 3 F5
Waipoua Forest (locality) 3 F5
Waipoua Settlement 3 F4
Waipounamu 72 H9
Waipu 4 J13 6 A8
Waipu Caves 4 J12
Waipu Cove 6 A8
Waipuku 23 D6 25 A1
Waipukurau 28 J9 32 A10
Waipuna, NI 26 D9
Waipuna, SI 46 D8
Waipunga Falls 20 G9
Waipuru 26 H14 27 H2
Wairakau 10 H10 12 A11
Wairakei 19 C5
Wairakei Village 19 C6
Wairamarama 9 F2
Wairapukao 20 B10
Wairata 14 J14 15 J3
Wairau Bar 35 J6 44 C11
Wairau Pa 35 J5 40 J10 44 B11
Wairau Park 88 H3
Wairau Valley 43 C7
Wairaurahiri Hut 76 G8
Waireia 3 C3
Waireka 12 H14 13 H3
Wairere (Northland - Far North) 3 C5
Wairere (Northland) 5 B6
Wairere Boulders Nature Park 3 C5
Wairere Waterfall - Whakatane 14 E11
Wairio 76 D14 77 A2
Wairoa (Bay of Plenty) 10 J13 12 B14 13 B3
Wairoa (Dunedin) 124 G2
Wairoa (Gisborne) 16 D12
Wairoa (Hawke's Bay) 21 H5
Wairoa Pa 10 J13 12 B14 13 B3 94 C1
Wairoa Reservoir 7 G7 9 B4
Wairua Falls - Whangarei 4 G9
Wairuna 78 B12
Wairunga 74 D13
Waitaanga 17 E6
Waitaha 50 C10 51 C1
Waitahanui 19 E5
Waitahora 30 D13 31 D7
Waitahu 46 A9
Waitahuna 73 J5 79 B3
Waitahuna Gully 73 J6 79 B4
Waitahuna West 73 J4 79 B2
Waitakaruru 8 J10 9 D7
Waitakere 7 D2 89 B1
Waitakere Regional Park 7 E2
Waitakere Reservoir 7 E2
Waitaki Bridge 68 F12
Waitane 78 C8
Waitangi 4 B9 81 A2
Waitangirua 110 B3
Waitanguru 11 J3 17 A7
Waitao 13 B4 94 D3
Waitapu, NI 3 D3
Waitapu, SI 38 D8
Waitara 17 G1 23 A6
Waitarere 29 F4
Waitaria Bay 35 J2 40 F10
Waitaruke 2 H10
Waitati 74 F12
Waitawa 61 H4
Waitawheta 10 F10
Waiteitei 6 D9
Waitekauri 10 E10
Waitepeka 79 E3
Waiterimu 9 F6
Waiteti (Bay of Plenty) 13 F4
Waiteti (Waikato) 11 J6 18 A10
Waitetoki 2 G8
Waitetoko 19 F4
Waitetuna 11 C4
Waitewaewae Hut 29 J5 33 A6
Waiti 10 G7
Waitiki Landing 1 B2
Waitoa 10 H9 12 A10
Waitohi, NI 29 C6

Waitohi, SI 61 G4
Waitoki 6 H8 7 B2
Waitomo Caves (locality) 11 H5
Waitotara 25 G5
Waituhi 22 D9
Waituna (Invercargill) 77 E7
Waituna (Waimate) 68 D12
Waituna Lagoon 77 G7
Waituna West 30 A8 31 A2
Waitutu Hut 75 G7
Waitutu Track 75 G7
Waiuku 7 J4 9 D1
Waiuna Lagoon 57 J2
Waiuta 46 D9
Waiuta - Big River Track 46 C9
Waiwaka 30 H8 31 H2
Waiwera (Auckland) 6 G10 7 A4
Waiwera (Manawatu) 30 G8 31 G2
Waiwera Hot Springs 6 G10 7 A4
Waiwera South 78 C13 79 E1
Waiwhetu 111 C4
Waiwhiu 6 E9
Wakamarina - Onamalutu Track 39 J7 44 B8
Wakanui 55 J3 62 D9
Wakapatu 76 H13
Wakapuaka 38 H13 39 F5
Wakarara 27 G6
Wakari 74 G11
Wakatipu Heights 125 B5 126 B3
Wakatu 116 B4
Wakefield 39 J2 43 B3
Wakelings Hut 27 G5
Waldronville 74 H10 124 G6
Walker Island 1 G6
Wall Island 41 G2
Wallacetown 77 D4
Wallaceville 111 B5
Wallingford 32 C10
Waltham 120 F2
Walton 10 J9 12 B10
Wanaka 65 C6
Wangaloa 79 E5
Wanganui 26 J8 108 B4
Wanganui East 26 H8 109 B5
Wangapeka Track 42 C9
Wanstead 32 B10
Waoku Coach Road Walk 3 E5
Waotu 12 G10
Warawara Forest 3 C3
Ward 44 F12
Wardville 10 J10 12 B11
Warea 23 D3
Warepa 79 E2
Warkworth 6 E9
Warkworth District Museum 6 E10
Waro 4 E11
Warren, The 52 F13 53 F4 55 B6
Warrington 74 F12
Warwick Junction 46 B12
Washdyke 61 J5
Washdyke Lagoon 61 J5
Washington Valley 115 B1
Washpool Hut 33 H6
Watchdog Hut 50 G11 51 G2
Waterfall Hut (Mackenzie Region) 59 C5
Waterfall Hut (Mt Cook) 50 J9 60 A10
Waterfall Hut (Ruahine FP) 27 H5
Waterloo 33 E3 35 A3 111 C4
Waterton 62 E8
Waterview 89 C3
Watlington 61 J4
Wattle Bay 7 F3
Wattle Downs 7 F5 9 A2
Waverley, NI 24 J9 25 G4
Waverley, SI (Dunedin) 74 H11 124 D4
Waverley, SI (Invercargill) 128 B2
Wawa 12 J12 13 J1
Wayby 6 D8
Wayby Valley 6 D9
Waynes 74 B12
Weavers Crossing 9 G4
Weber 30 E14 32 E8
Wedderburn 67 G4
Weedons 53 J6 56 E8
Weka Pass 54 C8
Wekaweka 3 E4
Welbourn 106 D6 107 C4
Welcome Bay 10 J13 13 B4 94 D2
Welcome Flat Hot Pools 59 A5
Welcome Flat Hut 59 A5
Wellington 33 F1 35 C4 110 D2 112 D5
Wellington Zoo 33 F1 35 C4

Wellsford 6 D8
Wendon 72 H9
Wendon Valley 72 H10
Wendonside 72 G8
Wentworth Falls - Whangamata 8 J13
  10 D10
Weraroa 29 G5
Wesley 89 C3
West End 104 D1 105 C3
West Eweburn Dam 67 G4
West Eyreton 53 F5 55 B7
West Harbour 89 B2
West Harper Hut 52 D8
West Melton 53 H5 55 D7
West Plains 77 E4 128 D1
West Sabine Hut 42 J12 47 A4
Westerfield 55 H1 61 C7
Western Heights (Auckland) 89 C2
Western Heights (Rotorua) 96 B2
Western Springs 89 C3
Westfield 90 D5
Westhaven (Christchurch) 120 F4
Westhaven (Te Tai Tapu) Marine Reserve
  37 B5
Westhaven (Wellington) 110 B2
Westlake (Auckland) 88 H4
Westlake (Christchurch) 120 C1
Westland Tai Poutini National Park 49 F6
Westmere (Auckland) 89 C3
Westmere (Waikato) 9 G4 11 A5
Westmere (Wanganui) 26 H8 109 A2
Westmere (Wellington) 34 C10
Westmorland 120 D1
Weston 68 H11
Westown 23 B5 107 C3
Westport 41 G3
Westshore 28 D12 103 B1
Westwood 74 H10 124 H6
Wetheral 53 G7 56 C9
Wetherstons 73 H5 79 A3
Weymouth 7 F5 9 A2
Whakaari/White Island 14 A13
Whakahoro 18 H8 24 B13
Whakahoro Hut 18 H8 24 B13
Whakaki 21 H6
Whakaki Lagoon 21 J6
Whakamara 24 H8 25 E3
Whakamarama 10 J12 12 B13 13 B2
Whakamaru 19 A3
Whakanui Track 33 F3
Whakapapa Skifield - Mt Ruapehu 26 A13
Whakapapa Village 18 J12 26 A12
Whakapapaiti Hut 26 A12
Whakapapaiti Hut Track 18 J12 26 A12
Whakapara 4 E11
Whakapirau 5 C6
Whakapourangi 16 E11
Whakarae 14 J11
Whakarewarewa 13 G4 96 D3
Whakarewarewa Thermal Valley - Rotorua
  13 G4 96 D3
Whakarongo 30 D8 31 D2
Whakataka Hut 20 D13 21 D1
Whakataki 34 A13
Whakatane 14 E11
Whakaterepapanui Island 40 B10
Whakatete Bay 8 G11 10 B8
Whakatina 24 E13 26 B8
Whakatiwai 8 G9 9 B6
Whakatu 28 E12 103 B4
Whakawhitira 16 D11
Whale Stream Hut 59 D6
Whananaki 4 D13
Whananaki South 4 D13
Whanarua Bay 15 B7
Whangaahei 8 B11 36 J5
Whangae 4 B9
Whangaehu (Wanganui) 26 J9 29 A4
Whangaehu (Wellington) 34 B10
Whangaimoana 33 G5
Whangamarino (Bay of Plenty) 13 F5
Whangamarino (Waikato) 9 E4
Whangamata 8 J14 10 D11
Whangamomona 17 J6 24 C11
Whanganui 18 E14 19 E2
Whanganui Hut 20 E14 21 E2
Whanganui Island 8 D10
Whanganui National Park 18 J8 24 D12
  25 A7
Whangaparaoa (Auckland) 6 H10 7 B4
Whangaparaoa (East Cape, NI) 16 A9
Whangaparapara 36 E4

Whangape 3 B2
Whangapoua 8 C12
Whangara 22 D12
Whangara Island (Auckland) 36 E4
Whangara Island (Gisborne) 22 D12
Whangarata 7 J6 9 D3
Whangarei 4 G11 84 B4
Whangarei Airport 4 G12
Whangarei Falls 4 F12
Whangarei Heads 4 H13
Whangaripo 6 D9
Whangaroa 2 H10
Whangaruru 4 C12
Whangaruru South 4 C12
Whangateau 6 D10
Wharanui 44 H12
Whare Creek Hut 70 F12 71 F1
Whare Flat 74 G11 124 F1
Whareama 34 B12
Wharehine 5 D7
Wharehuanui 65 G5
Wharehuia 23 D7 25 A2
Wharekahika Hut 14 H11
Wharekaho Beach / Simpsons Beach 8 D13
Wharekaka 22 A13
Wharekakahu Island 74 H13
Wharekauhau 33 G4
Wharekawa (Auckland) 8 G9 9 B6
Wharekawa (Waikato) 8 H14 10 C11
Wharekohe 4 G10
Wharekopae 21 C6
Wharepaina 20 A8
Wharepapa 5 J7 7 C1
Wharepapa South 12 G9
Wharepoa 8 J12 10 D9
Whareponga 16 F12
Wharepuhunga 12 H8
Whareroa 23 H7 25 E2
Wharetoa 78 A13 79 C1
Wharewaka 19 D5 98 D4
Wharfedale Hut 52 E12 53 E3 55 A5
Wharfedale Track 52 E12 53 E3 55 A5
Whariwharangi Hut 38 D9 39 B1
Whataroa 49 F7
Whatatutu 22 A9
Whataupoko 100 B4
Whatawhata 11 C5
Whatipu 7 F2
Whatipu Caves 7 F2
Whatitiri 4 G10
Whatoro 3 G6
Whatuwhiwhi 2 F7
Whau Valley 85 B1
Whawharua 11 H6
Wheatstone 62 E9
Wheki Valley 4 H10
Whenuahou 30 A14 32 A8
Whenuakite 8 E13
Whenuakura 24 J9 25 F4
Whenuanui 5 B4
Whenuapai 6 J9 7 D3 89 A2
Whenuapai Airforce Base 6 J9 7 D3
Whetukura 30 B14 32 B8
Whirinaki (Hawke's Bay) 28 C12
Whirinaki (Northland) 3 D4
Whirinaki Forest Park 20 D10
Whiritoa 8 J14 10 D11
Whiriwhiri 7 J4 9 D1
Whitby 110 A3
White Hut 50 B14 51 B5
White Island 14 A13
White Pine Bush 14 F10
White Rock 80 G5
White Rocks 35 F1 40 E13
Whitecliffs 52 H11 53 H2 55 D4
Whitecliffs Walkway 17 F4
Whitecraig 68 H11
Whitehall 12 D9
Whitemans Valley 33 D4
Whiterigg 78 A9
Whiterock 53 D6
Whitford 7 E6 9 A3
Whitiaga Airfield 8 D12
Whitianga (Bay of Plenty) 15 D5
Whitianga (Waikato) 8 D13
Whitikahu 9 H6 11 A7
Whitikau 15 H4
Whitiroa 91 C3 92 E3
Whitstone 68 H11
Whymper Hut 49 H7
Wigram Aerodrome - Christchurch 53 J7
  56 E9 120 C2

Wigram Park 120 V2
Wilden 72 G13 73 G2
Wilder Settlement 32 D9
Wilkinson Hut 50 D12 51 D3
Willowbank 78 A10
Willowbridge 68 D13
Willowby 55 J2 62 D8
Willowford 28 C8
Willows Hut 48 C9
Wills Hut 58 F12 59 F1
Wilsons Crossing 77 D5
Wilsons Siding 53 G7 56 C9
Wilsonville 4 E11
Wilton 110 D1
Wiltsdown 12 G11
Wimbledon 32 F9
Winchester 61 G5
Winchmore 55 H2 62 C8
Windermere 55 J1 61 D7
Windsor (Invercargill) 68 G10 127 A5
  128 B2
Windsor Park 68 G11
Windwhistle 52 H9 55 D2
Windy Hill 4 J8
Windy Ridge 88 J3
Wingate 33 E3 35 A3 111 C4
Wingatui 74 H10 124 G4
Winiata 27 F3
Winscombe 60 F12 61 F1
Winslow 55 J2 62 D8
Winton 77 B4
Wiri 7 F5 9 A2 90 E5
Wither Hills Walkway 35 K6 44 C10
Woburn 110 C3
Womens Island 80 D6
Wood Bay 89 D2
Wood, The 115 B5
Woodaugh 123 A4 124 D3
Woodbourne 44 C10
Woodbury 61 E4
Woodcocks 6 F9
Woodend (Invercargill) 77 F5
Woodend (Waimakariri) 54 F8 56 B10
Woodend Beach 54 F8 56 B10
Woodhill 5 J7 7 C1 84 C2
Woodlands Park 89 D2
Woodlands, NI (Bay of Plenty) 10 G11 14 F13
  15 F2
Woodlands, SI 77 E6
Woodlaw 76 D14 77 A2
Woodleigh 9 G2
Woodside, NI 33 C7
Woodside, SI 74 H9 79 A7
Woodstock (Tasman) 38 J8 42 A13
Woodstock (Westland) 45 J2
Woodville 30 D10 31 D4
Woolleys Bay 4 E13
Woolston 54 J8 56 E10 120 F2
Woolwich 103 D4
Wreys Bush 77 A3
Wrights Bush 77 D4
Wyllies Crossing 74 H10 124 J3
Wyndham 78 D9

Yaldhurst 53 H7 56 D9 120 A3
Yaldhurst Museum of Transport & Science -
  Christchurch 53 H7 56 D9
Yankee River Hut 77 J1 80 C3
Yeates Track 29 H6
Yeats Ridge Hut 50 B13 51 B4
Yellow Hut 74 F11
Yeoman Track 27 G6
York Track 23 D5
Young Hut 58 G9
Youngman Stream Hut 52 C13 53 C4
Yourk Bay 110 D3

ACKNOWLEDGEMENTS

We would like to thank the following people for their contributions to this manual: all the past participants on our training courses, for their enthusiasm and suggestions; the Occupational Therapists who introduced us to relaxation and stress-management - Gill Westland, Sue Bryson, Heather Lord, Debbie Harrison, Marie MacBean and Jo Spink; Dr Audrey Livingston Booth, Amber Lloyd and Jane Madders for permission to use their material and our colleagues in the Health Promotion Service for their patience and support.

We particularly want to thank Veronica Candy for the enthusiasm and commitment which she has brought to the unenviable job of seeing the manual through its final stages of production!

We also thank the Health Promotion Service of the East Anglian Regional Health Authority for funding the publication of this work.

© Cambridge Health Promotion 1989

ISBN 1 87228 100 1

Design, layout and illustration
Cambridge Health Promotion Studios

ABOUT THE AUTHORS

Marion Howell joined the Cambridge Health Promotion team in 1984. Formerly she worked at MIND Headquarters and had a particular interest in mental health promotion. Aware that stress is a topic everyone can identify with and an issue that many people see as a problem, Marion initiated Health Promotion's work in relaxation. She developed the relaxation project described in this manual, led relaxation groups in GP practices and has run many relaxation groups in the health service, voluntary sector and industry. Marion left Health Promotion in late 1987 after producing a son and daughter in quick succession. She is now involved in voluntary work and is hoping to develop her career as a freelance trainer.

Jane Whitehead has worked for Cambridge Health Authority since 1984, when she became involved in the Food and Health Programme as a researcher and co-ordinator. In 1986 she joined the Health Promotion Service as HEO with responsibility for developing publications, and after Marion's departure she took over the management of the relaxation project. She has run relaxation and stress management training courses for many groups within and outside the NHS, as well as running groups in the community.

Survive Stress brings together two of her main interests in health promotion, developing publications and providing training for other professional groups.

CONTENTS

SECTION 1
PRE-COURSE PREPARATION
Before running a course   12

SECTION 2
THE OPENING SESSION
The opening session   16

SECTION 3
WHAT IS STRESS?
Recognising and managing it effectively   20

SECTION 4
EFFECTS OF STRESS
Part 1   Fight/flight   28
Part 2   Perceptions of stress   31
Part 3   Breathing   35

SECTION 5
RELAXATION TECHNIQUES
Part 1.1   Background   40
Part 1.2   Loosening exercises   43
Part 2.1   Progressive relaxation   45
Part 2.2   Mitchell method of physiological relaxation   47
Part 2.3   Guided and unguided visualization   50
Part 2.4   Simple massage   51
Part 2.5   Biofeedback   54

SECTION 6
EVERYDAY RELAXATION
Relaxation in everyday situations   58

SECTION 7
RUNNING A GROUP
Running a relaxation group   64

SECTION 8
GUIDELINES AND COURSE OUTLINES
Planning a course   68

SECTION 9
FOLLOW-UP
Following up the course   74

SECTION 10
COURSE MATERIALS
Relaxation Texts 1-5   78-84
Case Studies 1-2   85-86
Handouts 1-11   87-104
Flipcharts 1-11   105-115

SECTION 11
RESOURCE LIST
Recommended reading and resource list   118

FOREWORD

We all have to cope with stress, and when it is well managed it becomes the spur to action, the challenge that is necessary for success at work and sport, and it is essential for survival. But when it becomes more than we can manage it can have ill effects upon health, work and personal relationships. The human cost is great: millions of work days are lost each year through stress related illness and the financial cost to the National Health Service is alarmingly high.

It is now being accepted by the medical profession that preventive measures which involve stress management and relaxation can give individuals greater responsibility for their own well being and can help them to avoid many of the stress related disorders. However, a plethora of self-help methods has sprung up during the past few decades, some of them soundly based and well taught, but others may be an expensive trap for vulnerable and gullible people suffering from the effects of stress. The Cambridge Health Authority Project which has initiated relaxation and stress management classes under the National Health Service is in the forefront by introducing sound, safe, preventive measures to the general public.

I believe this manual to be unique. It is a comprehensive guide for those who wish to train to run courses for the public. The authors have clearly had considerable experience in conducting classes in the community and in training courses for professionals. They recognise that individuals differ not only in their reactions to stress but also in the preventive methods most suitable for them. This book therefore covers a number of well authenticated methods, gives good factual information, makes suggestions for setting up classes and offers guidance into the content of lessons and the importance of follow up.

One of the problems of those first taking relaxation and stress management classes is lack of confidence and there will be some anxiety as to whether there will be sufficient material to last the series of classes. The detailed help given in this book in the form of charts, suggestions for discussion, the combination of factual information and ways of involving class members should go a long way to dispel doubts.

The promotion of mental health is only just getting the attention it deserves. People are more ready nowadays to take responsibility for their own stress management if they are given wise guidance. Because the methods given in this manual are flexible they can easily be adapted to use in hospitals, GP practices, schools, voluntary groups and in the workplace.

It is made clear throughout that this manual is directed at TRAINERS. The authors have drawn together material from a variety of sources and puts it firmly in the context of a coherent training programme. They state that they are not concerned with providing therapy which requires expert help but a framework for those who are preparing to conduct classes for the general public to help them manage their stress without distress.

Jane Madders
October 1988

INTRODUCTION

This manual is based on a series of workshops run by Cambridge Health Promotion Service over the last two years. It is intended as a practical guide to the basics of stress management and relaxation for health professionals and others who see a need to help combat the effects of stress in their own, their colleagues' and clients' lives.

The authors appreciate that this essentially individual-focused approach has limitations in combating stress which is often the result of social and economic forces over which individuals have little control. However we hope that for many people, raised awareness of personal stress and the development of personal coping strategies will be a starting point from which to explore the possibilities for individual or collective action to tackle the structural causes of stress in their lives.

Background

Relaxation groups are now established in many GP practices and other community settings throughout the Cambridge Health District. As a result of our training as group leaders and our experience of running relaxation groups in the community, we decided to offer our first 'Introduction to Relaxation' workshop as part of a series of training courses under the general title 'Skills for the Practice of Health Education'. The initial two-day course attracted a multi-disciplinary group which included NHS and Social Services employees, a yoga teacher, freelance counsellors, probation officers and workers from voluntary organisations. The materials used on that course have since been developed and expanded into a flexible training package which is suitable for use with many occupational groups.

Aims

The manual is intended as a resource for training health professionals and others to pass on basic stress management and relaxation techniques to colleagues and clients, either in groups, or on a one-to-one basis. By the end of a two-day course based on its contents, participants should be able to teach others how to:

- identify causes of stress in their lives
- understand the physical and psychological effects of stress
- use relaxation as a preventive measure and as a coping strategy
- combine relaxation techniques with other strategies to reduce and manage stress.

Evaluation of our courses shows that participants are also likely to benefit on a personal level from looking at the stress in their own lives and by learning simple but effective ways of coping with it.

Why Relaxation?

Relaxation techniques have been chosen as the central component of the course for several reasons. Learning relaxation skills helps people understand and take control of their own physical and psychological responses to stress. This sense of 'being in control' has been identified as an important factor in determining health status and behaviour. Practising relaxation offers opportunities for self-reflection and taking time for oneself, which can enhance self-esteem and contribute to general well-being. More specifically, relaxation has been shown to be effective in the management of stress-related health problems such as essential hypertension (Patel:1985; Jorgensen: 1981), and to be beneficial in the treatment of a variety of anxiety symptoms, hyperventilation, insomnia, and fears and phobias. Attendance at relaxation groups has also been associated in a recent local survey with reduced levels of smoking and tranquilliser consumption. (Kapila:1987)

Relaxation methods can be adapted for use by people of widely varying ages, backgrounds and ability, and they are quickly and easily learned by most people. Relaxation is of course only part of an effective stress-management programme, and the manual clearly places relaxation in the context of other strategies for stress reduction and control.

Who Are The Training Courses For?

Given time and practice, many people are capable of passing on basic relaxation and stress-management skills to others. There is no mystique involved! However, a two-day workshop is not going to turn people into stress-management therapists, and the idea is rather to disseminate basic relaxation skills. Some experience of working with groups is assumed, although there is a session on the practical aspects of running a relaxation group. We have found that participants who come on the course with a particular client group already in mind are more likely to use the skills they learn, so this should be taken into consideration when sending out pre-course information.

The workshops on which the manual is based have been run successfully with both uni- and multi-disciplinary groups. Participants have included: health visitors, school nurses, dental hygienists, physiotherapists, occupational health nurses, student nurses, nurse tutors, counsellors, probation officers, personnel managers, administrators, doctors, clergymen, voluntary workers, housing officers, college nursing sisters and health promotion officers.

Evaluation

Analysis of evaluation forms from a sample of three of the multi-disciplinary courses (thirty six participants) indicated that all participants had found the course helpful, both from a personal and from a professional point of view. Typical comments were:

'The course highlights the benefits of relaxation skills. It has certainly been of great help to me in maintaining my own good health and I intend to pass it on to others in my work.'

'It has confirmed my belief about the value of relaxation and encouraged me to believe that individuals can have control over their own health.'

'I realised how tense I am and how much I need to alleviate stress in my personal and work life.'

When asked about which parts of the course they found most useful, 57% said the discussion and presentations on stress, 40% the practical relaxation exercises, and others the sections on planning and leading relaxation sessions. A general comment on the whole course was:

'I found each session very useful, and each was preparation for the next.'

Asked whether they now felt confident about passing on relaxation skills to others, 72% felt that they could work with individuals, but felt lacking in confidence to lead a group. A number highlighted the need for an additional group-work course, and for 'refresher' sessions to reinforce what they had learned. Participants with previous experience of training or working with groups felt able to offer a 4 or 5 week course, with 'hot-line' support provided by the Health Promotion Service. (See Section 9 : Following up the course.)

How To Use The Manual

The manual contains all the material you need to run a basic introductory course on relaxation and stress management, including flip-chart/OHP material, relaxation texts, case studies, handouts for participants and evaluation forms. At the end you will find a selected reading list, and a list of addresses from which further information and resources can be obtained.

The manual is arranged in sections, some of which correspond directly to a single workshop session (Sections 2, 3, 6 and 7) and some of which contain material that will be spread out over a number of sessions (Sections 4 and 5). To help you in planning, sample course outlines are provided for two-day, one-day, half-day and two-hour workshops, with references to the relevant sections in the manual (Section 8). Although the format which we have used most often is the two-day workshop, there's no reason why the course should not be run as a series of shorter sessions. Sections can also be used on their own as the basis for single sessions on a particular topic.

Participatory methods are used wherever possible, as the emphasis is on the acquisition of personal skills, and on relating theory to practical experience. Each section contains the following elements, in different combinations:

- *INTRODUCTION (background information for leader)*
- *LEADER'S PRESENTATIONS (short inputs which can be expanded if necessary by referring to the information in the Introduction)*
- *GROUP EXERCISES*
- *CHECKLISTS* (to give you an idea of what kind of feedback to expect from the various exercises, and some suggestions as to how to structure discussion)

Material for photocopying (Flip chart/OHP, handouts, evaluation forms, case studies etc.) is all in Section 10. Participants will also need copies of some or all of the relaxation texts in Section 5.

We hope that you will enjoy running courses using this manual, and that you will find it a useful starting point from which to develop your own training in this fascinating and fast-growing area. Good luck - and don't forget to relax and enjoy it!

Jane Whitehead

Marion Howell

August 1988

References

Patel C et al., *Trial of relaxation in reducing coronary risk; four year follow-up,* Br Med J 1985; 290: 1103 - 1106

Jorgensen RS et al., *Anxiety management training in the treatment of essential hypertension,* Behav Res & Therapy 1981; 19:467 - 474

Kapila M, *Promoting Community Mental Health: An Experience of General Practice-based Relaxation Groups* (unpublished) 1987.

SECTION 1

PRE-COURSE PREPARATION

Before running a course   12

BEFORE RUNNING A COURSE

This section covers pre-course preparation and organisation, and should help you avoid some of the more stressful pitfalls of running a workshop of this kind!

Leading the course

We strongly recommend that the workshop should be run by two people rather than one, and that the two leaders have an equal input to both the practical relaxation exercises and the more theoretical elements. This will show participants two different styles of leadership, and help avoid the common misconception that only certain kinds of voice are 'good' for relaxation. If you have had little or no experience of leading relaxation sessions, we suggest that you experiment on each other for a few weeks beforehand!

Pre-course information to participants

Whatever kind of course you are running, information sent out to participants beforehand plays a vital part in helping shape their attitudes and expectations. When organising a workshop on 'Stress Management and Relaxation', it's particularly important to make the pre-course information as clear, comprehensive, and therefore stress-reducing as possible. For example, if you forget to tell people that the parking facilities at the venue are atrocious and that they are likely to have to choose between a fifteen-minute walk and a serious threat to their blood-pressure and no-claims bonus, they will be in a far from receptive mood by the time they arrive!

Information to include in pre-course letter:
- title of course and brief outline of aims
- names of workshop leaders (with invitation to participants to phone with any pre-course queries)
- venue (with map if necessary)
- date(s)
- times
- lunchtime arrangements
- details of parking facilities and any special parking arrangements
- costs

Participants should also be told that the course is practical and participatory, and that they might like to bring a blanket or rug and a cushion, for maximum comfort during the relaxation sessions. The information sent out should include a 'Stress Diary' for participants to complete during the week before the course, together with explanatory notes. (Handout 1).

NB. It is important to emphasise in the letter, and in any pre-course publicity, that the aim of the workshop is training, not therapy. In other words, it is not appropriate for people who are themselves suffering from deep-seated anxieties or seeking help with major personal problems. Participants generally do derive personal benefit from the course, but the emphasis throughout should remain firmly on the acquisition of skills and the exploration of strategies which can be passed on to clients and colleagues either in groups or on a one-to-one basis. It is also helpful to suggest that before coming on the course, participants think about potential clients and client groups, as this will help focus their learning and make it easier to relate theory to practice.

Numbers

A comfortable size for the group will be determined to some extent by the available space. We usually aim for 12, as it divides conveniently into pairs, 3s and 4s, but we have run sessions with as few as 8 people, which should probably be regarded as a minimum for a group training session.

Pre-course preparation

This will be much the same as for any other course, but here are a few points to bear in mind at the planning stage:

Venue:

- size - is there enough space for all participants to lie down comfortably at the same time?
- noise-level - is the room relatively quiet, so that concentration will not be too hard to maintain?
- lighting - in the absence of natural light, is there an alternative to fluorescent light?
- comfort - is the floor clean and carpeted? Are chairs comfortable enough for relaxation exercises to be done sitting down?
- heating - is this easy to regulate, to accommodate changes in body temperature during relaxation?
- window coverings - are there blinds or curtains, allowing the room to be darkened?
- availability of other rooms for work in small groups?
- kitchen facilities?

Refreshments

- avoid tea and coffee - try herbal teas (camomile, rosehip, mint etc.) or fresh fruit juice

Course information

In addition to material copied from the participants' handouts in Section 10 and the relaxation texts from Section 5, you will also need:

- participants' list
- course outline/timetable
- folders in which participants can keep all their course material together

Equipment

- flip-chart and stand
- newsprint or other large paper
- felt pens
- blutack
- cassette recorder
- relaxation music tape (see list of resources at end)
- bio-feedback machine (optional - see list of resources at end)

SECTION 2

THE OPENING SESSION

The opening session   16

THE OPENING SESSION

The opening session of a course sets the tone for everything that follows, and it is important to establish the right atmosphere from the beginning. The way in which you choose to do this will depend on several factors – your own experience, the composition of the group, participants' familiarity with each other - but the stages outlined below have proved useful in helping create a friendly, informal, supportive atmosphere in which people feel able to relax.

Introductions and welcome to the course

Have a 'Welcome to the course' sign displayed on the board or flipchart, and offer people herbal tea or fruit juice as they arrive.

Course leaders introduce themselves briefly.

Ice-breaker

Everyone will have their favourite way of beginning a course, and these ideas are offered only as suggestions. They are useful because they combine physical activity which helps people to loosen up (cushion game), with focusing on the positive side of things, which plays an important role in building self-esteem (round of names). The length of the opening session can be varied according to the time available. See the Course Outline Plans (Section 8) for suggested timings.

Cushion game

AIM: to help participants and leaders learn and remember each others' names; to help everyone relax.

TIME: 5 minutes

Everyone stands up in a circle. Leader explains the game as follows: the cushion is thrown round the room at random. For the first few rounds, everyone says their *own name* as they throw the cushion. Continue until everyone has said their name a few times. Then change to saying the name of the person you're throwing the cushion *to*, and continue until all members of the group can confidently name each other.

and/or Round of names

AIM: to help participants and leaders learn and remember each others' names; to set a precedent for concentrating on positives rather than negatives during the course.

TIME: 5 minutes

Group sits in circle. Leader asks everyone to write their name on a sheet of flip-chart paper which is passed around from person to person, and to say their name and one thing they like about themselves. (Give examples to help, eg. 'I'm Jane, and I like my sense of humour', 'I like the fact that I'm tall', 'I like myself for being a good listener' etc.)

Laying down the ground-rules

TIME: 3 minutes

Setting boundaries and laying down ground-rules is a vital part of working with any group. It is particularly important when the group may be addressing sensitive personal issues. The ground-rules for the course should include:

- complete confidentiality - nothing said on the course, either in the large group or in any small group, should be repeated outside.
- individual discretion - nobody should feel under pressure to reveal any more than they are willing to, or to take part in any exercise which they do not wish to join in.
- punctuality - the time on the course is limited, and there's a lot of ground to cover, so group members should make every effort to be on time for all sessions, and to let the leaders know if they are likely to be late.
- no smoking in any of the rooms used for the course - smokers should be told where they can go to smoke at breaks and lunchtime.

It may be useful to have these ground-rules written out on flip-chart paper beforehand, so that they can be stuck on the wall as a reminder throughout the course.

Content of Course

AIM: To give participants an outline of what to expect on the course, clarify misconceptions, allay anxieties, and, if appropriate, negotiate content of future sessions to meet participants' needs.

TIME: 5 minutes

This session can be run in different ways, depending on the format and duration of the course. For example, if the workshop is held on two consecutive days, the content is not really negotiable (unless the leaders are prepared to stay up all night re-thinking Day 2!), and all that is needed is a simple exercise clarifying expectations and allaying any concerns. If the course is spread out over several weeks, it may be possible to modify the content to meet expectations to some degree. It is important to be realistic about what you have to offer.

Exercise 1

AIM: To clarify participants' expectations and deal with any concerns.

TIME: 5 minutes in pairs, 10 minutes for feedback.

METHOD: In pairs, group members draw up 'shopping list' of five things they'd like to take away from the course, and a separate list of things they're worried about, eg. all the work piling up back at the office, feeling a fool, feeling guilty about taking time etc.

FEEDBACK: Lists are stuck up on the wall, and expectations compared with leaders' aims and objectives for the course. Leaders draw out any expectations which are unrealistic or seem unlikely to be met, and offer group members the opportunity to withdraw from the course if they really feel that they have been misled.

Looking at lists of concerns, leaders acknowledge any which are well-grounded, such as anxiety at work piling up elsewhere, but emphasise positive benefits of the course in providing time for reflection and offering skills which, with practice, will improve quality of personal and professional life. In order to make the course itself as anxiety-free as possible, as in all training exercises, it is important that leaders explain clearly the aims and content of each session. This applies particularly to relaxation exercises, which may be unfamiliar to many people.

Personal Coping Strategies

We all have our own ways of relaxing and 'unwinding'. It might be a workout on the squash court, collapsing in front of a soap on TV, a night down the pub with friends, or a gin and a hot bath. We're going to begin our exploration of stress management and relaxation by finding out what people do already.

Exercise 2

AIM: to allow group members to share some personal information; to give an idea of the range and variety of coping skills which we use to deal with stress.

TIME: 5 minutes in pairs, 10 minutes for feedback.

METHOD: In pairs, participants find out what their partner does to relax and unwind, in order to introduce her/him to the rest of the group.

FEEDBACK: Leader goes round the group, asking each person in turn to introduce her/his partner, and draws up collective list of activities mentioned.

The collective list will probably include a wide range of activities which can be grouped into several categories, such as physical exercise, eg. squash, swimming, walking, jogging; hobbies/activities requiring complete concentration, eg. singing, model-making;

pampering oneself, eg. buying treats, having a good night out, having a cigarette; escapism, eg. watching 'rubbish' on TV, drinking; and more contemplative activities, such as listening to music and reading.

Leader's presentation

Although there's a great variety of activities listed here, there seem to be a few underlying themes which we might pick out. Physical exercise, whether it's gardening, walking the dog or having a game of squash, is a very good way of dispelling tension - it actually helps us work out of the system the chemicals which fuel the stress response. Other activities which you've mentioned seem to share the characteristic of requiring complete concentration. In other words, you become so wrapped up in what you're doing that you aren't able to worry about anything else! Then there's that range of activities which are to do

with giving yourself a treat - the gin and tonic in the bath, splurge on a new dress or camera - something that makes you feel really good at the time.

Everything on the list is a useful coping strategy; a way of saying to the world : 'This is my time, and I'll do exactly what I like with it.' Problems might arise if the odd drink turns into an absolute necessity to numb you to the horrors of existence, or flashing the credit card becomes your reflex reaction to a bad day at work, but on the whole it's healthy to have a range of pleasures to choose from when it comes to relaxing. This is where relaxation techniques come in - after all, there are many occasions on which it just isn't possible to lounge in a hot bath or read a few soothing chapters of a fat historical romance. Relaxation can be practised in some form in almost any situation, which is why it is such a useful addition to our already well-developed repertoire of coping strategies.

SECTION 3

WHAT IS STRESS?

Recognising and managing it effectively

WHAT IS STRESS?
Recognising and managing it effectively

Introduction

'Stress is a threat to the quality of life, and to physical and psychological well being.' (Tom Cox, Stress, Macmillan 1978:1)

There is growing evidence that stress may be an important factor in the development of many of the diseases and conditions which take a high toll in developed Western countries. Among the conditions which seem in some way to be stress-related are: high blood pressure, coronary heart disease, asthma, migraine, diabetes, ulcers, insomnia, and a range of psychological disorders from persistent irritability to severe anxiety and depression.

If this is the case, then the effective management of stress is clearly a desirable goal to pursue, but before we can begin to think constructively about managing stress, we need first to clarify exactly what we mean by 'stress'. When we talk about 'stress' and 'stressful' situations in everyday conversation we use the terms loosely to refer to a wide variety of phenomena, and if we were forced to come up with a precise definition, we would probably all produce something rather different. This diversity of opinion is also to be found in the large body of literature on the subject. As Tom Cox says:

'The concept of stress is elusive because it is poorly defined. There is no single agreed definition in existence. It is a concept which is familiar to both layman and professional alike; it is understood by all when used in a general context but by very few when a more precise account is required ....' (Cox 1978:1)

In this session, we'll be looking at our personal experiences of stress, as a starting point for understanding and dealing with it successfully.

Exercise 1

AIMS: to differentiate between the causes and effects of stress; to show that 'stress' means different things to different people and to make the point that stress in an unavoidable part of life.

TIME: 3 minutes

METHOD: Brainstorm in group "What are the words which come to mind immediately when you think of 'stress'?"

Leader takes feedback on flip-chart.

CHECKLIST: A typical list generated by this exercise might include:

pressure	limits
trouble	aggression
despair	fatigue
lack of resources	fear
annoyance	other people
personalities	bills
deadlines	money
time	responsibility
speeches	tests
traffic	illness
Christmas	unemployment
weeds (in garden!)	work

Leader's presentation

The list we've produced is a mixture of causes and effects of stress. Some of the causes identified here are external - like bills, lack of resources and traffic. Others may be coming from within ourselves - responsibility, pressure, limits. Some of the effects mentioned are physical, like fatigue and illness, while others are emotional, like aggression and annoyance. Several words listed might be either cause or effect; my annoyance might cause you stress; your illness might cause me stress.

Three things which emerge from the words listed are:

- stress is an unavoidable part of everyday life, familiar to us all in one form or another
- 'stress' means slightly different things to all of us
- there's some confusion about whether we're talking about something 'out there', beyond our control, or something which we feel within ourselves; a physical, emotional and psychological phenomenon over which we may be able to exert some influence. Perhaps the most useful way of looking at stress is to see it as the product of an interaction between the individual and the environment.

Models of Stress

As noted in the Introduction to this section, there is a good deal of debate as to the exact meaning of 'stress'. The reason for this confusion is not hard to trace. Stress has been written about from many different perspectives, each with its own terminology and its own insights. The model which we present in the workshops is a version of the 'transactional' model, but leaders should be aware of the other two widely-used and influential models, the 'engineering' and 'biological' models. These are described briefly here. (For a fuller discussion, see Cox: 1978)

1. Stress as an interaction - Transactional Model

According to this model, stress is defined as the result of an imbalance between a perceived demand on the one hand, and a person's perception of his or her ability to meet that demand on the other. The crucial balance is not between actual demand and actual capability, but between perceived demand and perceived capability. Take as an example two people about to give a lecture. Objectively measured, their past performances have been very much on a par. Person A is self-confident, outgoing and thinks of herself as a good lecturer, so the prospect of performing in this way causes no great stress. Person B is shy and lacking in self-esteem, and thinks of himself as an awful lecturer, in spite of reassurance from his friends. The prospect of giving a lecture makes him feel ill for days beforehand. This illustrates that it is not the situation in itself (i.e. being about to give a lecture) which causes stress, but the individual's own perception of his or her ability to cope.

This model provides a useful framework for looking at stress as it emphasises the individual nature of the experience of stress, and introduces the concept of 'coping', or handling stress effectively.

2. Stress as a set of causes - Engineering Model

This model borrows its terms from Hooke's Law of Elasticity, a law of physical science which describes how loads produce deformation in metals. The load or demand placed on the metal is described as 'stress' and the resulting deformation is termed 'strain'. Hooke's law states that if the strain produced by a given stress falls within the 'elastic limit' of the material, when the stress is removed the material will return to its original condition. If the strain forces the material beyond its 'elastic limit', some permanent damage will result. When this principle is applied to people, it suggests that stress in the form of external demands can be tolerated up to a point, but that when it reaches a certain level, permanent damage may result. It also suggests that just as different materials have different 'elastic limits', so individuals vary in their ability to resist the damaging effects of stress.

When 'stress' is defined in this way as a set of causes, the question then arises of identifying the conditions likely to cause 'strain'. The problem here is that we all respond differently to a given situation or stimulus. For you, the thought of giving a lecture, playing a violin concerto, or climbing the north face of the Eiger might be a stimulating challenge while the idea of doing any of these things might reduce me to a state of complete panic. My playing Radio 1 at full blast all day may be giving me pleasure, but it might be considered a stressful stimulus by my elderly neighbours.

In spite of the difficulty of generalisation, much research has concentrated on trying to identify the common characteristics of conditions which will be universally experienced as 'stressful'. Some of these include:

- Extremes of sensory stimulation - noise, heat, cold, humidity, over-crowding
- Disrupted physiological function (possibly as a result of disease, drugs, sleep loss, etc.)
- Sensory deprivation - isolation, confinement, underwork
- Group pressure
- Perceived threat to cherished values and goals
- Lack of control over events

3. Stress as a response - Biological Model

According to this model, stress is defined as a person's physical and psychological *response* to a stimulus rather than as a cause or set of causes in the environment. The response-based model was first developed by the Canadian doctor and physiologist, Hans Selye. His definition of stress was 'the non-specific response of the body to any demand made upon it'. (Hans Selye, *Stress without Distress*, Hodder and Stoughton, 1975:27).

The three main ideas in Selye's concept of stress are:

- The physiological stress response does not depend on the nature of the stressor or cause of stress, and follows the same pattern in most species.

- If exposure to the stressor is continual or repeated, the defence reaction goes through three identifiable stages, collectively described as the General Adaptation Syndrome. The stages are:
  1. Alarm reaction - initial defence reaction, level of resistance reduced
  2. Stage of resistance - organism adapts to continual exposure to stressor
  3. Exhaustion and death - ability to adapt exhausted, and collapse occurs.

- The defence responses themselves, if severe and prolonged, cause 'diseases of adaptation' as the physiological system is extended beyond its resources.

- A distinction should be made between stress, which is an unavoidable part of being alive, and 'distress', which is damaging or harmful stress.

Selye's ideas have been enormously influential in the development of our concept of stress but the biological model as presented here has two main limitations.

- Its breadth - the absence of distinction between pleasant and unpleasant stimuli - all are classified as 'stressors'.

- The emphasis on the non-specific nature of the stress response. There is now evidence to suggest that the stress response may vary according to the characteristics of the stressor, and according to the psychological impact made by the stressor on the individual. (See Section 4, Part 2 - Perceptions of Stress).

N.B. If these definitions are introduced into the discussion, they should not be laboured too much. All the approaches outlined above have something to offer, and in much of the literature on stress there is considerable confusion as to which approach is being adopted. The important points to bring out in discussion are:

- the experience of stress is an individual phenomenon, although there are certain types of stimulus which may generally be experienced as 'stressful' by the majority of people

- situations in themselves cannot be categorically labelled 'stressful' or 'unstressful'

- stress is not something 'out there' by which we are bombarded. The experience of stress results from our relationship with our environment.

Leader's presentation

We can all think of major life events which are likely to cause us stress : the death of someone we love, the serious illness of a partner or friend, buying and selling a house, or coping with a new addition to the family. However, much of our day-to-day stress is caused not by such momentous events, but by a combination of petty annoyances, irritations and hassles, often caused by our own and other people's inflexibility.

Exercise 2 - Case Study 1, 'Bad News at Bedtime'.

AIMS : to illustrate the 'transactional' model of stress; to show how we raise our own levels of stress unnecessarily by the way we handle everyday situations; to provide a framework for looking at coping strategies.

TIME : 15 minutes for reading through and discussing in small groups, 15 minutes for feedback.

METHOD : Case Study

Divide participants into groups of 4 or 5. Hand out Case Study 1, 'Bad News at Bedtime'. Ask participants to read through, building up a picture of John and his family, then in their small groups to answer the questions: 'Why did John become stressed? How could he have handled the situation better?' Each group should elect a spokesperson to report back.

Case Study 1 - Bad News at Bedtime

John's wife has recently got an evening job. This means that John has to get home from work at 5:30 precisely so that his wife can leave the house immediately. The evenings in the Johnson household have a regular pattern: serve dinner to the four children, help with homework, baths, read stories and bed. Tonight John particularly wants to watch a programme on television which begins at 9 o'clock. He thinks to himself: "I'll have all my jobs finished by then, and I'll be able to sit quietly and relax. Why not? I've had a very busy day after all."

By 7:15 pm., Luke, the two-year-old had had his bath and been put to bed. Jane, aged ten, was doing her homework and asked her father to help find her ruler. To encourage her independence and teach her to keep track of her own possessions, John asked "Where did you last see it?" and carried on washing up the dishes. The next job was to bath the four-year-old, David, and John was only too grateful when Katie, aged eight, said she would also like a bath, and that she would help John by bathing David. "Great!" he thought, "So far, so good. They should all be in bed by 8:30 at the latest!"

While putting away the last of the dinner dishes, John's heart missed a beat - he could hear David running up and down in the bath. He ran up the stairs three at a time, his head filled with images of catastrophe - a split skull, a double drowning. As he flung open the bathroom door, he smashed the doorknob into Katie's eye.

Katie burst into tears. David carried on running up and down the bath. John shouted "Stop that at once", which startled the little boy so that he fell over and swallowed some of the bath water. He too began to cry. The sound of wailing was also heard in one of the bedrooms - the noise and chaos had woken Luke. Just at this point, Jane came into the bathroom and asked if John had found her ruler. John exploded. "We're in complete chaos, and all you can think about is your ruler!' She too burst into tears.

John treated Katie's eye, calmed David down, got Luke back to sleep, and persuaded Jane to go to bed without having found the missing ruler. It was just after 9:00, and with generous Scotch in hand, John collapsed gratefully in front of the television.

"I want a drink of juice, Dad", came a voice from upstairs. It was Katie. Still feeling bad about her eye, he took a drink up to her. She somehow managed to miss her mouth, and grape juice went all over her, her nightie, the carpet and the bedclothes. The last straw!

Finally, at 10:00 pm. he sat down just in time to see the credits roll at the end of the programme. His wife walked in and asked brightly "Is everything OK?"

"Just fine", he said grudgingly, "Absolutely fine."

(Adapted from *Coping with Stress* Donald Meichenbaum)

Leader takes feedback from each group in turn, compiling checklist on flip-chart.

A typical list of suggestions might include :

- Expecting too much of himself and others
- Unrealistic time limit - self-imposed
- Inflexibility - sticking to routine although inappropriate
- Over-reaction, leading to more problems
- 'Catastrophising' - imagining the worst
- Loss of self-control
- Build-up of resentment against his wife - suppression of feeling comes out in sarcasm.

Every workshop will come up with different suggestions as to how John might have handled the situation better - forget about bathing the children, leave the tidying up until later, invest in a video etc. It's always easier to see someone else's mistakes and prescribe the appropriate course of action than to analyse our own behaviour honestly and make stress-reducing changes!

On another piece of flip-chart paper break down the checklist into the following categories: Event, Appraisal, Reaction.

Event/Situation - bath-time in the Johnson household

Appraisal (how event or situation is viewed) - must get all the jobs finished and children in bed before 9.00pm.

Reaction (physical, mental and emotional) - displaces pressure on to children; exaggerates significance of events; becomes inflexible; feels guilty; becomes resentful; hits the bottle!

Leader's presentation

This three-part framework is a useful way of analysing stressful experiences as it shows the crucial role of our appraisal of a situation or event in determining our feelings and behaviour. A combination of calming 'self-talk', eg. 'It won't be the end of the world if I don't watch that programme after all', and 'emergency' relaxation techniques (as described in Section 6,) can help to induce a feeling of calm and control which is more likely to lead to a successful outcome than over-hasty panic reactions which often cause a situation to deteriorate, as poor John found to his cost! As this case study shows, it's easy to tell other people how to avoid stress. The difficult part is taking our own advice! The next step is to start trying to apply theory to practice, and look at areas of stress in our own lives.

Exercise 3

AIMS : to help participants identify areas of stress in their own lives; to make the distinction between positive stimulation and negative stress; to introduce the idea that choice and control are vital elements in the experience of stress.

TIME: 5 minutes to present matrix and take examples from the group; 5 minutes working individually; 10 minutes feedback in group.

METHOD: leader draws matrix as shown below on flip-chart, and asks group for examples of activities/situations which fit into the different boxes. Then, working individually, participants draw the matrix for themselves, and identify situations in their own lives which fit into each section (perhaps referring back to their stress diaries). Leader takes feedback from four participants, taking several examples from each box.

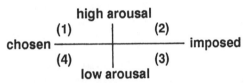

(Figures in brackets refer to key below. Do not draw on matrix.)

1. A challenging situation, i.e. one in which you have chosen to put yourself under a certain amount of pressure.

2. A situation in which you are under a lot of pressure, and over which you have little or no control.

3. A situation in which you are under-stimulated, and over which you have little or no control.

4. A situation in which you have deliberately chosen to keep your level of stimulation low.

Checklist

Typical examples in each box would be :

1. Playing a competitive game of squash; doing a demanding but rewarding job; acting; leading a climbing expedition; skiing.

2. Too many bills to pay; impossible deadlines to meet at work; looking after a sick relative; unhappy personal relationship with lots of rows; threat of redundancy/unemployment.

3. Any kind of repetitive, undemanding work which is seen as unrewarding, e.g. housework; work on a production line; routine shopping; or enforced leisure, as in unemployment or unwanted retirement.

4. Lying on a beach; reading a trashy novel; watching soap operas on T.V.; having a bath and locking the world out.

Points to bring out in discussion:
- Although patterns may emerge, people will come up with different examples in each box, again re-inforcing the importance of individual perception.
- The stress response is most likely to be experienced in situations combining high levels of arousal/demand with low levels of choice and control.
- Where low levels of arousal are combined with a low degree of choice and control, feelings of futility, apathy, depression, boredom and fatigue are likely to be experienced.

The matrix is a useful tool for helping participants to look at the balance in their lives between positive stimulation and stress. For example, if most of a person's working life is spent in the imposed/low arousal box, and most of her life outside work also comes into that category, the outlook for her physical and mental health is not likely to be good. In this situation, an appropriate stress-management strategy might be to choose some enjoyable and stimulating activity to balance the unavoidable routines of work and housework, if at all possible.

Similarly, the high-powered executive whose life is all compressed into the high arousal area of the matrix would benefit from choosing a few less demanding activities. A highly competitive game of squash with a business rival may not be the best way of unwinding after a tough day in the boardroom!

Exercise 4

AIM: to help participants use stress diaries as starting point for developing coping strategies.

TIME: 10 minutes, with 10 minutes feedback including presentation of Human Function Curve.

METHOD: In pairs, look at the 'high pressure, low control' and/or 'low stimulation, low control' situations identified in the diaries. Discuss how you felt in those situations, and anything you did which helped you to feel better.

FEEDBACK: was it useful to keep a diary? Any surprises, observations?

Leader's presentation

The importance of recognising signs of stress in ourselves and developing effective ways of coping is illustrated by Dr. Peter Nixon's Human Function Curve. **(Flip-chart 2)**

The Human Function Curve - Healthy tension or life-threatening stress?

Cardiologist Dr. Peter Nixon's Human Function Curve plots 'performance' against 'arousal' (Jane Madders, *Stress and Relaxation*, Macdonald Optima, 1979:22-4). The curve shows performance rising steadily with increased arousal (stimulation) until the point at which fatigue is reached.

While someone is on the upward left hand part of the curve, they will feel healthy, relaxed, alert, confident and energetic. They will probably enjoy a balanced lifestyle in which work and leisure play an equal part, and extra effort will lead to increased performance. They will appear adaptable and approachable to friends and colleagues, and enjoy high self-esteem. However, even someone being driven on to greater efforts by their own success will eventually reach the fatigue point, but as long as they take steps to recover either by catching up on sleep or using relaxation techniques, they will continue to cope successfully.

People get pushed over the top of the curve - often without realising it - when they become so entrenched in a routine or job that they do not allow enough time for rest and recuperation, but carry on regardless of increasing physical and mental tiredness. They continue to take on burdens greater than they can cope with, and drive themselves harder (increasing arousal) in the mistaken belief that this will result in better performance. Warning signs of being on this part of the curve are hours of fruitless activity in which performance falls off, so increasing anxiety and raising the level of arousal even further; inability to distinguish between minor details and major problems; bad temper; constant irritability; disrupted sleep and disrupted eating patterns. If no steps are taken to reduce fatigue, there is a serious risk of ill-health.

'P' on the curve represents the point at which even slight additional arousal may result in breakdown. Dr. Nixon reports that the event which finally pushes his patients into a heart attack can range from the death of a budgie to the death of a partner.

Points to bring out in discussion :

- the curve represents the cumulative response to arousal (demand, stimulation) from all sources, internal and external.

- everyone has their own 'function' curve. The important thing is to recognise when we are reaching our own 'fatigue point'.

- the function curve helps us recognise that the law of diminishing returns applies when we are constantly pushed beyond our optimum level of arousal.

- once we are familiar with our own 'function curve' and recognise the warning signs of over-arousal, we can take steps to restore the balance by resting. How do people recognise the 'fatigue point' in themselves? What are the warning signs? What corrective action can we take? Do we have to wait until we are actually physically ill before taking time off to recover, whether from employment or at home? Is it easier to take a couple of days off with a bad cold than to admit to feeling under stress and needing some time to restore the balance?

Managing Stress: a framework for action

(Flip-chart 3 - present main headings, and encourage discussion in large group about the fatigue point X, where coping strategies identified by participants fit in, and how they might be expanded.)

From the Case Study and our discussions of the stress matrix, the diaries and the Human Function Curve, we have begun to get an idea of the many dimensions of stress. Any strategy for managing stress must also therefore have several components, some of which we have already identified. Thinking back to the Case Study, we saw how John's disastrous evening could be analysed in terms of the *situation* itself, or rather the sequence of events which occurred; his *appraisal* of those events; and his subsequent *reactions*. We discussed the ways in which these were inter-related, and suggested ways in which he might have managed the situation better by modifying his expectations and attitudes and behaving more calmly.

This ability to make changes in attitudes and behavioural responses is an important element in any stress management programme, but it is only half the story. It's no use telling someone whose work environment is noisy, dirty and dangerous that all they have to do to combat their work-related stress is change their attitude and put in their ear-plugs! Changes in the environment, whether physical or social, may be an essential part of a stress-reduction programme. The flip-chart shows the different levels at which stress can be tackled.

1. Changing the actual situation

This involves dealing with the agents of stress in the environment, by one of four possible strategies: adding, subtracting, re-organising or avoiding. Environmental changes may be simple and within the control of individuals, such as improving the lighting, seating or heating in an office. (Although even these might not be straightforward for people who work in large bureaucratic organisations!) Examples of stress-reducing changes to the physical environment might include: adding an extra light source, removing a noisy telex machine, reorganising desks to make better use of space, providing ergonomically-designed seating for typists and glare-reducing shields for VDU screens.

Some situations cannot be tackled in this way, and avoidance or flight may be the only way of escaping the intolerable pressures of an unsatisfactory or unsuitable job, a poor relationship, overcrowding, poor housing etc. The same strategies can apply to people; we may need to take stock of current relationships with family, friends and colleagues.

Extreme forms of coping behaviour, eg. moving house to escape from noisy neighbours; leaving an unsatisfactory marriage or relationship, can often lead to new problems. The individual has to decide whether on balance it's worth substituting one set of problems for another, or whether other coping strategies might be more effective.

2. Improving ability to cope with situation

This can involve developing specific skills to cope with a given situation or demand, eg. training in dealing with child-abuse for health visitors, or in conducting 'health interviews' for school nurses. It also covers more general 'lifeskills' such as assertiveness, time-management, objective-setting and communication, which can help to reduce stress in personal life as well as in the context of employment.

3. Changing perception of the situation

This involves changing the way we think about a situation. We can *change our minds* about the nature of the demands being made of us - 'perhaps it's not so dreadful after all'; about our ability to cope - 'I've done more difficult things before'; and about the importance of coping - 'What's the worst thing likely to happen if I fail?'

'Self-talk', or the endless monologue which we carry on inside our heads, has a great influence on the way we perceive things. Significant shifts of perspective can be achieved by:

- Changing negative self-talk into positive eg. 'I mustn't make mistakes or fail' into 'I have a right to make mistakes and learn from them'.

- Avoiding 'catastrophising', ie. exaggerating the significance of problems by using words like 'terrible', 'awful', 'disastrous', etc. when what we really mean is 'inconvenient', 'annoying', or 'a nuisance'.

- Avoiding 'demand' words, whether applied to ourselves or other people. These, include 'must', 'should', 'have to'. When you hear yourself saying (or thinking) 'I must. .', or 'You ought to. .' etc., try changing to 'I would rather. . .', 'I would prefer. .', and notice the difference.

- Resisting the temptation to label things 'good' and 'bad'. Judging, criticising and moralising tend to generate resentment, frustration and self-righteous anger, all emotions which create stress.

4. Changing behaviour

This involves taking action to 'stress-proof' ourselves by making adjustments in the way we live. Examples of positive lifestyle factors include:

- good nutritious diet
- avoiding harmful substances, eg. tobacco, alcohol and other drugs
- taking enjoyable exercise
- having sufficient rest
- pursuing creative hobbies and interests
- learning and practising relaxation techniques to help unwind, and reduce physical, emotional and mental tension.

Summary

1. Stress is an unavoidable fact of life, and can have harmful consequences if not managed effectively.

2. Although there are certain types of stimuli which will generally be experienced as stressful, the experience of stress is also linked with *individual* perception of an imbalance between demands and ability to cope.

3. We often increase the pressure on ourselves by inappropriate attitudes, expectations and behaviour.

4. We are most likely to experience stress in situations which combine a high degree of pressure with a low degree of control.

5. If the warning signs of stress are not recognised, and effective coping behaviour not adopted, mental and/or physical ill-health and ultimately breakdown may result.

6. An effective stress-management programme may include: changes in actual demand; improving ability to cope with situation; cognitive change and behavioural change.

SECTION 4

EFFECTS OF STRESS

Part 1	Fight/flight	28
Part 2	Perceptions of stress	31
Part 3	Breathing	35

Part 1

FIGHT/FLIGHT

Introduction

This section will explore what happens to us physically when we are in stressful situations and look at how stress can undermine our health, if experienced over a period of time.

Exercise 1

AIM: for participants to become aware of how they respond *physically* when they are tense, anxious or stressed.

TIME: 8 minutes for discussion in small groups, 10 minutes for feedback in large group.

METHOD: In small groups of 3 or 4 discuss :

"How do *you* feel physically when you are tense?" (Refer back to the stress diary)

Discussion can be prompted by the following example : -

You've had a very busy day at work, with no time for tea or lunch break and when you arrive home, your partner and children are demanding tea and help with homework etc.

(The exercise can also be done by giving each group a cartoon body outline on flip-chart paper, and coloured felt pens, and asking them to represent their physical symptoms either graphically or by writing on appropriate parts of the figure.)

Take feedback from each group, noting points on a flip chart.

Checklist:

- backache
- headache
- tense shoulders
- neck ache
- aches and pains in joints
- indigestion
- nausea
- loss of appetite
- heart beating fast
- palpitations
- heart-burn
- breathing speeds up
- hyperventilation
- wanting to go to the toilet
- mouth goes dry
- itching
- rash
- skin problems
- blotchy skin
- sweaty palms
- fatigue
- dry throat

Leader's presentation

All these symptoms have their origins in a perfectly normal and healthy reaction to something we see as a danger. They are called Generalised Anxiety Symptoms, and they are part of the FIGHT/FLIGHT response which occurs automatically when we perceive a threat to our well-being. The body goes on to 'Red Alert', 'All Systems Go', and if we are facing a physical danger, the extra energy released enables us to run, jump or climb with more strength and speed than we ever imagined we possessed. The fight/flight response is controlled by the 'sympathetic' branch of the autonomic, or involuntary nervous system (the part which regulates all the body functions not usually under our conscious control, like blood pressure, heart rate etc.). This means we have no control over the *initiation* of the reaction– it is reflexive and almost instantaneous, which makes it very valuable as a primitive life-saving response.

We can easily see that such a reponse would have been a life-saver for our ancestors if the wild boar they had earmarked for supper turned too fierce to handle. In our own experience, we can think of situations in which instant physical action is needed to avert disaster; for example, as we slam on the brakes to avoid hitting a child who has run out in front of the car. In situations like this, as soon as the danger is over, the fight/flight reaction subsides, and the body returns to normal, even though we may feel 'shaken' for a while afterwards.

Problems occur when the fight/flight reaction is triggered by events and situations in which neither fighting nor running away is an appropriate response. When we perceive a situation as threatening to our status, livelihood, affections or health, the same response occurs. Examples of situations in which we might experience the reaction are: break-up of a relationship, threatened unemployment, diagnosis of serious illness, constant pressure at work, or conflict with family or colleagues. The same response can be triggered by something as mundane as the phone ringing, the alarm clock going off or having to sit in a traffic jam while the minutes tick away to the time of an important appointment.

Exercise 2

AIM: for participants to identify their personal triggers of the 'fight/flight' response.

TIME : 3 minutes

METHOD: group brainstorm - what makes you feel tense, edgy and vulnerable? Leader writes up on flip-chart.

Leader's presentation

Everyone will be able to identify situations which make them feel threatened. The threat may be real or imagined, but the perception of 'danger' will trigger the 'fight/flight' response. Unfortunately many contemporary problems are not of the kind that can be dealt with simply by physically battling it out, or running away.

What happens to the body in fight/flight

(Flip-chart 4; Handout 2)

Going back to the checklist of General Anxiety Symptoms, we can see how the fight/flight response enables us to cope with perceived danger. Messages are sent to the brain that the body needs a sudden burst of energy to cope with danger. Immediately the body reacts by increasing activity in organs which are essential for energy and movement and slowing down activity in the organs which are not required in the immediate emergency.

Increased activity occurs as follows :-

- Circulation increases to allow more blood and therefore oxygen to the brain, muscles and limbs.
- Heart beats quicker and harder. Blood pressure rises as peripheral blood vessels constrict; blood supply to skin is restricted.
- Coronary arteries dilate to increase blood supply to heart.
- Lungs take in more oxygen and release more carbon dioxide to enable increased tissue respiration during vigorous exercise.
- More sweat is produced to speed up heat loss.
- Skeletal muscles tense in preparation for physical activity– blood supply increases.
- Liver releases extra sugar to provide energy during activity– also releases cholesterol and fatty acids.
- Blood-clotting ability increases to protect against excess blood loss if injury occurs.
- Pupils dilate and eyelids are drawn back, giving expression of alertness and excitement.
- Adrenal glands continue to produce adrenalin, nor-adrenalin and cortisones to prolong the 'fight/flight' response.

Decreased activity occurs as follows:

- Digestion slows down or stops because the stomach and small intestine reduce their activity (who would eat a sandwich while running away from a sabre-toothed tiger !)
- Kidneys, large intestine and bladder slow down as they are not needed.
- Sphincter muscles close to prevent urination and defaecation. (It is noted that when confronted with extreme danger the sphincter muscles can open).
- Immune responses decrease.
- Blood vessels in salivary glands constrict, making mouth go dry.

Exercise 3

AIM: to raise participants' awareness of the effects of continuous tension and anxiety.

TIME: 3 minutes

METHOD: group brainstorm - 'What physical ailments or illnesses would you expect to occur if the fight/flight response was prolonged over a period of weeks, months or years?' Leader writes up on flip-chart, adding items from checklist if these are not mentioned.

Checklist

- High blood pressure
- Increased risk of coronary heart disease
- Habitual overbreathing, faintness and dizziness
- Digestive disorders such as duodenal and stomach ulcers
- Skin problems such as rashes and allergies
- Chest pains
- Dry throat and mouth due to constriction of the blood vessels in the salivary glands
- Aches and pains in muscles
- Headaches, migraines

Leader's presentation

What happens is that the parts of the body which are constantly stimulated in the fight/flight mode are becoming over-used and those which are 'shut down' will stop working effectively or efficiently.

Our individual physical reactions to stress will be influenced by many factors. We may have a 'weak spot' left by an illness, or an inherited predisposition to a particular ailment. Environmental, social and economic conditions, personality traits, and individual lifestyle all play a part in determining how resistant we are to the damaging effects of stress.

How can relaxation help?

Now for the good news! As we've already seen, the 'fight/flight' response occurs whether we want it to or not and whether it's appropriate or not. Relaxation techniques enable us to 'switch off' the fight/flight response by taking conscious control of two parts of the system we do have access to - breathing, and the voluntary muscles of the trunk and limbs (those are the muscles we can control). By consciously slowing down and deepening our breathing, and by releasing tension in the muscles, we can 'switch on' the opposite of the 'fight/flight' response. This is sometimes referred to as the 'REST/DIGEST' response, and happens as a result of parasympathetic stimulation.

In the 'rest/digest' response, the following changes occur:

(Flip-chart 5; Handout 2):
- Breathing becomes deeper and slower.
- Heartbeat slows down and lessens in force - blood pressure is lowered.
- Coronary arteries constrict, reducing the flow of blood to the heart.
- Activity in stomach and small intestine speeds up, allowing food to be properly digested and absorbed.
- Urethral and anal sphincter muscles relax, allowing urination and defaecation to occur.
- Tension in muscles is reduced, and flow of blood to skeletal muscles slows down.

By learning to counteract muscle tension and taking control of our breathing, the 'rest/digest' response can be activated and the body voluntarily 'relaxed' and rested.

Summary

1. When our body is showing signs of stress and tension, we must see them as early warning signs and take an opportunity to rest and recuperate, even if only for a short time.

2. The fight/flight response is an essential and healthy reaction to danger but if a high level of arousal continues over a prolonged period, health problems may result.

3. When danger is perceived, the brain automatically sends messages to the body to prepare for action. However, by taking conscious control of our limbs, muscles and breathing organs, we can send a message to the brain that we want to rest and restore energy, and this can be an effective way of controlling the feelings and physical reactions associated with stress.

Part 2

PERCEPTIONS OF STRESS

Introduction

This session is based on material from Dr. Audrey Livingston Booth's book, 'Stressmanship', (Severn House 1985, Chapter 2: 'Getting to grips with stress'.)

The fight/flight response is the body's primary reaction to stress. However, there are other secondary hormonal changes which take place when we are under stress. Unlike fight or flight, which is a reflex all-or-nothing reaction, the secondary response varies with our emotional state.

As we have seen in Section 3, the level of stress experienced is determined by the individual's perception of a situation. The nature of that perception determines the type and quantity of chemicals (hormones) released by the brain. The hormone cocktail will vary according to the nature, duration and severity of the stressful situation. For example, increasing anger leads to a corresponding rise in the production of the hormone Nor Adrenalin.

Adrenalin is perhaps the best known of these hormones. There are others such as Dopamine, Met Encaphalon, Beta Endorphin and Cortisol, and the amounts and combinations of these released into the system vary according to the individual's perception of the situation.

Leader's presentation

Dr. Audrey Livingston Booth describes the different patterns of reaction in her book *Stressmanship*. She characterises them by the following expressions :

"I want to ......"
"I have to (I'm being forced to) ......"
"I can't escape from ......"

(Flip-chart 6)

I want to....

A person in this state has high motivation to achieve and succeed over and above the normal level. There may be rewards for extra effort, such as higher status, greater recognition, financial remuneration or promotion.

NUMBER 7 LOOKS SET TO WIN

In this situation the cognitive (thinking) part of the brain activates the hormones Adrenalin, Nor Adrenalin, Dopamine and possibly Met Encephalon and Beta Endorphin. These speed up activity and increase energy levels, fuelling further effort which in turn leads to greater satisfaction.

While everything is going well this spiral will continue. Signs of this stage are that all activities speed up – walking, talking, thinking, eating, drinking. People in this state feel 'driven', and indeed they are being driven on to achieve more and more by their 'switched on' activating system. They feel full of energy and confidence in their ability to achieve anything.

However, problems may arise if the body's basic needs are neglected. A person in this state may not feel hungry (remember, the stomach reduces activity when under stress) and will not take time to eat properly although the body still needs food to provide energy for the extra demands being made of it. Regular eating and relaxation are vital elements to include at this stage. If this state continues week after week, the harmful effects of prolonged stress will begin to be felt and energy levels will decrease (see Human Function Curve, **Flip-chart 2**) with a resulting fall-off in performance. This state of arousal is fine in the short term, and indeed necessary from time to time when extra energy is needed and deadlines have to be met, but the body should be given a chance to return to normal once the extra demands have been met.

short-term solution to the problem. In this state, a different part of the brain is alerted, the limbic (emotional) system. Because Adrenalin is only a short-term answer to the increased demands on the body, it is not enough by itself to cope with longer term energy requirements. It needs to be bolstered by the action of the more powerful Cortico-Steroids or Cortisols which come from the adrenal cortex. These steroids break down the fat from the body's fatty stores to form usable energy. They also act on the body's stored sugars, changing them to glucose which can be used by the body tissues. This provides extra energy. Every hormonal change is geared to providing increased energy, so that the body will be able to cope with the extra demands being made of it.

A potentially damaging consequence of this is the accumulation of fats and sugars circulating in the bloodstream. If no action is taken to use up these products, there may be a build up of fatty deposits on the artery walls which can lead to heart and circulatory problems.

The risks of this kind of damage can be reduced by a combination of regular physical exercise which 'burns off' the excess fats and sugars, and relaxation exercises, which help prevent the build-up of waste products in the first place by reducing feelings of anxiety.

Symptoms of this stage may include: over-sensitivity, irritation, tiredness and fatigue, poor memory, anxiety, feeling 'driven' and always being aware of the pressure of time.

I have to...

This situation is one in which energy is demanded to cope with stress over a longer period of time and there is no immediate or

I can't escape from ...

In this state, the body is continuously consuming excessive amounts of energy in order to deal with apparently inescapable pressures. Energy stores are being depleted at a greater rate than that at which they are being restored by rest and sleep.

The fats, sugars and hormones continue to circulate in the bloodstream, clogging up the system and causing persistent fatigue and anxiety. By this stage, a person may well have been to see his or her G.P., complaining of feeling sluggish and tired, irritable and unable to concentrate. All aspects of health are likely to be affected: physical, intellectual and emotional.

Symptoms are likely to include some of the following: **(flip-chart 7)**

PHYSICAL
> Palpitations and chest pains.
> Recurrent headaches
> Heartburn, stomach cramps
> Stomach full of gas

INTELLECTUAL
> Loss of memory and concentration
> Feeling woolly headed
> Inability to make decisions
> Insomnia
> Sleep disturbance

EMOTIONAL
> Frequent feelings of anger and irritation
> Feeling dull and low
> Inability to love and care, feeling tearful

Exercise 1 Case Study 2, 'Three faces of stress'.

AIM: To illustrate the three phases of the stress response as described above; to help participants see the value of integrating 'stress proofing' measures into their lifestyle.

TIME: 25 minutes including feedback

METHOD: Case study in small groups.

Divide participants into groups of 4. Give everyone a copy of Case Study 2, and ask the groups to identify the causes of stress for each of the three characters. Ask them also to identify any 'safety valves' which might help them cope with their stress. Each group should choose someone to report their discussion to the whole group.

Case Study 2

Here are three brief case studies of people who work long hours. Discuss each situation in turn, identifying the stressors for Brenda, Julia and Sandra and the 'safety valves' which may help them cope with their stress. A safety valve is defined as 'an element within their lifestyle which helps prevent or defuse the build-up of stress'.

Brenda is working very hard for her A levels. Like a number of her friends she wants to go to university. She has been offered two provisional places, based on her past performance. Her friends and family believe she can achieve the necessary grades, although they are avoiding putting too much pressure on her.

Brenda's alarm goes off at 5.45 am. There are only three weeks before her first exam and she has breakfast and studies for two hours before cycling to school. After coming home from school she discusses her day with her parents, eats dinner and then works until 9.30 pm. She is very tired when she goes to bed, but enjoys reading novels before going to sleep. She looks forward to the weekend when she indulges in her hobby, horseriding. Her studying is going well but she will be glad when the exams are over.

Julia is a secretary to a Sales Director. She works for a boss who is very unreasonable. She feels she cannot make any decisions on her own about her work as he is inconsistent and changes his mind every day about the degree of responsibility he is willing to allow her. He smokes continuously, which she finds very irritating. When he is annoyed by colleagues' inefficiency or impatient customers, he gets into a rage and slams the adjoining door between their offices. Julia needs a job to pay her rent and living expenses, but no other local company can match her current salary. In her own time Julia is keen on keeping fit. She walks to and from work, twenty five minutes each way. She plays badminton twice a week, swims at the weekend and does relaxation exercises four times a week on average.

Sandra is a full-time housewife and mother. She has four children, aged seven, five, three, and four months. She is very tired as the baby is not sleeping and the 3-year-old is feeling displaced by the baby and is rebelling by being very irritable. Sandra loves her husband and appreciates that he has a very long day at work and needs 'peace and quiet' at home. She encourages the children to make life easier for their Dad, but they are fed up because he doesn't play games with them like other Dads. Sandra is constantly trying to keep the peace.

Sandra gets up at six in the morning, irons the children's clothes, makes packed lunches and breakfast and gets them all dressed for a five-minute walk to school. She comes home, does the housework, works in the garden where she is growing her own produce (to save money) and spends quite a lot of time making the children's clothes as it is more economical.

She gets headaches regularly and finds it difficult to concentrate. Her husband is a very organised person, and can't imagine what Sandra does during the day to make her so exhausted!

Leader's presentation

Have flip-chart prepared with the three names. Take feedback from each group in turn, identifying the stressors, the 'safety valves' and noting any practical suggestions. (Use the Checklist of Safety Valves as a guide.)

In terms of the three phases of stress identified at the beginning of this session, the situations of the three characters can be described as follows:

Brenda - 'I want to . . .'
Julia - 'I have to . . .'
Sandra - 'I can't escape from . . .'

Brenda

There's nothing much wrong with Brenda's situation - it's healthy! She is coping well as she values herself, is valued by her parents, and held in esteem by her peers. Physical exercise, eating regularly, keeping up hobbies, and optimism about the ultimate outcome all make for successful coping. Brenda's stress is also time-limited, and this makes coping very much easier.

Julia

The groups will have lots of recommendations for Julia! Her working environment is not healthy, she has no control over her work, and is not allowed to make any decisions. Her boss's smoking is a potential health hazard as well as an irritant. She probably dreads going to work on Monday mornings, and she needs to weigh up whether the salary is worth the hassle!

On the positive side, her commitment to regular physical exercise and relaxation will help to 'stress-proof' her at least in the medium-term, as they will help eliminate the build-up of dangerous products in the bloodstream. This will delay any serious damage, but she should consider making changes soon if at all possible.

Sandra

Sandra's life of endless drudgery is not to be envied. She has a tiring and demanding routine, and does not seem to value herself, or to be valued by her husband. She has to work hard to save money and keep the family together. Many groups will come up with radical solutions for Sandra - eg. leave them all to get on with it! The likely consequences of such a course must be taken into account; leaving may cause even more stress, and she may not want to escape the situation, but rather learn how to cope better with it.

Checklist of Safety Valves

BRENDA
- Self-esteem
- High motivation
- Peer/parental support
- Held in high esteem by colleagues
- Optimism about outcome - believes she can achieve the grades
- Eats regular meals
- Exercise - cycles
- Keeps up hobbies

The end is in sight!

JULIA
- Likes to keep fit
- Regular walk to work
- Badminton
- Swims
- Relaxation

SANDRA
- Nil

SUMMARY

1. In the stress response the hormonal changes which take place are determined by the individual's perception of a situation.

2. The important factors to take into account when analysing a stressful situation are:
  i)   duration
  ii)   individual's degree of control
  iii) individual's perception of ability to cope with situation.

3. Steps which can be taken to alleviate the harmful effects of stress include:
  i)   relaxation exercises
  ii)   physical exercise - walking, sport, games etc.
  iii) positive self-talk
  iv)   ensuring adequate rest
  v)   healthy diet and regular meals
  vi)   pampering yourself - make a 'treat' list of 10 things you enjoy, and reward yourself with one when you need a lift, or when you've done something which you found difficult

The main points to bring out in discussion are that it is important to be aware of the different stages of stress, in order to use appropriate stress reduction techniques before situations get out of hand and require radical and perhaps painful solutions.

Part 3

BREATHING

Introduction

There are few certainties in life but one is that we all breathe within seconds of being born and when we stop breathing we die.

Breathing is an unconscious activity that we tend to take for granted. We are aware that for special purposes such as swimming and singing, we can control our breathing, but the rest of the time we forget about it and this can lead to the development of bad breathing habits, which in turn can affect the way we feel, both physically and mentally.

Exercise 1

AIM: to identify a breathing pattern whilst undertaking brisk physical exercise.

TIME: 2 minutes

METHOD: In pairs, facing each other, participants run on the spot for one minute. After one minute, instruct both partners to sit down and observe each other's body movements as they breathe – is the most noticeable movement in the chest or abdomen?

FEEDBACK: It is likely that immediately upon sitting down the movement will be in the upper chest region. However, as time passes it will move downwards to the abdomen area.

Leader's presentation

Why do we breathe shallowly whilst exercising?

We begin by looking at how we breathe. There are two phases in the respiratory process: inhalation and exhalation. **(Flip-chart 8)**

Inhalation or breathing in

There are two basic movements which occur simultaneously.

The muscles of the diaphragm contract and cause it to flatten from its domed position. This pushes the organs beneath the diaphragm outwards.

The lower ribs are raised upwards and outwards by contraction of the intercostal muscles which run from rib to rib.

Both these movements increase the volume of the thorax and lungs and the increase in volume raises the capacity of the lungs so that atmospheric pressure forces air into them through the nose and trachea.

Exhalation or breathing out

Again the following movements occur simultaneously:

The muscles of the ribs and diaphragm relax.

The ribs move down under their own weight.

The organs below the diaphragm move back to their original position, and the diaphragm resumes its domed shape.

The lungs also move back to their original position by virtue of their own elasticity.

Breathing in is the active phase and breathing out is the passive or relaxing phase of the breathing process, which is why the emphasis is always placed on the out-breath in relaxation exercises.

All these movements are controlled by the respiratory centre of the brain which is sensitive to the carbon dioxide level in the blood. If the brain senses a drop in carbon dioxide in the blood, nerve impulses are sent to the diaphragm, ribs and muscles to increase the rate of breathing.

During vigorous exercise, such as running, we need to expel carbon dioxide more quickly in order to get more oxygen into the body as

there is an increased need for tissue respiration. We therefore breathe more shallowly and quickly as the oxygen does not have time to go to the base of the lungs.

Once exercise has ceased our bodies should return to their normal breathing pattern - abdomen swelling as we breathe in and decreasing in volume as we breathe out, with a pause after each out-breath. The breathing rate varies between individuals but will normally be around 12 - 14 breaths per minute.

Exercise 2

AIM: To show that breathing becomes shallow when we are under stress, and that we return to the normal abdominal breathing pattern when relaxed; to demonstrate the power of mental images in determining physical feelings.

TIME: 3 minutes

METHOD: leader instructs participants:

Place one hand high on your chest and the other on your abdomen, around the area of the navel. Sit forward on your chair, tensing your body. Think of a situation that frightens you, something very unpleasant. Close your eyes and imagine yourself in that situation now. (Allow 30 seconds for this visualization). Note what happens to your breathing. Then relax, sit back in the chair, keeping your hands on chest and abdomen. Now imagine something very pleasant and peaceful. For the next minute visualize yourself in that situation. Again, note how you are breathing.

NB. Before beginning this exercise, tell participants that the visualization of the unpleasant situation will only last for 30 seconds. If they become very anxious, it's fine for them to stop before you tell them to! It's also worth noting that if they try out this exercise with client groups, the visualization of the anxiety-inducing situation should be kept short - perhaps as short as 10 seconds for very anxious people, as half a minute could seem like a very long time!

FEEDBACK: Most participants will have noted the following pattern:

Threatening situation: shallow rapid breathing from the chest region.

Pleasant situation: slower, deeper breathing from the abdomen.

NB. Some people may have such deeply-entrenched poor breathing habits that even when 'relaxed' they continue to breathe from the thorax and upper chest. This may be partly explained by the wearing of tight clothing which restricts the abdomen, and by cultural norms of 'good' posture which involve keeping the stomach pulled in. (This applies particularly to women).

Another misconception which needs to be cleared up at this point is that a 'deep breath' is an exaggerated and unnatural movement which involves pulling in the abdomen, and raising the rib-cage and shoulders. The rigid, military posture which results is the opposite of relaxed! Deep breathing in this context means abdominal breathing, which allows air into the base of the lungs with minimum effort.

Leader's presentation

When we see situations as threatening or frightening the sympathetic nervous system takes over and we automatically go into the fight/flight mode as if getting ready to run. If running or direct physical action is not called for, we still breathe shallowly and quickly, inhaling too much oxygen and releasing too much carbon dioxide. We are overbreathing or 'hyper-ventilating'.

Hyperventilation can be defined as:

"Breathing in excess of bodily requirements" or "habitual overbreathing".

Hyperventilation is an exaggeration of the body's normal reaction to stress. Many people experience some of its effects, such as racing heart, weak knees and 'butterflies' in the stomach, perhaps before an examination, first date with a new girlfriend or giving a speech. These symptoms usually disappear once the stressful situation is over.

However, some people develop the habit of hyperventilating all the time. Their breathing becomes erratic and irregular with wide variations in the rate and rhythm of breathing.

Signs to look for in distorted breathing patterns:

- Irregular breathing with little movement of the abdomen or diaphragm
- Breathing from the thorax while at rest
- Frequent sighs
- Gulping for air yet continually feeling short of breath
- Frequent belching and saliva swallowing
- A respiratory rate of at least 15 breaths per minute - often over 20. During severe attacks this can reach 30 or more.

These erratic breathing patterns can often be observed in TV interviews and other similar 'high pressure' situations.

Hyperventilators get into a circle of increased anxiety, as their shallow irregular breathing sends messages to the brain that the body is preparing to run away from a threatening situation. The brain therefore continues to send messages to other parts of the body to remain in the fight/flight mode. **(Flip-chart 9)**

If a person hyperventilates continually, an alarming range of physical symptoms may begin to occur.

Listed below are the common symptoms of chronic and acute hyperventilation, as described by Rosemary Cluff of Papworth Hospital, Cambridge. *(Journal of the Royal Society of Medicine,* Vol.77, October 1984:856) (Write up on flip chart, or give out Handout 3)

Cardiac
• Palpitations, 'angina'.

Neurological
• Dizziness, faintness, visual disturbance, migrainous headache, numbness, 'pins and needles' in face and limbs.

Respiratory
• Shortness of breath, 'asthma', chest pain, excessive sighing.

Gastro-intestinal
• Heartburn, burping, air swallowing.

Muscular
• Cramps, fibrositic pains, tremors.

Psychic
• Tension, anxiety, 'unreal' feelings, depersonalisation, hallucination, fear of insanity, panic attacks, phobic states.

General
• Weakness, exhaustion, lack of concentration, sleep disturbance, nightmares, emotional sweating (armpits and palms).

Because of the strangeness and diversity of these symptoms, the sufferer may begin to worry that he or she is developing a life-threatening disease, and the hyperventilation and anxiety will increase. It has been estimated that between 6% and 10% of patients referred to medical specialists for symptoms such as heart problems are in fact suffering from hyperventilation.

Research has also shown that rather than hyperventilation being one manifestation of an anxiety state, chronic anxiety has actually been *caused* by habitual hyperventilation. (Dr L. C. Lum, *Journal of the Royal Society of Medicine,* Vol. 74, January 1981:1,4) Re-learning proper breathing patterns is therefore one of the most important steps we can take in learning to manage anxiety and tension.

The following exercises show how we can take control and use our breathing to reduce panic and anxiety.

NB. When demonstrating breathing exercises, leaders should be aware that there is a small risk of hyperventilation occurring. To avoid this, tell participants that if they feel anxious at any point in the exercises, they should stop immediately and allow their breathing to return to normal. It is a good idea to divide the group in two, and take the smaller groups through the exercises alternately, so that no-one runs the risk of overbreathing.

Exercise 3

(The breathing exercises which follow are reproduced in Handout 4)

AIM: to demonstrate the movements involved in breathing and to show that, with concentration and practice, we can control our breathing pattern.

TIME: 2 minutes

METHOD: The finger-tip touch (to be done lying down).

Let your hands lie on your abdomen, finger tips just touching.

Breathe gently twice, so that the fingers part slightly.

Pause.

Move hands to the outside of the lower ribs and repeat.

Pause.

Move your hands to the very top of your chest.

Breathe gently twice causing your hands to lift.

Pause.

Move hands back to the lower ribs and repeat.

Pause.

Move your hands back to your abdomen and repeat.

Pause.

Rest.

NB. The only purpose of this exercise is to increase body awareness. It has *no value* as a breathing exercise, and should only be practised until people become familiar with the feelings of breathing at different levels. (Taken from *Relaxation for Living* pamphlet, 'Better Breathing'.)

Exercise 4

AIM: to teach a calming breathing pattern for use in every-day situations such as interviews, meetings, hectic periods at work, demanding times at home etc. (Nobody need know you are feeling anxious!)

TIME: 2 minutes

Let the chair support your back.

Drop your shoulders, feel them widen from the spine outwards to your arms.

Allow your lungs and chest to expand fully.

Now take 5 slow deep breaths, starting with an exhaled breath. Do not hold your breath. As you breathe in, your abdomen swells out slightly and as you breathe out, it subsides again.

Continue by breathing in to a count of 1-2-3 and out to a count of 1-2-3-4. (The count can be varied to suit the individual. The important point to note is that the out-breath should be one count longer than the in-breath.)

Calming breathing can be used in any situation in which you feel tension mounting. By breathing in this way, you send messages to the brain that you are coping easily and calmly.

Exercise 5

AIM: to teach a breathing technique to reduce panic.

TIME: 2 minutes

As tension or panic are building up say to yourself "STOP", exhale a deep breath and inhale gently. Hold the breath for a moment, then breathe out and imagine letting go of all the tension.

This sends a message to the brain, through the respiratory organs, that you are in control of the situation, and that tension is inappropriate.

N.B. This exercise should not be done more than *once* as holding the breath distorts the natural breathing rhythm and may lead to hyperventilation.

Exercise 6

AIM: to teach a technique for releasing tension which has built up over a period of time, to be used eg. at lunch-time or before going home after work.

TIME: 2 minutes

Choose a comfortable chair for maximum support.

Breathe 6 slow, comfortable breaths.

With each outgoing breath, imagine yourself deflating slightly, like a balloon.

When you start to feel less anxious, begin to flop forward at the head and neck.

Gradually let your shoulders and arms fall further and further forward until you are hanging limp from the waist, like a rag doll.

Hang there for a minute or so, then come up very slowly and gently, letting your hands lie limp on your lap, like a rag doll.

Sit like this for as long as you like, although 4 minutes is sufficient to reduce your pulse-rate and blood pressure.

When you are ready, take a deep breath before getting up. (Adapted from *Stressmanship,* Livingston Booth:114)

Summary

1. The rate and depth of breathing are highly sensitive to physical and emotional stimuli such as fear, excitement and exercise.

2. The normal breathing pattern is that the abdomen swells slightly as we inhale and flattens as we exhale.

3. Rapid shallow breathing is a natural response to a perceived threat but once the threat is removed, we should return to the normal breathing pattern.

4. Persistent hyperventilation can lead to a vicious circle in which physical symptoms *caused* by overbreathing give rise to further anxiety about the sufferer's state of health.

SECTION 5

RELAXATION TECHNIQUES

Part 1.1	Background	40
Part 1.2	Loosening exercises	43
Part 2.1	Progressive relaxation	45
Part 2.2	Mitchell method of physiological relaxation	47
Part 2.3	Guided and unguided visualization	50
Part 2.4	Simple massage	51
Part 2.5	Biofeedback	54

Part 1.1

BACKGROUND

Introduction

There are many relaxation techniques in use today, most of them variants on one or two basic methods. Two main approaches can be identified.

The first treats relaxation as a physical skill which can be learned in the same way as any other skill. Progressive muscular relaxation and the Mitchell method fall into this category. The second type of approach lays more emphasis on the role of the mind's imaginative faculties in achieving a state of relaxation. Examples of this are the 'self-suggestions' made in autogenic relaxation, the focusing on a chosen object of contemplation, as in meditation, and the generation of a series of pleasant and calming images used in visualization techniques.

Some methods draw on both approaches, using physical exercises to initiate the relaxation response, and then using the imaginative powers of the mind to take the process a stage further. Whichever method is used, the basic principle is the same: that mental and physical tension go together, and that by consciously relaxing the body, a feeling of calm and well-being can be induced.

Individuals will respond differently to the various methods, and during the workshop, participants should have the opportunity to experience at least three sessions of relaxation, introducing them to different methods. Participants are also encouraged to lead a full relaxation session, with the help of the texts provided in this section.

Leader's presentation

As we saw in the session on the fight/flight response, relaxation techniques offer a way of switching off the reflex reaction to danger and threat, and switching on the relaxation response. We talked about the kind of health problems which might be experienced by someone who was constantly in a state of over- arousal. Now let's look at the other side of the coin, and see what the benefits of mastering relaxation might be.

(Flip-chart 10)

The benefits of relaxation

- Simple and effective way of reducing the stress response

- Increases self-awareness of effects of stress on body and mind

- Reduces fatigue by increasing awareness of inappropriate muscle tension, energy-wasting nervous tics, and enabling corrective action to be taken

- Increases confidence in ability to deal with feelings of anxiety, stress and panic, by offering method of controlling physical and emotional reactions. Having the appropriate skills to use in difficult situations makes people less likely to feel overwhelmed and unable to cope. Relaxation techniques can be used unobtrusively in most situations.

- Can improve personal relationships. Prolonged stress can lead to emotional strain, signs of which may be irritability, tearfulness and hyper-sensitivity to criticism, all of which can put a strain on relationships. Relaxation is an effective way of dealing with this potentially damaging emotional strain.

- Helps promote sleep. People with sleeping problems (insomnia, early waking etc.) often find that relaxation helps them to get to sleep more quickly in the first place, or to get back to sleep once they have woken up.

- Provides an alternative to potentially harmful medication and self-medication. People often use drugs (including alcohol and tobacco) to help them cope with the effects of stress. These are potentially harmful if abused. The same applies to medically-prescribed tranquillisers and sleeping pills, which can be invaluable for short-term use in times of crisis, but which may lead to addiction and dependency if used over long periods. Relaxation can induce similar feelings of calm and well-being, while allowing people to remain in control of their own bodies, and to avoid the harmful physical and psychological effects of reliance on drugs.

Guidelines for leading a relaxation session

(Handout 5)

Before starting the session:

- Give people time to make themselves comfortable, put on an extra layer for warmth, go to the loo if necessary etc.

- Describe the exercise you are about to do - make sure people have grasped the principle behind the exercise, and that they know what to expect, and how long it will take.

- Give people permission to choose their own position in which to relax, lying or sitting. If lying, suggest they might use a small cushion to support the lower spine, if this makes them more comfortable. People often find it more comfortable to lie with raised knees and feet drawn back towards the body, rather than completely flat out on the floor.

- Make sure that everyone has enough space, and that people are not touching.

- Check that people are lying or sitting straight before beginning. If sitting, get them to check that their shoulders are level, with the head upright. If lying, ask them to raise their heads slightly to make sure that the head is in line with an imaginary line drawn down the middle of the body.

- Advise everyone to loosen tight clothing at the neck and waist, and suggest that people wearing glasses take them off.

- Timing and speed of delivery - inexperienced leaders often rush the instructions out of nervousness and fear of silence. A useful guide is to do some of the exercises yourself as you give the instructions.

- Tone of voice - it's very common for people new to leading relaxation sessions to feel that they don't have the 'right' tone of voice. As long as instructions are given gently, yet firmly and clearly, practically anyone can successfully lead a relaxation session. Clients should *not* be encouraged to become dependent on the leader's voice; there's nothing magical about it, and they're the ones actually doing the relaxing!

- Advise people to adopt a passive attitude of just 'letting go' and allowing relaxation to happen, rather than trying too hard and becoming annoyed with themselves when they feel that it's not working immediately.

During the exercise

- **Laughing/giggling.** If this occurs, ignore it. It's usually a sign of embarrassment or nervousness, and will die down as you continue with the exercise.

- **Sleep.** It quite often happens that people drop off during a session. The problem here is that they usually see this as a sign of success, whereas in fact you have to point out to them that by falling asleep, they're missing out on most of the session! Falling asleep is very common among tense people who are poor sleepers at night, and great consumers of energy during the day. When they do finally let go, they fall asleep out of sheer exhaustion. To wake people, ask them by name to wake up, and if that doesn't work, gently touch them on the arm, having first told them that you will do so.

- **Feedback.** It is essential to allow time for feedback after every session.

- **Feelings of anxiety and panic.** People sometimes experience strange feelings when their bodies start to relax. They may feel 'heavy' or 'floaty', have pins and needles or tingling sensations in arms or legs, or feel disorientated. In people who habitually keep themselves tightly under control, these signs of 'letting go' may be anxiety- inducing. They should be reassured that such symptoms show that they are beginning to relax.

- **Dislike of a particular relaxation method.** It is not unusual in a group for opinion to be strongly divided as to the usefulness of a particular technique. For example, a very tense person may not respond to the tense/release method because he or she is unable to release the tension created during the exercises. Some participants may find visualization difficult, and prefer a more 'practical' physical method. Always point out that the choice of technique is a very personal matter, while emphasising that no method will be beneficial unless it is practised regularly.

- **Loss of concentration or 'wandering thoughts'.** Many people find it comparatively easy to relax the body, but have problems with 'racing' thoughts or wandering attention. Reassure them that concentration becomes easier with practice, and suggest that whenever disturbing thoughts intrude, or they find themselves 'miles away', they acknowledge the fact without berating themselves for the lapse, and bring their attention gently back to observing the natural rhythm of their breathing. Repeating a word like 'calm' on each in- and out- breath; or simply counting '1' on the in-breath and '2' on the out-breath can help concentration.

- **Crying.** This occasionally happens when someone has been under a lot of pressure, and has suddenly let go under the influence of relaxation. Reassure the person that this is a perfectly natural and healthy reaction, and a sign that they have begun to release pent-up feelings which are better out in the open than bottled up inside. The person concerned and the rest of the group will take their cue from you. If you accept crying as a natural part of 'letting go', and explain it as a healthy release of tension, nobody will be embarrassed.

NB. Most people can benefit from learning basic relaxation skills. However, specialist training is required if relaxation is to be offered to people suffering from severe depression, or from psychotic illness. It's also worth noting that certain physical conditions may be affected by relaxation, and if medication is involved (eg. as in diabetes, hypertension, heart disease, asthma, epilepsy), a doctor should be consulted before relaxation techniques are used.

Part 1.2

LOOSENING EXERCISES

Simple 'loosening' or warming up exercises have several uses and can be introduced at various stages in a relaxation training workshop.

Their main purpose is to begin the process of getting rid of muscular tension, and to raise awareness of the different parts of the body in which tension can be harboured. Exercise also helps relaxation, as warmed-up muscles are easier to relax.

Loosening exercises can be used:

- at the beginning of a course, day or session, as an ice-breaker and general warm-up
- before a relaxation session, to help muscles warm up and make relaxation easier to achieve
- after a session in which participants have been sedentary, to raise energy levels by introducing some physical activity.

NB. Always make it clear at the beginning of a session that participants must work within their own limitations. Stress that the exercises are not competitive in any way, and that participants have permission not to do an exercise if they know it is likely to cause them pain! Always tell them to stop an exercise the moment it causes any discomfort.

All the following exercises are to be done standing, feet slightly apart, although some of them can be done equally well in a sitting position. These are marked *. If possible, they should be done without shoes, as this improves foot and ankle mobility, and balance. Make sure that there is enough space between group members to allow everyone freedom of movement.

Hands and Arms

Swinging

(Check that there is enough space behind you before this one!)

Stretch out both arms in front of you at shoulder height. Let your arms and hands go limp and swing down by your sides. Let your arms swing to a standstill, then raise again to shoulder height and repeat several times. Each time, imagine your arms and hands becoming heavier and more limp.

Finally, raise arms slightly higher than your shoulders, and give them one last big swing.

Shaking

Shake your left hand. Imagine you are shaking out all the tension in your hand. Let the shaking spread all the way up your arm - feel the muscles begin to soften as you shake out all the tension.

Rest, then repeat with the right hand and arm.*

Shoulders

The heavy shopping bag exercise

Imagine you are carrying a heavy shopping bag in each hand. Really feel the weight pulling your shoulders down towards the floor. Then drop the bags - feel the sudden release of tension in your shoulders. Repeat - notice that your shoulders move downwards, leaving your neck feeling longer and less restricted.

Shoulder rolling

Roll your right shoulder backwards six times. Repeat with the left shoulder. Roll your right shoulder forwards six times. Repeat with the left shoulder. Roll both shoulders forwards together six times. Repeat, rolling them backwards.*

Neck

Slowly let your head drop forwards until your chin touches your chest. Feel the tension in the back of the neck. Slowly raise your head until it is back in the upright position. (Repeat three times)*

Keeping your shoulders completely level and still, lower your head gently to the right, as if you are trying to touch your shoulder with your ear. Feel the tension along the left hand side of the neck. Lift your head slowly back into the upright position. Repeat on left hand side. (Repeat three times).*

Keeping your head level, gently turn it from side to side, trying to see over your shoulder as far as you can on either side. (Repeat three times)*

Feet and Legs

Shaking

(To help with balance, participants may form a circle to support each other, or use the backs of chairs).

Lift your left foot and shake it. Shake it hard - imagine shaking out all the tension. Let the shaking spread up through your ankles ... calves ... thighs. Feel the muscles getting softer and softer as they begin to warm up and relax. Repeat with the right foot.

Soft-ball foot massage

Distribute soft balls - the ideal size is slightly larger than a tennis ball. Everyone puts his or her ball on the floor, and rolls it around gently with the foot. Imagine that the ball is covered with sticky black ink. The idea is to completely cover your foot in this ink - toes, sole of foot, instep, heel, sides and top of foot. Begin with the right foot - gently move the ball around with the foot, until all the surfaces of the foot have come into contact with the imaginary ink. (Half a minute). Now pause. Put your right foot on the floor again, and see if you can feel any difference between the two feet. Repeat with the left foot.*

Whole Body Warm Up

Slapping

This tones up the muscles as well as helping them to relax. First give your hands a good shake to relax them. Then, beginning with your calves, slap the muscles all over your body. Move up your legs to the thighs, buttocks, forearms, upper arms, and then move all the way down again.

Part 2.1

PROGRESSIVE RELAXATION

Introduction

Progressive relaxation is a technique developed by an American professor of physiology, Dr. Edmund Jacobson. He identified the relationship between inappropriate muscular tension and anxiety and discovered that exercises based on relaxing muscles and groups of muscles in sequence will reduce anxiety and initiate a feeling of calm. Progressive relaxation is a neuromuscular skill, just like standing, walking, runnning and throwing a ball. In each of these activities the mind and muscles learn to work together. In progressive relaxation the muscles obey the mind's decision to let go of tension.

As we saw in the session on the fight/flight response, muscles tense up when we are preparing to run from a threatening situation. We also saw that merely thinking about a threatening situation increases muscle tension. It needn't be a serious problem - we may be thinking about a piece of work that needs to be done before next week and which we can't bring ourselves to get down to. It may even be something quite insignificant such as thinking about the appalling mess we have left in the kitchen which we must clear up soon, after we've read another chapter of an engrossing novel. These thoughts are translated into muscular activity and so if we are continually thinking about what needs to be done *next*, our muscles are permanently tense and ready for action.

Before we can learn to let go of inappropriate muscular tension, we must first become aware of it in our own bodies.

Exercise 1

AIM: to identify muscular tension in participants.

TIME: 10 minutes, including discussion

METHOD: Ask all participants to freeze and try to remain still for the next minute. Leader goes round the group one by one identifying any of the following :-
- Ankle bending or tapping
- Coiled legs
- Arms folded
- Worried frown
- Tight, hunched shoulders
- Clenched teeth and jutting jaw
- A gripped thumb
- Clenched fists
- Interlaced hands
- Hair twirling

(It is worth noticing any of these characteristic 'stressed' positions or nervous tics at the beginning of the course when people are feeling apprehensive.)

Some people in the group may not be exhibiting any of these characteristics at this particular moment, but almost everyone will be aware of some personal tics and habits.

It is worth having a 5 minute discussion about nervous habits (hair twirling, nail biting, etc.) The discussion should conclude by highlighting that even as people are sitting listening to your presentation, their muscles may be working very hard, and all to no purpose!

Once people become aware of inappropriate muscular tension, they can begin to do something to correct it. In progressive relaxation, total relaxation is achieved in progressive stages, going over the whole body from toes to head or vice versa, while letting go of tension.

The basic instructions for progressive relaxation are TIGHTEN/TENSE a muscle or muscle-group; HOLD the tension; STUDY the feeling of tension; RELEASE; NOTE the difference between the feeling of tension and the feeling of relaxation.

Exercise 2 (Relaxation Text 1)

AIM: To identify particular areas of the body in which people are prone to hold tension; to help participants become aware of the difference between tense and relaxed muscles.

It is recommended that this exercise is done sitting in a comfortable chair.

TIME: 10 minutes

Exercise 3 (Relaxation Text 2)

TIME: 25 minutes

This exercise systematically goes from toes to head and ends with a simple formula for helping the mind to relax. People often say that they can control their muscular tension but have considerable difficulty in stopping their minds from racing. Simple mind-stilling techniques like breath counting, word-focusing and visualization can be helpful in overcoming this.

Conclusion

Progressive relaxation has been used successfully by many behavioural therapists, psychologists and relaxation teachers. The principles are simple, but some positive results will usually be felt almost immediately. Regular practice - at least 20 minutes daily - is essential in order to become proficient at using the technique and obtain maximum benefit.

It is important to acknowledge that progressive relaxation may not suit everyone. As Jane Madders points out in *Stress and Relaxation* (1980:31-2), anxious people using this method may find it difficult to dissipate the tension they have created, with the result that they feel more tense and anxious at the end of a session than at the beginning! She also differs from Laura Mitchell (see p. 47) in believing that the adoption of the 'readiness for action' posture (hunched shoulders, feet flexed up at the ankle, etc.) under stress is not universal, and that some individuals respond to a perceived threat by stiffening and straightening. Because people are individuals, it is important to recognise that no one method of relaxation is going to suit everyone. Many of the techniques build upon the works of others, and the desired end result may be achieved by many means. It is up to every individual to experiment with different exercises over a period of time, and then to decide which they find the most useful and beneficial.

Part 2.2

MITCHELL METHOD OF PHYSIOLOGICAL RELAXATION

Introduction

Physiological relaxation is a stress-reducing technique devised by Miss Laura Mitchell, a physiotherapist. In her book 'Simple Relaxation' she describes how she developed the foundations of the technique while confined to bed in hospital with severe arthritis.

No conventional relaxation technique - diaphragmatic breathing, visualization, tensing and releasing muscles, self hypnosis - brought any relief of the continuous ache in her neck, body and arms. She eventually realized that the only way to work her way out of the odd position in which she was lying was to systematically do the *opposite movement* in each joint, and so obtain relief. After years of trial and error with patients and students, she produced a set of instructions which apply this principle to the 'unravelling' of the positions which the body automatically adopts when under stress. We were not able to get permission to reprint her instructions in the present publication, as they are already available in the form of a pamphlet. A copy is provided in the folder at the end of the manual.

The Mitchell Method differs in some important respects from the other methods of relaxation included in the course, and should not be mixed up with other techniques.

The main points of difference are:
- unlike the tense/release techniques, which involve consciously *exaggerating* the characteristic 'stress' contractions of the muscles in order to contrast tension with relaxation, the method is based on the principle of learning to contract the *opposite* group of muscles to those habitually tensed, as this automatically causes relaxation to occur.
- the word 'relax' is not used at all. Instead, a set of precise orders is given to carry out specific actions which will result in the body being held in a position of ease.
- the method concentrates on those parts of the body which habitually tense for action under threat.

- since sensation is registered in the joints and through the skin, and not in the muscles themselves, the method focuses on joint position and skin sensation, rather than on 'letting go' of muscular tension.
- the method is not 'seductive', in that there is no suggestion of feelings of heaviness, warmth, calm etc. Instructions are given in a normal, conversational tone of voice, with no dimmed lights or lulling music.

Leader's presentation

As we saw in the section on the fight/flight response, our bodies react spontaneously when we perceive a threat of any kind. Laura Mitchell identified a definite 'stress' posture which is adopted by everyone, adult or child, at times of deep emotion, pain, danger or apprehension.

Exercise 1 (Handout 6)

AIM: to identify the characteristic 'stress' position

TIME: 5 minutes

METHOD: leader demonstrates on co-leader or volunteer, who adopts the positions described in turn, ending up as a living image of tension!

Head - the head comes forward. If cause of stress is grief or pain, the head may be bent right down with chin pulled in. If anger or fear are the causes, the chin juts forward and the whole head moves forward on the neck.

Shoulders - shoulders are raised towards the ears in a 'shrugged' position. Upper arms hug the body either at the sides or in front, while the elbows bend upwards. (The common defensive posture in which the arms are folded across the front of the body is a version of this.)

Hands - fingers and thumbs curl up as if to form a fist, or hands may be clenched together, or tightly clasping some object, eg. a pen, money, or be constantly active, eg. in the nervous rattling of change in trouser pockets.

Legs (sitting) - a person may sit sideways on the edge of the chair, with one leg wound around the other. (Most common in women.) Legs may be crossed, with the upper foot held rigidly upwards at the ankle, or with rapid movement up and down at the ankle, the accent on the upwards movement.

Legs (standing) - legs are crossed and uncrossed continuously, as the person is unable to keep still.

Body - whole body bends forward and is usually held fairly rigid.

Breathing - accent is on the inward breath, which is often taken in at a gasp. The upper chest moves rapidly up and down.

Face - jaw is clamped tightly shut, and teeth may grind together. Lips are tightly closed. The tongue is pressed against the roof of the mouth. The brows corrugate, and in grief or pain the eyes may screw up, or open wide in real or imagined danger.

Exercise 2

AIM: to help participants identify their own characteristic stress positions.

TIME: 10 minutes

METHOD: In the large group, go round the room asking everyone to identify the one position which they know is their most common response to stress.

Leader's presentation

The positions we've just identified are part of a reflex response to fear. The Mitchell Method teaches a pattern of movement which enables us to change the stress positions into positions of ease.

Patterns of movement are established very early in life. When a baby is learning to reach out for the toy or food he wants, his central nervous system is learning how to translate the brain's orders into appropriate muscle activity. When the desired result is achieved, and reinforced by practice and repetition, the action becomes imprinted in the brain, and a pattern of movement is established for grasping toys and food.

A vital part of the learning process involves distinguishing between appropriate and inappropriate patterns of movement. For instance, a child learns (eventually!) that spooning food into her ear does not produce the pleasurable sensation of taste which is obtained by getting it more or less in her mouth. Adults too make inappropriate movements when the messages between the brain and the muscles are incorrect. Next time you snap off the stem of an expensive wine-glass or drop someone's cut-glass bowl while drying up, try explaining that it's the result of an 'inappropriate pattern of movement'!

The stress positions we identified earlier are also often inappropriate, in that our bodies are preparing to fight or run away when we are sitting in a difficult meeting, or stuck in a traffic jam. As we saw in the discussion of the fight/flight respose, action *can* be taken to defuse the feeling of tension, by moving the voluntary muscles and slowing down the rate of breathing. The brain can learn a pattern of movement which changes feelings of tension into feelings of ease. As with any other pattern of movement, repetition and practice are needed before the pattern is imprinted in the brain and can be repeated at will. Physiological relaxation is a particular set of patterns of movement which can be learned, just as we once learned to eat, or to throw and catch a ball.

How does the Mitchell Method work?

(see also the pamphlet at the back of the manual, 'Mitchell Method of Relaxation'.)

Throughout the body, muscle groups work in pairs, so that when any group of muscles is working, its opposite number relaxes. In order to 'relax' the muscles which habitually work overtime when we are under stress, all we have to do is cause the opposite group to work. For example, as the characteristic stressed position of the shoulders is slightly hunched up towards the ears, relaxation can be achieved by ordering the shoulders to be pulled down towards the feet - which automatically relaxes the muscles used in the hunched position. The Mitchell Method gives a series of orders based on this principle of 'reciprocal relaxation'. The orders are given specifically to those parts of the body which habitually contract under stress.

For each part of the body, the sequence of orders is the same:

- To work into the opposite of the stress position (ie. the position of ease).
- To stop doing this.
- To register consciously the new position.

Since sensations are registered in the joints and through the skin, the orders are designed to help the brain record the new positions of ease by focusing attention on joint position and skin sensation. In this way, the new pattern of movement is established, as the brain registers that pleasant sensations can be obtained by initiating certain movements.

The instructions should be given *precisely as written* (no substituting 'relax' for 'stop', for example), and given in a normal conversa-tional tone of voice. There should be no soft, lulling music or any suggestion of hypnotism, which makes this method a particularly useful one for people to practise on their own, as once the orders have been memorized, the exercises can be used anywhere. There's no need to retire to a darkened room for half an hour in order obtain the benefits of relaxation by this method - it can be used while in the car, sitting at a desk, on the phone, doing the ironing or making a speech.

The method will appeal particularly to practical, down to earth people who prefer precise instructions to soothing injunctions to relax, and for this reason too it is a very useful additional technique to teach.

Exercise 3

AIM: to demonstrate the Mitchell Method in action; to make sure that participants clearly understand all the orders.

TIME: 10 minutes

METHOD: leader goes through instructions (see pamphlet), using volunteer in lying position to demonstrate movements. At the end of the exercise, go over again any movements which volunteer found difficult or unclear.

Part 2.3

GUIDED AND UNGUIDED VISUALIZATION

We have already seen that merely imagining, remembering or anticipating a stressful situation can provoke feelings of anxiety or even panic (Section 4, Part 3, Exercise 2). Visualization is a way of channelling imagination and memory, and making these powerful faculties work for us rather than against us. With practice, we can learn to rid the mind of unwanted thoughts and images, and substitute calming, pleasurable scenes which we come to associate with tranquillity and relaxation. The images we choose to project on our mental screen can be drawn from memory, or pure fantasy, or be a mixture of both.

Visualization exercises can be of several types. The first text given here (Relaxation Text 4) is a 'guided fantasy' in which you are taken into a scene and then encouraged to explore it, following the suggestions in the text. The second text (Relaxation Text 5) gives the outline for an 'unguided' visualization exercise, in which the choice of setting is left to you. Before trying this, you might find it helpful to focus your thoughts by calling to mind a favourite beauty spot, a holiday picture, or a painted landscape you can see clearly in your mind's eye.

As in other types of relaxation exercise, if worrying and unwanted thoughts intrude on your peaceful scene, acknowledge them, and let them drift away again without pursuing them. Bring your attention gently back to the scene you have created and remember that with practice, your concentration will improve. As you get used to using the technique, you may find that a certain element of your mental scene acts as a 'trigger' signifying 'relaxation', without your having to construct the whole image. This might be the comfortable chair you imagine yourself sitting in or the gate through which you enter your secret garden.

Visualization exercises can either be used on their own, in which case, use the general relaxation instructions given at the beginning in brackets, or in combination with other techniques as a 'tailpiece' to a session. When used in this way, they provide a way of dealing with the common problem of the mind still 'racing' even though the body is physically relaxed.

Part 2.4

SIMPLE MASSAGE

Introduction

Massage is a valuable aid to stress reduction as it can reduce muscular tension and associated pain, stimulate the circulation, speed up the elimination of waste products and promote a general feeling of well-being and relaxation.

Many misconceptions and taboos surround the subject of massage (see leader's presentation below). For this reason, we suggest that a session on massage should be included at a stage in the workshop/course when participants have got to know one another, and feel comfortable as a group. On a two-day course, for example, we have used this session successfully at the beginning of the second day. Although some participants may show slight initial reluctance to try out simple massage techniques, or claim that such techniques could never be used with their particular client group, many people have found this to be one of the most enjoyable and beneficial sessions on the course.

Leader's presentation

Touch is the first form of communication that we learn as babies. As we grow up, we discover that touch can relieve pain, convey warmth and reassurance, friendship and affection. We also learn the social taboos which surround physical contact, and as adults we may become embarrassed and self-conscious about any form of touching which falls outside certain clearly-defined boundaries. These feelings are likely to affect our attitudes towards massage, which is a particular kind of touching. Two images come to mind when we mention massage, both of them misleading. On one hand, massage is seen as the province of the expert, the physiotherapist or masseur. On the other hand, it is connected with shady goings-on in 'massage' parlours from Soho to Bangkok. The simple massage techniques which we'll be trying out in this session have nothing to do with either medical or erotic massage! Provided that a few basic rules are followed, almost anyone can learn to offer this relaxing

and beneficial form of physical contact to a client, colleague, partner or friend.

Benefits of massage

(Flip-chart 11)

- reduces muscular tension
- can relieve pain
- stimulates circulation
- promotes elimination of waste products from muscle cells
- reduces emotional tension and anxiety
- promotes feeling of relaxation and well-being

Guidelines for giving massage

(Handout 7)

(These points should be raised at the appropriate stage in your demonstration of the various techniques).

- good massage is a form of communication - it's important that the person giving the massage checks with the person receiving that the pace/pressure of touch/position is right.
- both giver and receiver should be in positions which allow them to be comfortable and relaxed.
- muscles cannot relax when cold, so check temperature of room and hands of person giving massage.
- make sure that nails are short, and remove jewellery likely to catch on skin, clothes or hair.
- before beginning massage, place hands on partner for a few moments, holding them still. Breathe calmly and slowly so as to transmit a feeling of relaxation. (Tension in the massager will quickly come across to the receiver).
- use firm, deliberate, rhythmical strokes - check that the pressure and pace are right for your partner.
- during the massage, always keep one hand in contact with the skin in order to maintain continuity.
- as you come to the end of the massage, indicate this by a few slower, more deliberate strokes.

- when the massage is complete, rest your hands on your partner for a moment while he or she 'comes round'.
- have confidence in yourself - trust your own instincts and your partner's feedback.
- massage is not masochism! It shouldn't hurt, and the receiver should let the massager know as soon as a movement becomes painful.

NB. Inexperienced people giving massage should avoid massaging over the spine itself.

For the reduction of stress, the most useful parts of the body to massage are the neck, shoulders and forehead. We're going to look at a few simple techniques for helping those areas to relax.

Exercise 1. Forehead

AIM: To demonstrate a simple massage technique.

METHOD: Leader demonstrates on volunteer or co-leader, making sure that participants all have a clear view. Participants then try the techniques themselves.

TIME: 20 minutes (including feedback)

EXERCISE: Receiver sits in chair in relaxed posture. Massager stands behind, close enough to allow receiver's head to rest against her/his body. Following the guidelines above, leader demonstrates two strokes.

1. (See Fig 1) Both hands are placed on the forehead, finger-tips lightly touching. The hands are moved out towards the temples, and then either up into the hairline in a sweeping-upwards movement, or down towards the cheek-bones in a downward movement finishing at the level of the ear. Repeat each movement several times before moving on to the next one, so that participants see each one clearly.

FIG 1

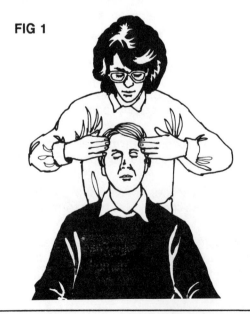

2. (See Fig 2) Using hands alternately, smooth up over the forehead from the bridge of the nose to the hairline. As one hand reaches the top of the head, begin smoothing upwards with the other, so that one hand is always in contact with the head.

In pairs, participants try these techniques for themselves, taking turns to give and receive massage. (5 minutes each way, with a reminder half way through each 5-minute period to change strokes.)

FIG 2

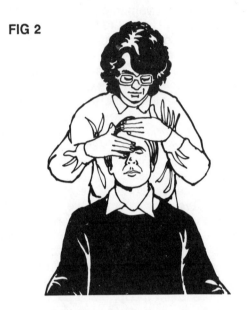

Feedback

This will probably take the form of contented sighs, pleas of 'more, more', and comments like 'And to think we're getting paid for this!' People may be surprised to find that giving massage can be a relaxing experience as well as receiving it. Some participants will find it hard to believe that they're doing it 'properly' - emphasise again the importance of communication between partners, and encourage people to believe their partners when they say 'That was lovely - I really enjoyed it'. The main worry is likely to be the fear of hurting people unintentionally, but this will not be a problem if good communication is established, and the guidelines given above are followed.

Exercise 2.
Shoulders and Neck

AIM: To demonstrate a simple massage technique.

METHOD: as above

TIME: as above

EXERCISE: Positions as described above. Shoulder massage is made easier if receiver is wearing a plain top without a collar, eg. T-shirt. Jewellery (dangling earrings, necklaces) should be taken off, and long hair should be put up or tied back if possible.

FIG 3

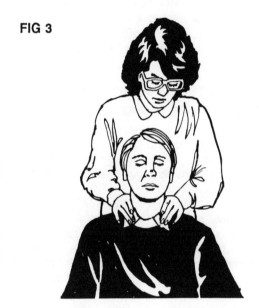

1. **(See Fig 3)** Stroking. Hands are cupped round the sides of the neck, just below the ears. Hands are then moved down the neck, over the tops of the shoulders, and off the ends of the shoulders in a sweeping movement, as if literally 'brushing away' tension. The movement is then repeated several times.

2. **(See Figs 4)** Thumb circling. Hands are placed on the tops of the shoulders, with fingers facing forwards and thumbs downwards. Using the rest of the hand to counterbalance the pressure, make small circling movements with the thumbs, systematically working outwards from the area near the spine, over all the upper back area which can be reached while still keeping the rest of the hands in place on the shoulders. NB. Do not massage over the area of the spine itself.)Use the fleshy part of the thumb and not the tip, and ask your partner for feedback about pressure and sensitive or tense areas. These often feel 'knotty', and with a little practice, are quite easy to identify.

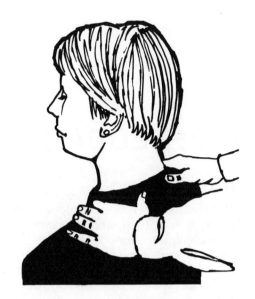

FIG 4

NB. Occasionally, there may be people in a group who really do not want to be touched by anyone else, and who find the idea of massage threatening. If this is the case, encourage them to try out the techniques on themselves, and point out that self-massage has many of the same positive effects as massage by another person. Self-massage of the forehead and temples is something we often do naturally if we feel a headache coming on. Another simple way of relieving 'tension' headaches is to take yourself 'by the scruff of the neck' with one hand, and to work from the top of the back to the base of the skull, kneading the muscles between thumb and fingers.

Summary

Simple massage is a useful tool in stress management as it:

- helps reduce muscular tension
- helps relieve pain
- stimulates circulation
- speeds up elimination of waste products
- promotes general feeling of well-being and relaxation
- requires no specialist training

Part 2.5

BIOFEEDBACK

Introduction

Biofeedback was developed in the 1960's. It is a term which covers a variety of techniques for monitoring physical functions and providing 'feedback' to the user in the form of a sound or light display.

Different types of biofeedback machines are used to monitor brain waves, blood pressure, muscle tone, body temperature and skin resistance. Their main use is to provide an objective measure by which people can learn to regulate body functions which are not usually under voluntary control. The machine we have used in the workshops is a battery-operated skin resistance galvanometer or 'relaxometer' (see Resource List for details). This indicates changes in levels of arousal by producing a sound of varying pitch. Biofeedback machines are useful teaching aids as they provide an objective measure of the user's physiological state, and demonstrate the effectiveness of relaxation techniques. What's more, they are great fun to use with a group!

Exercise 1

AIM: To demonstrate the uses and limitations of biofeedback machines.

TIME: 10 minutes

METHOD: Ask for a volunteer to demonstrate the biofeedback machine. Attach the electrodes to the fingers and allow the user time to settle down. Set the pitch/volume control to a level at which the sound is not too piercing. Encourage the group to continue chatting (this is a useful exercise to do during a break). Ask the volunteer to try relaxation techniques and diaphragmatic breathing to reduce her/his level of arousal. (Note that both movement and laughter can raise the pitch of the sound.) If the user succeeds in reducing the pitch of the tone produced by the machine, ask her/him to think of something stressful. The machine should register a corresponding increase in pitch. If a reduction in pitch is achieved, this usually takes the form of a wave-like pattern of sound in which the 'peaks' get lower and lower in pitch.

When the group has got the general idea, ask for another volunteer to demonstrate. Experiment with the effects of sudden loud noise, like a clap or the slamming of a door. Have the relaxometer available throughout the course, so that people can try it out in their own time, as it is quite difficult to relax when the attention of the group is focused on you!

How biofeedback works, and how it can be used

Leaders may like to present this section formally, using a flip-chart, or in a less structured way, encouraging the group to consider the possible uses and limitations of biofeedback.

The most common biofeedback machine in general use is called 'relaxometer' and this measures changes in levels of arousal as indicated by minute changes in the electrical conductivity of the skin, which is determined by the level of activity of the sweat glands. As shown in the session on the fight/flight response (Section 4, Part 1), sweating increases under stress, whether this takes the form of excitement, fear, pain or anger. The biofeedback machine measures the user's resistance to small electric currents being sent from the machine to the fingertips : if arousal is high, the skin moisture level is raised, resistance is reduced and the machine produces a correspondingly high-pitched sound. As the user relaxes, the skin moisture level decreases, resistance rises, and the noise produced by the machine lowers in pitch until it becomes a gentle purring sound, and then subsides into silence.

Uses and benefits of biofeedback

- Provides objective 'proof' that the body reacts to stress and that there is a direct connection between anxious thoughts and raised levels of physical arousal.

- Shows that, with practice, bodily reactions to stress can be brought under control.

- Provides objective measure by which people can monitor their progress in learning to relax. (Particularly useful for people who find it hard to trust the evidence of their own senses.)

- Simple to use
- Gives a 'reward' for controlling tension, in the form of lower-pitched sound. People can derive encouragement and a sense of achievement from having their success recorded by a machine.

Points to note when using biofeedback

- Each participant should be told to concentrate only on his/her own 'performance' and not to compare it with others. The level of perspiration varies from person to person, so everybody has a different starting point from which to work on reducing the pitch of the sound produced by the machine. Comparison between individuals is not possible.
- Perspiration rates may be affected by heat and exercise.
- Biofeedback is not a substitute for self-awareness. It can provide reinforcement during the early stages of learning relaxation techniques, and may be particularly helpful for people who are sceptical about their ability to relax. It should be emphasised that the machine does not *make* people relax - they do that for themselves. All the machine does is to record the results.

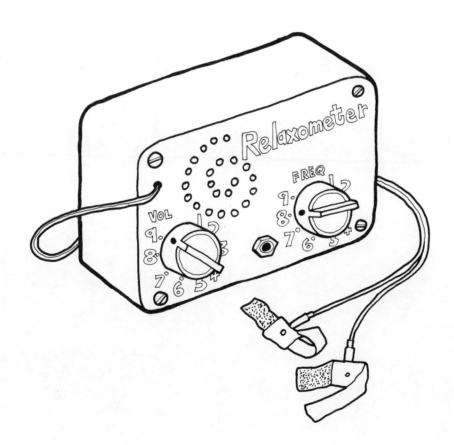

SECTION 6

EVERYDAY RELAXATION

Relaxation in everyday situations 58

RELAXATION IN EVERYDAY SITUATIONS

Introduction

Many people who would benefit enormously from using relaxation techniques claim that they just have not the time in their crowded schedules for any kind of relaxation. "I'm far too busy to relax", they say, rushing off to a vitally important meeting, or heading for the supermarket on Friday evening. Although regular relaxation periods of at least twenty minutes a day are highly beneficial, people should also be aware that relaxation techniques can easily be integrated into their daily routine. It doesn't take any extra time to pick up the phone in a relaxed manner instead of snatching it up or to sit in a meeting breathing calmly and deeply rather than tapping your feet and drumming your fingers on the table! Muscle-relaxing exercises, diaphragmatic breathing and 'quick release' tension reducers are invaluable when the going gets tough.

Leader's presentation

Emergency relaxation techniques

Jane Madders and Laura Mitchell both suggest techniques to try when pressure is mounting and it's not possible to get away completely and do a whole-body relaxation. Tension may be caused by a row with a difficult colleague, feeling harrassed by pressures and deadlines at work, panic at the thought of an unpleasant situation or a general build up of demands from the family. The principle behind both techniques is that mental stress will be reduced if corrective action is taken to relax the muscles, and calm the breathing.

Exercise 1

Jane Madders' 'Emergency Stop Technique'

AIM: to teach a 'quick release' method for reducing tension

TIME: 3 minutes

METHOD: Leader runs through instructions once, then takes group through following exercise:

Sit on the edge of your chair and visualize a situation in which you have recently felt threatened or anxious. Really imagine yourself in that situation. Remember how you felt. Feel your muscles becoming tighter. Now say sharply to yourself "STOP" (this means stop fussing or getting worked up), then breathe in and hold your breath for a moment. Then, breathe out slowly and as you do, relax your shoulders and hands. Pause for a moment then breathe in again. As you breathe out this time relax the forehead and jaw. Stay quiet for a few seconds, then continue with whatever you are doing, moving smoothly and slowly.

This emergency technique can usually be done without anybody noticing and will almost certainly reduce tension. It should be noted that generally you should not pause between inhaling and exhaling but in an emergency it may help.

Laura Mitchell's 'Key Positions'

Laura Mitchell doesn't prescribe a specific technique for reducing tension in emergencies. Instead she recommends that people find out which exercise in the physiological relaxation sequence brings about the most immediate relief.

She believes that everybody will be able to identify one particular exercise in the sequence which unlocks tension most effectively and easily for them. She calls this a 'key position'. Once you have identified your key position and practised it regularly in times of 'emergency', your appreciation of exact joint and skin sensations will increase enormously, as it is reinforced by repeated application. Laura Mitchell recommends that when people are in the process of identifying their key position, they should think aloud about the changes taking place in the joints and skin. She illustrates this as follows, taking changes in the hand as an example:

'I can feel my four fingers are straight and separated at the knuckles (the joints where the fingers meet the hand). When I then register the further two joints in each finger in turn, I can feel each joint is nearly straight. It is certainly not curled with the finger tips in towards the palm. Indeed if I stretch out the fingers actively a little bit more I can feel them straightening further and the skin on the underside of these joints being definitely stretched. Now I stop stretching the fingers and I feel the skin slacken and the finger tips on the support. Now I give all my attention to the finger tips. I am not going to move the fingers in any way. I am simply going to register the texture of what they are lying on.' (*Simple Relaxation*, John Murray, 1985:65)

Laura Mitchell suggests that people become aware of their 'triggers of tension' and use their key position whenever they anticipate a difficult situation.

Exercise 2

Identifying and using 'key positions'

AIM: to help participants identify their 'key' positions' for reducing tension; to try out the technique.

TIME: 10 minutes

METHOD: Leader recalls briefly the orders given in the Mitchell Method of relaxation. Next, each participant is asked to think about her/his own physiological response (as discussed in the fight/flight section) and try to identify the key position which will most effectively switch off her/his characteristic stress reaction.

Ask participants to sit on the edge of the chair and visualize a 'difficult' situation, then use their own key position to reduce tension. As they take corrective action they should dwell on the sensations produced by the changes taking place in the joints and skin, and enjoy the feeling of relaxation which they have achieved.

Feedback

Have a group discussion about the effectiveness of key positions. Were they easy to identify? What changes did people notice in the parts of the body they exercised?

Leader's presentation

Relaxed posture and differential relaxation

If you are interested in sport, you will notice that good athletes look poised and graceful even while they are enduring enormous physical pressures. Doesn't watching Sebastian Coe make you believe that it takes no great effort to break world records on the running track? Indeed, he shows such economy of movement and effort that you almost believe you could overtake him down the back-straight! What he is displaying is his ability to maximise energy and reduce wear and tear under enormous pressure. Relaxation techniques enable us ordinary mortals to maximise energy and reduce wear and tear by letting go of unnecessary tension whether standing, sitting, walking, running, driving a car, or engaging in any other everyday activity.

As we showed in the description of the Mitchell method of relaxation, muscle groups work in pairs - as one group contracts, the other relaxes. In daily activities, damage to the body can be minimised by using (contracting) only the muscles essential for any task, whilst those not needed are resting. Dr Edmund Jacobson calls this 'Differential Relaxation'. (*You Must Relax*, Unwin, 1980:128) The resulting activity looks balanced and poised. Differential relaxation can be achieved by becoming aware of which muscles are needed for an activity and which can remain at rest.

Exercise 3

Saving energy in everyday activities

AIM: to show how effort can be economised by using differential relaxation

TIME: 10 minutes

METHOD: participants try out the positions and activities described below:

Sitting in a relaxed position

Ideally, sit in a chair with head, back and arm rests, or have the chair pushed up against a wall so that the head is supported. Really get as much support as possible from the chair. Have legs a little apart and both feet flat on the floor. Support hands on the arms of the chair or on your lap. Relax the neck, and have the head and spine in perfect alignment. When standing up, lead with your head rising from the chair and move from the pelvis.

Writing (ask one person to sit at a table with pen and paper)

Use only the minimum pressure with the pen or pencil.

If you lean forward tilt from the pelvis, not the waist or the neck. This helps avoids the 'scholar's stoop', and the aches and pains in shoulders and neck which are often suffered by people who spend long hours hunched over books or writing at desks.

Rest your free arm on the desk or on your lap (often handwriting can improve after training in relaxation).

Bending, lifting, carrying

Reduce strain on the spine by bending from the hips, not waist or neck.

Squat down with the feet apart imagining you are picking up an object. Keep the head, neck and back aligned. When carrying a heavy object hold it against your body, as this reduces the load on the spine.

Reading (Hand out books, or ask participants to look at a newspaper, magazine etc.)

Relax the body by sitting in the position described above.

Hold your hands and arms in a relaxed position. Look at a book and read a few lines. Begin to let go with the eye and forehead muscles until you are not able to read the words, and can only vaguely see the print.

Next, increase tension until the eyes are focused just to the point at which the words can be read. Continue to read at this pressure as it is easiest on the eyes.

Exercise 4
Relaxation in everyday situations

AIM: to make participants aware of simple techniques which can be used in everyday situations, so as to prevent the build-up of harmful tension, minimise wasted energy and reduce wear and tear on the body.

TIME : 20 minutes

METHOD: Have flip-chart sheets written out in advance with the everyday situations given below. (Or if time allows, get participants to invent their own scenarios, based either on work or home life.) Allow space between the numbered 'stages' for participants to write in their suggestions to present to the group.

Divide large group into small groups of 3 or 4. If appropriate, arrange composition of groups so that participants are looking at situations which are particularly relevant to them (e.g.,if Ann has said a number of times that she doesn't like going to the dentist, suggest that she joins the group looking at situation B). The groups decide collectively

on appropriate relaxation techniques for use at each stage in their scenario and write these in felt-pen on the flip-chart. Each group appoints a spokesperson. Groups report in turn, reading out their scenario to the whole group before presenting their ideas.

Situation A

You were at a meeting late last night and have arrived for work feeling tired, overworked and undervalued. This morning you have a clinic at which you have to see 12 clients individually. This afternoon you have to give a talk. You are beginning to feel tense and feel that you need help with your heavy case-load. Think of appropriate relaxation techniques to use :
1. Before you see the first client in the morning.
2. After you have seen your last client.
3. Before the talk.
4. Standing outside your supervisor's door, preparing to tell him/her that you need help.

Situation B

You have agonising toothache. You dislike going to the dentist. At 4 pm you nerve yourself to ring the dentist and make an appointment for the next morning. Throughout the evening you are becoming nervous.

Decide on the best methods of relaxation to use :
1. During the evening.
2. As you wake up the next morning.
3. In the waiting room.
4. In the chair.

Situation C

You are late for work and have an important meeting at 9 am. You have a 20 mile drive to your office, 17 miles along the motorway and 3 miles in busy city traffic. As you leave the house you begin to feel tense. Decide on the best ways of relieving the tension:
1. As you sit in the car and start the engine.
2. As you are driving on the motorway.
3. As you are stuck in a traffic queue, one mile from the office.
4. As you stand outside the meeting room, 15 minutes late.

Checklists

Situation A

1. Before the first client
- Diaphragmatic breathing
- Check posture, making sure you are making economical use of muscles by practising differential relaxation
- Do your Laura Mitchell 'key position' exercise

2. After your last client
- If possible go to a room where you can be on your own, or a quiet room with no disturbances
- Try some loosening exercises - pay attention to hands, shoulders and jaw
- Check diaphragmatic breathing
- Do a sitting deep relaxation exercise or Laura Mitchell exercise

3. Before your talk
- Jane Madders' 'emergency' technique
- Diaphragmatic breathing
- Prepare to stand correctly - use differential relaxation
- Take 5 minutes to go through Laura Mitchell exercise, paying special attention to the eyes and mouth

4. Standing outside the supervisor's office
- Diaphragmatic breathing
- Check through the body for tension and do progressive relaxation exercises to correct any tension, or use Laura Mitchell 'key position'
- Stand correctly - use differential relaxation
- Smile - this tenses and relaxes the mouth

Situation B

1. During the evening
- Loosening exercises
- Full relaxation exercise - either Laura Mitchell, progressive or deep relaxation technique. During the mental relaxation at the end of the exercise you may like to visualize the waiting room and yourself sitting there feeling very relaxed. If this does make you tense, immediately think of something different!

2. As you wake up the next morning
- Full relaxation exercise
- Diaphragmatic breathing
- Loosening exercises, paying special attention to jaw and mouth

3. In the waiting room
- Emergency technique - Jane Madders or Laura Mitchell 'key position'
- Differential relaxation - sit in a position which allows maximum relaxation
- Make sure that you are breathing slowly and calmly from the diaphragm
- Prepare to smile at the dentist - this automatically relaxes your face and jaw, and may give him or her a pleasant surprise!

4. In the chair
- Relax your face with a sigh
- Tense and release your jaw and tongue
- Let your head roll back into the support
- Press your whole body into the support and release (Laura Mitchell technique)
- Support your arms and hands on the chair, having palms upwards (helps you to resist the impulse to clench the seat!)
- Tense your feet and release the tension, then let legs and feet flop outwards
- Imagine the pattern your body makes on the chair
- If having an injection - breathe out as the needle goes in
- If you become tense during the treatment do a Jane Madders emergency 'Stop' exercise

Situation C

1. As you sit in the car and start the engine
- Get maximum support form the car seat
- Laura Mitchell 'key position'
- Diaphragmatic breathing
- Open window so that you don't get too hot
- Positive self-talk - you will get there as soon as possible, but the journey takes a certain length of time, and worrying will not get you there any faster!

2. On the motorway
- Check that your head is centrally poised on your spine and that you are sitting in a relaxed position - use differential relaxation
- Rest your left leg on the floor - it serves no purpose hovering above the clutch Even one group of relaxed muscles is an indicator to the brain that all is well - no need to be on 'red alert!'
- Do not hold the wheel so tightly that your knuckles are white with tension. The steering wheel should be held just firmly enough to enable you to be in full control
- Drop your shoulders and hold your upper arms away from the body as Laura Mitchell recommends
- Let your field of vision be as wide as possible.This does not mean that you should not look where you are going ! Try to relax the eye muscles as much as possible by not focusing intensely and exclusively on the stretch of road ahead
- Diaphragmatic breathing

3. In the traffic jam
- Check whether there is any tension in your feet, legs, arms, hands, face and shoulders and do progressive relaxation exercises to reduce the tension
- Let go of the wheel, relax hands and arms and drop shoulders
- Check posture and make sure that you are sitting in the most economical position
- Self-talk - accept the traffic jam and use the enforced waiting time to restore your energy after the motorway drive

4. Outside the meeting room
- Diaphragmatic breathing
- Jane Madders' emergency technique.
- Prepare to smile as you enter the room - this automatically relaxes your face and jaw

Summary

Obviously, the group will have other suggestions to add to those on the checklist. These tips are intended to show participants that they can easily integrate relaxation techniques into their everyday routine. They don't take extra time or energy and the benefits are immediate. They reduce wasted energy, help beat tiredness, improve performance and can increase confidence in ability to deal with day-to-day situations by preventing the build-up of anxiety and tension. So next time someone tells you they "haven't time to relax" you can prove them wrong!

SECTION 7

RUNNING A GROUP

Running a relaxation group   64

RUNNING A RELAXATION GROUP

Introduction

In this section, we have assumed that all or most participants have some experience of working with groups. Those who do not will at least have gained an impression of how a relaxation group might be run from their experience of taking part in your course. Suggestions as to how a course might be structured are given in Handout 9, and detailed instructions for giving relaxation exercises are in Handout 5. This section covers some of the general, practical issues involved in running a group of this kind.

Leader's presentation

If you are planning to run a relaxation and stress-management group for clients, colleagues or friends, there are a number of practical issues which you need to think about. Questions of environment and leadership style and role, which are important in any kind of group, are perhaps even more important in groups which aim to help people cope with their fears and anxieties. People will not be able to relax unless they feel safe and comfortable, and a poor environment or the wrong kind of approach on the leader's part may leave them feeling more tense than ever!

Exercise 1

AIMS: to raise participants' awareness of practical issues involved in running a relaxation group; to raise awareness of importance of leader's style and technique.

TIME: 15 minutes

METHOD: group discussion of the two questions : What kind of environment would be suitable for a relaxation group? What does the leader's role involve? (If group numbers 8 or fewer, discuss both questions in whole group. If more than 8, divide into two groups, each looking at one question.) Take feedback on a flip-chart under two headings: 'Environment' and 'Leader's Role', allowing participants to expand on any areas of particular interest or concern.

Checklist

Environment

- quiet, free from interruptions (have sign on door) and distractions, eg. noisy radiators
- curtains or blinds for privacy and comfort as well as darkening the room
- pleasantly warm and free from draughts, with extra heating available for use during relaxation sessions. (If no extra heating available, advise people to bring an extra blanket with which to cover themselves, as body temperature drops during relaxation.)
- clean, carpeted floor (or mats provided) if people are going to lie down
- comfortable chairs
- enough space for everyone to lie down without touching. (Size of group will be limited by the available space, but the maximum size for a relaxation group is probably about 12, the minimum 4, with 8 being a happy medium.)
- facilities for making hot drinks, eg. herb teas, decaffeinated coffee

Leader's Role

- create friendly, relaxed atmosphere by allowing plenty of time for preparation of the room, being relaxed, open, organised but not inflexible, offering refreshments, giving all group members equal attention regardless of professional status, sex etc.

- build up participants' self esteem and confidence by noticing everyone as they come into the room, welcoming everyone by name; listening attentively; valuing contributions; encouraging people to support each other and not look to you for solutions; avoiding temptation to be the 'expert' and being honest about your limitations; acknowledging the collective experience and wisdom of the group; reassuring people that it is not selfish to spend time focusing on their own needs.

- set boundaries, by being clear about what the group is for, how often it will meet and for how long, the ground-rules by which it will operate.

- teach basic relaxation and stress-management skills - see Handout 5 (Leading a Relaxation Session - Guidelines) for guidance on issues specifically related to running relaxation sessions. (NB. Many participants may think that this is their main role, and that all the rest is secondary. They should be encouraged to consider whether learning and sharing are likely to take place at all if the factors likely to influence the group process and climate are not given priority. Building up participants' self-esteem is also crucial, because if people do not value themselves in the first place, they will not think it worthwhile to learn to protect themselves from stress.)

THE JONES' ARE CLOSING THEIR CURTAINS..... MUST BE HAVING A RELAXATION SESSION!

SECTION 8

GUIDELINES AND COURSE OUTLINES

Planning a course

PLANNING A COURSE
Guidelines and course outlines

Now for the crunch! You have read this manual, tried out a few of the exercises on friends or colleagues and perhaps used some emergency stress-reducing techniques when sitting in the car in a three mile traffic jam. But one sunny Monday morning you are asked to run a 2-day relaxation course for a multi-disciplinary group, most of whom would like to pass on simple stress-reducing techniques to their clients. Suddenly your stress levels reach previously unknown heights! Where do you start?

We felt it would be useful to conclude this manual with 4 outlines of training courses which we have run ourselves. We have used the material in the manual in workshops of varying length, from the original 2-day course to a one and a half hour session with Dental Hygienists on techniques for helping nervous patients relax at the dentist's. You will obviously have your own ideas to add but we believe the following points are useful to bear in mind when planning your course:-

- Allow participants to talk about either their own sources of stress or their personal reactions to stress as early in the course as possible.

- Be clear in your own mind about the aims of the course - i.e. training, not therapy. Discussions of stress can move rapidly into mutual moaning sessions (if the subject is stress at work) or amateur group therapy, if deeply personal issues emerge. The most effective way of dealing with this is to plan the session timing tightly (and stick to it!); acknowledge that deep seated problems, whether organisational or individual, cannot be dealt with in the context of the course, and re-state the aim of the course, which is training.

- Allow adequate time for recovery and other activities between practical relaxation sessions. Otherwise, participants will not be able to distinguish the benefits of individual exercises. They may also be confused by the different methods, and become dozy and unable to concentrate!

- Allow enough time at the end of a relaxation session for people to 'come round', especially just before lunch or the last session of the day when people may be driving home.

- If you are leading a short session, e.g. one and a half hours, it is probably more useful to concentrate on a few 'emergency' techniques (Section 6) rather than full relaxation exercises.

- On the longer courses, i.e. 2 days, structure the course so that each participant has a chance to lead a relaxation exercise in a small group. NB. need for additional rooms for these sessions.

TWO-DAY WORKSHOP

Day One

9.00 SESSION 1
Introductions and welcome.
(Section 2, ice-breaker, ground-rules,
course content, Exercise l)
Loosening exercises, e.g. arm
swinging, shoulder- rolling etc.
(Section 5, Part 1.2)
In pairs, find out how your partner
relaxes and unwinds and be prepared
to introduce them to the group.
(Section 2, Exercise 2)

9.35 How stress affects the body.
(Section 4, Part 1)
Physical effects of stress.
(Exercise 1 and presentation)
Identifying personal triggers of stress.
(Exercise 2 and presentation).
Effects of continuous tension and
anxiety, and role of relaxation in
combatting stress.
(Exercise 3 and presentation)
Summary

10.30 Break
(During the break, a biofeedback
machine can be introduced, if available.
Section 5, Part 2.5)

10.45 SESSION 2
What is stress? Recognising and
managing it effectively. (Section 3)
What does 'stress' mean to you?
(Exercise 1 and presentation)
'Transactional' model of stress
illustrated. (Case Study 1 and
presentation)
Dimensions of stress-choice and
control. (Exercise 3 and presentation)
Stress diaries as tools for working out
personal stress management strategies.
(Exercise 4 and presentation)
Summary

12.20 Relaxation exercise to identify muscular
tension.(Relaxation Text 1)

12.30 Full progressive relaxation exercise to
music (optional).
(Relaxation Text 2)

12.55 Feedback and questions
Give out copies of Relaxation Text 2 in
preparation for first participant-led
relaxation session in small groups.

1.00 Lunch

2.00 SESSION 3
Better breathing (Section 4, Part 3)
Breathing patterns during exercise.
(Exercise 1 and presentation)
Breathing patterns under stress.
(Exercise 2 and presentation)
Breathing exercises 3, 4, 5, and 6.
Summary

2.30 Deep relaxation with breathing
awarness. (Relaxation Text 3)
Summary

2.50 Benefits of relaxation.
(Section 5, Part 1.1)

3.00 Break

3.10 SESSION 4
Running a relaxation group. (Section 7)

3.25 Participant-led relaxation exercise in
small groups. (Relaxation Text 2)
Ask for volunteer in each group to
lead the session.
Give out Session Planner (Handout 10).
Suggest that groups allow 30 minutes
for the relaxation exercise (including
feedback) and 20 minutes for
beginning to plan the first 2 sessions
of a series of relaxation classes.

4.15 Feedback in large group.
Take feedback from leaders first -
how did it feel to lead the session?
Any problems? Observations?
Feedback from relaxers - was it easier
to relax, the second time around?
(Session plans will be discussed on
Day Two, when they have been
completed).

4.30 Close

Day Two

Before session begins, hand out
copies of Relaxation Text 3 and
Mitchell Method.

9.00 Simple Massage (Section 5, Part 2.4)

9.30 SESSION 5
Perceptions of stress.
(Section 4, Part 2)
'Secondary' response to stress.
(Presentation)
Three stages of stress.
(Case Study 2 and presentation)

10.10 Mitchell Method of
Physiological Relaxation.
Explanation of principles.
(Section 5, Part 2.2)
Rehearsal of instructions.
(See booklet in back flap)
Mitchell Method exercise (sitting).
Feedback

10.50 Break

11.00 Relaxation in every-day situations.
(Section 6)

11.45 Participant-led relaxation exercise
in small groups.
(Relaxation Text 3). Small groups
remain as before, a different volunteer
taking the session. Allow 20 minutes
for relaxation and feedback, 20
minutes for completing session plans.

12.25 Feedback from relaxation exercise.

12.30 Lunch

1.30 SESSION 6
Loosening exercises, muscle slapping,
heavy shopping basket, neck exercises,
etc. (Section 5, Part 1.2)

1.40 Participant-led relaxation exercise in
small groups (Mitchell Method).
Small groups remain as before,
session to be taken by participants
who have not yet tried leading an
exercise. Complete session plans if
not finished already. Think about
possible content of further sessions.

2.10 Feedback on relaxation exercise.

2.20 Taking relaxation back to the
workplace. Feedback on session plans,
and participants' plans for working with
colleagues and clients.
(Give out Handouts 8 and 9)
Discussion and questions.

2.50 In pairs, participants discuss any areas
about which they feel uncertain, or on
which they would like more
information. Each pair produces
a 'shopping list'.

3.00 Feedback. Leaders offer two follow-up
sessions within the next month, to deal
with issues identified by group as
most important. Also offer 'hot line'
support for dealing with problems.

3.15 Break

3.30 In whole group, guided and unguided
visualization.
Introduction to technique (Section 5,
Part 2.3)
Guided visualization exercise.
(Relaxation Text 4)
Unguided visualization exercise.
(Relaxation Text 5)

4.00 Feedback

4.10 Course evaluation (Handout 11)

4.15 Close

ONE-DAY WORKSHOP

9.30 **Session 1**
Introductions and welcome.
(Section 2, icebreaker followed by
course outline)

9.40 How does stress affect you?
(Section 4, Part 1)
Physical effects of stress. (Exercise 1
and presentation)
Effects of continuous tension and
anxiety, and role of relaxation in
combatting stress. (Exercise 3 and
presentation)
Summary

10.30 Break and biofeedback (if machine
available).

10.40 **SESSION 2**
What is stress? Recognising it and
managing it effectively.
Dimensions of stress - choice and
control. (Section 3, Exercise 3 and
presentation)
Present Human Function Curve.
(Flip-chart 2).
How does this relate to participants'
experience?
Discuss in large group : 'Is it OK to
take a couple of days off work with a
cold, but not because I'm at the end
of my tether?'
Summary : importance of recognising
own characteristic signs of stress and
taking appropriate action.

11.10 Benefits of relaxation.
(Section 5, Part 1.1)
Identifying muscular tension.
(Section 5, Part 2.1, Exercise 1,
followed by Relaxation Text 1)

11.35 Better Breathing. (Section 4, Part 3)
Breathing patterns during exercise.
(Exercise 1 and presentation)
Breathing patterns under stress.
(Exercise 2 and presentation)
Breathing exercises 3 and 4.

12.00 Deep relaxation with breathing
awareness to music if available.
(Relaxation Text 3)

12.20 **Feedback**

12.30 **LUNCH**

1.30 Loosening exercises - muscle
slapping, arm-swinging, neck
loosening. (Section 5, Part 1.2)

1.40 **SESSION 3**
Perceptions of stress.
(Section 4, Part 2)
'Secondary' response to stress.
(Presentation).
Three stages of stress. (Case study 2
and presentation)

2.20 Simple massage. (Section 5, Part 2.4)

2.50 **Break**

3.00 Relaxation in everyday situations.
(Section 6)

3.45 Taking relaxation back to the workplace.
In threes discuss how relaxation and
stress management can be used:
1. personally
2. professionally, with clients and
colleagues.

3.55 Feedback and discussion in whole
group.

4.05 Progressive relaxation.
(Relaxation Text 2)

4.25 Course evaluation. (Handout 11)

4.30 **Close**

HALF-DAY WORKSHOP

9.15 Ice-breaker, round of names. (Section 2)

9.20 **SESSION 1**
Introduction and welcome (Section 2, ground-rules, workshop content).

9.30 What is stress? Recognising and managing it effectively. (Section 3) Discussion in pairs: 'What does 'stress' mean to me?'

9.40 Feedback in whole group. Leader's presentation. (as for Exercise 1)

9.50 'Transactional' model of stress illustrated. (Case Study 1 and resentation)

10.20 How stress affects us. (Section 4, Part 1) Physical effects of stress. (Exercise 1 and presentation) How relaxation can help. (Leader's presentation as for Exercise 3)

10.45 Break and biofeedback (if machine available).

10.55 **SESSION 2**
Identifying muscular tension (Relaxation Text 1)

11.05 Better breathing (Section 4, Part 3) Breathing patterns during exercise. (Exercise 1 and presentation) Breathing patterns under stress. (Exercise 2 and presentation) Breathing exercises 3, 4, 5 and 6.

11.35 Deep relaxation with breathing awareness. (Relaxation Text 3)

11.55 Relaxation in everyday situations (Section 6) Emergency techniques. (Exercises 1 and 2) Stress-proofing in action. (Exercise 4)

12.45 Guided visualization.

12.55 Round: one way in which I am going to use relaxation: 1. For myself 2. In my work with clients and colleagues

1.00 **Close**

TWO-HOUR WORKSHOP

9.30 Round of names-participants identify one situation in which they'd like to learn to relax.

9.35 How stress affects the body. (Section 4, Part 1) Physical effects of stress. (Exercise 1 and presentation on fight/flight as for Exercise 2)

9.50 Identifying muscular tension. (Relaxation Text 1)

10.00 Better breathing. (Section 4, Part 3)

10.30 Deep relaxation with breathing awareness. (Relaxation Text 3)

10.45 **Feedback**

10.50 Relaxation in everyday situations. (Section 6) Emergency techniques. (Exercises 1 and 2) Stress proofing in action (in threes, work on car journey case-study from Exercise 4).

11.15 Guided visualization.

11.25 **Feedback**

11.30 **Close**

SECTION 9

FOLLOW-UP

Following up the course 74

FOLLOWING UP THE COURSE

One of the most important aspects of running workshops in relaxation is providing follow-up and support to people who have been on the course and are keen to use their newly-acquired skills, but perhaps rather diffident about doing so. With the right kind of support, even participants who can't imagine themselves ever leading groups can be encouraged to take the plunge and make a success of it, as many health visitors, school nurses and college nurses have found out.

Here are some suggestions as to how you can build on the enthusiasm generated by the course:

- Plan a three-month follow up meeting, at which everybody will report back on their relaxation activities, share successes and problems, and consider their further training needs.

- Before the course ends, encourage participants to plan to work together in pairs.

- With the agreement of participants, provide everyone with a list of each other's phone numbers, so that they can get informal support from each other.

- Offer the support of the course leaders as trouble-shooters in case of any crisis, and also offer consultation sessions to individual leaders or pairs of leaders, if this seems appropriate. Often, the knowledge that there is someone to turn to is enough to give people the confidence to have a go.

- As the final session of the course, allow participants time to discuss in pairs any aspects they feel uncertain of, and arrange two follow-up lunch-time sessions within the next month.

Building up a Network

In Cambridge, the existence of Health Authority-funded relaxation groups in the community means that there is already an extensive network of relaxation leaders working in the area. Most of these leaders, like the authors of this manual, have been through a training course devised and run by Occupational Therapists from Fulbourn Hospital (the local psychiatric hospital). The latest development in the relaxation programme is the integration into this network of the health professionals and others who have been on the two-day courses, so that people coming from very different backgrounds and with widely differing experiences now have a chance to exchange ideas and share their expertise.

The community group leaders have quarterly meetings at which they share the experiences of their current groups, and look at specific topic areas in which they feel the need for further information. In the past these have included tranquilliser withdrawal, hyperventilation and dealing effectively with GPs. These meetings are now open to all the leaders, irrespective of which course they came through. Training sessions will now be run jointly, and areas of need which have been identified recently are: simple massage; building self-esteem and confidence; and use of mind-stilling techniques. A newsletter has just been launched, which goes out to all leaders.

The Relaxation Project is run by the Health Promotion Service with the help of a Steering Group whose membership includes representatives of:
- Health Promotion Service
- Community Services (Adults)
- GPs
- Group leaders (NHS and non-NHS)
- Social Services
- Community Education

The Relaxation Project was initially set up to run relaxation and stress management groups in GP practices and other community settings. The early groups were run by enthusiastic volunteers, but after an experimental period in which the service proved its value to clients and GP's, it seemed appropriate to put the project on an official footing, by trying to secure funding from the Health Authority. This was an important step in several ways, as it showed recognition of the time and effort involved in preparing and running groups; made it easier to develop links with GP's; increased the credibility and public profile of the service, and provided a model for a new way of working within the NHS.

The project Steering Group made an application to the Health Authority, and recurrent funding of £4000 a year was made available from development money in the budget of the (then) Community Unit for Adults. The sum requested was calculated on the basis of session fees for group leaders equivalent to those paid to adult education tutors employed by the local authority.

With the current growth of interest in the promotion of mental health, you may be able to encourage your organisation to put money into the development of a similar project, using *Survive Stress* as the basis for your training programme.

Even if there is no Health Authority-sponsored relaxation or stress management programme in your area, there may well be people offering groups locally, either in community education, or in industry, or under the auspices of an organisation like Relaxation For Living. (See back for useful addresses). There is a relaxation component in the Look After Yourself Course, and local LAY tutors may well be interested to meet other people embarking on running relaxation groups. If you can identify a number of individuals and agencies who are active in the field, there may be the possibility of setting up joint training, and of 'placing' people fresh from the workshop as co-leaders of groups run by leaders with more experience. We have found this to be one of the most effective ways of consolidating skills and building up confidence.

SECTION 10

COURSE MATERIALS

Relaxation Texts	1-5	78-84
Case Studies	1-2	85-86
Handouts	1-11	87-104
Flipcharts	1-11	105-115

Relaxation Text 1

IDENTIFYING MUSCULAR TENSION

(10 minutes sitting)

This is an introductory exercise to help you learn to recognise the difference between the feelings of tension and relaxation, and to become aware of the areas of your body which usually harbour tension.

Posture Sit in the most restful position - feet flat on floor, feet directly below knees, thighs rolled out. (If feet do not reach the floor, support with a folded blanket or pile of books.)

Get as much support as possible from the back of the chair.

Forehead Frown hard and notice where your forehead feels particularly tense. Pay special attention to the bridge of the nose and the eyebrows. Slowly relax the forehead. Notice how it feels when you release the muscles.

Eyes Close your eyes very tightly. Notice any tension above and below the eyelid and on the inner and outer edges of the eyes. Gradually relax your eyes as you open them slowly. Note the difference between the feeling of tense and relaxed eye muscles.

Nose Wrinkle up your nose. The bridge and nostrils are the tense areas. Gradually relax your nose slowly, releasing all the tension. Notice how it feels to have those muscles loose and relaxed.

Mouth Give a forced smile. The upper and lower lips and cheeks on each side should feel tense. Your lips should be hard against your teeth. Gently relax the muscles around your mouth. Notice how this feels.

Tongue Press your tongue hard against the roof of your mouth. Notice where it feels tense. The tension areas are the inside of the mouth and the tongue and the muscles just below the jaws. Slowly relax these muscles by letting your tongue gradually sink to the bottom of your mouth. Notice how it feels to have these muscles loosened and relaxed.

Jaws Clench your teeth. Notice where this creates tension, particularly on the sides of your face and at your temples. Gradually relax your jaw and enjoy the sensation of 'letting go'. Notice how it feels when the muscles are allowed to loosen and relax.

Stomach/Abdomen Push your abdomen outwards and make it as fat as possible. Pay particular attention to the area round the navel. Gradually relax your abdomen and let it fall back in to its natural position. Notice how it feels to have the muscles loose and relaxed. Enjoy the feeling of softness in comparison with the feeling of tension you have just experienced.

Legs Lift your right leg. Turn your toes up towards your face and tighten your whole leg to its maximum tension. Notice where it feels tense, particularly the top and bottom and sides of your thigh, knee, calf and toes. Gradually relax and lower your leg until your foot is squarely on the floor, bending your knee as you relax. Make sure your leg goes back to its relaxed position. Notice how it feels for your leg to be relaxed. Become aware of the different sensations in your right and left legs.

Repeat this process with your left leg.

Shoulders Hunch your shoulders hard. Notice the tension, particularly around the shoulder blades and the top of your arms. Gradually release the tension. Notice the difference between tensed and relaxed shoulders.

Arms Put your arms out straight. Feel the tension. Notice the tension in the back of the arm, the elbow and above and below the wrist. Gradually relax your arms and bend your elbow slightly so they are loose and relaxed. Enjoy the difference between tense and relaxed arms.

Hands Clench your fists tightly. Notice the tension in your fingers and palms of your hand. Let the tension go. Notice the difference between tense and relaxed hands.

These exercises are designed to help you feel the difference between a tense and a relaxed body. Just spend a minute enjoying the feeling of relaxation you have created by letting go of tension in your muscles.

Relaxation Text 2

PROGRESSIVE RELAXATION

(25 minutes)

Tensing and relaxing muscles (lying down)

As you lie down check that your body is in a straight line. Take off your glasses if you wear them, and loosen any tight clothing at your neck and round your middle. Place your arms slightly out from your sides on the floor and have your palms upwards. Let your legs fall slightly apart. Become aware of your breathing. Breathe slowly and deeply. Try to breathe out all the tensions that are in your body. Imagine your body becoming warm and heavy. Enjoy the feeling of being completely supported by the floor. Allow your eyes to close, if that feels comfortable. Otherwise, choose a fixed spot on the ceiling to look at.

You are going to work through the body, from your feet up to your head (or from your head down to your feet, see note at end), tensing and relaxing different groups of muscles in turn. As you tense the muscles, really study the feeling of tension. Then, as you release the tension, enjoy the feeling of relaxing and letting go.

Feet

Become aware of any tension in your feet. Tense your feet by straightening them and pointing your toes towards your face. Hold the tension. Release the tension. When you are ready, do this again.

Legs

Become aware of any tension in the lower part of your legs. Straighten your legs and point your feet towards your face. Hold the tension. Release and let all the tension drain out of your legs. Again, when you feel ready, do this again.

Point the toes strongly away from you, contracting the calf muscles at the back of the lower leg. Hold the tension. Release, and let the tension flow out. Again, when you are ready try this again.

Next, tense your upper legs by bending at the knee and drawing your feet back towards you. Hold the tension. Release, and let the tension flow out of your legs. In your own time try this again.

Notice any tension in the lower part of your legs, in the calf muscles and behind your knees. Feel any tension in the front of your knees and in the thigh muscles, right up to the top of your legs. Imagine your feet feeling soft and floppy and your legs feeling heavy and lazy.

Hips and Buttocks

Now tense your buttocks by pushing them hard together. Hold. Slowly release, and let all the tension drain out of them. Feel the muscles soften against the floor. Repeat this when you are ready.

Abdomen

Next become aware of your abdomen muscles. When you are ready, tense your abdomen by pushing it out. Hold for a moment, then gently release the tension. Notice how comfortable you feel when the muscles across your abdomen are soft and relaxed. Again, in your own time, repeat this exercise.

If you are still aware of tension in the lower part of your body, take in another breath and send it away as you breathe out.

Back and Chest

Now become aware of any feelings of tension in your back. Very gently and carefully arch your spine towards the sky. Hold. Release. Let your back become soft and relaxed as it sinks back on to the floor. Again, when you are ready, repeat this exercise.

Next tense your back by drawing your shoulders back to meet behind you. Hold. Concentrate on the feeling of tension in your chest. Now release the tension. Then in your own time, try that again.

Now create tension by pressing your hands against your upper thighs. Feel your chest muscles bunching together. Release. Notice the feeling of relief once the pressure is lifted. Then in your own time, do the exercise again.

Hands and Arms

Keeping the feeling of relaxation in the rest of your body, clench your fists tightly. Hold the tension for as long as is comfortable and then slowly release the tension. Let your fingers and hands hang loosely and imagine that they are warm, heavy and relaxed. When you are ready, try this again.

Now become aware of your arms. First tense your lower arms by raising your hands off the ground. You will feel the tension running up your forearms. Hold. Release the tension and let your hands go limp. Notice that your arms are feeling heavy. When you are ready, repeat this exercise.

Now think about the front of your upper arms. With your palms facing upwards, bring your hands towards your shoulders. Hold. Release, returning your arms to their resting position. When you are ready, repeat this exercise.

Shoulders

Slowly raise your arms to a vertical position, concentrating on the pull from your shoulders. Hold the tension. Notice the muscle tension across the top of your shoulders. Release, and let the muscles relax. Let your arms become soft and heavy and let your shoulders move down as low as possible. When you are ready, try this again. Now shrug your shoulders up towards your ears, as high as they will go. Feel the tension in the middle of your upper back. Then release - let the shoulders move down again, and feel your shoulder blades flatten against the floor. In your own time, try that again.

Breathing

Now, take your attention to your breathing again. Enjoy your slow peaceful breathing. On your next in-breath, fill your lungs and hold your breath for a few seconds noting all the tension in your ribs and diaphragm.

Now release the tension and empty the lungs. Let the tension flow out with your breath.

Neck and Throat

Now take your attention to your neck muscles. Very gently rock your head from side to side, releasing any tension in your neck. Then become aware of your throat. Drop your chin down firmly on your chest. Hold for as long as it's comfortable. Release. Repeat when you are ready.

If there is any tension remaining in your shoulders or neck, very gently lift your head off the floor slightly. Feel the tension in your neck and shoulders, then gently lower your head back on to the floor, and enjoy the sensation of having your head completely supported.

Jaw

Clench your jaw by bringing your upper and lower jaw together. Hold the tension. Release, and let your jaw drop so that there is a slight gap between your upper and lower teeth.

Face

Now take your attention to your face. Become aware of any tension in your face - in your forehead, around your eyes, around your mouth. First press your lips together hard - sustain this pressure, then release, and let your lips go loose and soft. When you are ready try this again.

Next curl your tongue and press it back against the roof of your mouth. Press your tongue upwards, then release, and let it lie softly in the bottom of your mouth.

Keeping your eyes closed move the eyeballs round as if you are looking at an imaginary clock face - first upwards to 12 noon, then right to 3 o'clock, then downwards to 6 o'clock, then left to 9 o'clock.

Finally, take your attention up to your forehead and scalp. Frown hard, drawing in and tensing the muscles of the forehead. Hold for a moment. After frowning hard, relax the whole face, letting it widen and soften.

Imagine your skin becoming soft as your forehead and cheeks return to normal and your jaw sags. Your mouth may be slightly open. Your breathing is now slow and deep. Imagine that your arms, legs and head are heavy and your face, neck and shoulders and abdomen are soft.

Now you are going to lie for about 3 minutes enjoying the changes you have produced. Each time you inhale, imagine you are breathing in the word 'calm', and each time you breathe out, imagine you are breathing out the word 'tension' slowly and silently.

(3 minute gap)

Now I am going to bring the session to an end. In your own time, slowly count backwards from 5 to 1.

When you feel ready, clench your fists as tight as you can and then relax. Again, clench your fists and this time bring your hands together and rub them until they feel warm.

Bring your hands over your eyes and slowly open your eyes into the warmth of your hands. When you feel ready, take your hands away from your eyes and lie still for a few seconds. Slowly, turn on your side, and when you feel ready sit up, taking your time.

As you become more confident about leading relaxation exercises, you will probably want to adapt the text given above, which is only intended as a guide. The following summary instructions for obtaining relaxation in the various muscle groups can be used as a checklist on which to base your own exercises.

NB. This exercise can also be used in reverse, i.e. starting from the head and working down towards the feet. Some people may prefer this, and you should experiment with both ways in order to find out which suits you and your clients better.

Summary key to tense-release relaxation exercises :

No.	To contract the:	Movement:
1	foot	bend the toes
2	lower - leg (front)	bend up the foot
3	lower - leg (back)	point toes
4	upper - leg (front)	bend then straighten leg
5	upper - leg (back)	pull heel back
6	buttocks	push buttocks together
7	abdomen	tense abdominal wall by pushing out stomach
8	lower back	arch spine
9	upper back	shoulders back and in
10	breasts (pectorals)	hands in against thighs
11	hand	make tight fist
12	forearm	bend up hand
13	upper arm (front)	flex arm
14	upper arm (back)	straighten arm
15	shoulder	raise straight arm
16	diaphragm and thorax	deep breath and hold
17	trapezius (top of back)	shrug shoulders
18	neck	rock head from side to side
19	throat	press chin on to chest
20	jaw	clench teeth
21	lips	press lips together
22	tongue	teeth together, press tongue against roof of mouth
23	eyes	look right, left, up, down
24	mind	repeat words e.g. 'relax' on inhaling and 'tension' on exhaling, imagining breathing out tension from the body.

Relaxation Text 3

DEEP RELAXATION WITH BREATHING AWARENESS

(15minutes) Adapted from Jane Madders' 'Self Help Relaxation'

Find a comfortable position in which to relax, either lying or sitting in a chair.

Let your body sink into the floor or the chair. Enjoy the feeling of being supported.

Begin by breathing out first, and then breathe in easily just as much as you need.

Focus on your breathing as the breath moves in and out of your body.

As you breathe out, feel the tension beginning to drain away.

Now direct your thoughts to each part of your body in turn, to the muscles and joints.

Think about your left foot. Does your left foot feel warm or cold? Imagine it becoming warm and heavy. Are your toes relaxed and still? Let your foot rest easily on the floor.

Now your right foot (same instructions as for left foot).

Now become aware of your legs. Your thighs roll outwards when they are relaxed, so let them go, let your hips turn out. Feel your legs becoming heavy and warm.

Your back muscles will relax when your spine is supported by the back of the chair or the floor.

Let your abdominal muscles become soft and relaxed. There is no need to hold your tummy in tightly. Let it rise and fall as you breathe calmly and quietly.

Become aware of the fingers of your left hand. They are curved, limp and quite still. Now the fingers of your right hand. Let them become relaxed, soft and still. Allow this feeling of relaxation to spread up your arms to your shoulders.

Let your shoulders relax. Let them drop easily so that your neck feels long and supple. Then let them relax even further than you thought they could.

Have your head balanced evenly on the top of your spine so that the neck muscles do as little work as possible. If you are lying down, enjoy the feeling of having your heavy head completely supported. Feel its weight on the floor.

Now take your attention to your face. Let your face relax. Let go of all expression from your face.

Make sure your teeth are not held tightly together. Have a little space between your top and bottom teeth and allow your jaw to hang loosely. Have your tongue lying softly in the bottom of your mouth.

Your cheeks become soft because there is no need to keep up an expression. Your lips are soft and hardly touching.

Relax your forehead. Imagine all the lines of worry and care being smoothed out and imagine it feels a little higher and a little broader than before.

Now, instead of thinking of yourself in parts, become aware of the all-over sensation of letting go, of quiet and rest.

When your muscles are relaxed and you are breathing calmly and slowly you begin to feel peaceful and rested and quiet.

Enjoy this feeling of relaxation. Try to keep your attention focused on your breathing. Passively observe the breath as it comes into and leaves your body. You may find that once your body has relaxed, your mind becomes busy and active again. If this happens, don't fight the thoughts and images which crowd into your mind. Acknowledge them, and let them drift away without pursuing them. Gently bring your attention back to your breathing, and the sensations in your body. Work back through the different parts of the body, and if you become aware of any tension, imagine it draining away as you breathe out.

(3 minute gap)

Now I am going to bring the session to an end, so in your own time, bring yourself back into the room, open your eyes, have a stretch or a yawn, and if you have been lying down, sit up slowly. Try to hold on to the feeling of relaxation that you have just achieved.

Relaxation Text 4

GUIDED VISUALIZATION

(10 minutes)

If using this exercise on its own, take participants through the short general relaxation instructions at the beginning.

[First make yourself completely comfortable, whether you are sitting in a chair or lying on the floor. If you are wearing glasses, take them off, and loosen any tight clothing at your neck and waist. Allow your body to sink into the chair or floor. Let your legs and feet flop outwards. If you are lying on the floor, have your arms resting on the floor beside you, slightly apart from your body. If you are sitting in a chair, move your upper arms slightly away from your body, and have your hands resting comfortably on your thighs, or on the arms of the chair. Enjoy the feeling of resting, of being completely supported. Let your eyes close. Don't make any effort to keep them shut, just lower your eyelids gently over your eyes. Make sure that your lower jaw is loose - that your teeth are not clamped together, and that your tongue is is not pressed against the roof of your mouth. Let your tongue lie gently in the bottom of your mouth. Have a slight gap between your upper and lower teeth, and let your lips be slightly parted.

Now become aware of your breathing. Follow the breath as it comes into and goes out of your body. Don't try to control it in any way - just observe the natural rhythm of your breathing. As you breathe out, imagine your whole body deflating, growing limp and heavy. Each time you breathe out, imagine that you are letting tension flow out of your body and mind. Focus on the word 'calm' as the breath flows gently in and out of your body].

(Pause)

Now that your body is relaxed, take yourself in your imagination to the garden of a cottage by the sea. You are sitting in a comfortable garden chair with plump cushions. All around you are the flowers of the cottage garden, and you have a wonderful view out to sea. You sit in the warmth of the sun, listening to the lazy drone of insects, and the sound of gulls crying overhead. In the distance, you hear the rhythmic beating of the waves on the beach below.

(Pause)

After a while, you get up from your chair, walk across the brilliant, sun-warmed grass of the lawn, and go down a short flight of steps which leads you directly on to the wide, smooth, sandy beach. You are quite alone on your stretch of sand, although you can see tiny figures playing in the distance, and hear the faint sound of their voices from far away. You take off your sandals, and walk over the pale, warm, dry sand down towards the water's edge. Feel the warmth coming up from the sand beneath your feet - feel the sand between your toes. As you get nearer to the sea, the sand becomes smooth and hard and damp. Feel this new texture - the sand is perfectly smooth, with only here and there a tiny pink shell glinting in the light of the sun. Now you come to the water's edge. You watch the sparkling foam running up the beach towards you, and you let the warm, shallow water flow round your ankles. You look out to sea, and notice a sail on the horizon - you follow it with your eyes as it moves smoothly round the headland and out of sight. Then you walk along the water's edge, enjoying the rhythmic swish of the waves swirling round your ankles, the sunlight dancing on the water.

(Pause)

Now you turn back to go towards the house, and you walk back over the smooth, hard sand, and then over the dry, pale, powdery sand. You go up the steps which lead back on to the lawn, and the grass feels cool and refreshing to your warm, bare, sandy feet. You sit down in your chair again, allow your eyes to close, and bask in the warmth of the late afternoon sun.

(Pause)

Now I am going to bring this session to a close, so in your own time, count back from five to one, and when you get to one, open your eyes, stretch, yawn, and slowly bring yourself back into the room. When you do sit up, remember to take your time. Try to hold on to the sense of relaxation which you have created for yourself.

Relaxation Text 5

UNGUIDED VISUALIZATION

(10 minutes)

If using this exercise on its own, take participants through the short general relaxation instructions at the beginning.

[First make yourself completely comfortable, whether you are sitting in a chair or lying on the floor. If you are wearing glasses, take them off, and loosen any tight clothing at your neck and waist. Allow your body to sink into the chair or floor. Let your legs and feet flop outwards. If you are lying on the floor, have your arms resting on the floor beside you, slightly apart from your body. If you are sitting in a chair, move your upper arms slightly away from your body, and have your hands resting comfortably on your thighs, or on the arms of the chair. Enjoy the feeling of resting, of being completely supported. Let your eyes close. Don't make any effort to keep them shut, just lower your eyelids gently over your eyes. Make sure that your lower jaw is loose - that your teeth are not clamped together, and that your tongue is is not pressed against the roof of your mouth. Let your tongue lie gently in the bottom of your mouth. Have a slight gap between your upper and lower teeth, and let your lips be slightly parted.

Now become aware of your breathing. Follow the breath as it comes into and goes out of your body. Don't try to control it in any way - just observe the natural rhythm of your breathing. As you breathe out, imagine your whole body deflating, growing limp and heavy. Each time you breathe out, imagine that you are letting tension flow out of your body and mind. Focus on the word 'calm' as the breath flows gently in and out of your body].

(Pause)

Now that your body is relaxed, let yourself drift in your imagination to a place of great beauty and peace. This might be somewhere you know well in real life, or remember from a holiday, or from childhood, or it might be completely imaginary. It might be by the sea, in the mountains, by a lake, in a garden, in a wood, in a town or a city, indoors or out. Breathe easily and peacefully as you let the picture of your scene take shape in your mind.

(Pause)

Become aware of the harmony and tranquillity of your surroundings. You feel perfectly calm and at peace in this place.

(Pause)

Become aware of the position of your body- notice what you are touching with the different parts of your body. Become aware of the objects nearest to you - how close are they? Can you reach out and touch them? What are their shapes, textures, colours, smells? Can you hear anything? What kind of sound is it? Is it nearby or in the distance? Is there any movement in your scene, or is everything completely still? If there is movement, what kind of movement is it - who or what is making it?

(Pause)

Now, take your attention away from your immediate surroundings, and look into the distance. What can you see as you follow your gaze to the very edge of sight? If you are inside a building, you might look out through a window, or an open door, or think about the scene outside. Is anything happening in this wider scene? Can you describe it to yourself?

Listen intently for a moment to any sounds. What kind of sounds are there? Become aware of the things which are closest to you. Notice their colours, shapes, size, smells. Because you feel relaxed and calm, all your senses are unusually alert, and you feel, see, taste and smell things more vividly than in everyday life. Enjoy this feeling of being completely alive and responsive to your surroundings.

(Pause)

Enjoy the freedom to do anything you like- to stay inside your scene and explore it more fully, or to move on to another place altogether.

(Long pause)

Shortly, I am going to bring this session to an end, so in your own time, begin to move slowly away from your scene. Become aware of the feelings of peace and tranquillity which you are bringing back with you.

(Pause)

When you are ready, have a good stretch and a yawn, and slowly bring yourself back into the room. Take your time before getting up, and when you do sit up, remember to do so slowly.

Case Study 1

BAD NEWS AT BEDTIME

Questions

Why did John become stressed?

How might he have handled the situation differently?

John's wife has recently got an evening job. This means that John has to get home from work at 5:30 precisely so that his wife can leave the house immediately. The evenings in the Johnson household have a regular pattern: serve dinner to the four children, help with homework, baths, read stories and bed. Tonight John particularly wants to watch a programme on television which begins at 9 o'clock. He thinks to himself: " I'll have all my jobs finished by then, and I'll be able to sit quietly and relax. Why not? I've had a very busy day after all."

By 7:15 pm., Luke, the two-year-old had had his bath and been put to bed. Jane, aged ten, was doing her homework and asked her father to help find her ruler. To encourage her independence and teach her to keep track of her own possessions, John asked "Where did you last see it?" and carried on washing up the dishes. The next job was to bath the four-year-old, David, and John was only too grateful when Katie, aged eight, said she would also like a bath, and that she would help John by bathing David. "Great!" he thought, "So far, so good. They should all be in bed by 8:30 at the latest!"

While putting away the last of the dinner dishes, John's heart missed a beat - he could hear David running up and down in the bath.

He ran up the stairs three at a time, his head filled with images of catastrophe - a split skull, a double drowning. As he flung open the bathroom door, he smashed the doorknob into Katie's eye.

Katie burst into tears. David carried on running up and down the bath. John shouted "Stop that at once", which startled the little boy so that he fell over and swallowed some of the bath water. He too began to cry. The sound of wailing was also heard in one of the bedrooms - the noise and chaos had woken Luke. Just at this point, Jane came into the bathroom and asked if John had found her ruler. John exploded. "We're in complete chaos, and all you can think about is your ruler!' She too burst into tears.

John treated Katie's eye, calmed David down, got Luke back to sleep, and persuaded Jane to go to bed without having found the missing ruler. It was just after 9:00, and with generous Scotch in hand, John collapsed gratefully in front of the television.

"I want a drink of juice, Dad", came a voice from upstairs. It was Katie. Still feeling bad about her eye, he took a drink up to her. She somehow managed to miss her mouth, and grape juice went all over her, her nightie, the carpet and the bedclothes. The last straw!

Finally, at 10:00 pm. he sat down just in time to see the credits roll at the end of the programme. His wife walked in and asked brightly "Is everything OK?"

"Just fine", he said grudgingly, "Absolutely fine."

(Adapted from *Coping with Stress* Donald Meichenbaum)

Case Study 2

THREE FACES OF STRESS

Here are three brief case studies of people who work long hours. Discuss each situation in turn, identifying the stressors for Brenda, Julia and Sandra and the 'safety valves' which may help them cope with their stress. A safety valve is defined as 'an element within their lifestyle which helps prevent or defuse the build-up of stress'.

Brenda is working very hard for her A levels. Like a number of her friends she wants to go to university. She has been offered two provisional places, based on her past performance. Her friends and family believe she can achieve the necessary grades, although they are avoiding putting too much pressure on her.

Brenda's alarm goes off at 5.45 am. There are only three weeks before her first exam and she has breakfast and studies for two hours before cycling to school. After coming home from school she discusses her day with her parents, eats dinner and then works until 9.30 pm. She is very tired when she goes to bed, but enjoys reading novels before going to sleep. She looks forward to the weekend when she indulges in her hobby, horseriding. Her studying is going well but she will be glad when the exams are over.

Julia is a secretary to a Sales Director. She works for a boss who is very unreasonable. She feels she cannot make any decisions on her own about her work as he is inconsistent and changes his mind every day about the degree of responsibility he is willing to allow her. He smokes continuously, which she finds very irritating. When he is annoyed by colleagues' inefficiency or impatient customers, he gets into a rage and slams the adjoining door between their offices. Julia needs a job to pay her rent and living expenses, but no other company can match her current salary. In her own time Julia is keen on keeping fit. She walks to and from work, twenty five minutes each way. She plays badminton twice a week, swims at the weekend and does relaxation exercises four times a week on average.

Sandra is a full time housewife and mother. She has four children, aged seven, five, three, and four months. She is very tired as the baby is not sleeping and the three-year-old is feeling displaced by the baby and is rebelling by being very irritable. Sandra loves her husband and appreciates that he has a very long day at work and needs 'peace and quiet' at home. She encourages the children to make life easier for their Dad, but they are fed up because he doesn't play games with them like other Dads. Sandra is constantly trying to keep the peace.

Sandra gets up at 6 am., irons the children's clothes, makes packed lunches and breakfast and gets them all dressed for a five minute walk to school. She comes home, does the housework, works in the garden where she is growing her own produce (to save money) and spends quite a lot of time making the children's clothes as it is more economical.

She gets headaches regularly and finds it difficult to concentrate. Her husband is a very organised person, and can't imagine what Sandra does during the day to make her so exhausted!

Handout 1

STRESS DIARY

NB. Keeping a diary during the week before the course is essential pre-course preparation, and all participants are asked to do this.

Keeping a detailed diary for a short period of time can be a useful way of identifying sources of stress in your life. You are probably already thinking that having to write everything down will create *more* stress rather than help in any way! It may help to look on keeping a diary in the short-term as an investment for the future. All time-management exercises for harassed executives begin with some kind of audit of present use of time, and there's no reason why you can't do the same kind of exercise for yourself. You will find out exactly where the time goes, begin to identify situations in which you feel under stress, become aware of your physical and emotional responses to stress, and note how you cope with these.

How to do it

Use the sheet attached, or write out the same headings on another piece of paper.

Keep the diary during the week before the course. Don't give up if you miss a day, or worry about it being a 'typical' week.

Throughout the day, note things down under the various headings as often as possible; every half-hour would be ideal, but once an hour is enough. Don't wait until the end of the day - you'll find it impossible to remember enough detail.

What you can learn from the diary

Keeping a diary like this will not only give you a good idea of where your time goes, but will help you begin to see where your stress is coming from. You will be able to distinguish between stress which is self-generated (coming from your own thoughts and actions), and that which comes from outside (from other people, or circumstances over which you have no control).

You probably know all too well what are the chronic, continuing causes of stress in your life - difficult relationships, low income, poor housing, caring for an elderly relative or juggling a job and a family. For many of these situations, there will be no easy or short-term solutions, and stress-management strategies will concentrate on damage-limitation (eg. by learning relaxation skills, giving some time to your own needs etc.) On the other hand, the diary may well make you aware of ways in which you are needlessly creating pressure for yourself. Patterns of behaviour which have come to seem normal and inevitable over the years (always having lunch with parents on Sundays, although no-one enjoys it; always cleaning the kitchen floor on Monday because your mother always did; always shopping on Friday evenings although it's the busiest time etc.) can be challenged and changed if you become aware that they're sources of stress. Bad planning and lack of organisation are also potent (and curable) causes of self-imposed stress, which the diary will reveal (as in the example below!)

Ways of coping vary enormously between individuals. You may find it hard at first to recognise your own coping behaviour, but again the diary will point up ways of behaving which you adopt when under stress eg. spending money, eating, smoking or drinking more than usual, working out on the squash court etc. Relaxation techniques are just another form of coping behaviour which can be added to your repertoire.

NB. The stress diary is primarily for your own use. During the course, you will be asked to share some of its contents with one other person, in complete confidence. Discussion in the whole group will focus on general principles and not on individual situations.

Example Diary
DAY: MONDAY

TIME	ACTIVITY/ SITUATION	HOW I FELT	HOW I COPED
9.00am.	Still at home, couldn't get out of bed when alarm went, no clothes ironed, threw on any old thing, dashed out of house	Hung-over, cross with myself, hungry, tight feeling in stomach- worried about meeting	Drove fast
10.00am.	Stuck in traffic jam on way to meeting. No time to prepare - papers lost	Cross. Incompetent, hot and flushed. Tense feeling in shoulders	Told myself to calm down

Stress Diary

Week beginning:

Day:

TIME	SITUATION/ ACTIVITY	HOW I FELT	HOW I COPED

Handout 2

FIGHT/FLIGHT and REST/DIGEST RESPONSES

The 'fight/flight' response is a reflex reaction to a perceived danger or threat. It results from stimulation of the 'sympathetic' branch of the involuntary or autonomic nervous system (the part which regulates all the body functions which are not under our conscious control, like blood pressure, heart rate etc.) Messages are sent to the brain that a sudden burst of energy is needed to cope with danger. Immediately the body reacts by increasing activity in organs and muscles which are essential for energy and movement and slowing down activity in those which are not needed in the immediate emergency.

Increased activity occurs as follows :-

- Circulation increases to allow more blood and therefore oxygen to the brain, muscles and limbs.
- Heart beats quicker and harder. Blood pressure rises as peripheral blood vessels constrict, blood supply to skin is restricted.
- Coronary arteries dilate to increase blood supply to heart.
- Lungs take in more oxygen and release more carbon dioxide to enable increased tissue respiration during vigorous exercise.
- More sweat is produced to speed up heat loss.
- Skeletal muscles tense in preparation for physical activity - blood supply increases.
- Liver releases extra sugar to provide energy during activity - also releases cholesterol and fatty acids.
- Blood-clotting ability increases to protect against excess blood loss if injury occurs.
- Pupils dilate and eyelids are drawn back, giving expression of alertness and excitement.
- Adrenal glands continue to produce adrenalin, nor-adrenalin and cortisones to prolong the 'fight/flight' response.

Decreased activity occurs as follows:

- Digestion slows down or stops because the stomach and small intestine reduce their activity (who would eat a sandwich while running away from a sabre-toothed tiger !)
- Kidneys, large intestine and bladder slow down as they are not needed.
- Sphincter muscles close to prevent urination and defaecation. (It is noted that when confronted with extreme danger the sphincter muscles can open).
- Immune responses decrease
- Blood vessels in salivary glands constrict, making mouth go dry.

The opposite of the 'fight/flight' response is sometimes referred to as the 'rest/digest' response. This results from stimulation of the parasympathetic branch of the autonomic nervous system. When this part of the system is stimulated, the following changes occur:

- Breathing becomes deeper and slower.
- Heartbeat slows down and lessens in force - blood pressure is lowered.
- Coronary arteries constrict, reducing the flow of blood to the heart.
- Activity in stomach and small intestine speeds up, allowing food to be properly digested and absorbed.
- Urethral and anal sphincter muscles relax, allowing urination and defaecation to occur.
- Tension in muscles is reduced, and flow of blood to skeletal muscles slows down.

By learning to counteract muscle tension and taking control of our breathing, the 'rest/digest' response can be switched on and the body voluntarily 'relaxed' and rested.

Handout 3

HYPERVENTILATION

What it is, and how to recognise and avoid it

When we see situations as threatening or frightening the sympathetic nervous system takes over and we automatically go into the fight/flight mode as if getting ready to run. If running or direct physical action is not called for, we still breathe shallowly and quickly, inhaling too much oxygen and releasing too much carbon dioxide. We are overbreathing or 'hyperventilating'.

Hyperventilation has been defined as: "Breathing in excess of bodily requirements" or "habitual overbreathing".

Hyperventilation is an exaggeration of the body's normal reaction to stress. Many people experience some of its effects, such as racing heart, weak knees and 'butterflies' in the stomach, perhaps before an examination, first date with a new girlfriend or giving a speech. These symptoms usually disappear once the stressful situation is over.

However some people develop the habit of hyperventilating all the time. Their breathing becomes erratic and irregular with wide variations in the rate and rhythm of breathing.

Signs to look for in distorted breathing patterns:

- Irregular breathing with little movement of the abdomen or diaphragm
- Breathing from the thorax whilst at rest
- Frequent sighs
- Gulping for air yet continually feeling short of breath
- Frequent belching and saliva swallowing
- A respiratory rate of at least 15 breaths per minute - often over 20. During severe attacks this can reach 30 or more.

These erratic breathing patterns can often be observed in TV interviews and other similar 'high pressure' situations.

Hyperventilators get into a circle of increased anxiety, as their shallow irregular breathing sends messages to the brain that the body is preparing to run away from a threatening situation. The brain therefore continues to send messages to other parts of the body to remain in the fight/flight mode.

If a person hyperventilates continually, an alarming range of physical symptoms may begin to occur.

Listed here are the common symptoms of chronic and acute hyperventilation, as described by Rosemary Cluff of Papworth Hospital, Cambridge. (*Journal of the Royal Society of Medicine,* Vol.77, October 1984:856)

Cardiac
- Palpitations, 'angina'.

Neurological
- Dizziness, faintness, visual disturbance, migrainous headache, numbness, 'pins and needles' in face and limbs.

Respiratory
- Shortness of breath, 'asthma', chest pain, excessive sighing.

Gastro-intestinal
- Heartburn, burping, air swallowing.

Muscular
- Cramps, fibrositic pains, tremors.

Psychic
- Tension, anxiety, 'unreal' feelings, depersonalisation, hallucination, fear of insanity, panic attacks, phobic states.

General
- Weakness, exhaustion, lack of concentration, sleep disturbance, nightmares, emotional sweating (armpits and palms).

Because of the strangeness and diversity of these symptoms, the sufferer may begin to worry that he or she is developing a life-threatening disease, and the hyperventilation and anxiety will increase. It has been estimated that between 6% and 10% of patients referred to medical specialists for symptoms such as heart problems are in fact suffering from hyperventilation.

Research has also shown that rather than hyperventilation being one manifestation of an anxiety state, chronic anxiety has actually been *caused* by habitual hyperventilation. (Dr L.C. Lum, *Journal of the Royal Society of Medicine*, Vol. 74, January 1981:1,4) Re-learning proper breathing patterns is therefore one of the most important steps we can take in learning to manage anxiety and tension.

Better Breathing

Breathing badly is a habit, not a disease, and like all habits it can be overcome with awareness and practice.

Here are some simple guidelines which will help remedy over-breathing (hyperventilation).

1. Aim to develop a slower, more even rhythm of breathing, with inhalation running smoothly into exhalation. After each out-breath, make a tiny pause, during which you should consciously relax. Try to aim for a breathing rate of 10 - 12 breaths per minute.

2. Observe your breathing while resting. Place one hand on your navel, and consciously move your breathing down to the abdomen area, so that there is very little movement in the upper chest.

3. Become more aware of your breathing while you are carrying out every-day activities.

4. Ask a friend or partner to observe your breathing patterns and check for any unconscious mannerisms, particularly sighs.

5. Visualize difficult situations in which you anticipate feeling anxious, and then relax, and see how quickly you can return to your normal, calm, breathing pattern. This will give you confidence in your ability to get back in control when you feel under pressure.

6. Practise general relaxation either lying or sitting as much as possible, as this will automatically slow down your breathing.

7. Avoid wearing tight clothing which restricts the movement of the abdomen (eg. jeans). Tight clothes are a problem for both men and women, but women also have to fight against cultural conditioning which encourages them to keep their stomachs pulled in. This makes it very difficult to breathe properly!

8. Avoid smoking - taking deep puffs at a cigarette distorts the natural breathing pattern, and could lead to hyperventilation.

Emergency Technique

The effects of hyperventilation can be reversed by breathing into and out of a paper bag several times, as this restores the carbon dioxide level in the bloodstream. A similar effect can be achieved by cupping your hands tightly round your mouth and breathing into and out of your hands a few times.

Handout 4

BREATHING EXERCISES

Guidelines for demonstrating and practising breathing exercises

Breathing exercises are among the most useful and popular relaxation techniques, as they can be used unobtrusively in many situations. However, there are a few points which you should be aware of before introducing them to clients.

1. When practising breathing exercises, there is a small risk of hyperventilation occurring. To avoid this, tell clients beforehand that if concentrating on their breathing makes them feel anxious at any point during the exercises, they should stop immediately and allow their breathing to return to normal.

2. Some people have such deeply-entrenched poor breathing habits that even when 'relaxed' they continue to breathe from the thorax and upper chest. This may be partly explained by the wearing of tight clothing which restricts the abdomen, and by cultural norms of good posture which involve keeping the stomach pulled in. (This applies particularly to women).

3. There may be misunderstandings about what is meant by 'deep breathing'. What many people understand by a 'deep breath' is an exaggerated and unnatural movement which involves pulling in the abdomen, and raising the rib-cage and shoulders. The rigid, military posture which results is the opposite of relaxed! Deep breathing in this context means relaxed, abdominal breathing, which allows air into the base of the lungs with the minimum of effort. The key point to emphasise is that on the IN breath, the abdomen moves OUT, and on the OUT breath, the abdomen FLATTENS again.

Breathing awareness

AIM: to demonstrate the movements involved in breathing and to show that, with concentration and practice, we can control our breathing pattern.

METHOD: the finger-tip touch (to be done lying down).

Let your hands lie on your abdomen, finger tips just touching.

Breathe gently twice, so that the fingers part slightly.

Pause.

Move hands to the outside of the lower ribs and repeat.

Pause.

Move your hands to the very top of your chest. Breathe gently twice causing your hands to lift.

Pause.

Move hands back to the lower ribs and repeat.

Pause.

Move your hands back to your abdomen and repeat.

Pause.

Rest.

NB. The only purpose of this exercise is to increase body awareness. It has *no value* as a breathing exercise, and should only be practised until people become familiar with the feelings of breathing at different levels. (Taken from *Relaxation for Living* pamphlet, 'Better Breathing'.)

Calming breathing

AIM: to teach a calming breathing pattern for use in everyday situations such as interviews, meetings, hectic periods at work, demanding times at home etc. (Nobody need know you are feeling anxious!)

- Let the chair support your back.
- Drop your shoulders, feel them widen from the spine outwards to your arms.
- Allow your lungs and chest to expand fully.
- Now take 5 slow deep breaths, starting with an exhaled breath. Do not hold your breath. As you breathe in, your abdomen swells out slightly and as you breathe out, it subsides again.
- Continue by breathing in to a count of 1-2-3 and out to a count of 1-2-3-4. (The count can be varied to suit the individual. The important point to note is that the out-breath should be one count longer than the in-breath.)

Calming breathing can be used in any situation in which you feel tension mounting.

By breathing in this way, you send messages to the brain that you are coping easily and calmly.

Emergency panic-reduction

AIM: to teach a breathing technique to reduce panic.

As tension or panic are building up say to yourself "STOP", exhale a deep breath and inhale gently. Hold the breath for a moment, then breathe out and imagine letting go of all the tension.

This sends a message to the brain, through the respiratory organs, that you are in control of the situation, and that tension is inappropriate.

NB. This exercise should not be done more than *once* as holding the breath distorts the natural breathing rhythm and may lead to hyperventilation.

'Rag doll' tension-reducer

AIM: to teach a technique for releasing tension which has built up over a period of time, to be used eg. at lunch-time or before going home after work.

Choose a comfortable chair for maximum support.

Breathe 6 slow, comfortable breaths.

With each outgoing breath, imagine yourself deflating slightly, like a balloon.

When you start to feel less anxious, begin to flop forward at the head and neck.

Gradually let your shoulders and arms fall further and further forward until you are hanging limp from the waist, like a rag doll.

Hang there for a minute or so, then come up very slowly and gently, letting your hands lie limp on your lap, like a rag doll.

Sit like this for as long as you like, although 4 minutes is sufficient to reduce your pulse, heart-rate and blood pressure.

When you are ready, take a deep breath before getting up. (Adapted from *Stressmanship,* Livingston Booth:114)

Handout 5

LEADING A RELAXATION SESSION - GUIDELINES

Before starting the session:

- Give people time to make themselves comfortable, put on an extra layer for warmth, go to the loo if necessary etc.

- Describe the exercise you are about to do - make sure people have grasped the principle behind the exercise, and that they know what to expect, and how long it will take.

- Give people permission to choose their own position in which to relax, lying or sitting. If lying, suggest they might use a small cushion to support the lower spine, if this makes them more comfortable. People often find it more comfortable to lie with raised knees and feet drawn back towards the body, rather than completely flat out on the floor.

- Make sure that everyone has enough space, and that people are not touching.

- Check that people are lying or sitting straight before beginning. If sitting, get them to check that their shoulders are level, with the head upright. If lying, ask them to raise their heads slightly to make sure that the head is in line with an imaginary line drawn down the middle of the body.

- Advise everyone to loosen tight clothing at the neck and waist, and suggest that people wearing glasses take them off.

- Advise people to adopt a passive attitude of just 'letting go' and allowing relaxation to happen, rather than trying too hard and becoming annoyed with themselves when they feel that it's not working immediately.

- Timing and speed of delivery - inexperienced leaders often rush the instructions out of nervousness and fear of silence. A useful guide is to do some of the exercises yourself as you give the instructions.

- Tone of voice. It's very common for people new to leading relaxation sessions to feel that they don't have the 'right' kind of voice. As long as instructions are given gently, yet firmly and clearly, practically anyone can successfully lead a relaxation session.

Clients should *not* be encouraged to become dependent on the leader's voice; there's nothing magical about it, and they're the ones actually *doing* the relaxing!

- Hearing difficulties. Ask people to raise their hand if they are having difficulty hearing, so that you can raise your voice or change position.

During the exercise

- **Laughing/giggling.** If this occurs, ignore it. It's usually a sign of embarrassment or nervousness, and will die down as you continue with the exercise.

- **Sleep.** It quite often happens that people drop off during a session. The problem here is that they usually see this as a sign of success, whereas in fact you have to point out to them that by falling asleep, they're missing out on most of the session! Falling asleep is very common among tense people who are poor sleepers at night, and great consumers of energy during the day. When they do finally let go, they fall asleep out of sheer exhaustion. To wake people, ask them by name to wake up, and if that doesn't work, gently touch them on the arm, having first told them that you will do so.

- **Feedback.** It is essential to allow time for feedback after every session.

- **Feelings of anxiety and panic.** People sometimes experience strange feelings when their bodies start to relax. They may feel 'heavy' or 'floaty', have pins and needles or tingling sensations in arms or legs, or feel disorientated. In people who habitually keep themselves tightly under control, these signs of 'letting go' may be anxiety-inducing. They should be reassured that such symptoms show that they are beginning to relax.

- **Dislike of a particular relaxation method.** It is not unusual in a group for opinion to be strongly divided as to the usefulness of a particular technique. For example, a very tense person may not respond to the tense/release method because he or she is unable to release the tension created during the exercises. Some participants may find visualization difficult, and prefer a more 'practical' physical method. Always point out that the choice of technique is a very personal matter, while emphasising that no method will be beneficial unless it is practised regularly.

- **Loss of concentration - 'wandering thoughts'.** Many people find it comparatively easy to relax the body, but have problems with 'racing' thoughts or wandering attention. Reassure them that concentration becomes easier with practice, and suggest that whenever disturbing thoughts intrude, or they find themselves 'miles away', they acknowledge the fact without berating themselves for the lapse, and bring their attention gently back to observing the natural rhythm of their breathing. Repeating a word like 'calm' on each in- and out- breath; or simply counting '1' on the in-breath and '2' on the out-breath can help concentration.

- **Crying.** This occasionally happens when someone has been under a lot of pressure, and has suddenly let go under the influence of relaxation. Reassure the person that this is a perfectly natural and healthy reaction, and a sign that they have begun to release pent-up feelings which are better out in the open than bottled up inside. The person concerned and the rest of the group will take their cue from you. If you accept crying as a natural part of 'letting go', and explain it as a healthy release of tension, nobody will be embarrassed.

NB. Most people can benefit from learning basic relaxation skills. However specialist training is required if relaxation is to be offered to people suffering from severe depression, or from psychotic illness.

It's also worth noting that certain physical conditions may be affected by relaxation, and if medication is involved (eg. as in diabetes, hypertension, heart disease, asthma, epilepsy), a doctor should be consulted before relaxation techniques are used.

Handout 6

RECOGNISING SIGNS OF STRESS IN POSTURE

(adapted from Laura Mitchell "Simple Relaxation")

HEAD - the head comes forward. If cause of stress is grief or pain, the head may be bent right down with chin pulled in. If anger or fear are the causes, the chin juts forward and the whole head moves forward on the neck.

SHOULDERS - shoulders are raised towards the ears in a 'shrugged' position. Upper arms hug the body either at the sides or in front, while the elbows bend upwards. (The common defensive posture in which the arms are folded across the front of the body is a version of this.)

HANDS - fingers and thumbs curl up as if to form a fist, or hands may be clenched together, or tightly clasping some object, eg. a pen, money, or be constantly active, eg. in the nervous rattling of change in trouser pockets.

LEGS (sitting) - a person may sit sideways on the edge of the chair, with one leg wound around the other. (Most common in women.) Legs may be crossed, with the upper foot held rigidly upwards at the ankle, or with rapid movement up and down at the ankle, the accent on the upwards movement.

LEGS (standing) - legs are crossed and uncrossed continuously, as the person is unable to keep still.

BODY - whole body bends forward and is usually held fairly rigid.

BREATHING - accent is on the inward breath, which is often taken in at a gasp. The upper chest moves rapidly up and down.

FACE - jaw is clamped tightly shut, and teeth may grind together. Lips are tightly closed. The tongue is pressed against the roof of the mouth. The brows corrugate, and in grief or pain the eyes may screw up, or open wide in real or imagined danger.

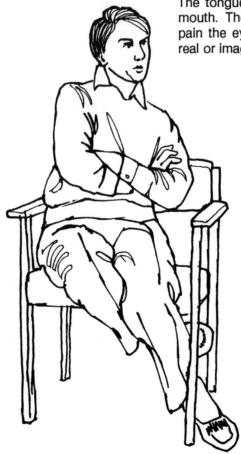

Handout 7

SIMPLE MASSAGE

Benefits of massage

- reduces muscular tension
- can relieve pain
- stimulates circulation
- promotes elimination of waste products from muscle cells
- reduces emotional tension and anxiety
- promotes feeling of relaxation and well-being

Guidelines for giving massage

- good massage is a form of communication - it's important that the person giving the massage checks with the person receiving that the place/pressure of touch/position is right.
- both giver and receiver should be in positions which allow them to be comfortable and relaxed.
- muscles cannot relax when cold, so check temperature of room and hands of person giving massage.
- make sure that nails are short, and remove jewellery likely to catch on skin, clothes or hair.
- before beginning massage, place hands on partner for a few moments, holding them still. Breathe calmly and slowly so as to transmit a feeling of relaxation. (Tension in the massager will quickly come across to the receiver).

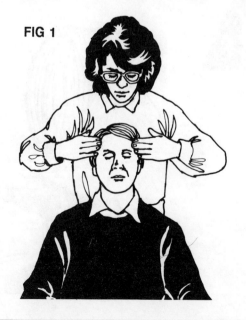

FIG 1

- use firm, deliberate, rhythmical strokes - check that the pressure and pace are right for your partner.
- during the massage, always keep one hand in contact with the skin in order to maintain continuity.
- as you come to the end of the massage, indicate this by a few slower, more deliberate strokes.
- when the massage is complete, rest your hands on your partner for a moment while he or she 'comes round'.
- have confidence in yourself - trust your own instincts and your partner's feedback.
- massage is not masochism! It shouldn't hurt, and the receiver should let the massager know as soon as a movement becomes painful.

NB. Inexperienced people giving massage should avoid massaging over the spine itself.

For the reduction of stress, the most useful parts of the body to massage are the neck, shoulders and forehead.

Techniques for massaging forehead, shoulders and neck

Exercise 1. Forehead.

Receiver sits in chair in relaxed posture. Massager stands behind, close enough to allow receiver's head to rest against her/his body. Following the guidelines above, try the two 'strokes' descibed below. (Figs. 1 and 2)

i. Both hands are placed on the forehead, finger-tips lightly touching. The hands are moved out towards the temples, and then either up into the hairline in a sweeping-upwards movement, or down towards the cheek-bones in a downward movement finishing at the level of the ear. (Fig.1)

ii. Using hands alternately, smooth up over the forehead from the bridge of the nose to the hairline. As one hand reaches the top of the head, begin smoothing upwards with the other, so that one hand is always in contact with the head. (Fig. 2)

Exercise 2. Shoulders and Neck.

Positions as described above. Shoulder massage is made easier if receiver is wearing a plain top without a collar, eg. T-shirt. Jewellery (dangling earrings, necklaces) should be taken off, and long hair should be put up or tied back if possible.

i. Stroking. Hands are cupped round the sides of the neck, just below the ears. Hands are then moved down the neck, over the tops of the shoulders, and off the ends of the shoulders in a sweeping movement, as if literally 'brushing away' tension. The movement is then repeated several times. **(Fig. 3)**

ii. Thumb circling. Hands are placed on the tops of the shoulders, with fingers facing forwards and thumbs downwards. Using the rest of the hand to counterbalance the pressure, make small circling movements with the thumbs, systematically working outwards from the area near the spine, over all the upper back area which can be reached while still keeping the rest of the hands in place on the shoulders. (NB. Do not massage over the area of the spine itself.) Use the fleshy part of the thumb and not the tip, and ask your partner for feedback about pressure and sensitive or tense areas. (These often feel 'knotty', and with a little practice, are quite easy to identify.) **(Fig. 4)**

NB. Occasionally, there may be people in a group who really do not want to be touched by anyone else, and who find the idea of massage threatening. If this is the case, encourage them to try out the techniques on themselves, and point out that self-massage has many of the same positive effects as massage by another person. Self-massage of the forehead and temples is something we often do naturally if we feel a headache coming on. Another simple way of relieving 'tension' headaches is to take yourself 'by the scruff of the neck' with one hand, and to work from the top of the back to the base of the skull, kneading the muscles between thumb and fingers.

FIG 3

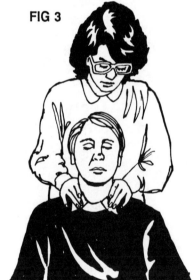

FIG 2

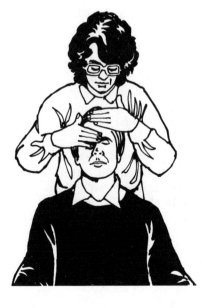

FIG 4

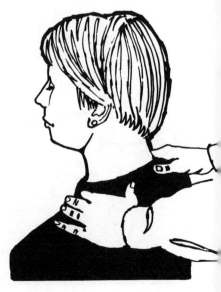

Handout 8

RUNNING A RELAXATION GROUP
The environment and the role of the leader

Environment

- quiet, free from interruptions (have sign on door) and distractions, eg. noisy radiators
- curtains or blinds for privacy and comfort as well as darkening the room
- pleasantly warm and free from draughts, with extra heating available for use during relaxation sessions. (If no extra heating available, advise people to bring an extra blanket with which to cover themselves, as body temperature drops during relaxation.)
- clean, carpeted floor (or mats provided) if people are going to lie down
- comfortable chairs
- enough space for everyone to lie down without touching. (Size of group will be limited by the available space, but the maximum size for a relaxation group is probably about 12, the minimum 4, with 8 being a happy medium.)
- facilities for making hot drinks, eg. herb teas, decaffeinated coffee

Leader's Role

- create friendly, relaxed atmosphere by allowing plenty of time for preparation of the room, being relaxed, open, organised but not inflexible, offering refreshments, giving all group members equal attention regardless of professional status, sex etc.
- build up participants' self esteem and confidence by noticing everyone as they come into the room, welcoming everyone by name; listening attentively; valuing contributions; encouraging people to support each other and not look to you for solutions; avoiding temptation to be the 'expert' and being honest about your limitations; acknowledging the collective experience and wisdom of the group; reassuring people that it is not selfish to spend time focusing on their own needs.
- set boundaries, by being clear about what the group is for, how often it will meet and for how long, the ground-rules by which it will operate.
- teach basic relaxation and stress-management skills - see Handout 5 (Leading a Relaxation Session - Guidelines) for guidance on issues specifically related to running relaxation sessions.

NB. You may think that this last is your main or even your only role, and that all the rest is secondary. It's natural that you should be keen to pass on your newly-developed skills, but essential to remember that the learning and sharing process which will enable this to happen will not take place in a vacuum. The *processes* at work in the group are as important as the overt 'content'. Building group-members' confidence and self-esteem is also vital, because if people do not value themselves in the first place, they will not think it worthwhile to learn to protect themselves from stress.

Handout 9

GUIDE TO PLANNING YOUR RELAXATION COURSE

Course Outline for 6-session course

NB. This is intended only as a guide. Groups vary enormously in their needs, and a rigid structure is often inappropriate. As you gain in confidence, you will feel much better able to judge the mood of the group and its response to different exercises.

The content suggested here would fill a session of 2 hours - obviously it can be adapted to suit shorter periods. Whatever the length of your sessions, don't be tempted to cut down on the time allowed initially for group members to get to know each other. This is vital to the creation of an atmosphere of trust and mutual support which will allow people to relax.

One common worry among people just starting groups is that they won't have enough material to last through the agreed number of sessions. This fear will evaporate when you begin to tap into people's own experiences, and encourage them to get support from each other. There's no need either to feel that each session has to contain completely new material - people like to repeat exercises they've enjoyed, and only by repetition will they become familiar enough with the relaxation techniques to use them in every-day life.

Session 1

Arrive in good time to organise room e.g. seating, lighting, heat, sign on door, drinks etc.

Welcome people with juice or herbal teas (avoid coffee and tea)

Introductions Leaders introduce themselves

Warm-up exercise - cushion game (5 minutes)

Everyone stands up in a circle. Leader explains the game as follows: the cushion is thrown round the room at random. For the first few rounds, everyone says their *own name* as they throw the cushion. Continue until everyone has said their name a few times. Then change to saying the name of the person you're throwing the cushion *to*, and continue until all members of the group can confidently name each other.

Exercise - round of names (5 minutes)

Group sits in circle. Leader asks everyone to write their name on a sheet of flip-chart paper which is passed around from person to person, and to say their name and one thing about it, eg 'My name's Jane, but I've always wanted to be called Arabella', or 'My name's Christine and I hate being called Chris.'

Laying down the ground-rules (5 minutes)

Setting boundaries and laying down ground-rules is a vital part of working with any group. It is particularly important when the group may be addressing sensitive personal issues. The ground-rules for the course should include:

- complete confidentiality - nothing said on the course, either in the large group or in any small group, should be repeated outside.

- individual discretion - nobody should feel under pressure to reveal any more than they are willing to, or to take part in any exercise which they do not wish to join in.

- punctuality - group members should make every effort to be on time for all sessions, and to let the leaders know if they are likely to be late or unable to attend. It can be very unsettling for the group if there's a lot of hanging around at the beginning wondering whether people are going to turn up.

- no smoking during sessions.

In pairs, group members discuss 'Why I'd like to learn to relax and what I hope to get out of the course.' (5 minutes each)

Feedback in group

- not putting pressure on people to talk - just to get general flavour of discussion.

Give outline of course content - ask group to think of issues they'd like to deal with.

Loosening exercises

Sitting relaxation - identifying muscle tension. (Relaxation Text 1)

Feedback

Break - for people to go to the loo etc. Give out evaluation forms if required.

Full relaxation, lying down, with or without background music. (Relaxation Text 2)

Feedback. How did lying compare with sitting? Which did they prefer? Emphasise that relaxation will come with practice, and that people will respond to different methods.

Session 2

Round of names - everyone says name and one good thing which has happened during the week, ie. something which has given them pleasure. This could be something quite small like buying a bunch of daffodils, husband unexpectedly cooking supper. Encourage group to focus on positive things which have happened during the week.

Ask participants to choose a partner they didn't work with last week and discuss in pairs what kind of week they've had. Have they been able to do any relaxation? (5 minutes each)

Feedback - note blocks to relaxation - get group to discuss how these might be overcome.

Exercise - The body under stress

Put group into 3s and give each group a body outline drawn on a large sheet of paper and a felt pen. Ask them to think about what happens when they are under stress, tense and anxious. What happens physically, emotionally, intellectually, behaviourally? Each group draws or writes its collective response on the figure. (Allow at least 10 minutes)

Feedback in group - compare drawings

Explain why physical reactions happen - fight/flight.

Explain how relaxation techniques allow us to control this automatic reaction.

Better breathing - begin with group members' experiences of breathing - do they notice anything different about breathing when under stress? Has anyone done yoga, or learned breathing exercises? etc.

Take group through breathing exercises, sitting or lying.

Feedback

Break

Relaxation - progressive (Text 2), if the group liked this, or Text 3 (deep relaxation with breathing awareness) if they would like to try something different.

Feedback

Encourage group to monitor own breathing patterns during coming week - to notice *how* they're breathing, and how fast, and the effect of slowing it down. Again emphasise need to incorporate relaxation into everyday life - breathing ideal for this.

Session 3

Round - one thing I enjoyed this week; one thing I'm looking forward to next week.

In pairs, talk about what kind of week it's been, how they've used relaxation - were the breathing exercises any use? (5 minutes each way.)

If finding time to relax is a problem, this exercise may help: in pairs, each person outlines their daily routine. The partner suggests times and places at which they could relax. After discussion, the pair make a contract to try out each other's suggestions in the coming week. (NB. This may need to be preceded by some basic work on setting realistic goals - see references to books on Assertiveness for help with this.)

Loosening exercises

Deep relaxation with breathing awareness, sitting (Text 3)

Feedback

Break

Guided visualization exercise, lying down, with or without music (Text 4)

Feedback and homework- ie. continue to practise and remember commitment made to partner (if goal-setting exercise was used).

Session 4

Round - one good thing during week/or one occasion on which I was able to relax.

Pairs (same as last week) - everyone reports back to partner on how well they got on with putting last week's goals into practice.

Feedback in whole group. What did people learn from the exercise?

Introduce Mitchell Method - allow time for group members to identify their own 'stress' positions.

Use volunteer to run through instructions before using the method with the group.

Mitchell Method - lying down

Feedback - how did it compare with other methods? How will they be able to use it in everyday life? (Explain 'key' positions.)

Break

Identifying sources of stress - brainstorm what 'stress' means to people. Look at Human Function Curve - how do people recognise when they're on the down-side of the curve? What do they do about it?

Present stress matrix (high stimulation/low stimulation/control/ no control) - in group, find examples in each box. Working individually, ask group members to think about which aspects of their lives fit in the different boxes. In pairs, discuss their findings. Is there a good balance between stimulation and relaxation, or are there things they'd like to change?

Feedback in group.

Explain use of stress diaries - ask everyone to try and keep one for a day in the following week. Emphasise that it's for their use only - there's no point in making it up if they haven't managed to do it!

Homework - try out the Mitchell exercises at home. Become aware of individual 'stress' positions, and use appropriate exercise to release tension. Keep the stress diary for a day.

Session 5

Round - one thing I like about myself

Feedback - how easy was it to say something good about yourself? Did it feel like boasting? Why? What does that tell us about our culture?

In pairs, look at **stress diaries**. Each person listens to the other for 5 minutes, without speaking, as she/he goes through her/his own diary and comments on anything which was interesting, surprising, predictable etc. Then discuss in pairs anything which might be changed, and make a contract with each other to change one thing which is causing stress. (Remember rules for effective goal setting!)

Feedback in whole group. What was it like to be given attention, and not interrupted? What did people learn from the stress diaries? Was it a useful exercise? Relaxation exercise - Mitchell Method (sitting).

Feedback

Break

Massage

If the group seems ready for it, introduce simple massage techniques. Demonstrate on a volunteer, then encourage people to work in pairs.

Feedback - what was it like to give and receive massage? Would they feel comfortable doing massage with people outside the group?

Ask in group what people would like to do in the last session. Is there anything they'd like to go over again? Anything they particularly enjoyed and would like to try again?

Homework - try out massage with friends and family; work on the commitment to change one stressful aspect of their lives.

Session 6

Round - one thing I'll take away from this course/one thing I'm going to change as a result of coming to the group.

Pairs (same as last week): How I got on with the commitment to change. What was the result? If it didn't work, what was getting in the way? Could I tackle it in a different way? (5 minutes each way.)

The content of the rest of the session will probably be determined by the group's requests from the previous week. Specific subjects which they might like to explore include: saying 'no' and other aspects of assertive behaviour; sleep; food; worrying; biofeedback (if machine available); tranquillisers; smoking; alcohol etc.

Resources

Give out address list of organisations connected with relaxation and stress-management; reading list; list of recommended tapes; information on local sources of help and support.

Evaluation

Allow time for filling in final evaluation form.

If the group seems enthusiastic, arrange a follow-up meeting in three months' time so that everyone can get together and compare notes.

Handout 10

SESSION PLANNER

You are going to lead a series of 2-hour relaxation sessions for a group of eight people. Use the Session Planner to plan the first two sessions for this group, paying attention to the structure of the sessions (ie. timing, balance of activities etc.) and to the content and aims of each section. You also need to consider what materials/aids (flip-charts, handouts, tapes, cassette recorder etc.) may be needed.

TIME	CONTENT	AIMS	MATERIALS/AIDS

Handout 11

PARTICIPANT'S EVALUATION

Venue: **Dates:**

Please tick as appropriate, and feel free to expand as much as you like in the comment sections.

1. Did you find the course helpful?

Yes   No

Why/why not?

_____
_____
_____
_____
_____
_____
_____

2. Which part did you find the most useful?
Please say why?

_____
_____
_____
_____
_____
_____
_____

3. Which part did you find the least useful?
Please say why?

_____
_____
_____
_____
_____
_____

4. Are there any other areas/issues/ techniques which you would like to have been included?

_____
_____
_____
_____
_____
_____

5. How do you intend to use what you have learned on the course

i) Personally?

_____
_____
_____
_____
_____
_____
_____

ii) Professionally?

_____
_____
_____
_____
_____
_____

6. Would you be interested in further training in aspects of relaxation and stress-management and related subjects?

Yes   No

If yes, please specify which aspects would interest you particularly:

_____
_____
_____
_____
_____

If yes, which of the following would suit you best:
One-day workshop
Half-day workshop
Short series of 2-hour daytime workshops
Short series of 2-hour evening workshops
Other

Many thanks for filling in this questionnaire. Your comments will be very useful to us in planning future courses.

Flip-chart 1

TRANSACTIONAL MODEL OF STRESS

Stress as the result of an Interaction between the Individual and the Environment

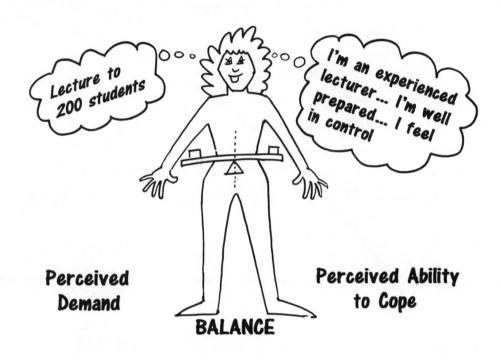

Perceived Demand   Perceived Ability to Cope

BALANCE

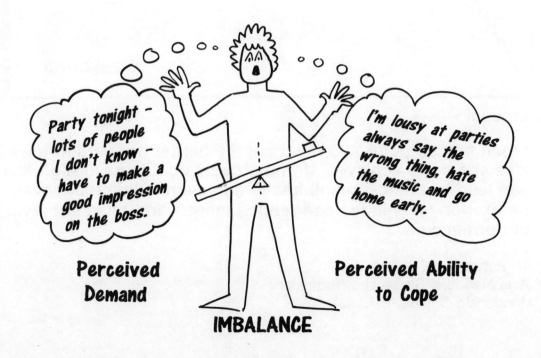

Perceived Demand   Perceived Ability to Cope

IMBALANCE

Flip-chart 2

HUMAN FUNCTION CURVE

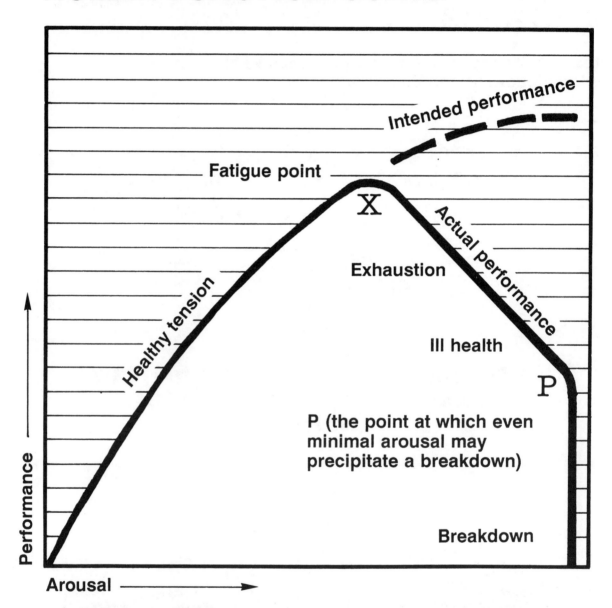

When fatigue point X is reached, the harder the person tries the less she or he achieves. If the arousal continues at high level it can lead to exhaustion, ill health and eventually breakdown. Relaxation techniques can reduce fatigue and raise the level of performance.

(Dr Peter Nixon - adapted from
Jane Madders' Stress and Relaxation,
Macdonald Optima, 1979:23)

Flip-chart 3

MANAGING STRESS - A FRAMEWORK FOR ACTION

CHANGING ACTUAL SITUATION
- adding
- subtracting
- re-organising
- avoiding

IMPROVING ABILITY TO COPE WITH SITUATION
- training
- developing new skills
- time-management
- assertiveness
- objective-setting
- communication

STRESS

CHANGING PERCEPTION OF DEMANDS AND COPING ABILITY
- positive self-talk
- avoiding 'catastrophising'
- avoiding 'shoulds', 'musts' and 'oughts'
- curbing self-righteousness

CHANGING BEHAVIOUR
- healthy eating
- cutting down on tobacco, alcohol and other drugs
- taking enjoyable exercise
- having enough rest
- having creative hobbies and interests
- practising relaxation

Flip-chart 4

FIGHT/FLIGHT RESPONSE (SYMPATHETIC STIMULATION)

INCREASED ACTIVITY

- Pupils dilate.
- Circulation increases blood supply to brain, muscles and to limbs (more O_2).
- Heart beats quicker and harder - coronary arteries dilate.
- Blood pressure rises.
- Lungs take in more O_2 and release more CO_2.
- Liver releases extra sugar for energy.
- Muscles tense for action.
- Sweating increases to speed heat loss.
- Bloodclotting ability increases.
- Adrenal glands secrete adrenalin to fuel response.

DECREASED ACTIVITY

- Digestion slows down or stops - stomach and small intestines reduce activity.
- Mouth goes dry - constriction of blood vessels in salivary glands.
- Kidney, large intestine and bladder slow down.
- Immune responses decrease.
- Sphincter muscles close to prevent urination and defaecation.

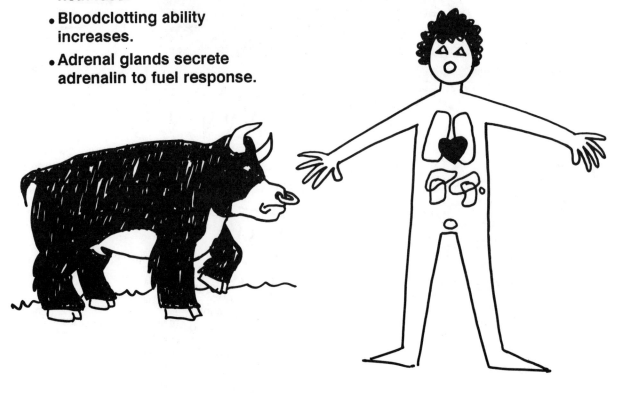

Flip-chart 5

REST/DIGEST RESPONSE (PARASYMPATHETIC STIMULATION)

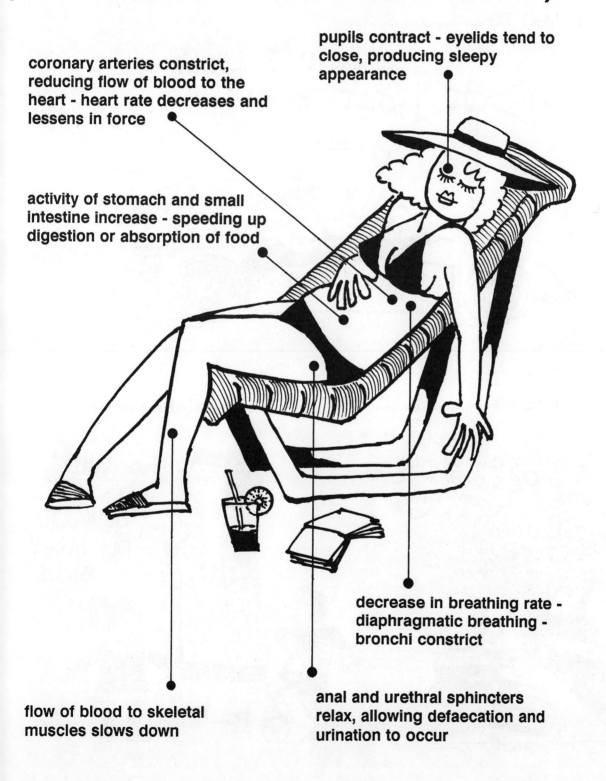

coronary arteries constrict, reducing flow of blood to the heart - heart rate decreases and lessens in force

pupils contract - eyelids tend to close, producing sleepy appearance

activity of stomach and small intestine increase - speeding up digestion or absorption of food

decrease in breathing rate - diaphragmatic breathing - bronchi constrict

flow of blood to skeletal muscles slows down

anal and urethral sphincters relax, allowing defaecation and urination to occur

Flip-chart 6

PERCEPTIONS OF STRESS

I WANT TO ....

I HAVE TO ....

I CAN'T ESCAPE FROM..........

Flip-chart 7

WARNING SIGNS OF PROLONGED STRESS

Physical	Intellectual	Emotional
Palpitations and chest pains	Loss of memory and concentration	Frequent feelings of anger and irritation
Recurrent headaches	Feeling woolly headed	Feeling dull and low
Heartburn, stomach cramps	Inability to make decisions	Inability to love and care, feeling tearful
Stomach feeling full of gas		Sleep disturbance

Flip-chart 8

MECHANICS OF BREATHING

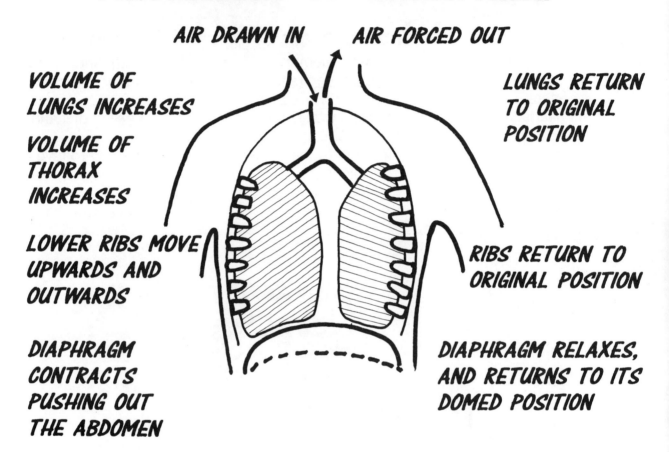

AIR DRAWN IN   AIR FORCED OUT

VOLUME OF
LUNGS INCREASES

VOLUME OF
THORAX
INCREASES

LOWER RIBS MOVE
UPWARDS AND
OUTWARDS

DIAPHRAGM
CONTRACTS
PUSHING OUT
THE ABDOMEN

LUNGS RETURN
TO ORIGINAL
POSITION

RIBS RETURN TO
ORIGINAL POSITION

DIAPHRAGM RELAXES,
AND RETURNS TO ITS
DOMED POSITION

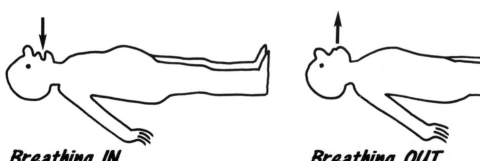

Breathing IN
abdomen swells slightly

Breathing OUT
abdomen flattens

Relaxed Abdominal Breathing

Flip-chart 9

THE ANXIETY CIRCLE

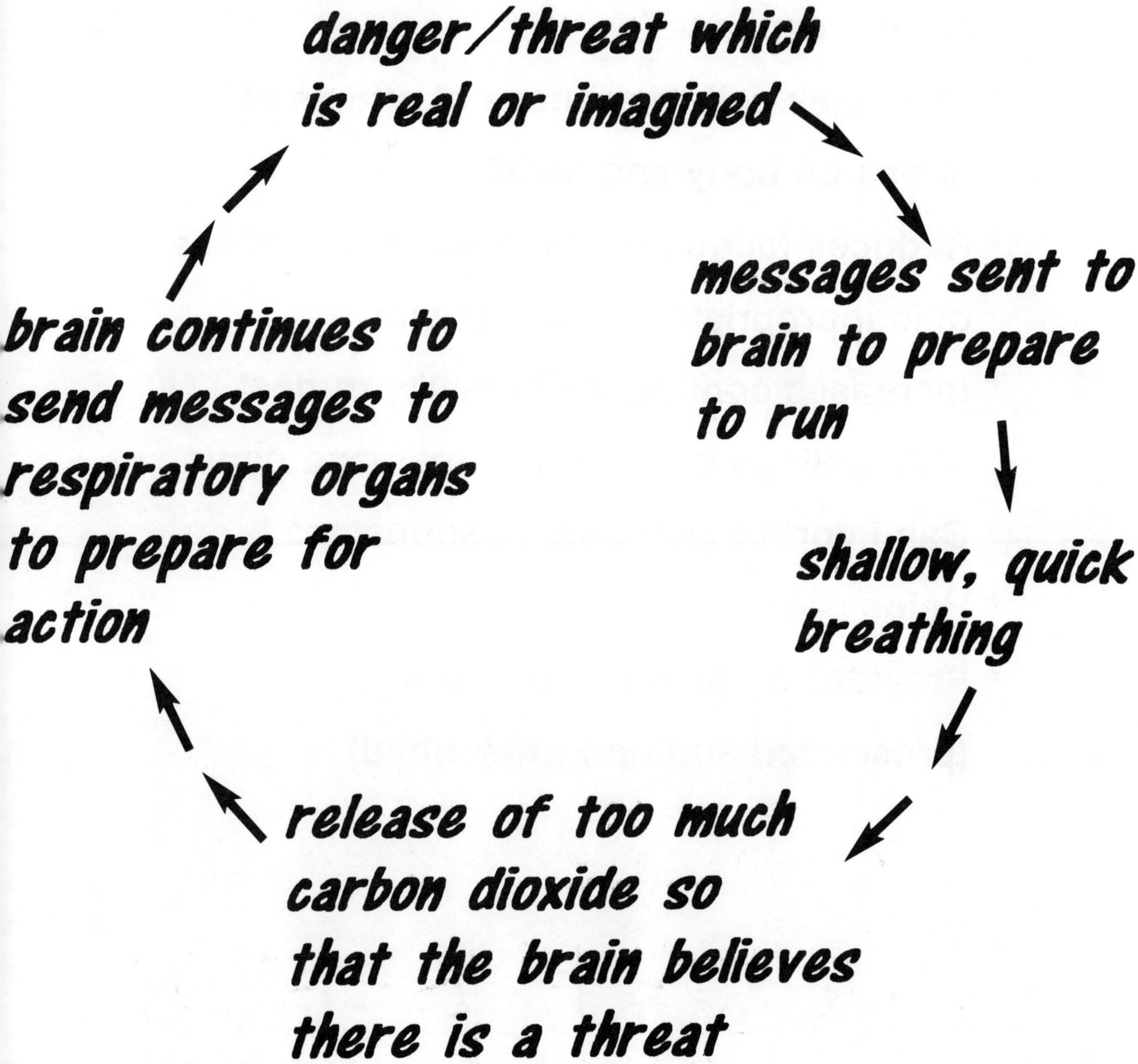

danger/threat which
is real or imagined

messages sent to
brain to prepare
to run

brain continues to
send messages to
respiratory organs
to prepare for
action

shallow, quick
breathing

release of too much
carbon dioxide so
that the brain believes
there is a threat

<u>Flip-chart 10</u>

BENEFITS OF RELAXATION

* Simple and effective way of reducing the stress response

* Increases self-awareness of effects of stress on body and mind

* Reduces fatigue by increasing awareness of inappropriate muscle tension

* Increases confidence in ability to deal with feelings of anxiety, stress and panic

* Can improve personal relationships

* Helps promote sleep

* Provides an alternative to drugs (prescribed and non-prescribed)

Flip-chart 11

BENEFITS OF MASSAGE

*Reduces muscular tension

*Relieves pain

*Stimulates circulation

*Promotes elimination of waste products

*Reduces emotional tension and anxiety

*Promotes feeling of relaxation and well-being

SECTION 11

RESOURCE LIST

Recommended reading and resource list   118

RECOMMENDED READING AND RESOURCE LIST

Stress is a growth industry, and there is now a bewildering array of publications on all aspects of the subject. This list is not comprehensive, but aims to give an idea of the range of material available to trainers and clients. We have also included the addresses of organisations which supply training and materials in stress-management, relaxation and related fields.

We strongly recommend that anyone planning to run a course based on this manual should read at least some of the books listed under the heading Basic Background.

BASIC BACKGROUND

Stress and Relaxation, Jane Madders, 1979 (Macdonald Optima, £4.95)

Stressmanship, Dr Audrey Livingston Booth, 1985 (Severn House, £4.95)

Simple Relaxation: The Physiological Method for Easing Tension, Laura Mitchell, revised ed. 1987 (John Murray, £4.95)

You Must Relax, Dr Edmund Jacobson, 1976 (Unwin, £2.95)

Living with Stress, Cary L. Cooper, Rachel D. Cooper and Lynn H. Eaker, 1988 (Penguin, £4.95)

Stress, Tom Cox, 1978 (Macmillan, £7.95)

GENERAL

Understanding Stress, 1988 (Consumers' Association/Hodder & Stoughton, £6.95)

Taking the Strain, Robert Eagle, 1982 (BBC, £2.75)

The Relaxation Response, Herbert Benson, 1975 (Fount, £1.75)

Stress-Proofing Programme, Leon Chaitow (Thorsons, £1.95)

Coping with Stress, Donald Meichenbaum (Century, £2.95)

Coping with Stress: A Practical Self Help Guide for Women (Sheldon Press, £2.50)

Overcoming Stress, Dr Vernon Coleman (Sheldon Press, £4.95)

Less Stress More Success, Dr Audrey Livingston Booth, 1988 (Severn House, £5.95)

Relax and Be Happy, Jane Madders, 1988 (Unwin, £6.95)

STRESS AT WORK

How to Survive the Nine to Five, Martin Lucas, Kim Wilson, Emma Hart, 1986 (Methuen, £3.95)

Coping with Stress at Work - Case Studies from Industry, Judi Marshall, Cary L. Cooper (eds.) 1981 (Gower, £22.50)

Stress in the Public Sector - Nurses, Police, Social Workers & Teachers, March 1988 (Health Education Authority, available free from HEA Supplies Dept.)

Stress in Teaching, Jack Dunham, 1986 (paperback ed.) (Croom Helm, £9.95)

Stress in Nurse Managers, P. Hingley, C. Cooper, P. Harris (King's Fund Project Paper No 60) Published as *Stress and the Nurse Manager,* 1986 (Wiley, £17.95)

Staff burnout: job stress in the human services, Cary Cherniss, 1981 (Sage Publications, £16.50)

Job Stress and Blue Collar Work, Cary Cooper & Michael Smith, 1985 (Wiley, £30.95)

Women's Health Work and Stress, broadsheet produced by Women and Work Hazards Group. Available from 9 Poland St., London W1, or from Women's Health Information Collective, 52 Featherstone St., London EC1

ASSERTIVENESS

Asserting Yourself, Dr Marsha Lineham & Dr Kelly Egan, 1983 (Century, £2.95)

Assertiveness at Work, Ken & Kate Back, 1982 (McGraw Hill, £12.50)

A Woman in Your Own Right, Anne Dickson, 1982 (Quartet, £3.95)

ANXIETY & DEPRESSION

Self Help for your Nerves, Dr Claire Weekes, 1962 (revised eds.1969,) 1981 (Angus and Robertson, £5.95)

Understanding Stress and Anxiety, Charles Speilberger (Harper and Row, £2.95)

Don't Panic - A Guide to Overcoming Panic Attacks, Sue Breton, 1986 (Macdonald Optima, £4.99)

For People Who Panic, Martin Landau-North, 1985 (Anthos Park Publishing Co., £7.35)

Beyond Fear, Dorothy Rowe, 1987 (Fontana £4.95)

Depression - The Way out of Your Prison, Dorothy Rowe, 1983, (Routledge, £4.95)

Dealing with Depression, Kathy Nairne and Gerrilyn Smith, 1984 (The Women's Press, £3.95)

The Social Origins of Depression, George Brown and Tirril Harris, 1978 (paperback ed. 1979) (Tavistock Press, £9.50)

TRANQUILLISERS

Bottling it up, Valerie Curran & Susan Golombok, 1985 (Faber & Faber, £3.25)

Coming off Tranquillisers and Sleeping Pills, Shirley Trickett, 1986 (Thorsons, £2.50)

'That's Life' Survey on Tranquillisers, Ron Lacey and Shaun Woodward, 1985 (BBC, £2.95)

OTHER RESOURCES

TRAINING MATERIALS

The Stress Pack, Neil Boot, Angus Buck, Elizabeth Perkins, 1986 (Nottingham and Bassetlaw Health Education Unit/University of Nottingham Department of Adult Education, £10). Available from: Nottingham and Bassetlaw Health Education Unit, Memorial House, Standard Hill, Nottingham, NG1 6HA.

Skills for Health 1. Relaxation Teaching Resource Pack, Lee Adams and Chrissie Smith, 1988. £15 inc. p.& p. from Positive Health Promotions, 2 Craigmore, Brampton, Cumbria CA1 1PY

Lifeskills Teaching Programmes, 1,2 and 3, Barrie Hopson and Mike Scally, 1980, 1982, 1986 (Lifeskills Associates, Ashling, Back Church Lane, Leeds LS16 8DN, £29.95 each) Designed for use in secondary schools, but includes much material which can be adapted for use with groups of any age. Sections on: time management, coping with transitions, building self-esteem, effective communication, assertiveness, managing negative emotions, preventing and managing stress, creative problem-solving and decision-making.

Living Skills Pack, Bob Wycherley (ed.), 1987 (South East Thames Regional Health Authority, £45) Available from Marketing and Public Relations Dept. Tel: 0424 730073 ext. 2158. Includes background information on stress, with practical sections on: Caring for Yourself, Assertion and Fighting, Rational Thinking, Relationships, Stress Management and Planning and Organising.

Women and Well Being: a Resource Pack for Women's Groups looking at aspects of Health and Well Being, Jane Groves, Susan Moffat and Sylvia Somerville, (Lothian Health Board Health Education Dept.) Includes material for workshops on: mental health,

assertiveness, stress, relaxation and exercise, drugs, alcohol, smoking and images of women.

Assertion Training: A Handbook for those involved in Training, Anni Townend, 1985, (FPA Education Unit, £6.50)

RELAXATION TAPES

Professionally-produced relaxation tapes can be useful both to trainers and clients. They are valuable sources of new ideas and techniques, and can help provide the necessary motivation for practising relaxation at home. They vary considerably in quality and approach, and it is difficult to make firm recommendations as people's tastes vary so widely. Individuals respond to different approaches - type of instruction, tone of voice, sex of voice etc. and one person's favourite may be completely unhelpful to someone else. The tapes listed below have been found useful by both relaxation leaders and clients. (See list of organisations for addresses).

I Can Relax, Jane Madders (for children, roughly from 4 -11) £6.00. From Relaxation for Living, Order Dept.

Sleep Well, Jane Madders, £6.00. Also available from Relaxation for Living.

Self-Help Relaxation, Jane Madders (for older children and adults) £6.00. Also available from Relaxation for Living.

Designed to accompany Jane Madders' book, *Stress and Relaxation,* the tape covers: relationship between muscle tension and anxiety, breathing, developing awareness of tension in different parts of body. A useful feature is the combination of 'quick release' methods on one side with a longer session on the other. A good, practical, basic tape.

Relax and Enjoy It!, Dr Robert Sharpe, £6. From Lifeskills. One of a series of 'Lifeskills' tapes. A good introduction to the tense/release technique, with some awareness of breathing. Covers both full and quick-release relaxation routines. Dr Sharpe gives instructions clearly and in a pleasant voice. A good basic tape for people who prefer a male voice.

Just Relax, Matthew Manning, £4.25 + p. & p. From Matthew Manning, Listening for Health.

One of a series of tapes called 'Listening for Health', *Just Relax* includes: awareness of breathing, creating feelings of peacefulness, visualization of a country walk and a walk along a beach, positive affirmations about relaxation.

Matthew Manning has a soothing, pleasant voice, and his method, which relies on visualization and suggestion, can be useful for people who do not like, or who should not use the tense/relax method (e.g. because of high blood-pressure, or high levels of anxiety). The method may not appeal to down-to-earth, pragmatic people who like to be given precise instructions.

Physiological Relaxation, Laura Mitchell, £4.50 + p. & p. From International Stress and Tension Control Society.

Should be used in conjunction with Laura Mitchell's book *Simple Relaxation,* which explains in detail her 'physiological' method of relaxation. Side 1 explains the principles on which the method is based, and Side 2 contains the instructions for full relaxation. Instructions are given clearly and precisely, and there is no element of auto-suggestion or visualization. The method appeals to practical, common-sense people who like clear instructions, and a down-to-earth approach.

MUSIC FOR RELAXATION

Soothing music can be a valuable aid to relaxation, whether used on its own or as a background to instructions. Again, people's tastes vary widely and the banality and monotony of some 'relaxation' music have been known to cause acute distress to music-lovers! Trial and error is really the only method we can recommend in this area, although the two tapes mentioned below have an enthusiastic following:

The Fairy Ring, Mike Rowland, £5.95 + p. & p. from Matthew Manning

Silver Wings, Mike Rowland, £5.95 + p. & p. from Matthew Manning

Other music tapes and recordings of soothing natural sounds (waves, running water, singing birds, woodland noises etc) can be obtained from:

New World Cassettes, Freepost, Paradise Farm, Westhall, Halesworth, Suffolk IP19 8BR

The Whole Thing, 188 Old Street, London EC1V 9BP

Coda Records, 17/19 Alma Road, London SW18

VIDEOS/FILMS

Videos can be useful in training, and for prompting discussion of specific issues, but they can never be a substitute for live discussion. This is particularly important to bear in mind in an area like stress-management in which self-awareness and self-analysis (whether at the individual or organisational level) are vital parts of the learning process.

Stress - ITV series of 6 programmes presented by Jane Madders.

Programme 1 - Stress and heart disease. Effects of hyperventilation. Different therapies used at Charing Cross Cardiac Unit. Use of biofeedback in stress management.

Programme 2 - The Alexander Technique. Meditation. Environmental pressures.

Programme 3 - Children and stress. Parents under stress. Relaxation techniques for children. Quick relaxation practice.

Programme 4 - Marylebone Holistic NHS Health Centre - the role of doctors, befrienders, priests, healers, music and other therapies. Stress caused by serious illness - effects on patients and their carers. Yoga.

Programme 5 - Relationships; how they can cause and alleviate stress. 'Rolfing' (form of massage). Effects of environmental pollution.

Programme 6 - Dr Patrick Pietroni, President of British Holistic Medical Association on a holistic approach to health & well-being. 'Biodynamic' massage. Alcohol and stress. Effects of diet - the good, the bad and the cranky.

Available individually as VHS video cassettes price £14.95 each including VAT and p. & p., or £60 for all six including VAT and p. & p.

For details, contact:
HTV Enterprises
The Television Centre
Culverhouse Cross
Cardiff CF5 6XJ
Tel: 0222 590150
Accompanying booklet available free from Stress, P.O. Box 2000, Cardiff CF5 6XS.

Teachers and Stress (Scottish Health Education Group) Catalogue reference : SHEG VHS 453

30-minute video focusing on stress in teaching, available from: Scottish Central Film and Video Library, 74 Victoria Crescent Road, Glasgow, G12 9JN. Tel: 041 334 9314

Available for hire or purchase. Details available on request from address above.

Stress (16 mm film/VHS) examines causes of stress in today's highly competitive society, and suggests ways of combating it, including job enrichment and relaxation. Available for hire or purchase. Hire: video £10 per day excluding p. & p. and VAT, film £7.60 per day Purchase: VHS video only £70
From:
Concord Films
201 Felixstowe Road
Ipswich
Suffolk
P3 9BJ
Tel: 0473 726012

Stress at Work looks at effects of too much pressure at work on people in different occupations, including catering manager, secretary, bus mechanic, airline clerk, social worker and shop steward. Available for hire or purchase from above address. Hire: Video £9 per day excluding p. & p. and VAT. Film £11 per day excluding p.& p. and VAT. Purchase: VHS video only £70 (to educational organisations) £150 (to non-educational organisations)

The Stress Mess (16 mm film) takes a humorous look at the sources and signs of stress in our lives, and suggests ways of reducing and managing stress. Hire: £13 per day excluding p. & p. and VAT. Available from:
Concord Films
201 Felixstowe Road
Ipswich
Suffolk
P3 9BJ
Tel: 0473 726012

Stress: Recognising the Causes focuses on an industrial manager. Available for hire or purchase from:
Video Arts Ltd.
Dumbarton House
68 Oxford Street
London WIN 9LA
Tel: 01 637 7288
Hire: 2-day rental : £105, 7-day rental : £140 Purchase: £650. Can be previewed at a number of regional centres.

USEFUL ADDRESSES

Relaxation for Living
Dunesk
29 Burwood Park Road
Walton on Thames
Surrey
KT12 5LH
Tel: Walton (0932)227826
Relaxation cassettes and self-help literature. Produces newsletter and organises study days and training for relaxation leaders. (Send SAE with requests for information.)

International Stress and
Tension Control Society (UK branch)
The Priory Hospital,
Priory Lane,
Roehampton,
London SW15 5JJ
Aims to disseminate information on the 'scientific aspects of human stress, tension related disorders and tension control methods' to professionals and the public. Produces newsletter and organises workshops and conferences.

Listening for Health
Matthew Manning
39 Abbeygate Street
Bury St. Edmunds
Suffolk IP33 1LW
Tel: 0284 69502/2364
Wide range of cassettes on various aspects of mental health. General titles include: Just Relax; Breathe; Why Worry?; Laugh your way to Health

Lifeskills
3 Brighton Road
London N2
Tel: O1 346 9646
Range of cassettes on relaxation and related topics, including assertiveness, sleep and giving up smoking

Aleph One Ltd.
The Old Courthouse
Bottisham
Cambridge
CB5 9BA
Tel: 0223 811679
Suppliers of 'relaxometers' and related cassettes and literature. Prices range from £60 for a 'mini-relaxometer' for personal use to £230 for the Model Q, which has a visual feedback facility and can be used in conjunction with a home computer. The middle of the range model S, (£105) which has a loudspeaker and headphone socket, is ideal for use both with groups and individuals. All prices include VAT and p.& p.

NOTE: Prices correct at time of going to press. Purchasers are advised to check current prices with retailers before sending orders.